SUSTAINING
NATURES

CULTURE, PLACE, AND NATURE

STUDIES IN ANTHROPOLOGY AND ENVIRONMENT

K. Sivaramakrishnan, Series Editor

Centered in anthropology, the Culture, Place, and Nature series encompasses new interdisciplinary social science research on environmental issues, focusing on the intersection of culture, ecology, and politics in global, national, and local contexts. Contributors to the series view environmental knowledge and issues from the multiple and often conflicting perspectives of various cultural systems.

SUSTAINING

NATURES

AN ENVIRONMENTAL
ANTHROPOLOGY READER

EDITED BY SARAH R. OSTERHOUDT
AND K. SIVARAMAKRISHNAN

UNIVERSITY OF WASHINGTON PRESS

SEATTLE

Design by Derek George
Composed in Garibaldi, typeface designed by Henrique Beier

UNIVERSITY OF WASHINGTON PRESS
uwapress.uw.edu

LIBRARY OF CONGRESS CATALOGING-IN-PUBLICATION DATA
Names: Osterhoudt, Sarah R., editor. | Sivaramakrishnan, K., 1957- editor.
Title: Sustaining natures : an environmental anthropology reader /
edited by Sarah R. Osterhoudt and K. Sivaramakrishnan.
Description: Seattle : University of Washington Press, [2023] |
Includes bibliographical references and index.
Identifiers: LCCN 2022055986 (print) | LCCN 2022055987 (ebook) |
ISBN 9780295751443 (hardcover) | ISBN 9780295751450 (paperback) |
ISBN 9780295751467 (ebook)
Subjects: LCSH: Human ecology—Case studies. | Sustainability—Case studies.
Classification: LCC GF41 .S87 2023 (print) | LCC GF41 (ebook) |
DDC 304.2—dc23/eng20230429
LC record available at https://lccn.loc.gov/2022055986
LC ebook record available at https://lccn.loc.gov/2022055987

CONTENTS

PREFACE

This is in some ways an unusual reader in the field of environmental anthropology. Given the enormous growth of scholarship by anthropologists on the environment in the last few decades, no reader can reasonably hope to be comprehensive. In this case, the question for us became: how should we choose what to include in this volume? One consideration that influenced our choices was that the selections should bring together accessible, engaging, and ethnographic examples of recent work that also considered key themes of sustainability. Within this frame, we wanted the volume to highlight intersections between environmental anthropology, with its abiding interest in nature variously understood, and sustainability, with its emphasis on fostering human and nonhuman forms of life.

Given these goals, we organized *Sustaining Natures* into key themes that speak to both environmental anthropology and sustainability studies. These themes include farming and food, urban environments, energy and energy alternatives, multispecies relationships, and landscapes and identity. The urgency and importance of environmental justice, decolonial approaches to environmental studies, and confronting the enormous challenge of planetary-scale climate change through innovative ethnographic research remains a concern across the sections. The reader addresses these

—

topics through ethnographic examples that span different continents, relying on a diversity of perspectives and voices, broadening the representation of the discipline. We selected articles published in the last decade or so, mostly by a new generation of researchers whose work we see as moving the field of environmental anthropology in exciting new directions. We have maintained the authors' original format for figures, references, and notes, except for converting footnotes into endnotes when applicable. Each thematic section begins with a short overview of the topic, along with several questions to help guide classroom discussion.

We have kept the reader deliberately selective in themes and articles so that the volume is a reasonable length and can be used in conjunction with other materials that individual instructors may wish to build into their curricula. It was not an easy task to arrive at the selections themselves, but our sense of students' interests—in topics like sustainable food systems, alternate energy, environmental justice, the ethics of human relations with nonhumans, and the environmental perspectives of historically oppressed and excluded groups—guided us. We hope both emergent concerns and diverse treatments of them in recent scholarship are well represented here.

All our editorial decisions, of course, occurred within the shadow of the vigorous discussion of the Anthropocene. We understand this concept to convey, at a minimum, that human inhabitation going forward will always be of a deeply altered planet—one that is perhaps losing its ability to recover from continuing shocks. While acknowledging the power of this idea, we wished to remain sensitive to the important caution raised by many scholars against a facile use of the term Anthropocene that ascribes equal culpability in planetary destruction across all humans. We thus placed emergent themes in environmental anthropology in dialogue with topics including environmental justice and social and economic inequality.

Environmental anthropology has always been astute and even relentless as a field in offering critique of the human condition with all its oppressions, inequalities, and exploitative relations among humans. It has also provided critical evaluation of human relations with the nonhuman world. This tradition, in its many forms, can be found in this volume. Beyond critique, however, we also offer selections that attend to the urgent work of repair and restorative justice, where people learn to treat those historically marginalized with respect and strive to forge alliances across past divisions

—

for crafting lasting, equitable solutions to the grave planetary crisis of this moment in history.

Ultimately, our goal in *Sustaining Natures* is to foreground the anthropological perspectives on sustainability, while retaining an interest in the way nature as an organizing concept for human relations with the nonhuman continues to be powerful. We hope this volume will be used by future scholars and practitioners seeking solutions to global challenges, who will glean from this volume that cultural understanding is integral to imagining and enacting sustainable and equitable futures.

Sarah R. Osterhoudt
BLOOMINGTON, JULY 2022

K. Sivaramakrishnan
NEW HAVEN, JULY 2022

ACKNOWLEDGMENTS

We first spoke about the project nearly four years ago and found that the executive editor at the University of Washington Press, Lorri Hagman, was actively interested in realizing it as part of the press's distinguished portfolio in environmental studies. With her encouragement, we set out to assemble the collection and wrote our introduction and the short pieces that frame each section of the volume. In putting the manuscript together, we had terrific research and editorial help from Amy Johnson, then a graduate student in the Department of Anthropology at Yale University. Her timely and efficient work allowed us to compile the selections and begin the process of seeking permissions from the authors and publishers.

The comments of three anonymous readers for the University of Washington Press affirmed our selections and helped us further refine the reader's main introduction and the introductions for each section. We thank them for their careful and generous reading and valuable suggestions.

As we moved through the logistical stages of securing formal permissions for reproducing the articles in this volume, Jennifer DeChello in the Department of Anthropology at Yale University provided crucial support in making sure all payments and permissions were completed and documented. We thank her for her diligent and timely support. We also thank

—

Marnie Lamb for casting her expert eye over the page proofs and preparing the index.

We are grateful to the Office of the Vice Provost of Research at Indiana University Bloomington for making an award from their Grants in Aid Program to Sarah R. Osterhoudt for funding to support the preparation of an index for the volume. Our thanks also go to Yale University for providing approval to use research funds at the disposal of K. Sivaramakrishnan to pay costs of permissions received from publishers and copyright holders for selected articles included in this volume.

We must thank, most of all, the authors whose articles are included here. They have done amazing work that makes environmental anthropology such a vibrant and innovative field at this time. They extended their wholehearted support for the inclusion of their scholarship in this reader and generously worked with us in making sure their materials were properly presented in this collection.

As this volume goes to press, a global pandemic continues to hold much of the world in its grip, even as some parts of the world seem to be finally gaining some relief from its deadly effects. Most of the work on this project was carried out while the pandemic was in full swing, and we remain grateful to each other and our families for the support that made this project possible and allowed it to move forward without a lot of delay or disruption in difficult circumstances.

—

INTRODUCTION

SARAH R. OSTERHOUDT
AND K. SIVARAMAKRISHNAN

W e are in a period of unrivaled human transformation of nature, leading to unprecedented extinctions, changes in climate, and levels of pollution. These escalating environmental challenges intersect with the urgent concerns of social and racial justice and human well-being. In fact, as is becoming increasingly evident, many of the baneful effects on the environment are a direct consequence of profound and persistent human inequality, leading to severe exploitation of many humans by the few who pursue extravagant, unsustainable lifestyles that require extreme forms of extractive regimes to maintain.

Yet despite such challenges, there are reasons for hope and an opportunity to meaningfully reimagine human engagements with nature. Demands for instituting more sustainable economic, political, social, and environmental policies are gaining momentum. Energy industries in the global North, for example, seem to have reached a turning point, as nonrenewable, highly toxic energy sources are losing favor with governments and corporations, many of which are increasingly adopting green and renewable energy programs. These and other sustainability efforts are led by a new generation of environmental leaders, from activists to scientists, from inventors to poets.

The field of environmental anthropology is well positioned to build on this positive momentum. Environmental anthropologists have long investigated the multifaceted dimensions of human and nonhuman relationships, exploring questions of power, meaning, value, knowledge, and history. They draw from ethnographic methods that provide an up-close view of how individuals experience, understand, and give meaning to their everyday relationships with nature. Such research perspectives are vital to address the "wicked problems" of sustainability, which necessitate a nuanced and multidisciplinary approach to understanding nature in its many forms.

Our aim with this reader is to highlight the intersections between environmental anthropology, with its abiding interest in nature variously understood, and sustainability, with its emphasis on fostering mutually supportive relationships between human and nonhuman forms of life. Bringing nature and sustainability together enables a consideration of the generative relation between the two concepts, as ideas of nature are reimagined and sustainability initiatives realize socially inclusive, environmentally just, and nature-respecting alternatives for human life on Earth.

In bringing together these two fields of inquiry, however, we must first grapple with how to contextualize the two main concepts of this volume: nature and sustainability. Both terms elude precise definition. The term *nature* is one of the most expansive, enduring, and contested concepts in human thought (Castree 2005; Kimmerer 2017). It is used to describe the entirety of the nonhuman world as well as the totality of human and nonhuman surroundings. Nature may denote an essence, a force, or an idealized state. Yet despite this suggestion of universality, ideas of nature often contain a distinct narrowness, connecting to particular Northern genealogies that depict nature as pristine, wild, and existing apart from human influence (Cronon 1996; Nash 2014). This conception characterizes nature by its absences—a view that may lead to justifying human dominance of nature. This characterization of nature affects the treatment not only of the environment but also of people. As scholars of critical race and gender studies have shown, those people considered lesser humans in any sense are often described as being more of, and in, nature. At the same time, framing nature as untouched and pristine is not always taken as a sign of nature's inferiority. As seen with the rise of ideals around pristine wilderness, for instance, these views of nature may signify integrity and purity in urgent need of rescue, preservation, and care (Delaney 2009).

The understanding of a reified nature apart from humans has proved influential, propagating forms of power that tend to erase the multiplicity of ways of knowing and experiencing nature, including those rooted in non-Western religious, epistemological, philosophical, and aesthetic traditions (Dungy 2009; Finney 2014). The narrow definition of nature is more than a semantic debate. Such definitions of nature—and what counts as natural—have justified violent and unjust actions against particular groups of people, including seizing Indigenous land and resources in the name of nature conservation (Neumann 1998; Shiva 2016). They have further undergirded violence against nonhuman species, as certain forms of life are deemed less natural and subsequently of lesser value, falling outside human priorities of conservation or cultivation (Marris 2013).

Environmental anthropologists have long countered the epistemic and political violence of taking a singular view of nature by advocating for theories that address the social construction of the natural world. This work situates knowledge production about nature among other things, in specific political and historical perspectives. It argues against the easy universalization of any one knowledge system as definitive, especially when it relies on creating a division between nature and culture to establish its own claims to authenticity. Instead, environmental anthropologists highlight the political conditions and philosophical motivations that separate human from nonhuman life and other facets of the inanimate world. Some environmental scholars, following the suggestions of thinkers like Georges Canguilheim (2008), are examining the cultural processes that lead to locating nature as something that exists a priori, outside of human conception. Equally, they have begun to challenge, in the spirit of the French philosopher Bruno Latour (2004), the idea that nature is purely a cultural artifact produced by humans through their interactions with the nonhuman world.

Work in environmental anthropology draws from detailed ethnographic studies around the world, to widen our ideas of what nature is and can be. It points to the polysemantic and multivocal properties of nature—hence that use of the plural term *natures* in this volume's title. As feminist theorists, Indigenous thinkers from the Americas and elsewhere, and spiritual traditions from Asia and Africa have long observed, the human condition is only fully imaginable when its deep connection to nature is acknowledged and respected (de la Cadena 2015; Duara 2015; Haraway 2016; Iheka 2018; Weller 2006). Such views are garnering increased attention. For environmental anthropologists, for example, becoming more attuned to such perspectives, which have long been marginalized within the field, opens new perspectives to understanding nature and its value across cultures. These perspectives bring much-needed insights to the urgent questions of how to reimagine more sustainable, fulfilling, and equitable relationships with nature.

Any discussion of the social constructions of nature, and human experiences of the natural world, must attend to the violence of human histories, including the experiences of slavery and the near extinction of Native Americans. The mutual shaping of Black intellectuals' reflections on nature through the experience of slavery and Native Americans' ideas about nonhuman life are deeply influenced by their shared history of European expansion into the Americas. These traumatic experiences have shaped alternatives to the hegemonic understandings of nature, as landscapes of forests and fields may denote memories of fear, suffering, and injustice, as well as specific forms of community solidarity, refuge, and resistance (Deming and Savoy 2011; Finney 2014; Murray et al. 2011). Such historical relationships with nature, and their shifts over time, are often obscured and devalued. Centering such narratives can form a basis for decolonial understandings of nature. They offer powerful examples of processes of learning among and across groups who have jointly seen their lives and cultures cruelly curtailed by the juggernaut of imperial conquest and its economic projects of accumulation (King 2019). Such studies are not only inquiring into transatlantic connections but also rethinking similar encounters and shared suffering elsewhere, including the realm of Pacific Island societies (Shilliam 2015).

Collectively, then, the field of environmental anthropology underscores that there is no single way to define, know, or experience nature. There is no one type of landscape where nature may be found. As new work in anthropology moves beyond forests, fields, farms, rivers, mountains, and wilderness, it finds nature in the heart of cities, in postindustrial landscapes, and in intensely traveled ocean routes, including the heavily

—

polluted deep sea (Elias 2019; Gordillo 2014; Helmreich 2009; Rademacher and Sivaramakrishnan 2017; Tsing [2017] 2021). Despite having such broad reach, however, we hesitate to claim that the idea of nature is entirely a human construct. To stand in a meadow teeming with life, to look out to the ocean from the shore, or to contemplate the consciousness of another form of life is to acknowledge the agency, power, and beauty of nonhuman nature. Even as we walk in the crowded city center and see an old, magnificent wolf tree that has miraculously survived among the concrete and glass structures that have sprung up around it, admiration for nature may well up within us as we pause to reflect on the wonder of what has come to pass.

Thus, while there are many entry points to arrive at what nature is, we argue that it remains a salient and vital category for understanding all human and nonhuman life. This is precisely because ideas of nature have shaped the visions and politics, the violent and peaceful relations, and the patterns of coexistence and domination that have marked human history. Human understandings of nature have similarly shaped the treatment of all entities regarded as nonhuman, in the process creating a gradient for organizing (and often valuing) life on the planet.

Arguably such pervasiveness and persistence of nature as both source and setting for the human condition has led to its ubiquitous translation as the environment. The popularity of this term is noted, for example, in departments for environmental science, by the field of environmental conservation, and by the political collectives promoting environmental movements. If the best work in environmental anthropology currently interrogates both nature and humanity with equal rigor, it is also participating in vibrant debates that question the relationships between nature and the environment. As some scholars have suggested, the notion of the environment as the totality of our surrounding conditions provokes a different understanding of the environment as both present everywhere and always under threat or in shock (Benson 2020).

The turn to the study of the environment, in part, brings into view a growing interest in sustainability. In many respects, the term *sustainability* is similar to the word *nature*, albeit more recently prominent. Like nature, sustainability proves difficult to define. In its broadest sense, sustainability considers human-environment relations in all their multifaceted dimensions. Sustainability also describes the drive to understand what will

—

degrade and destroy these relationships and how they might be renewed within more nurturing ecological, social, and political systems.

Notions of sustainability gained traction in the 1970s as people paid increased attention to escalating environmental challenges such as pollution, food insecurity, soil erosion, and species loss (Brundtland et al. 1987). However, like nature—which we have already argued owes its contemporary formations to the transformations wrought in the world by European expansion, modern slavery, and colonialism—sustainability seems to have emerged through similar processes that joined modern state formation with the rise of contemporary biological, physical, and social sciences, including the fields of political economy, demography, and development theory. In such emerging frameworks of sustainability, the human population was linked to the abuse of nature, including the wanton destruction of natural resources and the insufficient long-term husbandry of the earth and its bountiful biodiversity (Warde 2018).

Today, references to sustainability are ubiquitous. There are sustainability programs across the spheres of government, policy, education, business, and nonprofits. We see claims for sustainable fashion, energy, tourism, transportation, and fruit drinks. The proliferation of the term has led some scholars to warn that its overuse is eroding its meaning and power to make positive change (Thiele 2016). Yet like *nature*, the term *sustainability* has largely endured. In its ambiguity, it proves to be a compelling concept, with the potential to bring disparate groups and disciplines together to articulate shared visions and priorities (Brondizio et al. 2016; Leach et al. 2018). For such reasons, we do not abandon the term *sustainability* in favor of an alternative term. As with nature, however, we call for sustainability initiatives to be attendant to whose voices, experiences, and aspirations are meaningfully included in the conversation (Agyeman, Bullard, and Evans 2003; Davenport and Mishtal 2019).

Environmental anthropology has much to contribute to the evolving conversations on both nature and sustainability, as well as the connections between them. Research in environmental anthropology illustrates that questions of nature are also questions of materiality, power, meaning, knowledge, history, and justice. With its methodological attention to individual lives and narratives, environmental anthropology elevates the qualitative and indeterminate aspects of being human as essential to understanding nature and crafting sustainable futures. What moves us? What haunts us? And what forms of nature do we aspire to sustain? Such research highlights the commonalities in human experiences and meanings without erasing the diversity and validity of different views. In this volume, we have included work that both builds from these foundational strengths of environmental anthropology and charts new paths forward for the discipline—paths that are ever more inclusive of the multiplicity of voices and perspectives on what nature may be and on how to create a world where both human and nonhuman life can flourish.

OVERVIEW: TRAJECTORIES OF ENVIRONMENTAL ANTHROPOLOGY

Environmental anthropology has long been a vibrant subdiscipline of cultural anthropology, emerging over the course of the twentieth century. In this volume, however, we do not focus on the earlier work of the discipline but, instead, highlight scholarship from the past decade or so. We have made this decision for several reasons. First, there are many good resources already available that present a chronological view of the evolution of environmental anthropology, underscoring the key scholars and theoretical debates of the twentieth century (e.g., Dove and Carpenter 2008; Haenn, Wilk, and Harnish 2016). Second, moving toward more recent scholarship in environmental anthropology allows us to move away from an organization centered around somewhat narrow academic debates toward one with an emphasis on common themes that are key to sustainability work. While drawing from some of the foundational research in environmental anthropology, the pieces included in this reader present exciting new directions in the theory, methods, and applications of the field.

Although we do not focus on historical work in environmental anthropology, a brief overview of the field's history and trajectories is helpful to situate the more recent scholarship we include in the volume. Earlier work in environmental anthropology, sometimes referred to as cultural ecology, broadly examined how material environments shaped and were shaped by cultural and social systems. Seminal research included how subsistence land practices in the Great Basin Shoshone influenced the social connections between households (Steward 1938) or explored the

–

connections between seasonal variations in the Arctic and certain patterns of social organization for the Inuit people (Mauss [1979] 2013). As the field expanded, it investigated relationships between ecological systems and symbolic meanings, such as the nutritional and ecological implications of the rituals of hunting wild pigs in New Guinea (Rappaport [1968] 2000) or the mapping of cultural conceptions of purity and pollution onto particular elements of nature (Douglas 1957). Others examined the ecological knowledge and agrarian expertise of people practicing subsistence agriculture, situating these practices within broader historical, political, and spiritual frames (H. Conklin 1957).

Collectively, this work established many of the enduring themes of environmental anthropology. It destabilized dichotomies of nature and culture, pointing instead to the recursive relationships between the two and placing humans as integral parts of ecological landscapes (Geertz 1972). It called attention to the variety of human languages, knowledge, practices, and meanings connected to the natural world. Much of this work also, however, replicated the larger trends of sociocultural anthropology during this period. For example, it tended to describe "primitive" societies as largely bounded, static, and isolated entities, instead of as fundamentally interconnected to wider trajectories of political, economic, and social history. Within the field, a power dynamic existed whereby white, usually male anthropologists traveled from academic centers in the North to "study" Indigenous groups and people of the global South, extracting knowledge to bring back with them for publication for academic audiences (Bruchac 2018). As a result, understandings of the environment were largely filtered through Northern epistemologies and traditions, obscuring the multitude of other ways of knowing and appreciating nature (L. Smith 2013).

Beginning around the 1970s, environmental anthropology intersected with the emerging field of political ecology—an interdisciplinary field fashioned by human geographers and social anthropologists in collaboration with others interested in the human dimensions of environmental change (Robbins 2004; Zimmerer and Bassett 2003). People were becoming more aware of the interconnectedness of humans and ecosystems across the planet. The escalating challenges of air, water, and land pollution underscored how environmental issues crossed space and species boundaries (Carson [1962] 2002). Environmental anthropology, like other subfields

—

in sociocultural anthropology, also responded to growing social protest, especially led by students and young people around the world in the 1960s and 1970s. Throughout the 1980s and 1990s it reckoned with antiwar movements, as well as movements for the rights of Indigenous peoples, and responded to the rapid processes of decolonization around the world. Growing awareness of toxic waste dumping, dangers and risks posed by nuclear and other nonrenewable energy industries, and global deforestation for agribusiness and wood industries also became prominent concerns.

The displacement and destruction generated by high-modernist development came under the critical gaze of political ecologists. Political ecologists emphasized the multiscalar and dynamic nature of seemingly local environmental issues (Biersack 2006; Blaikie [1985] 2016; Paulson and Gezon 2005). They considered the processes, policies, and actions that played out on the international stage and their connection to local habitat loss, species endangerment, and livelihood destruction. This body of work examined environmental issues across space and time, bringing together analytics of environmental health, global economic markets, and political power (Duffy 2007; Rocheleau 2008). Political ecology also combined with poststructural scholarship, foregrounding how discourse and representation played a key role in how environments and resources were managed and which groups had the power to frame and co-opt these environmental narratives for their own benefit (e.g., Dove 1983; Escobar [1995] 2011; Fairhead and Leach 1996; Ferguson 1990).

Political ecology approaches to the environment similarly examined the workings of power, while also considering how landscapes and the people who made livelihoods on them were transformed, even disciplined, by powerful discourses like conservation, sustainable land management, and efficient resource use (Scott [1998] 2008). Scholars illustrated how international development and conservation activities generated forms of governing nature that controlled land, identified species to be preserved, and shaped human subjects by regulating their sense of responsibility for the environment (Agrawal 2005; West 2006). Also key to political ecology was the emphasis on not only critiquing existing structures but also working to improve them—a commitment that continues to appeal to scholars who would like their research to make a discernable difference in the world (Peet, Robbins, and Watts 2011).

—

The late 1990s and early 2000s brought another environmental crisis to the forefront: the rapid loss of biodiversity across the globe (E. Wilson 1992). With the loss of species, researchers pointed to the concurrent loss of potentially valuable genetic resources (Heywood and Watson 1995); the risks to integral ecosystem health (Perrings et al. 1997); and threats to the continuation of certain forms of environmental knowledge, practice, and meaning (Nazarea 2006). Attention to these issues led to a flourishing of anthropological scholarship in the 1990s and early 2000s on environmental knowledge, identity, and politics, especially as related to Indigenous groups (B. Conklin and Graham 1995; Ellen, Parkes, and Bicker 2003; Li 2000). Environmental anthropologists complicated the mainstream conservation narratives that placed much of the blame for biodiversity loss and global deforestation on small-scale farmers in the tropics (Kull 2002). Instead, research in anthropology pointed to broader economic and political drivers of resource degradation, including extractive industries, poor governance structures, and global capitalistic systems (Tsing 2005). Anthropologists also documented the human rights implications of removing people from their land in the name of conservation, advocating instead for community-based models of conservation that respected community priorities and practices (Alcorn 1989; West, Igoe, and Brockington 2006).

The attention to conservation projects reflects another abiding interest of the discipline of environmental anthropology—research into environmental institutions and policies. These institutions may include government forestry departments (Mathews 2005; Sivaramakrishnan 2009), international aid agencies (Corson 2016; Shipton 2010), or nonprofit conservation and development organizations (Agrawal and Gibson 1999; Muehlmann 2012), as well as more informal networks for natural resource governance (Barnes 2014, Lansing 2012). Such work examines the cultural dimensions of institutions and traces the material impacts that specific policy initiatives have on human and nonhuman landscapes.

More recently, anthropologists note a shift in much environmental policy and governance toward programs that take an ecocentric, rather than human-centric, approach to nature. These programs—which include ecosystem services (McElwee 2012), carbon offset models (Bidaud, Schreckenberg, and Jones 2018), and "rewilding" campaigns (Jørgensen 2015)—emphasize the regenerative capacity of minimally managed ecosystems.

—

The shift in policy away from counting the number of species in an eco-system, toward a consideration of the holistic health of landscapes more generally, opens space for more expansive and emergent views of nature. Such work has creatively engaged other fields, including landscape ecology, architecture and design studies, and sacred geographies.

Decentering humans in approaches to nature reflects a broader movement in environmental anthropology, often referred to as multispecies ethnography, or new materialism (Kirksey and Helmreich 2010; Ogden, Hall, and Tanita 2013). This scholarship takes seriously the agency and power of nonhuman species to shape the trajectories of culture and history. It brings forward "more-than-human" and posthumanist frameworks to understand how multiple ontological understandings of being and becoming in nature may coexist in any given landscape or assemblage of species. The work challenges us, for example, to consider the social relationships of forests from the point of view not only of humans but of trees (Kohn 2013) or points to the power of seemingly passive species such as mushrooms to influence human economic, social, and cultural relationships (Tsing [2017] 2021).

In its attention to how humans shape and are shaped by their material environments, multispecies anthropology echoes the work in cultural ecology of the mid-twentieth century. It differs, however, in closely thinking through the multiple positionalities contained in both human and nonhuman worlds (Velásquez Runk, Ismare, and Conquista 2019). In many ways, the interest in nonhuman life and how it is essential for human consciousness draws on much older philosophies and traditions of thought as much as it is born out of growing concerns with human destruction of the environment and the rapid extinction of nonhuman life in service of the human quest for prosperity (Dove 2021).

Collectively, posthumanist work underscores the interconnectedness of species (Lorimer 2016) and the ethical imperative for humans to be mindful of how their actions affect the continued existence of all forms of life. Often summarized as the ontological turn in the study of life beyond the human, or the pluriverse of life, these approaches offer a variety of new approaches to understanding the ways human and nonhuman agency are coproduced. These approaches consider how to acknowledge and comprehend forms of nonhuman thought, feeling, and sociality. They thus

—

examine other types of potential personhood beyond humans, including the existence of distinct ecological selves. Together, these diverse beings coexist in complex webs of relations and may express themselves as both individuals and collectives (Pandian 2014).

The ontological turn has further questioned a fundamental differentiation that has undergirded modern ideas of nature, between subjects capable of perception and knowledge and subjects who are, simply, targets of perception and knowledge production (Povinelli 2016). In complicating this divide, environmental anthropologists closely examine aspects of nature considered to have no discernible signs of biological life, from wind to sand, from glaciers to wood (Cruikshank 2006; Dudley 2014; Howe 2019; Zee 2017). These scholars identify the tendencies of such entities to resist or enhance human intention and endeavor, shaped by the entanglement of human agency with the material world. Such approaches are at times characterized as new materialism (O'Reilly, Isenhour, McElwee, and Orlove 2020).

Work in multispecies ethnography and new materialism also responds to the increasing interest across scholarly fields in the concept of the Anthropocene. The initial definition of the Anthropocene, fashioned by scientists, sought to identify a start for the epoch in which human activity had left an indelible imprint on biogeochemical cycles and created a geological signature (Mathews 2020). The concept of the Anthropocene potentially offers fundamentally new ways to think about human impact on the planet and how it has permanently altered relations between humans, nonhumans, and the material world. Just as the first views of the earth from space sparked concerns for the fragility of the earth as a system (Ingold 1993), earth systems modeling seems to have unleashed anxieties about the irreversible human destruction of the planet.

Unlike scientists searching for a definitive start date for the Anthropocene, historians and anthropologists are seizing on these planetary concerns to debate, disagree, and propose alternate theorizations of when such planetary-scale processes were initiated and accelerated. Relatedly, at least some environmental anthropologists have offered sustained critiques of the Anthropocene concept for wrongly distributing equal responsibility to all humans (Yusoff 2019). Instead, they argue that some humans should bear most of the responsibility for the Anthropocene, as a consequence of

—

their empire building, slave trading, and relentless resource extraction. Such activities affect nature from ocean depths to mountain tops, as they build unsustainable, inequitable, and exploitative lifestyles (Bonneuil and Fressoz 2016; Patel and Moore 2017).

However, much of the discussion around the Anthropocene remains enchanted by the ability to analyze planetary consequences and prescribe planetary solutions, thus favoring the same ideas of technological mastery of nature that have created the environmental crisis in the first place. This thinking results in ambitious and expensive solutions, such as climate engineering, which remain unmoored from historical, social, and ecological processes—processes that will inevitably influence the uneven consequences of such global projects, taken across space and over time (Demos 2017).

Anthropological studies are beginning to offer alternate perspectives to the planetary focus of the Anthropocene that attend to the interweaving of the human condition with the historical processes of nature making (Mathews 2020). These approaches appear generative and more likely to foster just and sustainable outcomes. They respond to the rather one-dimensional generality of the discourses on the Anthropocene by turning our attention back to the localities where the severe disturbances of the Anthropocene, including climate change, are often manifested as practical and moral crises. One such model study along these lines (Gagne 2019) offers an examination of an ethics of care that emerges within the environmental challenges of the Anthropocene—one directed toward other people and nature in all its forms. Through such work, we are reminded that the biggest environmental crises of the day remain locally experienced as both physical and cultural phenomena that shape the everyday conduct, values, livelihoods, and sentiments of communities.

Another ethnographic study working with an Indigenous community in the Philippines considers the historical, moral, and politically inequitable processes through which people experience and react to climate disruption (W. Smith 2020). The Indigenous farmers in this region are no strangers to the climate variations produced by El Niño currents and the storms that beset coastal areas. Currently, they experience changed weather patterns as transformations that reorganize their agricultural and social relations, including their immediate relations to plants and soil. Like the high

—

Himalayan herders described by Gagne (2019), the Indigenous farmers of upland Philippines find the wider environmental challenges and their personal ethical or cultural dilemmas to be a product of the changes that have overtaken their lives as global extractive economies intersect with local desires.

Such work in environmental anthropology underscores the ways that planet-altering environmental challenges generate new relationships between people and nature and remind us that environmental crises are always also moral crises. In the case of the Philippines, even as farmers acknowledge the powerful large-scale forces of marginalization and environmental degradation that affect their land, they also seem to regret how these changes have altered their personal lives (W. Smith 2020). For many such Indigenous and other marginalized people who continue to farm, fish, live with forests, or work with animals for their livelihoods, they are facing quite personal ethical dilemmas. These moral assessments, in turn, may spur wider conversations and legal innovations that help to ensure the flourishing of more-than-human lives across varied conditions (Sivaramakrishnan 2015).

While there are many exciting possibilities presented by emerging anthropological work on posthumanism and the Anthropocene, this work also presents certain caveats. For example, such discussions run the risk of flattening the textured meanings of the human condition, imposing on it an artificial sense of uniformity and cohesiveness. Posthumanist studies, innovative and rich as they are, also work best when they examine specific situations in which humans are conjoined with nonhumans to produce individual ecologies of self—ways of navigating and understanding notions of identity, meaning, and personhood in relation to other beings. An additional challenge is to situate individual examples into wider political, economic, and social processes, thereby placing posthuman complexes within uneven and conflict-ridden global environments. This is where some emerging work in environmental anthropology, including some presented in this volume, combines political ecology and posthuman perspectives. Here we are particularly pointing to the ability of political ecology to track the working of power across scales and sites and to understand the influence of inequality on varied human and nonhuman entities, ecological systems, and socionatural relations (Andrews and McCarthy 2014).

—

When effectively combined with political ecology, posthumanist ethnographic understandings of nature lead to renewed calls for ecological equity and justice (Kopnina 2017; Strang 2020). Environmental anthropologists have long foregrounded structures of environmental injustice in their research (Agyeman, Bullard, and Evans 2003; Taylor 2014). Important early work made visible the racial and economic disparities that shape which communities are most exposed to environmental risks and hazards, such as environmental toxins (Bullard 2008; Pellow 2007). Environmental justice scholarship also helped to broaden notions of the "environment" to encompass cities and suburbs, regarding these landscapes as human-ecological systems (Rademacher 2015).

Bringing together perspectives on environmental justice, political ecology, and posthumanism illustrates how intimate human and nonhuman relations interface with questions of human justice, ecological complexity, international economic systems, and global conservation politics. In the United States, such work calls for legal and restorative justice for the abuses of natural resources, including the seizure of Indigenous lands (Tuck and Yang 2012). As we look at the exploitative processes unleashed by global capital in other parts of the world, a wider picture of land dispossession, commodity violence, and environmental justice comes into view (Fairbairn 2020; Li 2018; Osterhoudt 2020). For instance, anthropological research documenting Indigenous struggles against extractive industries in Papua New Guinea brings environmental justice scholarship into international arenas and concerns (Kirsch 2007). As shown in the case of the Maasai in Kenya, displacement from ancestral homelands can frequently occur in the name of nature conservation (Goldman 2011). Moore (2012) and Swanson (2022) provide fine examples of such integrative work through studies of fisheries in the Bahamas and Japan, respectively.

As these examples suggest, in the realm of environmental policy, as well as cultural and economic anthropology, frameworks for environmental justice are increasingly adopting a more ecocentric approach toward defining legal rights and responsibilities, with some nations conferring legal standing to animals, rivers, and nature (Kopnina 2017). At the same time, there are calls to not abandon commitments to humanistic projects that advocate for environmental equality and justice for all people, whether through the lens of food, water, energy, climate, or land (Allen and Jobson

—

2016; Todd 2016). At the international level, these efforts take the form of tribunals on environmental issues as international law and activist networks confront issues that transcend national borders, such as multinational corporations that violate basic human rights by posing what might be seen as global hazards in addition to local injustices (Prete and Cournil 2019). Such work has the capacity to unite food justice, climate justice, and struggles for sovereignty among communities seeking sustainable futures.

AIMS AND ORGANIZATION

Selective in coverage of immense and diverse scholarship though it may be, the above genealogy of anthropological work on nature and sustainability showcases several foundational themes. One is an abiding interest in the recursive relationships between humans and their environment, and a close attention to how people locate themselves both within and outside of understandings of nature. Much of this scholarship draws from ethnographic methods that seek up close accounts of the practices, knowledge, politics, and meanings that shape our interactions with the natural world. Additionally, there is a strong connective thread of action-oriented research that closely interrogates questions of power, access, representation, and justice. These understandings further intertwine relationships of global capitalism, with its reliance on extractive, reductive, and exploitative practices toward people and nature.

Today, we find the field of environmental anthropology at an exciting and generative moment. Emerging research on nature, culture, and sustainability is expanding conceptions of both humanism and nature, opening the field up to creative ways to understand the multifaceted relationships of our world. Collaborative, participatory, interdisciplinary, and action-oriented research models are gaining momentum, as the narrow traditions of who does anthropology, and where and why, are being increasingly overturned. Similarly, there is growing attention to rethinking the long-standing theoretical underpinnings of the field and to incorporating a richer diversity of epistemological, empirical, and interpretative views. These shifts include centering nonhuman entities—including plants, animals, rocks, soils, and spirits—in our analytical frameworks. Such repositionings are occurring within the urgent context of escalating

—

global sustainability concerns of climate change, biodiversity loss, economic inequities, and environmental justice, raising the stakes for inclusive and meaningful environmental research.

In compiling pieces for this reader, we looked for work that captures this momentum. We focused on articles published after 2010 that orient themselves along a theoretical arc from political ecology to multispecies ethnography, bringing these frameworks to new theoretical arenas that creatively consider emerging relationships between humans and nature. All the authors we include in the collection ground their theoretical approaches in ethnographic methodologies that give fine-grained attention to people's everyday practices and meanings. Many of the authors adopt participatory and activist approaches to their ethnographic research, widening perspectives of what may "count" as nature, and why. Each piece, in our opinion, exemplifies ethnographic writing that is both rigorous and engaging. For this reason, we present articles in their entirety, rather than as excerpts, inviting readers to draw their own connections and insights from the complete works.

Collectively, the articles bring environmental anthropology from the more conventional sites of seemingly untouched or isolated landscapes, to places vibrant and overflowing with a diverse array of human and nonhuman life. These sites include renewable energy company meeting rooms in US cities, organic-certification projects in Indian rice fields, and urban waste disposal sites in China. Several authors consider individual bodies as multispecies landscapes of sorts, which contain their own topographies of environmental identities, memories, trauma, and healing. Finally, all pieces speak to the evolving relationships between ideas of nature and aspirations toward sustainability. Through insights garnered in patient and respectful ethnography, the authors each consider what a true vision of sustainability may look like. They challenge us to interrogate what realizing such futures may entail, including forms of political activism, historical reckoning, economic restructuring, and an individual mindfulness toward cultivating beauty, wonder, and care.

We organize the ten articles along five themes that each speak to key issues in both environmental anthropology and sustainability. These themes are farming and food; urban environments; energy and energy alternatives; nonhuman life; and climate, landscapes, and identity. We

—

begin each theme with a brief introduction that frames the topic and considers its implications for environmental anthropology and sustainability studies. We also suggest a few questions to encourage classroom reflection and discussion.

These five themes represent topics we have seen drawing increasing interest from both undergraduate and graduate students. For example, sustainable food and agriculture programs are expanding across the United States in both major universities and smaller colleges. It is exciting to see a growing number of students engage questions of environmental impact, health, and equity through the lens of food systems across the spheres of production, distribution, and consumption. Similarly, as animals, plants, and ethics of care come alive for students, posthumanist scholarship, including multispecies anthropology, currently resonates strongly; students are increasingly examining how more-than-human frameworks of analyses may be brought to bear on sustainability initiatives. Environmental justice, long a field of strong scholarship and activism, is being used more rigorously to evaluate sustainability debates, to ask who benefits from mainstream sustainability efforts and who may be left behind.

In identifying themes that organize the selection of essays presented in the volume, we carefully considered how to incorporate the topic of climate change. The urgent realities of climate change underlie all discussions of nature, whether through the lens of food, mining, energy, biodiversity, or justice. We have included questions of human relationships to climate in relation to grassroots activism, health, and knowledge production but have resisted the temptation to include additional work and themes specifically addressing climate change. We do this in recognition of the growing number of excellent collections and monographs that address this topic. We also do so because we consider climate change to be a manifestation of various other environmental problems caused by energy industries, environmental pollution, species extinctions, and deleterious land use practices, among other human actions. In many places, the effects of climate change are primarily experienced through more immediate environmental changes and livelihood disruptions, including forced migration, lost land, or living in toxic and imperiled landscapes.

Respecting the methods and lessons of ethnography, we have preferred to approach global dimensions of the environment, including climate

—

change, from local and situated vantage points. Such an approach also avoids what has been discussed as climate reductionism, or the tendency to blame complex environmental and social-economic changes broadly on climate change (Hulme 2011). A lot of the work that relates the question of climate change to the themes we have addressed in the introduction is also discussed in the representative articles included in this volume. A recent overview of the anthropological approaches to climate change seems to confirm our assessment of the potential key areas of broader interest in climate change studies (see O'Reilly et al. 2020).

Overall, we found that the most difficult challenge in compiling the reader lay not in finding scholarship and themes to include but rather in being able to select only a few examples among the wide array of compelling emerging scholarship in the field. Below we briefly discuss the articles we selected and how we see them contributing to new intellectual pathways that foreground anthropological perspectives on sustainability while retaining an interest in the way nature remains a powerful organizing concept that shapes human and nonhuman relationships in all their forms.

DISCUSSION OF ARTICLES

A vital criterion guiding the choice of articles was that authors build their arguments and case studies from fine-grained and often evocative ethnography, as we were keen to ensure that the collection foregrounded diverse voices, views, and experiences of nature. In identifying the subject areas to be covered, we have also selected topics that appear to be drawing increasing interest from undergraduate students.

We open with the theme of sustainable agriculture and food. As environmental anthropology increasingly bridges long-established fields of study like agrarian studies and urban studies, there have been growing concerns with food quality and the harmful consequences of industrial food production and transgenics (Aga 2021; Heller 2013). Food systems are being reimagined in ways that foster community while also respecting the environment, as evidenced in the slow-food movement (Petrini 2010). Such developments have created conditions for the growth of both organic agriculture (Guthman 2014) and food-sovereignty politics around the world (Aistara 2018). However, sustainability initiatives in agriculture

—

come with many challenges and pose new struggles for smallholder farmers who find their livelihoods already perched precariously on the edge of an economic and environmental precipice (Fitzmaurice and Gareau 2016).

Chapters 1 and 2 consider sustainable agriculture and food across the spheres of production, consumption, and exchange. In chapter 1 Shaila Seshia Galvin (2018) undertakes a study of organic agriculture and the institutions that grow around it for support and certification among small farmers in northern India. Both traditional crops and modern varieties participate in the reimagination of this corner of India as organic. Galvin shows how these transformations of farming, and integration into sustainability practices and aspirations, produce various moral discourses and questions of trust and uncertainty. If Himalayan northern India becomes a site for drawing on simplicity and relative innocence of farmers with respect to capitalist and green revolution agriculture to craft organic futures, then chapter 2, also on food, by Hiʻilei Julia Hobart (2017), considers the way food preferences in Hawaiʻi became a way to colonize the region. She shows the deep imbrication of taste and style of food materials and preparation in larger imperial civilizing processes. The inability of contemporary Hawaiʻi to provide sustainable food systems in the state is traced to the region entering international food commodity markets in the age of European expansion, through sugar plantations in particular. In this process, not only was the diversity and autonomy of Hawaiian food systems severely undermined, but a variety of traditional foods like poi became denigrated as signs of unwelcome primitivity in Hawaiian society.

The second theme of the reader moves from agrarian to urban landscapes. The relentless pursuit of modernity and greening ventures in the rural world has been matched, and perhaps exceeded, in the urban domain in the last few decades. At times working on a more ambitious scale, modern city making, infrastructure projects, and sustainability initiatives have reproduced a high-modernist hubris of an earlier period in the late twentieth century (Dennis 2008; J. Wilson 2021). Urban greening projects and reorganization of waste industries in the city, be it in Asia or Europe, have been signature initiatives in the pursuit of urban sustainability. In chapter 3 Cindy Isenhour (2011) shows how various ecological estimation and evaluation techniques, like life-cycle analyses, carbon footprints, and climate change projections, shape the imagining and realization of

—

urban sustainability as technoscientific utopia in Stockholm, Sweden. These high-modernist rubrics emerge even as some individuals propose an alternate vision of sustainability—one that connects to respecting land and promotes greater self-sufficiency. The arguments about the role and place of metrics of efficiency and networking in the making of green cities might well be creating an imaginary of cyborg urbanism in the name of smartness and sustainability (Gandy 2005).

One form these cyborg urban formations are taking, especially in Asian cities, is the invention of various waste-to-value projects, which bring a fascination with large-scale incinerators and big technology solutions to the growing problems of urban solid waste, consumer discards, and recycling industries. Such apparently sustainable solutions seem to overcome the problem of spreading landfills (Reno 2016). In chapter 4 Amy Zhang (2020) is concerned with the misgivings urban residents in China have with big technology and state-driven waste management. She documents their increasing interest, in the spirit of multispecies anthropology, in alternate approaches to waste that draw from interconnected human and nonhuman life-cycle patterns. Ordinary people take great interest in how they might control waste and use biological techniques of decomposition to both conserve and reuse matter considered either useless or toxic. Here sustainability imaginaries of ordinary city residents enroll local human action and nonhuman agency in rethinking poisons and pollutants, pests, and disease vectors, to tackle contamination and the excesses of throwaway cultures. In this sense, they are participating in a reevaluation of death and life of nature in urban Asia (Rademacher and Sivaramakrishnan 2021).

For the third theme, we turn to questions of energy and energy alternatives. The development of capitalism, green or otherwise, has spawned vast investments in energy infrastructure. Such technologies likely began with the damming and channeling of major rivers in various places but have since expanded to the exploitation of subterranean stores of energy in fossils, including oil and coal. Some of the most devastating environmental consequences of energy-intensive development have been visited on the planet in the twentieth century (Holleman 2018; McNeill and Engelke 2016). However, like so many things we have discussed in this volume, the origins of contemporary patterns of energy development and consumption have their roots in imperial projects of European expansion during

—

the eighteenth and nineteenth centuries that built massive regimes of extraction ranging across plant resources, fossil fuels, minerals, and precious metals (Grove 1996; Tucker 2000). Such energy infrastructures were coupled with scientific innovations in thermodynamics to serve colonial domination and power. Daggett (2019) reveals how thermodynamics was deployed as an imperial science that combined fossil fuel exploration and industrial expansion, mobilizing forms of inhuman and cruel labor via the hierarchical ordering of humans and nonhumans.

These troubling histories have generated research interest in rethinking energy production and use. In environmental anthropology, this focus has led to a strand of inquiry on the topics of energy science and politics, including newer renewable forms of energy of wind, solar radiation, biofuels, and waste gases (Boyer 2019). It has also led to ethnographic studies of how coal, oil, and natural gas, which have been infrastructurally foundational to modern capitalist and industrial societies, may become part of alternative local imaginations for livelihoods, political autonomy, and community development (Gardner 2012; Kikon 2019).

Chapters 5 and 6 speak to energy politics from the perspective of grassroots action in the United States and bring together discussion of sustainability with struggles for justice among Black and Indigenous people. In chapter 5 Dana E. Powell and Dáilan J. Long (2010) document protest movements against dominant forms of energy development, while also putting forward Indigenous visions for alternate energy and alternate economies. As they show, moving to renewable energy by itself may not suffice; such energy policies and new structures will need to address concerns around Indigenous sovereignty and dignity. Alternative energy projects should also aim to restore life chances and respect to minorities, marginalized communities, and people recovering from centuries of colonial oppression and exploitation.

In chapter 6 Myles Lennon (2017) brings questions of decolonizing energy to large US cities and to the Black Lives Matter movement of the last decade. As urban democracy movements in Black neighborhoods mobilize technoscientific expertise to galvanize their constituencies, energy technology companies in places like Wall Street seem to be discovering the value of holistic, socially just, and environmentally sustainable energy-industry innovations as worthy of their investments, both financially and

—

in terms of corporate culture. In some cases, they seem to undertake a fascinating journey toward diversification of their portfolios and offices, bringing an unusual and inspiring convergence between social justice activism and green technologies in urban centers.

The next two themes of the reader explore the multispecies relationships humans forge with animals, plants, and seemingly inanimate facets of landscapes such as sand and sea. The growing field of human-animal studies examines questions of animal agency, sentiment, and coexistence with humans. Some groups have long used animals to index degrees of humanity, as in racist ideas or pejorative accounts of tribes by people who considered themselves superior, and hence justified in their social dominance. Equally, certain species of animals have been transfigured as gods, spirits, creatures possessed of superhuman powers, exhibitors of venerable qualities, and respected occupants in lands shared with their human neighbors, worshippers, benefactors, and caretakers. Much of the writing on animals, in modern times, has become preoccupied with questions of wildness and domestication (Cassidy and Mullin 2007). This has spawned literature on wildlife conservation, pet industries for companion species, animal energy and labor, and commerce in animal body parts. Other recent writing deals with meat industries, with their large captive breeding programs for cattle or fowl in the global North as well as the politics of eating meat in the global South (Blanchette 2020; Staples 2020).

In chapter 7 Radhika Govindrajan considers the production of interspecies kinship in the Indian Himalaya by studying animal sacrifice and how it is anchored in culturally embedded ideas of care, love, reciprocity, and filial duties. In her account, animal agency operates in both corporeal and spiritual planes as goats raised as members of human families acquiesce in their own death to serve the family. As environmental crises like earthquakes, floods, and forest fires devastate hill economies and societies in northern India, Govindrajan (2015) finds that intimate relations of care deepen among humans and animals who reside together and grow up in mutual respect and affection. Such relations encompass local deities who are often fierce but always cognizant of the suffering and aspirations of their faithful. In this triad of human, animal, and supernatural or divine arise the multilayered forms of care and belonging that enable the meaningful death of one to sustain life for the other.

—

Some of the most exciting new developments in environmental anthropology are occurring in plant studies. At one level, plant-focused political ecology is generating alternatives to Eurocentric studies of plant circulation and the rise of plant sciences (Schiebinger and Swan 2007; Szczygielska and Cielemęcka 2019). In one case, for example, such research gives us a glimpse into how Chinese traditions shaped the formation of modern botanical knowledge (Menzies 2021). Other work takes us beyond botanical classification to examine the relation of plants to territory, to show how plants participate in more-than-human ways in projects of inclusion and exclusion, legibility, and surveillance. When plants are introduced to advance colonial missions in plantations, or nation-state projects of agrarian development, they continue to shape relations with other plants, soils, water, and human companions (Besky and Padwe 2016). It is even possible, as Mancuso (2021) shows in his playful manifesto, to narrate the history of the world from the perspective of plants and realize how their destruction has imperiled all life on the planet.

In chapter 8 John Charles Ryan (2012) takes the reader on a tour of the emerging field of human-plant studies. As he notes, the fields of ethnobotany and sustainable food studies tend to emphasize how humans act on plants. In that sense, they share a unidimensional perspective with other fields and environmental movements that were generated from colonial processes. Even when some might describe in more caring ways human love of plants beyond their utility for human prosperity and power, it is human action on plants that shapes their narrative. In contrast, Ryan invites the reader to consider how plants might act on humans and be involved in coproducing the social and natural milieu in which all life interactively unfolds.

Finally, we move to consider how landscapes produced in colonial encounters of the modern period become sites for reimagining postcolonial and just futures. Such landscapes are also in many instances being transformed again in material and cultural terms at the intersections between climate programs, community development, and the production of knowledge. For many decades participation and community inclusion have been buzzwords in economic development and nature conservation projects. The literature on how such projects failed to transfer real power to the people whose lives were most directly disrupted by these projects is

—

expansive. For example, the history of contamination and poisoning was often shrouded in secrecy. The study of such dangers and hazards also contributed a source of new knowledge in service of governmental control or capitalist innovation for profit in abatement and sequestration of poison and pollution, including medical applications (Arnold 2016; Walker 2011). In some cases, like the aftermath of the nuclear disaster and tsunami in Japan, it also led to renewed and diversified citizen science practices (Sternsdorff-Cisterna 2019).

Rather than present a somewhat arbitrary selection of such negative outcomes, we have chosen an article that showcases examples of citizens joining forces with scientists and governments to imagine resilient futures in the face of climate change. In chapter 9 Sarah E. Vaughn brings us to Guyana, focusing on floods, climate change research, and the building of resilient communities. It documents the participation of ordinary people in the investigation of disasters and the outlining of measures for prevention and adaptation. Vaughn (2017) shows how the newest wave of climate adaptation technologies and programs work in concert with longer histories of neoliberal development and technocratic governance. She notes that postcolonial states like Guyana remain enmeshed in colonial legacies and the powerful vestiges of imperious visions of national socioeconomic transformations.

In contrast to such totalizing views, some of the people Vaughn worked with in her ethnographic research recall this colonial history with misgivings and insist that today varied forms of knowledge should shape data collection and interpretation in participatory climate change projects. Such a proposal represents in many ways a radical democratization in the way climate-resilient futures may be imagined in service of climate justice. It counters the dominant world of market-based approaches to climate change mitigation and adaptation, including new waves of development that support large-scale community displacement in the name of responding to climate change vulnerability (O'Reilly et al. 2020; Paprocki 2021). In this context, Vaughn describes a struggle to reinforce the value of ordinary, placed-based knowledge to find more humane and just solutions to climate change challenges.

In chapter 10 Vanessa Agard-Jones keeps us in the Caribbean, where she links queer studies and new materialism through a meditation on sand

—

and the kinds of memories of land, intimate relations, and histories of eco-logical transformation that they invoke. Vanessa Agard-Jones (2012) finds affinity between sands, that which join land and sea in much of the Carib-bean, and the messy reality of human bodies too easily partitioned into inflexible gender categories. Queerness and sexual alterity are emplaced in her account. She considers struggles of Martinican belonging, for those who cannot easily move (to become diasporic) and must find, like the shift-ing sands of overexploited Caribbean beaches, a place within oppressive colonial legacies that weigh on sexual identity and nature in similar ways. From the perspective of gender, gay, and lesbian studies, Agard-Jones is asking us to consider the plight of those whose lives and environments are enmeshed in intersecting systems of extraction. In this sense, her work resembles accounts of other struggles, whether of poor farmers in Papua New Guinea (Halvaksz 2020) or artisanal gold miners in Colombia (Tubb 2020), whereby people articulate themselves in and through a sense of place, seemingly against all odds.

CONCLUSION

As these selections reveal, environmental anthropology is at its best when firmly grounded in careful, respectful, and systematic ethnographic research and writing that brings to the fore uncommon perspectives on widely recognized issues confronting the world. These articles, all of which appeared in the last decade, offer innovative approaches and original con-ceptual syntheses as they examine issues ranging from climate change to food and agriculture, energy politics, and urban environments. Always tilting toward studies that showcase diverse voices and consider questions of justice and sustainability, they illustrate new approaches to the study of nature as something always human but also much more than human.

Further, these pieces collectively push the boundaries of *how* environ-mental anthropology is conducted, reflecting the increased call within the discipline for collaboration, inclusivity, and practical applications for ethnographic research. Our short introduction to each theme connects the selected articles and the history of the discipline, while highlighting ques-tions for reflection and discussion. The reader is thus attuned to learning from past work in the field but is more intent on highlighting some of the

---

discipline's rich new trajectories along an axis that allows for an examination of the continuing relation between ideas of nature and ideas of sustainability and their consequences for human and all other forms of life on the earth.

REFERENCES

Aga, Aniket. 2021. *Genetically Modified Democracy: Transgenic Crops in Contemporary India*. New Haven, CT: Yale University Press.

Agard-Jones, Vanessa. 2012. "What the Sands Remember." *GLQ: A Journal of Lesbian and Gay Studies* 18 (2–3): 325–46.

Agrawal, Arun. 2005. *Environmentality: Technologies of Government and the Making of Subjects*. Durham, NC: Duke University Press.

Agrawal, Arun, and Clark C. Gibson. 1999. "Enchantment and Disenchantment: The Role of Community in Natural Resource Conservation." *World Development* 27 (4): 629–49.

Agyeman, Julian, Robert Doyle Bullard, and Bob Evans, eds. 2003. *Just Sustainabilities: Development in an Unequal World*. Cambridge, MA: MIT Press.

Aistara, Guntra. 2018. *Organic Sovereignties: Struggles over Farming in an Age of Free Trade*. Seattle: University of Washington Press.

Alcorn, Janis B. 1989. "Process as Resource: The Traditional Agricultural Ideology of Bora and Huastec Resource Management and Its Implications for Research." *Advances in Economic Botany* 7:63–77.

Allen, Jafari Sinclaire, and Ryan Cecil Jobson. 2016. "The Decolonizing Generation: (Race and) Theory in Anthropology since the Eighties." *Current Anthropology* 57 (2): 129–48.

Andrews, Eleanor, and James McCarthy. 2014. "Scale, Shale, and the State: Political Ecologies and Legal Geographies of Shale Gas Development in Pennsylvania." *Journal of Environmental Studies and Sciences* 4:7–16.

Arnold, David. 2016. *Toxic Histories: Poison and Pollution in Modern India*. Cambridge: Cambridge University Press.

Barnes, Jessica. 2014. *Cultivating the Nile: The Everyday Politics of Water in Egypt*. Durham, NC: Duke University Press.

Benson, Etienne. 2020. *Surroundings: A History of Environments and Environmentalisms*. Chicago: University of Chicago Press.

Besky, Sarah, and Jonathan Padwe. 2016. "Placing Plants in Territory." *Environment and Society: Advances in Research* 7:9–28.

Bidaud, Cécile, Kate Schreckenberg, and Julia P. G. Jones. 2018. "The Local Costs of Biodiversity Offsets: Comparing Standards, Policy and Practice." *Land Use Policy* 77:43–50.

Biersack, Aletta. 2006. "Reimagining Political Ecology: Culture/Power/History/Nature." In *Reimagining Political Ecology*, edited by Aletta Biersack and James B. Greenberg, 3–40. Durham, NC: Duke University Press.

—

Blaikie, Piers. (1985) 2016. *The Political Economy of Soil Erosion in Developing Countries.* Abingdon: Routledge.

Blanchette, Alex. 2020. *Porkopolis: American Animality, Standardized Life, and the Factory Farm.* Durham, NC: Duke University Press.

Bonneuil, Christophe, and Jean-Baptiste Fressoz. 2016. *The Shock of the Anthropocene: The Earth, History and Us.* London: Verso.

Boyer, Dominic. 2019. *Energopolitics: Wind and Power in the Anthropocene.* Durham, NC: Duke University Press.

Brondizio, Eduardo S., Efi Foufoula-Georgiou, Sylvia Szabo, Nathan Vogt, Zita Sebesvari, Fabrice G. Renaud, Alice Newton, et al. 2016. "Catalyzing Action towards the Sustainability of Deltas." *Current Opinion in Environmental Sustainability* 19:182–94.

Bruchac, Margaret M. 2018. *Savage Kin: Indigenous Informants and American Anthropologists.* Tucson: University of Arizona Press.

Brundtland, Gro Harlem, M. Khalid, S. Agnelli, S. Al-Athel, and B. J. N. Y. Chidzero. 1987. *Our Common Future.* Oxford: Oxford University Press / United Nations World Commission for Environment and Development.

Bullard, Robert D. 2008. *Dumping in Dixie: Race, Class, and Environmental Quality.* 3rd ed. New York: Routledge. First published in 1990 by Westview Press.

Canguilheim, Georges. 2008. "The Living and Its Milieu." In *Knowledge of Life*, edited by Paola Marrati and Tood Meyers, translated by Stefanos Geroulanos and Daniela Ginsburg, 98–120. New York: Fordham University Press.

Carson, Rachel. (1962) 2002. *Silent Spring.* New York: Houghton Mifflin.

Cassidy, Rebecca, and Molly Mullin. 2007. *Where the Wild Things Are Now: Domestication Reconsidered.* London: Routledge.

Castree, Noel. 2005. *Nature.* London: Routledge.

Conklin, Beth A., and Laura R. Graham. 1995. "The Shifting Middle Ground: Amazonian Indians and Eco-politics." *American Anthropologist* 97 (4): 695–710.

Conklin, Harold C. 1957. *Hanunoo Agriculture: A Report on an Integral System of Shifting Cultivation in the Philippines.* Rome: United Nations Food and Agricultural Organization.

Corson, Catherine A. 2016. *Corridors of Power: The Politics of Environmental Aid to Madagascar.* New Haven, CT: Yale University Press.

Cronon, William. 1996. "The Trouble with Wilderness: or, Getting Back to the Wrong Nature." *Environmental History* 1 (1): 7–28.

Cruikshank, Julie. 2006. *Do Glaciers Listen? Local Knowledge, Colonial Encounters, and Social Imagination.* Vancouver: University of British Columbia Press.

Daggett, Cara New. 2019. *The Birth of Energy: Fossil Fuels, Thermodynamics, and the Politics of Work.* Durham, NC: Duke University Press, 2019.

Davenport, Sarah Grace, and Joanna Mishtal. 2019. "Whose Sustainability? An Analysis of a Community Farming Program's Food Justice and Environmental Sustainability Agenda." *Culture, Agriculture, Food, and Environment* 41 (1): 56–65.

de la Cadena, Marisol. 2015. *Earth Beings: Ecologies of Practice across Andean Worlds.* Durham, NC: Duke University Press.

Delaney, David. 2009. *Law and Nature.* Cambridge: Cambridge University Press.

—

Deming, Alison Hawthorne, and Lauret E. Savoy. 2011. *The Colors of Nature: Culture, Identity, and the Natural World*. Minneapolis, MN: Milkweed Editions.

Demos, T. J. 2017. *Against the Anthropocene: Visual Culture and Environment Today*. Berlin: Sternberg Press.

Dennis, Richard. 2008. *Cities in Modernity: Representations and Productions of Metropolitan Space, 1840–1930*. Cambridge: Cambridge University Press.

Douglas, Mary. 1957. "Animals in Lele Religious Symbolism." *Africa* 27 (1): 46–58.

Dove, Michael R. 1983. "Theories of Swidden Agriculture, and the Political Economy of Ignorance." *Agroforestry Systems* 1 (2): 85–99.

———. 2021. *Bitter Shade: The Ecological Challenge of Human Consciousness*. New Haven, CT: Yale University Press.

Dove, Michael R., and Carol Carpenter, eds. 2008. *Environmental Anthropology: A Historical Reader*. Malden, MA: Blackwell Publishing.

Duara, Prasenjit. 2015. *The Crisis of Global Modernity: Asian Traditions and a Sustainable Future*. Cambridge: Cambridge University Press.

Dudley, Kathryn. 2014. *Guitar Makers: The Endurance of Artisanal Values in North America*. Chicago: University of Chicago Press.

Duffy, Rosaleen. 2007. "Gemstone Mining in Madagascar: Transnational Networks, Criminalisation and Global Integration." *Journal of Modern African Studies* 45 (2): 185–206.

Dungy, Camille T., ed. 2009. *Black Nature: Four Centuries of African American Nature Poetry*. Athens: University of Georgia Press.

Elias, Ann. 2019. *Coral Empire: Underwater Oceans, Colonial Tropics, Visual Modernity*. Durham, NC: Duke University Press.

Ellen, Roy, Peter Parkes, and Alan Bicker. 2003. *Indigenous Environmental Knowledge and Its Transformations: Critical Anthropological Perspectives*. London: Routledge.

Escobar, Arturo. (1995) 2011. *Encountering Development*. Princeton, NJ: Princeton University Press.

Fairbairn, Madeleine. 2020. *Fields of Gold: Financing the Global Land Rush*. Ithaca, NY: Cornell University Press.

Fairhead, James, and Melissa Leach. 1996. *Misreading the African Landscape: Society and Ecology in a Forest–Savanna Mosaic*. Cambridge: Cambridge University Press.

Ferguson, James. 1990. *The Anti-Politics Machine: "Development," Depoliticization and Bureaucratic Power in Lesotho*. Cambridge: Cambridge University Press.

Finney, Carolyn. 2014. *Black Faces, White Spaces: Reimagining the Relationship of African Americans to the Great Outdoors*. Chapel Hill: University of North Carolina Press.

Fitzmaurice, Connor J., and Brian Gareau. 2016. *Organic Futures: Struggling for Sustainability on the Small Farm*. New Haven, CT: Yale University Press.

Gagne, Karine. 2019. *Caring for Glaciers: Land, Animals, and Humanity in the Himalayas*. Seattle: University of Washington Press.

Galvin, Shaila Seshia. 2018. "The Farming of Trust: Organic Certification and the Limits of Transparency in Uttarakhand, India." *American Ethnologist* 45 (4): 495–507.

—

Gandy, Matthew. 2005. "Cyborg Urbanization: Complexity and Monstrosity in the Contemporary City." *International Journal of Urban and Regional Research* 29 (1): 26–49.

Gardner, Katy. 2012. *Discordant Development: Global Capitalism and the Struggle for Connection in Bangladesh*. London: Pluto Press.

Geertz, Clifford. 1972. "The Wet and the Dry: Traditional Irrigation in Bali and Morocco." *Human Ecology* 1 (1): 23–39.

Goldman, Mara. 2011. "Strangers in Their Own Land: Maasai and Wildlife Conservation in Northern Tanzania." *Conservation and Society* 9 (1): 65–79.

Gordillo, Gaston. 2014. *Rubble: The Afterlife of Destruction*. Durham, NC: Duke University Press.

Govindrajan, Radhika. 2015. "'The Goat That Died for Family': Animal Sacrifice and Interspecies Kinship in India's Central Himalayas." *American Ethnologist* 42 (3): 504–19.

Grove, Richard. 1996. *Green Imperialism: Colonial Expansion, Tropical Island Edens and the Origins of Environmentalism, 1600–1860*. Cambridge: Cambridge University Press.

Guthman, Julie. 2014. *Agrarian Dreams: The Paradox of Organic Farming in California*. Berkeley: University of California Press.

Haenn, Nora, Richard Wilk, and Allison Harnish, eds. 2016. *The Environment in Anthropology: A Reader in Ecology, Culture, and Sustainable Living*. 2nd ed. New York: New York University Press.

Halvaksz, Jamon Alex. 2020. *Gardens of Gold: Place-Making in Papua New Guinea*. Seattle: University of Washington Press.

Haraway, Donna. 2016. *Staying with the Trouble: Making Kin in the Chthulucene*. Durham, NC: Duke University Press.

Heller, Chaia. 2013. *Food Solidarity: French Farmers and the Fight against Industrial Agriculture and Genetically Modified Crops*. Durham, NC: Duke University Press.

Helmreich, Stefan. 2009. *Alien Ocean: Anthropological Voyages in Microbial Seas*. Berkeley: University of California Press.

Heywood, Vernon Hilton, and Robert Tony Watson. 1995. *Global Biodiversity Assessment*. Cambridge: Cambridge University Press.

Hobart, Hi'ilei Julia. 2017. "A 'Queer-Looking Compound': Race, Abjection, and the Politics of Hawaiian Poi." *Global Food History* 3 (2): 133–49.

Holleman, Hannah. 2018. *Dust Bowls of Empire: Imperialism, Environmental Politics, and the Injustice of "Green" Capitalism*. New Haven, CT: Yale University Press.

Howe, Cymene. 2019. *Ecologics: Wind and Power in the Anthropocene*. Durham, NC: Duke University Press.

Hulme, Mike. 2011. "Reducing the Future to Climate: A Story of Climate Determinism and Reductionism." *Osiris* 26 (1), https://doi.org/10.1086/661274.

Iheka, Cajetan. 2018. *Naturalizing Africa: Ecological Violence, Agency, and Postcolonial Resistance in African Literature*. Cambridge: Cambridge University Press.

Ingold, Tim. 1993. "Globes and Spheres." *Environmentalism* 32:31–42.

Isenhour, Cindy. 2011. "How the Grass Became Greener in the City: On Urban Imaginings and Practices of Sustainable Living in Sweden." *City and Society* 23 (2): 117–34.

Jørgensen, Dolly. 2015. "Rethinking Rewilding." *Geoforum* 65:482–88.

—

Kikon, Dolly. 2019. *Living with Oil and Coal: Resource Politics and Militarization in Northeast India*. Seattle: University of Washington Press.

Kimmerer, Robin. 2017. "Speaking of Nature." *Orion Magazine*, June 12, 2017. https://orionmagazine.org/article/speaking-of-nature/

King, Tiffany. 2019. *The Black Shoals: Offshore Formations of Black and Native Studies*. Durham, NC: Duke University Press.

Kirksey, S. Eben, and Stefan Helmreich. 2010. "The emergence of multispecies ethnography." *Cultural Anthropology* 25 (4): 545–76.

Kirsch, Stuart. 2007. "Indigenous Movements and the Risks of Counterglobalization: Tracking the Campaign against Papua New Guinea's Ok Tedi Mine." *American Ethnologist* 34 (2): 303–21.

Kohn, Eduardo. 2013. *How Forests Think: Toward an Anthropology beyond the Human*. Berkeley: University of California Press.

Kopnina, Helen. 2017. "Beyond Multispecies Ethnography: Engaging with Violence and Animal Rights in Anthropology." *Critique of Anthropology* 37 (3): 333–57.

Kull, Christian A. 2002. "Madagascar Aflame: Landscape Burning as Peasant Protest, Resistance, or a Resource Management Tool?" *Political Geography* 21 (7): 927–53.

Lansing, J. Stephen. 2012. *Perfect Order: Recognizing Complexity in Bali*. Princeton, NJ: Princeton University Press.

Latour, Bruno. 2004. *Politics of Nature: How to Bring the Sciences into Democracy*. Translated by Catherine Porter. Cambridge, MA: Harvard University Press.

Leach, Melissa, Belinda Reyers, Xuemei Bai, Eduardo S. Brondizio, Christina Cook, Sandra Díaz, Giovana Espindola, Michelle Scobie, Mark Stafford-Smith, and Suneetha M. Subramanian. 2018. "Equity and Sustainability in the Anthropocene: A Social-Ecological Systems Perspective on Their Intertwined Futures." *Global Sustainability* 1.

Lennon, Myles. 2017. "Decolonizing Energy: Black Lives Matter and Technoscientific Expertise amid Solar Transitions." *Energy Research and Social Science* 30:18–27.

Li, Tania Murray. 2000. "Articulating Indigenous Identity in Indonesia: Resource Politics and the Tribal Slot." *Comparative Studies in Society and History* 42 (1): 149–79.

——. 2018. "After the Land Grab: Infrastructural Violence and the 'Mafia System' in Indonesia's Oil Palm Plantation Zones." *Geoforum* 96:328–37.

Lorimer, Jamie. 2016. "Gut Buddies Multispecies Studies and the Microbiome." *Environmental Humanities* 8 (1): 57–76.

Mancuso, Stefano. 2021. *The Nation of Plants*. Translated by Gregory Conti. New York: Other Press.

Marris, Emma. 2013. *Rambunctious Garden: Saving Nature in a Post-Wild World*. New York: Bloomsbury Publishing.

Mathews, Andrew S. 2005. "Power/Knowledge, Power/Ignorance: Forest Fires and the State in Mexico." *Human Ecology* 33 (6): 795–820.

——. 2020. "Anthropology and the Anthropocene: Criticisms, Experiments, and Collaborations." *Annual Reviews of Anthropology* 49:67–82.

Mauss, Marcel. (1979) 2013. *Seasonal Variations of the Eskimo: A Study in Social Morphology*. London: Routledge.

—

McElwee, Pamela D. 2012. "Payments for Environmental Services as Neoliberal Market-Based Forest Conservation in Vietnam: Panacea or Problem?" *Geoforum* 43 (3): 412–26.

McNeill, John, and Peter Engelke. 2016. *The Great Acceleration: An Environmental History of the Anthropocene since 1945*. Cambridge, MA: Belknap Press.

Menzies, Nicholas. 2021. *Ordering the Myriad Things: The Transition from Traditional Knowledge of Plants to Scientific Botany in China, 1850–1960*. Seattle: University of Washington Press.

Moore, Amelia. 2012. "The Aquatic Invaders: Marine Management Figuring Fishermen, Fisheries, and Lionfish in the Bahamas." *Cultural Anthropology* 27 (4): 667–88.

Muehlmann, Shaylih. 2012. "Rhizomes and Other Uncountables: The Malaise of Enumeration in Mexico's Colorado River Delta." *American Ethnologist* 39 (2): 339–53.

Murray, Wendi Field, María Nieves Zedeño, Kacy L. Hollenback, Calvin Grinnell, and Elgin Crows Breast. 2011. "The Remaking of Lake Sakakawea: Locating Cultural Viability in Negative Heritage on the Missouri River." *American Ethnologist* 38 (3): 468–83.

Nash, Roderick Frazier. 2014. *Wilderness and the American Mind*. 5th ed. New Haven, CT: Yale University Press.

Nazarea, Virginia D. 2006. *Cultural Memory and Biodiversity*. Tucson: University of Arizona Press.

Neumann, Roderick P. 1998. *Imposing Wilderness: Struggles over Livelihood and Nature Preservation in Africa*. Berkeley: University of California Press.

Ogden, Laura A., Billy Hall, and Kimiko Tanita. 2013. "Animals, Plants, People, and Things: A Review of Multispecies Ethnography." *Environment and Society* 4 (1): 5–24.

O'Reilly, Jessica, Cindy Isenhour, Pamela McElwee, and Ben Orlove. 2020. "Climate Change: Expanding Anthropological Possibilities." *Annual Reviews of Anthropology* 49:13–29.

Osterhoudt, Sarah R. 2020. "'Nobody Wants to Kill': Economies of Affect and Violence in Madagascar's Vanilla Boom." *American Ethnologist* 47 (3): 249–63.

Pandian, Anand. 2014. "Thinking like a Mountain." *Hau: Journal of Ethnographic Theory* 4 (2): 245–52.

Paprocki, Kasia. 2021. *Threatening Dystopias: The Global Politics of Climate Change Adaptation in Bangladesh*. Ithaca, NY: Cornell University Press.

Patel, Raj, and Jason W. Moore. 2017. *A History of the World in Seven Cheap Things: A Guide to Capitalism, Nature, and the Future of the Planet*. Oakland: University of California Press.

Paulson, Susan, and Lisa Gezon, eds. 2005. *Political Ecology across Spaces, Scales, and Social Groups*. New Brunswick, NJ: Rutgers University Press.

Peet, Richard, Paul Robbins, and Michael J. Watts, eds. 2011. *Global Political Ecology*. London: Routledge.

Pellow, David Naguib. 2007. *Resisting Global Toxics: Transnational Movements for Environmental Justice*. Cambridge, MA: MIT Press, 2007.

Perrings, Charles, Karl-Göran Mäler, Carl Folke, C. S. Holling, and Bengt-Owe Jansson, eds. 1997. *Biodiversity Loss: Economic and Ecological Issues*. Cambridge: Cambridge University Press.

—

Petrini, Carlo, ed. 2010. *Slow Food: Collected Thoughts on Taste, Tradition, and the Honest Pleasures of Food*. New York: Chelsea Green.

Povinelli, Elisabeth. 2016. *Geontologies: A Requiem to Late Liberalism*. Durham, NC: Duke University Press.

Powell, Dana E., and Dáilan J. Long. 2010. "Landscapes of Power: Renewable Energy Activism in Diné Bikéyah." In *Indians and Energy: Exploitation and Opportunity in the American Southwest*, edited by Sherry L. Smith and Brian Frehner, 231–62. Santa Fe, NM: School for Advanced Research Press.

Prete, Giovanni, and Christel Cournil. 2019. "Staging International Environmental Justice: The International Monsanto Tribunal." *Political and Legal Anthropology Review* 42 (2): 191–209.

Rademacher, Anne. 2015. "Urban Political Ecology." *Annual Review of Anthropology* 44: 137–52.

Rademacher, Anne, and K. Sivaramakrishnan, eds. 2017. *Places of Nature in Ecologies of Urbanism*. Hong Kong: Hong Kong University Press.

———, eds. 2021. *The Death and Life of Nature in Asian Cities*. Hong Kong: Hong Kong University Press.

Rappaport, Roy A. (1968) 2000. *Pigs for the Ancestors: Ritual in the Ecology of a New Guinea People*. 2nd ed. Long Grove, IL: Waveland Press.

Reno, Joshua. 2016. *Waste Away: Working and Living with a North American Landfill*. Oakland: University of California Press.

Robbins, Paul. 2004. *Political Ecology: A Critical Introduction*. London: Blackwell.

Rocheleau, Dianne E. 2008. "Political Ecology in the Key of Policy: From Chains of Explanation to Webs of Relation." *Geoforum* 39 (2): 716–27.

Ryan, John Charles. 2012. "Passive Flora? Reconsidering Nature's Agency through Human-Plant Studies (HPS)." *Societies* 2 (3): 101–21.

Schiebinger, Londa, and Claudia Swan, eds. 2007. *Colonial Botany: Science, Commerce, and Politics in the Early Modern World*. Philadelphia: University of Pennsylvania Press.

Scott, James C. (1998) 2008. *Seeing Like a State*. New Haven, CT: Yale University Press, 2008.

Shilliam, Robbie. 2015. *The Black Pacific: Anti-Colonial Struggles and Oceanic Connections*. London: Bloomsbury.

Shipton, Parker MacDonald. 2010. *Credit between Cultures: Farmers, Financiers, and Misunderstanding in Africa*. New Haven, CT: Yale University Press.

Shiva, Vandana. 2016. *Staying Alive: Women, Ecology and Development*. London: Zed Books.

Sivaramakrishnan, K. 2009. "Forests and the Environmental History of India." *Journal of Peasant Studies* 36 (2): 299–324.

———. 2015. "Ethics of Nature in Indian Environmental History." *Modern Asian Studies* 49 (4): 1261–1310.

Smith, Linda Tuhiwai. 2013. *Decolonizing Methodologies: Research and Indigenous Peoples*. Zed Books.

Smith, Will. 2020. *Mountains of Blame: Climate and Culpability in the Philippine Uplands*. Seattle: University of Washington Press.

—

Staples, James. 2020. *Sacred Cows and Chicken Manchurian: The Everyday Politics of Eating Meat in India*. Seattle: University of Washington Press.

Sternsdorff-Cisterna, Nicolas. 2019. *Food Safety after Fukushima: Scientific Citizenship and the Politics of Risk*. Honolulu: University of Hawai'i Press.

Steward, Julian Haynes. 1938. *Basin-Plateau Aboriginal Sociopolitical Groups*. Washington, DC: US Government Printing Office.

Strang, Veronica. 2020. "Re-imagining the River: New Environmental Ethics in Human Engagements with Water." *One Earth* 2 (3): 204–6.

Swanson, Heather Anne. 2022. *Spawning Modern Fish: Transnational Comparison in the Making of Japanese Salmon*. Seattle: University of Washington Press.

Szczygielska, Marianna, and Olga Cielemęcka. 2019. "Plantarium: Human–Vegetal Ecologies." Introduction to "Plantarium: Human–Vegetal Ecologies." Special section, *Catalyst* 5 (2): 1–12.

Taylor, Dorceta. 2014. *Toxic Communities: Environmental Racism, Industrial Pollution, and Residential Mobility*. New York: New York University Press.

Thiele, Leslie Paul. 2016. *Sustainability*. 2nd ed. Cambridge, UK: Polity Press.

Todd, Zoe. 2016. "An Indigenous Feminist's Take on the Ontological Turn: 'Ontology' Is Just Another Word for Colonialism." *Journal of Historical Sociology* 29 (1): 4–22.

Tsing, Anna L. 2005. *Friction: An Ethnography of Global Connection*. Princeton, NJ: Princeton University Press.

———. (2017) 2021. *The Mushroom at the End of the World: On the Possibility of Life in Capitalist Ruins*. Princeton, NJ: Princeton University Press.

Tubb, Daniel. 2020. *Shifting Livelihoods: Gold Mining and Subsistence in the Chocó, Colombia*. Seattle: University of Washington Press.

Tuck, Eve, and K. Wayne Yang. 2012. "Decolonization Is not a Metaphor." *Decolonization* 1 (1): 1–40.

Tucker, Richard. 2000. *Insatiable Appetite: The United States and the Ecological Degradation of the Tropical World*. Berkeley: University of California Press.

Vaughn, Sarah E. 2017. "Imagining the Ordinary in Participatory Climate Adaptation." *Weather, Climate, and Society* 9 (3): 533–43.

Velásquez Runk, Julie, Chindío Peña Ismare, and Toño Peña Conquista. 2019. "Animal Transference and Transformation among Wounaan." *Journal of Latin American and Caribbean Anthropology* 24 (1): 32–51.

Walker, Brett. 2011. *Toxic Archipelago: A History of Industrial Disease in Japan*. Seattle: University of Washington Press.

Warde, Paul. 2018. *The Invention of Sustainability: Nature and Destiny, c. 1500–1870*. Cambridge: Cambridge University Press.

Weller, Robert P. 2006. *Discovering Nature: Globalization and Environmental Culture in China and Taiwan*. Cambridge: Cambridge University Press.

West, Paige. 2006. *Conservation Is Our Government Now: The Politics of Ecology in Papua New Guinea*. Durham, NC: Duke University Press.

West, Paige, James Igoe, and Dan Brockington. 2006. "Parks and Peoples: The Social Impact of Protected Areas." *Annual Review of Anthropology* 35:251–77.

—

Wilson, Edward O. 1992. *The Diversity of Life*. Cambridge, MA: Harvard University Press.

Wilson, Japhy. 2021. *Reality of Dreams: Post-Neoliberal Utopias in the Ecuadorian Amazon*. New Haven, CT: Yale University Press.

Yusoff, Kathryn. 2019. *A Billion Black Anthropocenes or None*. Minneapolis: University of Minnesota Press.

Zee, Jerry. 2017. "Holding Patterns: *Sand* and Political Time at China's Desert Shores." *Cultural Anthropology* 32 (2): 215–41.

Zhang, Amy. 2020. "Circularity and Enclosures: Metabolizing Waste with the Black Soldier Fly." *Cultural Anthropology* 35 (1): 74–103.

Zimmerer, Karl S., and Thomas J. Bassett. 2003. *Political Ecology: An Integrative Approach to Geography and Environment-Development Studies*. New York: Guilford Press.

—

FARMING AND FOOD

INTRODUCTION

Everyone needs food in some form to survive; eating is a universal human activity that connects people through time and space. Anthropological studies of food bring together the material and symbolic facets of being human, encompassing both the physical nature of procuring and consuming food as well as the meanings that people and groups confer upon experiences that revolve around eating. More than the ingestion of calories, preparing, eating, sharing, and savoring meals connect to realms of memory, identity, and community. Food accompanies humans as they move to new places, as they forge social bonds, as they celebrate, and as they mourn. Examining questions of food access, food justice, and the social dimension of taste reveals the deeply situated forms of historical, social, and economic power connected to food. In this way, eating is always, in part, a political act.

Food, whether from plants or animals, comes from somewhere. Anthropologists examine food production across differing strategies and scales, from backyard gardens to large-scale plantations to factory farms. As with consuming food, producing food bridges material, social, and symbolic realms. Patterns of land ownership, as well as which crops are cultivated where, by whom, and for whose benefit, reflect entrenched patterns of

—

political and economic power, often based on relations of colonialism and the capitalistic exploitation of people and nature. Agrarian relationships also shape more personal notions of identity and community—of being, belonging, and becoming in the world. These relationships include those between humans, plants, and animals, as the practice of agriculture is inherently a multispecies enterprise.

The spheres of food production and consumption do not exist in isolation. Increasingly, ethnographies of food and agriculture focus on the "in-between" spaces of food systems, including regulators, transporters, inspectors, and food scientists, as well as the people who stock shelves and work the checkout lines in grocery stores. These studies often follow a commodity as it moves (or does not move) between spheres of production, exchange, and consumption, gaining and shedding forms of meaning and value along the way.

Chapters 1 and 2 each address to some degree the spheres of food production, trade, and consumption and the connections between them. Both authors foreground the everyday experiences that connect individuals to global food systems. They illustrate how these systems not only produce certain types of food but also attempt to fashion particular types of agrarian and political subjects. For example, Shaila Seshia Galvin brings us to the rice fields of the Doon Valley in the northern Indian state of Uttarakhand to consider how organic certification simultaneously projects work across material, ethical, and affective realms. She notes that, for farmers, the processes of organic certification come to rely on qualitative assessments of "morally uncontaminated character as much as on chemically uncontaminated land" (57). Hiʻilei Julia Hobart analyzes the discourses that both Indigenous Hawaiians and outsiders to the region circulate about poi, a pudding-like substance fashioned from taro root that occupies an important place in Indigenous diets and cosmologies. Hobart connects the derogatory and racialized narratives that outsiders have long crafted about poi to the historical seizure of Indigenous land within Hawaiʻi's settler-colonial context, illustrating the violent ways that "taste and territory are profoundly co-produced" (79).

Both articles in this section point to ways that a close ethnographic understanding of the cultural and affective dimensions of food systems help address broader sustainability challenges including food justice,

—

agrobiodiversity, and food sovereignty. They underscore how food systems touch upon the intimate relations that humans forge with each other, with their own ideas of self, and with nature. It is only with close attention to these integral, more qualitative dimensions of growing and eating food that we can imagine more sustainable, just, and diverse food systems—systems designed to enhance the nourishment of all human and nonhuman beings that together make up agrarian landscapes.

DISCUSSION QUESTIONS

1. As Hobart notes, "Because food is both edible and agricultural, we must keep one eye carefully trained on its historical context and the other on the construction of taste" (79). How are questions of which foods people find delicious relevant to issues of sustainability? Consider some foods that you find delicious, and place your personal preferences into broader social, historical, economic, environmental, and cultural contexts.

2. The case of organic rice certification in India shows how northern consumer ideals of pureness, transparency, and trust influence how farmers are required to act to obtain certification. What images and ideals come to mind when you hear the term *organic*? Why? Did the ethnographic example of rice certification alter any of your assumptions about organically certified products? If so, how?

3. You are placed on a committee in charge of designing more sustainable food programs for your campus. What are some initial questions you would ask to better understand the existing dynamics of food at your school? What are some initiatives or programs you may explore? In your response, consider the differing scales of food systems—local, regional, and national—as well as the social, cultural, and economic dimensions of sustainability.

1

THE FARMING OF TRUST

ORGANIC CERTIFICATION AND THE LIMITS OF TRANSPARENCY IN UTTARAKHAND, INDIA

SHAILA SESHIA GALVIN

In the summer of 2008, some 4,500 diaries lay neatly stacked in the foyer of Uttarakhand's Organic Commodity Board, awaiting distribution to organic farmers across this largely Himalayan state in northern India. The Organic Board, which administers organic agriculture and certification for the state government, obliges organic farmers registered under its auspices to regularly document their agricultural activities in these diaries as part of third-party organic certification requirements. Details that farmers were required to record included how they procured and treated seeds, cleaned agricultural tools, sourced livestock feed, and used veterinary medicines, as well as what inputs they applied to their fields, in what quantities, and at what times of year. In other regions of the world, writing practices such as this are familiar to farmers as an integral element of agriculture (Joly 2010), but for many farmers in Uttarakhand, diary keeping, and the larger regime of record keeping of which it forms a part, only recently became a routinized element of their work.

Originally published as, Seshia Galvin, S., 2018. The Farming of Trust: Organic Certification and the Limits of Transparency in Uttarakhand, India. *American Ethnologist*, 45(4), pp. 495–507. Reprinted with permission from John Wiley & Sons, all rights reserved.

—

Farmers' diaries are the foundational document of organic certification, a documentary filament that connects organic farmers in the Doon Valley to a wider world of national and international organic standards. On them rests an elaborate scaffold of certification documents, institutions, and procedures linking cultivated fields in the valley to bureaucratic and corporate offices in the state capital of Dehradun, as well as in Delhi and beyond. The diaries are the primary written record through which compliance with nationally and internationally defined organic standards can be monitored and evaluated by certification inspectors and master trainers. The latter act as important liaisons and advisers who provide farmers with agricultural extension advice and assist them with certification processes, in addition to facilitating links among the Organic Board, organic producer groups, and private-sector buyers. Unlike other kinds of certification documents, farmers' diaries remain with the farmer at his or her home, where they are intended to make transparent, classifiable, and translatable the everyday work of organic farming.

So great was the detail called for in these diaries that they were described to me as a "mirror of the field" by Prakash Sharma, technical adviser for Hira Foods, a major Indian rice retailer that procured organic basmati rice paddy (unmilled rice) through contract farming with Doon Valley farmers.[1] Likening the diaries to mirrors that reflect daily agrarian practices, his metaphor resonated uncannily with Michel Foucault's (1988, 30) understandings of diary keeping as a key constituent of the technologies of the self. Early confessional diaries offer an illustration of Foucault's ideas: "Puritans replaced Catholic confession to a priest with the confessional diary, an account book of one's state of sin. . . . The 'work' of the journal was precisely to effect this linkage of self with biblical standards of measurement" (Paden, 1988, 70–71). The functional qualities of 17th-century confessional diaries—as both a mirror and a metric—are also replicated in 21st-century farmers' diaries in Uttarakhand. In a manner akin to early confessional diaries, they are supposed to serve as an "account book" of an individual farmer's "organicness."

The advent of organic certification in Uttarakhand, then, heralds new forms of agrarian governmentality as farmers, via the requirements and practices of document keeping, become subjects of agricultural bureaucracies, national and transnational regulatory frameworks, and international

—

audit practices. Farmers' diaries became part of a repertoire of standard-ization and documentary practices associated with organic agriculture in 2003, when the newly created state government of Uttarakhand embarked on a strategy to promote and develop certified and commercially ambitious organic agriculture among the region's smallholder farmers. The year is significant. The advent of state-led organic agriculture followed closely on the heels of Uttarakhand's formation in the year 2000, when it was carved out of the larger, more populous state of Uttar Pradesh. Uttarakhand's new senior civil servants, some of whom hailed from its mountainous districts, sought to define a strategy for agricultural development better suited to Himalayan agriculture and distinct from the yield-focused agricultural policies pursued on the plains of Uttar Pradesh. The Uttarakhand state government's promotion of organic farming also emerged in the wake of more than a decade of India's liberalizing economic reforms, which promised access to lucrative export markets at precisely a time when sales of organic products were beginning to grow rapidly in Europe and North America.

When I first encountered the regime of documentation necessitated by organic certification, its mechanisms for recording, quantifying, and clas-sifying agrarian practices and farmers themselves appeared to exemplify a modernist project of legibility (Scott 1998). Its requirement that farmers participate in making agrarian practices transparent also seemed illustra-tive of neoliberal and audit governmentality (Ballestero 2012, 160; Heth-erington 2011, 7). The expansion of international and national organic certification regimes may therefore be understood as a "neoliberal trade strategy" and a Weberian "extension of revised forms of bureaucratic ratio-nality through a national and transnational institutional matrix" (Muters-baugh 2005, 397).

The instruments and practices by which certification is intended to afford transparency, visibility, and legibility, among them documents and inspections, align it with audit cultures (Strathern 2000a). As a mecha-nism for producing transparency, audit is intended to establish account-ability and trust by affording "external visibility of internal processes" (Power 1996, 21), often using third-party agencies to verify compliance. Indeed, in Europe and North America, which together account for 90 percent of global retail sales of organic food (FiBL and IFOAM 2018, 68),

—

regulatory agencies frequently posit a causal relationship in which organic certification ensures accountability and thereby engenders public trust.

But the qualities of bureaucratic rationality and neoliberal governmentality ascribed to certified organic agriculture, and broadly similar certifications such as fair trade, may also be at odds with established forms of sociality and morality in agrarian settings and food systems. On the one hand, for farmers and laborers, fair trade and organic certifications may conflict with and undermine historically situated moral economies (Besky 2014; Moberg 2014). On the other hand, as consumers, "we are continually asked to place our trust in standards and certification processes at the expense of our trust in interpersonal relationships and daily interactions informed by wisdom locally generated and grounded in place" (DeLind 2000, 200). Thus, while regulatory authorities hail certification as the guarantor of public trust in organic agriculture and other domains, the everyday practices of certification may displace or erode forms of sociality and morality that inform relations of production.

As organic agriculture becomes established under state government auspices in the Doon Valley, trust can be understood neither as solely emergent in personalized relations and situated moral economies nor as simply an outcome of certification processes. Instead, trust is conditioned through practices of organic certification, and, paradoxically, it also sustains them. During my fieldwork in 2007 and 2008, farmers' diaries, perhaps unsurprisingly, did not prove to be "mirrors of the field."[2] They did not reveal or make transparent actual agricultural practices, for they were often not filled in by farmers but rather by master trainers who worked for the Organic Board.

In many settings, bureaucratic practices, including audit and certification, rarely achieve transparency (Mathur 2016) or legibility (Das 2004). Instead, the instruments intended to realize these objectives frequently produce opacity and ignorance (Anand 2015; Hull 2003, 2008; Mathews 2005, 2008). While similar observations may also be made about organic certification in the Doon Valley, they do not capture the whole story. Certification's failure to produce transparency not only generated impulses for more expansive and intensive forms of surveillance but also encouraged certification inspectors and master trainers to rely on their evaluations of farmers' moral character and on what they described to me as *viśvās* (trust, belief, or faith).

As these officials grappled with documents that were both vitally important and frequently incomplete, and with the impossibility of visiting and monitoring all the fields of every organic farmer, many came to understand organic agriculture as a moral enterprise and to describe organic farming as *viśvās kī khetī*, the "farming of trust." This understanding, along with their own sentiments of *viśvās*, allowed them to carry out organic certification. Precisely because documents were so central to certification and their production was recognized to be so imperfect, *viśvās* became integral to how certification officials managed forms of uncertainty that emerged from systems intended to yield certainty and knowledge. In the Doon Valley, then, organic fields are also moral fields, and *viśvās* is a managerial sentiment that sustains certification.

THE ROOTS OF ORGANIC CERTIFICATION IN UTTARAKHAND

Organic agriculture is popularly regarded as an alternative to industrial agriculture and the factory farm, especially in those regions of the world where food and agricultural production assume such forms. Uttarakhand does not share these experiences of agricultural modernization, and the origins of certified organic agriculture lie less in the environmental movements and activism for which the region is known (Guha 1989; Linkenbach 2006) than in a series of World Bank Projects undertaken in the 1990s and early 2000s. Building on long-standing anxieties about erosion and environmental degradation in the Himalaya (Karan and Iijima 1985; Thompson, Warburton, and Hatley 1986), initial projects focused on halting soil loss. In later interventions, aims shifted to enhancing the income of farmers by expanding agricultural markets. Presaging subsequent organic farming initiatives, farmers were encouraged not only to adopt new composting methods and pest-management techniques, but also to diversify their production from "traditional and low value food grains cereal crops to other high value crops" (World Bank 2002, iii), such as basmati rice, spices, and horticultural crops (see also World Bank 1999, 2004).

—

In the early 21st century, certified organic agriculture in Uttarakhand has become a unique site of convergence for processes of subnational state formation and liberalizing economic reforms. As a part of its organic strategy, the state established the Organic Commodity Board to offer agricultural extension advice and training, encourage the development of group organic certification, and connect cultivators to food wholesalers and retailers in India's growing private sector. It also established India's first state-run third-party organic certification agency. These newly created agricultural bureaucracies implement and enforce national and international standards for organic production and certification, drawing farmers into novel relations with the state government.

Farmers who register with the state's Organic Board are required to cultivate their crops in accordance with standards set out in the Government of India's National Programme on Organic Production and to maintain a daily record of their practices in their farmers' diaries. Since most farmers cultivate fewer than two hectares of land and because the costs of certification would be too much for them to bear individually, organic farmers are grouped in federations for the purpose of group certification and contract farming. In the Doon Valley, there are four such federations, each of which had from 300 to 400 members in 2007 and 2008. As the bedrock of group certification, farmers' federations constitute an internal control system (ICS), mandated under national and international protocols for organic certification. ICSs have been adapted to the context of smallholder organic agriculture from audit procedures more typically associated with financial accounting and public management, where they provide organizations with in-house mechanisms for ongoing monitoring, measurement, and surveillance.

The Organic Board's own in-house or "internal" inspectors conducted inspections of each farm twice a year as part of the ICS system in the Doon Valley, at which time they reviewed the farmers' diary and other farm-level documentation. They then prepared reports that were forwarded to a third-party certification agency. Once a year, third-party inspectors reviewed the ICS inspection reports and other documents and prepared risk assessments that identified which farmers were at greatest risk of noncompliance. Third-party inspectors conducted their own inspections on the basis of these assessments, focusing their efforts on those farmers

—

who, in the words of one inspector, were deemed "risky." If certification was granted, the federation (not the individual farmer) would qualify as certified organic in India. As a result of efforts to harmonize and create equivalence among organic standards across different national jurisdictions, crops that are certified organic in Uttarakhand may also be sold as such in the European Union and the United States. What enables harmonization and equivalence of organic production in such vastly different agrarian settings is not only shared standards of production but also a recognized infrastructure of audit, founded on document keeping and inspections, to enforce them.

CONFIGURING TRUST THROUGH AUDIT AND CERTIFICATION

As a technology of government that proliferated in the late 20th century, audit is designed to bring transparency and trust into relation with each other. Built on mechanisms that afford visibility and legibility, in which document keeping and inspections figure heavily, audit is supposed to generate other normative outcomes, such as public trust and accountability (Cavanaugh 2016). While audit culture is often thought to have emerged because of a "general decline of trust" (Brown 2010, 746), audits themselves paradoxically demand that trust be placed in their procedures and conclusions (Strathern 2000b, 7). Thus audits are not simply regimes of "trust-making" (Corsín Jiménez 2011, 178), in the sense that they are designed to enable widespread public trust; they are also internally premised on trust (Freidberg 2004, 83–86; Power 1997, 13).

Trust has long been understood as a sentiment kindled through personal relations and forms of solidarity forged over a period of time, often through institutions and practices involving the circulation of money or material objects, and couched in terms of kinship, friendship, exchange, reciprocity, and obligation (Hart 1988; Malinowski 1984; Mauss 2016). In influential bodies of social and political theory (Giddens 1990; Karpik 2010; Putnam 2000; Seligman 1997), trust is frequently conceptualized as a synthetic or binding force within society and taken as the basis of social capital, associational life, markets, and even democracy. But trust—and its counterpart, betrayal—may also be understood ethnographically as

—

involving historically contingent and culturally conditioned sentiments that "influence and shape material production" (Yanagisako 2002, 11). Following Yanagisako's exploration of sentiments as "forces of production," I take the invocation of *viśvās* by master trainers and certification inspectors as an ethnographic and conceptual cue to explore how trust emerges and what it means in processes of organic certification.

On many occasions, certification inspectors and master trainers described organic farming to me as *viśvās kī khetī* or *viśvās wālī chīz* (something to do with trust). *Viśvās* is usually translated into English as "trust," "faith," or "belief." Woven through everyday speech and popular culture in Hindi-speaking North India, it shares with its English analogues a resistance to precise specification. Trying to pinpoint its meanings lays bare "the difficulty of putting into words what is clearly a matter of feeling" (Kakar 1982, 39). For example, in Indian healing practices relating to mental health, *viśvās* inspired in a patient by a healer emerges "below the level of consciousness [as] the patient is busy registering how well the healer opposite him fits into his culturally determined idea of the ideal healer" (Kakar 1982, 39). Despite the difficulty of describing its meanings and foundations, *viśvās* is nonetheless distinguished from the more pejorative term *andha viśvās* (blind beliefs) in medical or healing relationships (Ecks 2013, 56; Kakar 1982; Pinto 2004, 343). In the realm of friendship, *viśvās* conveys intimacy and is associated with *prem* (love) or relations that are enduring and sometimes ritualized (Cohen 2010; Desai 2010). Under these different conditions, *viśvās* is personal and relational, a sentiment inspired by and placed in people. My interlocutors spoke of either *viśvās* or trust depending on whether we conversed in Hindi or English, and while I retain the Hindi term *viśvās*, I also use it interchangeably with trust to make links between my own ethnographic material and wider scholarly debates.[3]

Certification inspectors and master trainers did not understand *viśvās kī khetī* in terms of personal relations, nor for them was *viśvās* wholly inspired by farmers who conformed to a "culturally determined ideal." On the contrary, citing their often brief and cursory interactions and relations with farmers, as well as the inevitable practical constraints on their power to monitor and inspect, they invoked *viśvās* and trust as a way of managing these limits. By doing so, they suggested that these sentiments are not necessarily the consequence of long-standing personal relations, or

—

widely held values and practices—they may emerge also in circumstances in which knowledge and certainty are far more tenuous. In a similar vein, trust has been theorized by the sociologist Diego Gambetta (1988, 218) as "a tentative, intrinsically fragile response to our ignorance," while Parker MacDonald Shipton (2007, 34), studying credit, exchange, and entrustment among the Kenyan Luo, builds on this by making the broad claim that "to trust is to risk betrayal." Understandings of trust in these ethnographic and theoretical realms suggest that it remains also a sentiment inextricably tied to, and emerging out of, uncertainty and ignorance as much as knowledge.

This is relevant because audits are recognized by auditors themselves to amount to the "certification of the unknowable" (Pentland 1993, 611; Power 1997). In the Doon Valley, despite efforts to make agricultural practices legible and visible through documents and inspections, certification inspectors and master trainers readily acknowledged that much remained unknowable to them. In some cases, this arose from a lack of knowledge, as when inspectors spoke of the impossibility of fully knowing every farmer's agricultural practices; in other instances, unknowns were actually generated by the processes of certification itself, such as when inspections interviews with farmers yielded contradictory responses. However they arose, these unknowables produced feelings of uncertainty, and on occasion doubt and suspicion, in inspectors and master trainers.[4] *Viśvās* thus emerged as a necessary and crucial response to certification's prolific uncertainties.

WRITING THE FIELD

In organic certification, elaborate arrays of documents are intended to render agrarian practices legible by standardizing the meanings of "organic" within and across regulatory jurisdictions. Producing and maintaining written documentation—including farmers' diaries and farm files, spreadsheets called actual farmers' lists (AFL), inspection reports, risk assessments, and evaluations—comprises much of the work of organic certification in the Doon Valley. These documents pass through the hands of many people, such as farmers, master trainers, farmers' federation officials, private-sector buyers, ICS inspectors, and inspectors from third-party certification agencies.

Of all the records in the elaborate regime of certification, the AFL appears as the quintessential example of this project of legibility. A continually changing spreadsheet, the AFL succinctly presents all the production details for every farmer registered with the Organic Board. Each row of the spreadsheet represents an individual farmer and details his or her agricultural production, including the cultivated area and expected yield of each crop variety in each year since conversion to organic methods, along with the date when the farmer was first enrolled in the ICS system. The Organic Board's staff generate and maintain the AFL at their headquarters; internal inspectors update the AFL during their inspections with several more columns that note the date of the inspection, the initials of the inspector, and any observations of noncompliance that could compromise organic status. Though farms are geographically dispersed and farmers' cultivated lands are often small and noncontiguous, the AFL makes it possible for certification inspectors, master trainers, managers, and government bureaucrats to know in any given agricultural season who is producing how much of what, and where.

While it is tempting to see this sort of documentation as a contemporary phenomenon, even one associated specifically with neoliberalism, in this region of the Indian Himalaya, land surveys and revenue assessments were introduced in the mid-19th century. They have meant that the monitoring, surveillance, and documentation of agricultural land has long been part of how agriculture and people are governed (Smith 1985). What is new about certification documentation is that farmers participate in producing it. A leaflet distributed to farmers to inform them about the requirements for certification notes that "the documentation of all agricultural activities is an important point of the certification process" and explains the tasks of maintaining a farmer's diary as follows:

> The diary contains the farmer's full name, address, code, total area, and organic area. It also contains all the activities relating to farming such as ploughing of the field, sowing of the seeds, harvesting, quantity of seeds, expected production, actual production, manure used and quantity of insecticides etc. These details are filled daily or weekly. During the inspection, these details are carefully examined

—

by the inspector. Farmers are expected to fill this diary carefully and with responsibility.[5]

Farmers responded to the documentary demands of certification in a variety of ways. Some willingly embraced practices of document making. Comparing organic certification to a degree certificate, a large joint family of brothers, several of whom had retired from the Indian army, characterized organic farming as *ām kisān se alag khetī* (cultivation different from that of the common farmer). They emphasized that their adherence to requirements of documentation in organic agriculture distinguished them from those who had adopted high-yielding seeds and fertilizer packages during the Green Revolution. For them, the farmers' diary was not a technical, bureaucratic document but one with broader social and symbolic meaning. In a setting in which literacy practices do not saturate agricultural life, the farmers' diary proved important as a way of exercising and displaying particular literacy skills (Street 1995; Street and Besnier 1994) that asserted social and cultural distinction.

For others, diaries were important because they effected sought-after linkages to the state. One afternoon, I sat with Nisha Chauhan and her mother, Usha Devi, discussing organic agriculture and certification. With her husband involved in trucking and sand mining in the Doon Valley, in addition to farming their two hectares of land, Usha Devi had spent much of her married life raising their four children and maintaining her home and livestock. Of organic certification, she remarked to me, "What is there to understand? We got it, and that is enough. Now we know that we are organic farmers. What else is there to know about it?" At this point, Nisha, who had recently graduated with a degree in business administration, interjected:

> Proof is necessary. [. . .] This is a government rule, and you have to follow it. Government is emphasizing the benefits of organic farming and giving several facilities [training to make compost, providing organic seeds]. [. . .] If we have this certificate, we can attend the meetings, otherwise not, and you have to return home without attending the meeting.

—

Showing her familiarity with the way that paper artifacts may confer identity and status, and that they are needed to receive other kinds of benefits, she went on, "This certificate is like a passport and visa. Farmers are getting so many facilities from the government." Her analogy highlighted how official documents also afford opportunities for different kinds of mobility—as passports and visas enable travel across national borders, organic certification permits farmers to participate in far-flung domestic and global markets.

Organic agriculture entails literacy practices and skills of "writing the field," as much as cultivating it. In this regard, it is significant that some organic farmers also held (or had recently retired from) positions as schoolteachers, officers in the army or the bureaucracy; others had experience working in banks, insurance companies, and businesses in the state capital. It was usually these farmers who completed their diaries most consistently, suggesting that familiarity and experience with other genres of writing and record keeping helped them "write the field" more readily than others.

Although the rate of basic literacy is quite high in Uttarakhand, not all farmers were familiar with the literacy practices presupposed by the diaries, nor were they all equally inclined to view the completion of farmers' diaries as a worthwhile and meaningful exercise. Laxmi, a widow with two small children, told me that she had received a diary from employees of what she called the Organic Department and explained, "The employees come, they fill up whatever is required, sign it, and go away. We don't write anything in it. We only sign it." Gita, a recently married young woman now living in the home of her husband's family, corroborated this, saying that employees of the Organic Board would complete farmers' documentation. She recalled her father-in-law's response when asked to enroll in the organic basmati export program: "My father-in-law said, 'No, we will not do it [complete the diary]. Who will do it? [. . .] They said that your daughter-in-law can do it. They said that you simply go to the meetings, we will fill up all the forms, but I did not do it." Unlike those for whom farmers' diaries offered the possibility of refashioning agrarian identity, Gita, Laxmi, and many others like them expressed indifference. For them, the farmers' diary did not work as a technology of the self, an account book of their organicness, or a way of being different from the "common

—

farmer." Instead, it was a place where Organic Board officials could narrate organic status.

Writing practices are at the heart of what it means to be certified organic, and farmers become disciplined adherents to organic norms and rules as much through the process of keeping records "carefully and with responsibility," as described in the Organic Board's aforementioned leaflet, as they do through working their fields. But farmers did not produce themselves as compliant subjects in a uniform way.[6] Many experienced the task of daily record keeping as tedious and alien to their practices of cultivation, choosing to engage with it minimally or not at all, and exposing some of the deep fractures in what appears, and aspires, to be a system of agrarian governmentality. Over time, it became clear to me that theoretical moorings such as governmentality and legibility, which have so powerfully anchored analyses of audit and certification, were inadequate for understanding the practices of certification I observed. Puzzled and conceptually adrift, I wondered, How does certification actually proceed?

INSPECTIONS, AND (NOT) KNOWING THE FIELD

"It's all an idea," remarked Dilip Kumar, one of the Organic Board's internal inspectors, with some resignation. He went on,

> It all depends on interviews, documents. What we find in the plot or here, in interviews. Not in foods. Whenever farmers use chemicals, they do not express this in the interview. I do not declare that they use chemicals because it is out of our standard. I am not finding chemicals on the spot.[7]

It was late February 2008, and I was accompanying Dilip and Mohan Singh, a master trainer, while they conducted ICS inspections in the Doon Valley before the wheat harvest at the foot of the Himalaya in Dharampur Block (one of several development "blocks," or government subdistricts, in Uttarakhand). Forgoing meals and breaks, we had spent the day walking from house to house, through several villages, searching out farmers registered with the Organic Board as Dilip updated and annotated the AFL, and recorded his observations and comments in individual inspection reports.

In many instances, inspections interviews were brief. Dilip asked the farmers how much of their land was registered with the Organic Board, which crops they were growing, and where they procured their wheat seeds. The responses farmers gave were often as uniform as the questions Dilip posed, but he recorded each one in his inspection reports. Visits concluded with Dilip asking for the signature or thumbprint of the individual interviewed, an audit ritual (Harper 2000, 23) that hinted at the fact that even if land and agricultural practices are the focus of inspections, farmers are its real subjects. Dilip's weary reflection revealed his sense that there was possibly little correspondence between interviews and documents, on the one hand, and organic practices and food on the other. Instead, producing organic quality hinged on the communicative and literacy practices surrounding organic certification, words exchanged during interviews and recorded in documents.

Though documents are undoubtedly fetishized objects of audit practice, communicative encounters and interactions that take place between inspectors and food producers may be as crucial to production processes as the documents themselves. Among Italian heritage food producers, generating "economic sociability"—banter, laughter, and light conversation—with inspectors and other authorities proved vital to the functioning of neoliberal food production's audit cultures when documents themselves could "only ever partially represent what they were meant to capture" (Cavanaugh 2016, 698). This sort of economic sociability, Jillian Cavanaugh (2016, 696) argues, helps produce what she terms "relationships of responsibility" that run parallel to, or buttress, "structures of accountability" established by documentary requirements of food safety inspections.

Such sociality was rarely evident during certification inspections I observed Dilip and other inspectors undertake. Being obliged to complete hundreds of interviews in a few weeks, he kept pleasantries and conversations to a perfunctory minimum. In most encounters I observed, inspectors directed the exchange, straying little from topics necessary to obtain responses they needed to complete their inspections reports. Inspections, therefore, offered limited opportunity for the development of wider economic sociability and personal relations that Cavanaugh (2016) identified to be so essential for production processes in Italy. To the contrary, Dilip's

—

FIGURE 1.1. An agricultural extension worker, known as a master trainer, inspects a farmer's production diary as part of the process of certifying the crop as organic (Doon Valley, Uttarakhand, India, March 2008). Such diaries played a key role as objects, as much as instruments, of certification inspections. [This figure appears in color in the online issue.]

admission that he was required to take farmers' words and documents at face value, and his self-awareness of the limits of his inspectorial powers, conveyed a pervasive sense of uncertainty about the processes he was charged with certifying. By relying on what was said or documented, and on what could be seen in fields and farms at the time of inspection, Dilip implied that documents and inspections worked performatively to enact "an idea" of organic agriculture.

It was during these inspections that it often became apparent that farmers had not made entries in the diaries that were given to them. Dharampur's master trainer, Mohan, accompanied Dilip on the internal inspections I observed in the winter of 2008. When he found the diary incomplete, Mohan would often speak with members of the farming household and fill in some of the diary as Dilip conducted his inspection interview (see Figure 1.1). This was a fairly common occurrence, and master trainers' practice of completing diaries on behalf of farmers was well

—

known among inspectors, the Organic Board's managers, the external certification agency, and representatives from the company procuring organic basmati. It was, to some extent, also sanctioned by the Organic Board in the abovementioned leaflet, which explained that the diary "may be filled by the farmer himself or by the *mukhiyā* [village leader]." Such allowances recognized that—as managers in the Organic Board's headquarters and field-level master trainers noted—farmers were not in the habit of maintaining written records and that many were not accustomed to such genres of record keeping. To be sure, I never encountered master trainers knowingly entering false data in the diaries. Rather, such explanations were offered to reconcile the realities that master trainers and inspectors faced with the exigencies exacted by certification.

Nonetheless, the importance of documentation was not diminished by the manner in which diaries were often produced. Affirming their central role in certification, Raju, a master trainer, remarked that

> only a document will prove anything. A verbal statement can be changed every two minutes. Documents cannot be changed again and again. Once an entry is made that in this much area there is basmati, then it will remain that much. Documents are necessary, proof is necessary. In organic farming you will find documents with every farmer. Documents are a must. Otherwise there will be no certification. On what basis will the certificate be given if there is no record?

As he emphasized their necessity, Raju made the practice of document keeping tantamount to producing proof, deliberately privileging the written word as something inherently more reliable and less malleable than oral accounts. The qualities of being organic thus came to be constituted through paperwork as much as through agricultural practices, rendering documents objects rather than instruments of certification efforts. In this manner, documents and inspections were marshaled to create a semblance of certainty and transparency even as inspectors and others relayed their sense of uncertainty and their awareness of the unknowables that abounded within the certification process itself. As this happened, certification inspectors and others recast farmers as moral and not purely agrarian subjects.

—

MORAL FIELDS

"There are four pillars of organic farming: trust, honesty, transparency, and honor to commitment," said Prakash Sharma on our first meeting in the grounds of Raiwalla's block headquarters in December 2007, as we waited for farmers to bring their recently harvested organic basmati paddy to be inspected, weighed, and formally purchased by Hira Foods. This depiction of organic agriculture as dependent on a morally uncontaminated character as much as on chemically uncontaminated land was something I repeatedly encountered. Captured in these terms, organic certification required more than adherence to national and international standards. Notably, none of Prakash Sharma's "pillars" referenced land or agricultural practices, the focus of so much documentary labor. Instead, organic certification probed the moral character of farmers. For those charged with certification authority and procurement power, compliance with organic standards became a means through which they could articulate judgments about the moral qualities of organic cultivation and cultivators.[8]

The use of organic agriculture and its certification to register a farmer's honesty and commitment was often brought into sharpest relief when instances of noncompliance surfaced. One such occasion arose in the summer of 2008, when it came to the attention of the Organic Board that several farmers in Raiwalla Block revealed to the third-party certification agency—but not to the Organic Board's own internal inspectors—that they used prohibited chemicals. As we left the office that evening, Satish, the quality manager charged with overseeing the certification program, said to me with some exasperation, "The farmers are very clever. They disclose to the external agency, but they do not disclose to us. We went to check, and they told us no one came. But they have signed the forms [inspection reports]. They are telling lies." In practice, I learned, such divergent accounts might arise quite reasonably. Third-party inspectors often deliberately chose to interview family members who had not been previously interviewed by the internal inspectors, and they said they preferred interviewing women, whom they took to be more honest than men. But these interviewing techniques could also generate uncertainties about the reality of agrarian practices when discrepancies arose between accounts of farming practice given by different household members.

These circumstances pushed Satish to extend Raju's suggestion that

—

"only a document will prove anything." Signed forms did more than provide proof, as Raju had suggested; when interviews yielded contradictory responses, Satish implied that they could become arbiters of farmers' morality. Satish went on to claim that these discrepancies reflected a weakness of the ICS system. He added that

> one cannot blame the ICS inspectors. They apply their methodology. They ask questions, survey fields. We need a different methodology. ICS does not do inspections like the CBI [Central Bureau of Investigation]. Presently, the ICS method is like a police constable. The external certification agency is like the CBI. Like if there is a crime and the local police cannot solve it, they will make a complaint to the CBI. They [the CBI] can easily find out. We need to apply this methodology and be like the CBI.

Far from enacting economic sociability, Satish conceived of certification inspection interviews as comparable to those undertaken by state institutions of policing and intelligence gathering.

Satish's remarks also underscore how logics of audit and certification create pressure for ever-finer modes of inspection, monitoring, and surveillance. More intensive surveillance may take different forms: Satish advocated detailed information and intelligence gathering targeting farmers, while others advocated residue testing of the grain itself. Although more stringent testing may appear to decrease uncertainty, the intensification of these audit procedures—the push for "continuous improvement"—always produces "a domain of wildness" beyond the range of audit oversight, which then calls for its further expansion (Dunn 2007, 49).

The intractable incompleteness of audit made sentiments of frustration, disappointment, and even betrayal common in the work of certification, but, I came to learn, they were not unique to master trainers and inspectors. Aside from those farmers who embraced certification enthusiastically and those who participated minimally or not at all, there were a number of farmers who had once participated in the organic program but had since become disillusioned. Sunder Lal, a relatively prosperous farmer whose main income came from his nonfarm employment in Dehradun's private sector, expressed what many others conveyed to me:

—

> At that time [of participation in the organic program] we thought that the federation people [farmers' federation] are going to make much more improvements, and we will be benefit. If we had known that we are not going to get anything from the federation, then nobody would have taken this headache. We thought that the federation had given us this book, and that by doing the fill up we would get some facilities or benefits from the federation, or maybe they are going to tell us some new methods.

In these remarks, Sunder Lal located diary keeping in a larger moral economy of certification, one that entailed different but reciprocal obligations and commitments. Although he had once enthusiastically kept the diary, he had been disappointed by organic production and had recently decided to leave the program. He was not alone in his disenchantment. A number of farmers I met in 2007 and 2008 expressed disillusion and frustration with the program, and even anger. Many were dismayed that the money they received under the contract arrangement was not significantly higher than the market price of basmati, even though producing it organically required additional costs and labor; compounding this, they lamented that the yields of organic basmati they were contracted to grow for Hira Foods were lower than their own local variety of basmati.

Others felt that their trust had been betrayed and contractual commitments breached. Much of their disillusion centered on their farmers' federation, which was responsible for distributing payments to farmers for the basmati rice they sold to Hira Foods. Several farmers told me they had not been paid for basmati they sold six months before. For farmers, this breach was also a breach of trust based on exchange and reciprocity, and late payment or nonpayment was the most common reason why farmers abandoned the program. "When it is time to pay, the payment does not come. We are poor people. How can we manage if we don't get payment in time?" explained Savita Devi, who farmed with her husband and his brothers. Sunder Lal shared his own reasoning for leaving the program: "People have to invest in bulls, labor, seeds, and we give the paddy, but still the payment is not made on time. What is the benefit of doing this?" These sentiments show that farmers and officials alike perceive a gap between what is said and what is done, and that farmers calibrated their participation in

—

the program according to a larger moral economy. Yet farmers were positioned differently from officials as subjects of certification's power—not only through the new agricultural practices they were required to adopt, but also through expectations of honesty, trustworthiness, and commitment by which they were to abide.

In the Doon Valley, organic certification is a form of audit that aims to promote transparency and compliance but, in practice, often does not accomplish either of these things. The inevitable limits on certification's panoptic power and the impossibility of transparency seemed to stymie and exasperate officials, generating uncertainty about the realities of agrarian practices and prompting calls for more stringent surveillance and testing. But this uncertainty gave rise to other sentiments as well. In the same conversation in which Raju, Rawalnagar's master trainer, extolled documents as immutable proof that farmers adhered to organic standards, he made an entirely different appeal, one that seemed deeply paradoxical. Observing that at certain times of year he could not visit and monitor all the fields of every farmer, that uncertainty was unavoidable in his work, he reflected, "Organic farming jō hai, vō viśvās kī khetī hai" (Organic farming, that is the farming of trust).

VIŚVĀS KĪ KHETĪ: THE FARMING OF TRUST

As master trainers and inspectors acknowledged the impossibility of knowing the agricultural practices of each individual farmer enrolled in the program, they sometimes invoked the notion of *viśvās* to describe organic agriculture. Toward the end of my fieldwork in late 2008, I drove back to the Organic Board's headquarters with Birendra, one of the internal inspectors. We had spent the day with representatives from Hira Foods, visiting farmers in advance of the basmati harvest to assess the crop's quality and estimated yield. Recent internal inspections were on Birendra's mind as he told me that he had found instances of noncompliance among a large swath of farmers. Farmers do not always know what organic means, he indicated with some sympathy, corroborating what others had also told me. While they recognized the white granules of urea, a common nitrogen fertilizer, to be a form of *rāsāyinak khād* (chemical fertilizer), during the early years of the program they did not recognize that earth-colored DAP

—

(diammonium phosphate) was also prohibited. Noncompliance, he intimated, was often unwitting.

But Birendra was also clearly troubled by the possibility that as farmers became better acquainted with organic standards and certification, they were intentionally noncompliant. Speaking in Hindi, he described organic farming as *viśvās wālī chīz* (something involving or based on trust). Why, I asked him, given all the documents and all the inspections, does certified organic agriculture have so much to do with *viśvās*? He replied, "Farmers can go secretly to the field at night and apply chemicals to their fields. His neighbors will not know, we will not know." Birendra made this point less to suggest that farmers really did secretly use prohibited chemicals, but rather to underscore the utter inability of field officers and inspectors to be all-knowing and all-seeing. Inspectors cannot go to the fields at night or be there all the time, and thus organic agriculture necessarily depends on *viśvās*. Third-party certification inspectors—those whom Satish had likened to the CBI—voiced similar views. As we sat around a boardroom table in the offices of the third-party certification agency, one inspector, speaking in English, volunteered, "Certification is based on trust. You have to believe that what they are saying is true, unless there is a reason to doubt it."

How do the practices of organic certification and the circumstances that structure inspectors' labor condition what *viśvās* means and what work it does? The manner in which inspectors and master trainers invoked and relied on *viśvās* resembles Georg Simmel's (1950, 318n1) conceptualization of trust that entails "some additional affective, even mystical, 'faith' of man in man" (see also Simmel 1990, 178). This additional quality of faith is distinct from trust based on "good reasons" (Möllering 2001). These "good reasons" may be created through personal relations over a period of time, conceived in terms of friendship or reliability; plausibly, they may also be connected to the kinds of economic sociability and "relations of responsibility" that arise through conversation and social interaction during inspections in other settings (Cavanaugh 2016).

But "good reasons" are not what inspectors and master trainers relayed when they called on the notion of *viśvās*. Instead, by emphasizing the limits on their power, they drew attention to how uncertainty, doubt, and lack of knowledge make *viśvās* an indispensable part of organic certification. According to Simmel (1950, 318), trust arises in the midst of uncertainties;

—

it is not a result of complete knowledge. In the Doon Valley, master trainers and inspectors are all too aware that such affectively charged conditions exist despite—and also because of—an extensive documentary and inspections apparatus to promote transparency. Ultimately, it is their understanding of organic agriculture as *viśvās kī khetī*, instead of as a transparency regime, that enables those wielding certification authority to "bracket" or "suspend" (Möllering 2001, 414) what they do not, and cannot, know or see and to proceed with the work of certification. What makes *viśvās* of this sort crucially different from the "good reasons" for trust is that it is not a feeling kindled through confidence and certainty based on personal connections or shared history. On the contrary, it is a sentiment that emerges as a way of reckoning with the impossibility of complete knowledge and under conditions that demand a resolution of lingering uncertainty. *Viśvās* "bridges the synapse between evidence and conclusion" (Shipton 2007, 34) and thereby simplifies the material, cognitive, and social complexities that abound in organic certification.

At the time of my fieldwork in 2007 and 2008, the system of certification in place at the Organic Board depended almost exclusively on documents and inspections, on the materiality of forms, reports, and spreadsheets that moved among inspectors and offices. But with impulses toward "continuous improvement," certification and audit are not static systems (Dunn 2007, 49). In March 2016, I returned to the Doon Valley and the Organic Board, visiting farmers and meeting again with many of the same officials I had earlier come to know. During the intervening years, the membership of farmers' federations had declined because many farmers had left the program; each of the four federations now had fewer than 100 farmers. Satish, who remained in charge of overseeing the certification program, told me about a number of changes that had also been introduced to the Organic Board's system of certification. Internal inspectors, he said, no longer forwarded their reports to the third-party certification agency, but instead entered data from their reports directly into TraceNet, an online database hosted by the Government of India through the Agricultural and Processed Food Products Export Development Authority in the Ministry of Commerce. Promoted as the world's first online system of traceability at the national level, TraceNet centralizes the management of certification in a manner that expands surveillance by the central government

—

of the nation's organic farmers and certifiers. Lists of farmers to be visited by third-party inspectors are now generated on computers instead of compiled by certification inspectors. In this way, TraceNet quite radically transforms how documents and data are shared among, used by, and mediated through bureaucratic entities, seemingly expanding the scope of the central government's audit oversight.

In addition to participating in TraceNet, the Organic Board had also initiated routine chemical residue testing of basmati paddy for each farmers' federation. Although testing seemed at first glance to be a move in the direction of ever-greater surveillance, its method suggested otherwise. For it was not samples supplied by individual farmers that were tested, but instead a composite sample—a mixture of grains from all farmers in a federation—put together by a third-party inspector. While the composite sample made all farmers equally subject to the test, it prevented traceability to the farm level should prohibited residues be detected. In this regard, the composite sample had another important purpose: it created, Satish explained to me, "social pressure" among all farmers to comply with organic standards. Foreclosing the possibility of isolating one or two noncompliant farmers from the larger group, all members of the federation faced the possibility of having their organic status revoked if their shared sample failed testing. The composite sample, Satish emphasized, makes it "their moral duty to comply." Residue testing, it seemed, had been deployed not only to ensure the purity of the grain but also to further cultivate and police the moral purity of farmers themselves.

By 2016, then, new practices of certification seemed to increase transparency even as they were associated with proliferating opacities and uncertainties. Although TraceNet extended audit oversight up to the central government, it neither deepened its reach in the field nor altered the practices through which inspectors produced farm-level documents. Indeed, as they conducted inspections and completed diaries and forms, *viśvās* remained as important as ever. The introduction of routine residue testing, however, appeared to make *viśvās* obsolete by offering a means to overcome the doubts that inspectors had earlier expressed about their ability to evaluate compliance. But the procedure of composite sampling accomplished something quite different. Forms of knowing (about the presence of forbidden residues) and not knowing (about who was responsible) were

—

produced simultaneously. Emergent in these new unknowables were fresh sites for certification's disciplinary power as new opportunities were seized to make compliance a matter of "moral duty," and as participation in group certification required a commitment not only to comply but to have faith in one's fellow farmers to do the same. Insofar as residue testing has made it both more possible to discover noncompliance, and more impossible to identify the individuals responsible, *viśvās* is now a sentiment necessary not only for inspectors but also for certified organic farmers, whose fates as such are conjoined through the mixing of grains.

TRUST AT THE LIMITS OF TRANSPARENCY

Audit cultures have taken root in the Doon Valley's agricultural fields in the form of organic certification as requirements of document keeping and regular inspections endeavor to make agricultural practices legible and transparent. In so doing, certification seeks to refashion farmers as agents of their own surveillance and as compliant subjects of national and international certification regimes. But documents, particularly farmers' diaries, that were so central to certification's infrastructure, did not work in Foucauldian ways. More often than not, farmers did not complete the documents required of them—sometimes because it was not a literacy practice with which they were familiar, but at other times because their own trust in contract farming and in the promise that becoming certified organic might hold had been disappointed when the farmers' federation had failed to pay them on time or at all. This betrayal of trust proved to be an important reason why some farmers rejected fashioning themselves as compliant subjects by minimally engaging with the program or sometimes abandoning it altogether. The incompleteness of documents also created considerable uncertainty for certification authorities, who relied on farm-level documents to perform their work. In the end, much came to lie beyond the realm of what one could know through documents or what one could realistically inspect and audit. To grasp how organic certification works, therefore, requires more than exploring how farmers engage with it. It also demands focused attention on how those who wield certification authority come to reconcile the need for transparency and knowledge with the not infrequent reality of their incompleteness.

—

Gaps, fissures, and failures in audit practice specifically, and governmentalized schemes more generally, often produce calls for their expansion and intensification (Dunn 2007; Ferguson 1994; Riles 2004). A reading of organic certification along these lines may cast it as an ever-widening and self-reinforcing circle of technocracy in which the shortcomings of neoliberal technocratic practices such as audit create the conditions and impulses for their proliferation. I do not dispute that in many instances this is borne out. In the Doon Valley the inability of documents and inspections to capture the practices of agriculture brought forth calls for more stringent certification procedures, leading to routine residue testing.

But by invoking and describing *viśvās* as a critical part of certification, master trainers and certification inspectors foregrounded a different though equally significant dynamic latent in the apparent failures of certification. Uncertainty about agrarian practices and compliance was at times generated by farmers' diaries and other documents, as well as during inspections—in other words, by the very mechanisms of certification intended to create transparency and visibility. Compelled by the intractability of such uncertainty, *viśvās* became vitally important because of the limits of certification and the elusiveness of transparency. For this reason Raju, a master trainer, articulated two apparently contradictory ideas about organic certification—that "only a document will prove anything" and that organic farming is ultimately *viśvās kī khetī*. Raju shows how certification thoroughly relies on sentiments of trust to atone for uncertainty and all that cannot be known, thereby enabling documents to remain the ultimate, material source of proof. For master trainers and certification inspectors, then, *viśvās* was not simply the outcome of certification but a sentiment on which the whole edifice of certification thoroughly depended.

Raju, and others in his position, complicate and challenge critical perspectives contending that audit and its associated documentary infrastructures replace or erode relations of trust (Shore and Wright 2000). They urge us to attend to trust as a sentiment emanating from something other than the kinds of personal or long-standing relationships, mutuality and reciprocity, forms of exchange, or robust knowledge that have been documented in many anthropological and sociological accounts. The significance of *viśvās* in their work directs our attention to the way that trust

—

is also powerfully configured through the opacities generated by transparency regimes. In this manner, their experience offers a point from which to push further an abiding anthropological curiosity about the kinds of institutional, social, and cultural practices that shape and condition the emergence and natures of trust relations. At this moment, in the early 21st century, audit firms profess their intention to "build trust in society" (PwC, n.d.). The proliferation of audit and certification may lead us, then, to look more closely at trust born of, and at work within, these systems—to ask, What are the forms of trust in audit culture, and how are they being built and mobilized? Expanding infrastructures of certification and audit initiate new forms of surveillance and subjectivity, regimes of documentation and accountability. As they do, we must pay heed to how they reformat and redefine the way that trust works across many dimensions of social and economic life.

NOTES

Acknowledgments. I am grateful to everyone in India who made it possible for me to undertake this research. Detailed comments from Michael R. Dove, K. Sivaramakrishnan, Karen Hébert, James C. Scott, Chris Galvin, Nikhil Anand, Radhika Govindrajan, Alessandro Monsutti, Grégoire Mallard, Filipe Calvão, and Michelle Niemann were invaluable in developing this article. I also thank the anonymous reviewers for their detailed comments, as well as Angelique Haugerud and Niko Besnier for their careful reading of this work and their thoughtful editorial guidance. My research was greatly facilitated by the research assistance of Nuri Rawat in the latter part of 2008, and by Tiwariji, who transcribed and translated interviews I conducted in Hindi and Hindi-language printed materials. I am grateful to them, as well as to Meenakshi Nair Ambujam, Sijo John, Amishi Panwar, and Usha Singh Panwar, who worked to translate the abstract into Hindi. The Social Sciences and Humanities Research Council of Canada, the Wenner-Gren Foundation, the Yale Center for International and Area Studies, the Yale Program in Agrarian Studies, and the Graduate Institute of International and Development Studies funded fieldwork for this research. Any errors and omissions are mine alone.

1. I use pseudonyms throughout this article for individuals, for different areas of the Doon Valley, and for the company procuring organic basmati.
2. I conducted fieldwork in several phases, from 2005 to 2008, and later in March 2016. Moving across locations the Doon Valley, the Dehradun headquarters of the Organic Commodity Board, and corporate offices of Hira Foods in Delhi and Haryana, I spent extended periods of time with farmers, certification inspectors, the Organic Board's field officers, and managers. This afforded me access to documents of different kinds

—

and allowed me to observe how they were produced and used. It further enabled my observations of processes of certification from different vantage points. Conversations and interviews quoted in this article took place in Hindi or English.

3. This is not to suggest that the terms always mean the same thing and are equivalent in every context. Indeed, the meanings of *viśvās* in Hindi, and of trust in English, are complex and must therefore be grasped contextually. I attend to their nuances in this article, while maintaining that they share expansive, internally varied meanings that create sufficient overlap to allow for this translation.

4. For further discussion of different forms of ignorance, and the relations among ignorance, knowledge, and power, see also studies by Andrew Mathews (2005, 2008), Linsey McGoey (2012), and Nikhil Anand (2015). Ethnographic accounts of the relations among transparency, opacity, suspicion, and conspiracy may be found in West and Sanders (2003).

5. This leaflet, written in Hindi, was translated into English by my translator, Tiwariji, and later reviewed by me to ensure accuracy.

6. In a similar vein, Michael Cepek (2011) found that Cofán communities in Ecuador did not produce themselves as compliant subjects of community-based conservation projects requiring their participation.

7. While Dilip conducted his interviews with farmers in Hindi, many of our own conversations—including the one quoted here—took place in English.

8. The way that organic certification provides a framework for assessing moral conduct resonates with arguments that standards and grading test not only the "goodness" of things but also the "goodness" of people (Busch and Tanaka 1996, 4).

REFERENCES

Anand, Nikhil. 2015. "Leaky States: Water Audits, Ignorance, and the Politics of Infrastructure." *Public Culture* 27, no. 2 (May): 305–30.

Ballestero, Andrea S. 2012. "Transparency in Triads." *PoLAR* 35, no. 2 (November): 160–66.

Besky, Sarah. 2014. *The Darjeeling Distinction: Labor and Justice on Fair Trade Tea Plantations in India*. Berkeley: University of California Press.

Brown, Michael F. 2010. "A Tale of Three Buildings: Certifying Virtue in the New Moral Economy." *American Ethnologist* 37, no. 4 (November): 741–52.

Busch, Lawrence, and Keiko Tanaka. 1996. "Rites of Passage: Constructing Quality in a Commodity Subsector." *Science, Technology, and Human Values* 21, no. 1 (Winter): 3–27.

Cavanaugh, Jillian R. 2016. "Documenting Subjects: Performativity and Audit Culture in Food Production in Northern Italy." *American Ethnologist* 43, no. 4 (November): 691–703.

Cepek, Michael L. 2011. "Foucault in the Forest: Questioning Environmentality in Amazonia." *American Ethnologist* 38, no. 3 (August): 501–15.

Cohen, Lawrence. 2010. "M's Book." In *Muslim Portraits: Everyday Lives in India*, edited by Mukulika Banerjee, 11–20. Bloomington: Indiana University Press.

———

Corsín Jiménez, Alberto. 2011. "Trust in Anthropology." *Anthropological Theory* 11, no. 2 (June): 177–96.

Das, Veena. 2004. "The Signature of the State: The Paradox of Illegibility." In *Anthropology in the Margins of the State*, edited by Veena Das and Deborah Poole, 225–52. Santa Fe, NM: School of American Research Press; Oxford: James Currey.

DeLind, L. B. 2000. "Transforming Organic Agriculture into Industrial Organic Products: Reconsidering National Organic Standards." *Human Organization* 59, no. 2 (Summer): 198–208.

Desai, Amit. 2010. "A Matter of Affection: Ritualized Friendship in Central India." In *The Ways of Friendship: Anthropological Perspectives*, edited by Amit Desai and Evan Killick, 114–32. New York: Berghahn.

Dunn, Elizabeth. 2007. "Escherichia Coli, Corporate Discipline and the Failure of the Sewer State." *Space and Polity* 11, no. 1: 35–53.

Ecks, Stefan. 2013. *Eating Drugs: Psychopharmaceutical Pluralism in India*. New York: New York University Press.

Ferguson, James. 1994. *The Anti-politics Machine: "Development," Depoliticization, and Bureaucratic Power in Lesotho*. Minneapolis: University of Minnesota Press. First published 1990.

FiBL (Research Institute of Organic Agriculture) and IFOAM (International Federation of Organic Agriculture Movements). 2018. *The World of Organic Agriculture: Statistics and Emerging Trends 2018*. Frick, Switzerland: FiBL; Bonn, Germany: IFOAM.

Foucault, Michel. 1988. "Technologies of the Self." In *Technologies of the Self: A Seminar with Michel Foucault*, edited by Luther H. Martin, Huck Gutman, and Patrick H. Hutton, 16–49. Amherst: University of Massachusetts Press.

Freidberg, Susanne. 2004. *French Beans and Food Scares: Culture and Commerce in an Anxious Age*. New York: Oxford University Press.

Gambetta, Diego. 1988. "Can We Trust Trust?" In *Trust: Making and Breaking Cooperative Relations*, edited by Diego Gambetta, 213–38. New York: Basil Blackwell.

Giddens, Anthony. 1990. *The Consequences of Modernity*. Stanford, CA: Stanford University Press.

Guha, Ramachandra. 1989. *The Unquiet Woods: Ecological Change and Peasant Resistance in the Himalaya*. Delhi: Oxford University Press.

Harper, Richard. 2000. "The Social Organization of the IMF's Mission Work: An Examination of International Auditing." In *Audit Cultures: Anthropological Studies in Accountability, Ethics and the Academy*, edited by Marilyn Strathern, 21–53. London: Routledge.

Hart, Keith. 1988. "Kinship, Contract and Trust: Economic Organization of Migrants in an African Slum." In *Trust: Making and Breaking Cooperative Relations*, edited by Diego Gambetta, 176–93. Oxford: Blackwell.

Hetherington, Kregg. 2011. *Guerrilla Auditors: The Politics of Transparency in Neoliberal Paraguay*. Durham, NC: Duke University Press.

Hull, Matthew S. 2003. "The File: Agency, Authority, and Autography in an Islamabad Bureaucracy." *Language and Communication* 23, no. 3–4 (July–October): 287–314.

—

———. 2008. "Ruled by Records: The Expropriation of Land and the Misappropriation of Lists in Islamabad." *American Ethnologist* 35, no. 4 (November): 501–18.

Joly, Nathalie. 2010. "Tracing Cows: Practical and Administrative Logics in Tension." In *The Anthropology of Writing: Understanding Textually-Mediated Worlds*, edited by David Barton and Uta Papen, 90–108. London: Bloomsbury.

Kakar, Sudhir. 1982. *Shamans, Mystics and Doctors: A Psychological Inquiry into India and Its Healing Traditions*. New York: Alfred A. Knopf.

Karan, P. P., and Shigeru Iijima. 1985. "Environmental Stress in the Himalaya." *Geographical Review* 75, no. 1 (January): 71–92.

Karpik, Lucien. 2010. *Valuing the Unique: The Economics of Singularities*. Translated by Nora Scott. Princeton, NJ: Princeton University Press.

Linkenbach, Antje. 2006. "Nature and Politics: The Case of Uttarakhand, North India." In *Ecological Nationalisms: Nature, Livelihoods, and Identities in South Asia*, edited by K. Sivaramakrishnan and Gunnel Cederlöf, 151–69. Seattle: University of Washington Press.

Malinowski, Bronislaw. 1984. *Argonauts of the Western Pacific: An Account of Native Enterprise and Adventure in the Archipelagoes of Melanesian New Guinea*. Long Grove, IL: Waveland. First published 1922.

Mathews, Andrew S. 2005. "Power/Knowledge, Power/Ignorance: Forest Fires and the State in Mexico." *Human Ecology* 33, no. 6 (December): 795–820.

———. 2008. "State Making, Knowledge, and Ignorance: Translation and Concealment in Mexican Forestry Institutions." *American Anthropologist* 110, no. 4 (December): 484–94.

Mathur, Nayanika. 2016. *Paper Tiger: Law, Bureaucracy and the Developmental State in Himalayan India*. Delhi: Cambridge University Press.

Mauss, Marcel. 2016. *The Gift*. Edited and translated by Jane I. Guyer. Chicago: Hau Books. Distributed by University of Chicago Press. First published 1925.

McGoey, Linsey. 2012. "Strategic Unknowns: Towards a Sociology of Ignorance." *Economy and Society* 41, no. 1: 1–16.

Moberg, Mark. 2014. "Certification and Neoliberal Governance: Moral Economies of Fair Trade in the Eastern Caribbean." *American Anthropologist* 116, no. 1 (March): 8–22.

Möllering, Guido. 2001. "The Nature of Trust: From Georg Simmel to a Theory of Expectation, Interpretation and Suspension." *Sociology* 35, no. 2 (May): 403–20.

Mutersbaugh, Tad. 2005. "Just-In-Space: Certified Rural Products, Labor of Quality, and Regulatory Spaces." *Journal of Rural Studies* 21, no. 4 (October): 389–402.

Paden, William E. 1988. "Theaters of Humility and Suspicion: Desert Saints and New England Puritans." In *Technologies of the Self: A Seminar with Michel Foucault*, edited by Luther H. Martin, Huck Gutman, and Patrick H. Hutton, 64–79. Amherst: University of Massachusetts Press.

Pentland, Brian T. 1993. "Getting Comfortable with the Numbers: Auditing and the Micro-production of Macro-order." *Accounting, Organizations and Society* 18, no. 7–8 (October–November): 605–20.

Pinto, Sarah. 2004. "Development without Institutions: Ersatz Medicine and the Politics

—

of Everyday Life in Rural North India." *Cultural Anthropology* 19, no. 3 (August): 337–64.

Power, Michael. 1996. *The Audit Explosion*. London: Demos.

———. 1997. *The Audit Society: Rituals of Verification*. Oxford: Oxford University Press.

Putnam, Robert D. 2000. *Bowling Alone: The Collapse and Revival of American Community*. New York: Simon and Schuster.

PwC. n.d. "Our Purpose, and Values." Accessed September 13, 2017. https://www.pwc.com/gx/en/about/purpose-and-values.html.

Riles, Annelise. 2004. "Real Time: Unwinding Technocratic and Anthropological Knowledge." *American Ethnologist* 31, no. 3 (August): 392–405.

Scott, James C. 1998. *Seeing Like a State: How Certain Schemes to Improve the Human Condition Have Failed*. New Haven, CT: Yale University Press.

Seligman, Adam B. 1997. *The Problem of Trust*. Princeton, NJ: Princeton University Press.

Shipton, Parker MacDonald. 2007. *The Nature of Entrustment: Intimacy, Exchange, and the Sacred in Africa*. New Haven, CT: Yale University Press.

Shore, Cris, and Susan Wright. 2000. "Coercive Accountability: The Rise of Audit Culture in Higher Education." In *Audit Cultures: Anthropological Studies in Accountability, Ethics and the Academy*, edited by Marilyn Strathern, 57–89. London: Routledge.

Simmel, Georg. 1950. *The Sociology of Georg Simmel*. Translated by Kurt H. Wolff. New York: Free Press; London: Collier Macmillan.

———. 1990. *The Philosophy of Money*. 2nd ed. Translated by David Frisby. London: Routledge. First published 1900.

Smith, Richard Saumarez. 1985. "Rule-by-Records and Rule-by-Reports: Complementary Aspects of the British Imperial Rule of Law." *Contributions to Indian Sociology* 19, no. 1 (January): 153–76.

Strathern, Marilyn, ed. 2000a. *Audit Cultures: Anthropological Studies in Accountability, Ethics and the Academy*. London: Routledge.

———. 2000b. "Introduction: New Accountabilities." In *Audit Cultures: Anthropological Studies in Accountability, Ethics and the Academy*, edited by Marilyn Strathern, 1–18. London: Routledge.

Street, Brian. 1995. *Social Literacies: Critical Approaches to Literacy in Development, Ethnography and Education*. London: Longman.

Street, Brian, and Niko Besnier. 1994. "Aspects of Literacy." In *Companion Encyclopedia of Anthropology: Humanity, Culture and Social Life*, edited by Tim Ingold, 527–62. London: Routledge.

Thompson, Michael, Michael Warburton, and Tom Hatley. 1986. *Uncertainty on a Himalayan Scale: An Institutional Theory of Environmental Perception and a Strategic Framework for the Sustainable Development of the Himalaya*. London: Ethnographica.

West, Harry G., and Todd Sanders. 2003. *Transparency and Conspiracy: Ethnographies of Suspicion in the New World Order*. Durham, NC: Duke University Press.

World Bank. 1999. *Project Appraisal Document, Integrated Watershed Development (Hills-Ii) Project*. N.p.: World Bank.

———. 2002. *Status Report, Prepared for World Bank Review Mission November 18–22 2002,*

———

Diversified Agricultural Support Project (Cr-3106l / Ln-4365), Uttaranchal. Washington, DC: World Bank.

———. 2004. *Project Information Document (PID) Appraisal Stage, Uttaranchal Decentralized Watershed Development Project.* N.p.: World Bank.

Yanagisako, Sylvia Junko. 2002. *Producing Culture and Capital: Family Firms in Italy.* Princeton, NJ: Princeton University Press.

2

A "QUEER-LOOKING COMPOUND"

RACE, ABJECTION, AND THE POLITICS OF HAWAIIAN POI

HI'ILEI JULIA HOBART

n 1866, American novelist Mark Twain (born Samuel Langhorne Clemens) arrived in Hawai'i on assignment for the Sacramento *Union*. Over the course of the following four months he prodigiously scribbled notes that reported on life in the islands, producing a detailed record of how visitors might experience nineteenth-century Hawaiian place and culture. His letters and newspaper articles portray the environment, the people, and—importantly—the foodways that he encountered. Like many travelogues of the time, poi in Twain's work acts as metonym for Native sense and sensibility: their tastes, their manners, and their commensal relationships. At first mention in his correspondence series, which was later compiled, narrativized, and published as *Roughing It* (1872), readers are oriented toward the material dimensions of Hawai'i's food and its preparation:

> The poi looks like common flour paste . . . and is prepared from the
> *taro* plant. The taro root looks like a thick, or if you please, a corpulent

Originally published as, Hobart, H. J., 2017. A "Queer-Looking Compound": Race, Abjection, and the Politics of Hawaiian Poi. *Global Food History*, 3(2), pp. 133–49. Reprinted with permission from Taylor & Francis Group, all rights reserved.

—

sweet potato, in shape, but is of a light purple color when boiled . . .
The buck Kanakas bake it underground, then mash it up well with
a heavy lava pestle, mix water with it until it becomes a paste, set
it aside and let it ferment, and then it is poi—and an unseductive
mixture it is, almost tasteless before it ferments and too sour for a
luxury afterward.[1]

In this passage, Twain takes a comparative approach: kalo is somewhat
like a sweet potato. But lest readers mistake the soured kalo root for the
"sweet" potato of the Americas, and its corpulence for soft curves, they are
warned that their appetites will not be satisfied by this Native stand-in.
While Twain concedes that, "nothing is more nutritious," he nevertheless
articulates a politics of taste that maps onto settler/Native relationships
as they developed across the nineteenth century and into the twentieth:
that Indigenous foods, while abundant and healthful, fail to offer suitable
gustatory pleasure for white eaters. Those familiar with contemporary
travel writing will recognize Twain's description as relatively common to
the English-language literature of the Pacific, which at once primitivized
and sexualized Native culture through material and affective registers.[2]

At the time that Twain's letters were written, the Kingdom of Hawai'i
maintained an uncertain grasp on its sovereignty. Foreign missionaries,
who had begun arriving in the 1820s, promoted Christian ideals that dis-
couraged many Hawaiian cultural practices, including commensal habits.
Forty years later, a civilizing mission in Hawai'i was in full, if not complicated swing: missionary descendants entered into sectors of business and
government, influencing lawmaking that valued Western social ideals;
the predominantly foreign-owned sugar industry continued to expand,
bringing with it imported contract laborers from Asia and elsewhere; and
the Hawaiian monarchy adopted cosmopolitan forms of diplomacy that
blended Native and Western manners.[3] The development of foodways,
particularly within the urban center of Honolulu, reflected Hawai'i's
cultural and economic development: imported goods and their modes of
consumption contended with Native foodways, bringing to the fore larger
colonial concerns about intimate relations between bodies within tropical
environments.

These concerns were made legible through rich descriptions of poi

—

consumption that outsiders narrated, where adjectives of corpulence, tastelessness, pasty texture, and sourness indexed the Indigenous staple food as unpalatable. It is therefore not surprising that the question of poi's deliciousness has historically been a settler concern—a question about Hawai'i's traditional, everyday cuisine nearly always posed by an outsider looking in (indeed, the very definition of a staple food suggests normativity for its eaters). Likewise, Hawaiian language sources from the same time period reveal a food of unremarkable flavor—in that the deliciousness of poi appears far less worthy of debate among those who enjoyed it as part of their daily foodscape.[4] While there are certainly moments when Kānaka Maoli (Native Hawaiians) discuss the flavor of poi, its taste appears predominantly used as a metric for determining food safety—particularly as poi manufacture industrialized at the turn of the nineteenth century. Broader debates on "good" taste were, in contrast, at their most vigorous via colonial organs: the stomachs, mouths, and mouthpieces of haole (foreign) settlers. This article therefore focuses on Western, instead of Native Hawaiian, reactions to poi in order to show how sensory flavor and social taste comprised ideological overlaps that have persisted into the twentieth and twenty-first centuries.

CONTEXTUALIZING POI'S FLAVOR

While it is often suggested that the taste for poi is merely a matter of individual preference—that it's "an acquired taste"—an historical view shows that collective palates are inextricably bound up in colonial histories, in which diet, labor, and race help determine the parameters of what is delicious.[5] For readers unfamiliar, poi is a Native Hawaiian staple food made from the baked or steamed corm of the kalo (taro) plant.[6] To elaborate on Twain's description, the corm (or underground stem) of the plant is traditionally cooked in an imu (underground oven) for several hours and then hand-pounded with a pōhaku ku'i 'ai (stone pounder) on a papa ku'i 'ai (a wooden board).[7] Small amounts of water are incrementally added as the corm is mashed to produce foods known as pa'i 'ai (kalo diluted with very little water) or poi (with enough water incorporated as to create a pudding-like consistency). Over the course of several days after its initial preparation the water catalyzes a natural fermentation process; as lactic

—

acid builds within the food, poi increasingly takes on its characteristically sour flavor.[8] Regular consumers of poi thus often refer to its "age" to indicate their preferred sourness. A humorous, but popular, book on "local" food, *Pupus to da Max* explains:

> Depending on the amount of water you add, you get different consistencies. More water: two-finger or three-finger poi. Less water: one-finger poi. Note: You can buy fresh or day-old (or two- or three-day old poi). The older the poi, the more sour. Some people like it fresh, some like it sour.[9]

Partiality toward sourness—even today—often stands in as shorthand for indigeneity: the more sour the poi, the more culturally literate the eater.

Ideas that Hawaiianness can be expressed through taste preference extend back to the colonial encounter. For example, in 1893, the *Hawaiian Gazette* published an extensive piece on kalo ("particularly for the information of tourists and other newcomers to these islands"), which correlated palate to race, explaining that,

> White folks who sometimes, for a change, indulge in a little poi, prefer it when it is fresh, but the natives like it to be somewhat sour or fermented, and some even have a strong partiality for very sour poi, or poi akia.[10]

Tastes for sour poi were furthermore often used to mark a Hawaiian's lack of civility or masculinity. One 1882 travelog noted that, "however civilized a native may become, he invariably prefers his dish of sour poi to the choicest dainties eaten by haoles."[11] This is a common refrain, in which descriptions for foreign audiences of what poi tasted like characterize the food as either inedible or unlike food at all. The editor of the *Atchison Globe, Kansas*, who published his experiences of visiting Hawai'i in November 1905, recounted his visit to a well-to-do household, where he dined with Mr. Emmeluth, a haole, who resided with his Native wife:

> The taro is ground into a paste, and after fermentation, becomes poi, on which the natives mainly live. I tasted the poi. It tasted like sour

—

paste, and Mr. Emmeluth says it may be used as paste . . . When the taro crop fails the natives make poi out of American flour, and it seems to answer the purpose, though it is light in color, instead of dark.[12]

Within these descriptions, the enjoyment of poi is used to police the boundaries between Kānaka Maoli and haole, and the inevitable transgressions of daily life. The proximate relationships between Native bodies and foods has been a strong locus for haole (white) abjection, with many scholars recognizing that racist logics of edibility have long been central themes in works on "ethnic" foodways, including those of Pacific Island communities.[13] Today, too, many visitors to Hawai'i continue to enact the ambivalence of Twain and others by discretely discarding the small portions of poi that decorate their "luau plates" believing that they simply lack a personal preference.[14] Without denying the biological function of flavor—that sour poi will taste equally sour on most tongues—the interpretation of poi's tastes and textures have been shaped by colonial histories that racialized differential palates.

'ĀINA (LAND) IDEOLOGIES

A brief review of how Hawai'i's twentieth-century transition from sovereign nation to United States settler state has shaped its contemporary food system is a helpful place to begin considering this broader trajectory of tastemaking. In recent years, the State of Hawai'i has come under significant criticism for its inability to provide sustainable food sources for its residents. An oft-cited 2013 report on the archipelago's food supply shows that only 11.6 percent is locally produced, with an alarming 88.4 percent of Hawai'i's food imported primarily from continental United States distribution hubs located over 2,300 miles away.[15] This current state of precarity contrasts sharply with its historic agricultural productivity: in the Hawai'i of pre-Western contact in 1778, diversified Native agri- and aquacultures sustained a relatively dense population throughout the islands.[16] Such a radical change in provisioning had everything to do with food and land. Over the course of the nineteenth century, foreign economic interest grew in Hawai'i as a potential source for commodity sugar, resulting in the development of sugarcane plantations that overtook large tracts

—

of agricultural land, diverted and monopolized fresh water sources for their irrigation, consolidated capital in the hands of American business leaders, and utilized a contract labor system that reinforced racial hierarchies.[17] By 1893, some of those large business owners executed a forceful government takeover. Despite significant resistance from Kānaka Maoli, the newly formed Republic of Hawai'i (1894) remained in place until the enactment of the Newlands Resolution in 1898, through which the United States unilaterally annexed Hawai'i as one of its Pacific Territories.[18] By the early twentieth century, the sugar industry began a steady decline, and Hawai'i's primary economy shifted once again. With cheaper export markets developing overseas by the 1980s and 1990s, the State of Hawai'i instead invested in a tourism industry that overtook a substantial percentage of its total income, rising from less than 3 percent in 1949 to becoming the State's "largest single contributor to [its] gross domestic product" in 2013, with over $14 billion in annual revenue.[19] The proliferation of resorts and hotels, as well as housing developments to accommodate Hawai'i's growing population, has often come at the expense of agricultural land, further limiting any remaining ability to grow sufficient foodstuffs for the islands.[20]

Against the backdrop of these radical economic and political changes, the Native Hawaiian population became systematically divested from their traditional subsistence modes.[21] The health implications have been profound. By the 1960s, studies estimated that Hawaiians suffered from the second highest rates of obesity in the United States, as well as disproportionately high levels of diabetes, hypertension, and cardiovascular disease mortality (this in a State ironically ranked as one of the "healthiest" in America).[22] The statistics were, in part, connected to diet. A "local" cuisine, comprised of multicultural foodways introduced by plantation laboring populations in the 1900s, along with industrial products—like SPAM— popularized during World War II, became an adopted culinary standard for Hawaiians.[23] High in sugar, fats, and salts, the cuisine known today as "local" food differs from the traditional diet, which is generally low in fat, high in complex carbohydrates, and moderate in protein.[24] Without wanting to construct artificial causality (indeed, two hundred years of complex Hawaiian history cannot be satisfactorily distilled in two paragraphs) I offer these statistics as evidence of the structural dispossession—through

—

loss of life, culture, and land—that settler colonialism articulates. For Patrick Wolfe, health epidemics, the seizure of territory, and cultural erosion are interlocking parts of a "structure" that always seeks a dual purpose: to "eliminate" Native lives and, in turn, make land available for white settlement.[25]

Just as settler dominance structures the contemporary foodscape in the islands, so too has the concept of place been pulled into capitalist frameworks that elide Native orientations. Kānaka Maoli use the term ʻāina to distinguish their understanding of land from Western ideas of private property and national territory. ʻāina importantly translates into "that which feeds," by etymologically elaborating the word ʻai, which refers to both the act of eating and the object of food itself. So central is poi to this epistemology that Samuel Elbert and Mary Kawena Pukui assert in the *Hawaiian Dictionary* that the term ʻai, "often . . . refers specifically to poi."[26] Thus Hawaiian worldviews show the production of their staple food to be fundamental to the construction of place through reciprocal relations: if you care for the land, the land will care for you. As a result, the Western idea of territory as introduced to Hawaiʻi effects what Mishuana Goeman terms a "settler-colonial grammar of place," where Native peoples' spatial constructions are contorted in order to accommodate legibility demanded by the settler state.[27] Constraints of capitalism (i.e. the 1848 Māhele, the plantation economy, contemporary real estate development) and governance (i.e. American Pure Food and Drug Laws, land use zoning laws) at once ruptured constructions of Indigenous space and kalo production within it.[28] The ecological, cosmological, and genealogic meanings of kalo and the foods made from it bind the practice of eating poi to both material and cultural concepts of Hawaiian identity.

EMBODYING GOOD TASTE

Scholars like Parama Roy, Christy Spackman, and Jessica Hayes-Conroy and Allison Hayes-Conroy have shown how social and political power shape interpretations of sensorial taste by showing that taste is a sensation that not only operates upon the nose and the tongue, but also onto racialized, sexualized, and classed bodies as a whole.[29] Recently, a special double issue "On the Visceral" in *GLQ: A Journal of Lesbian and Gay Studies*

—

(2014) also interrogated this approach to embodiment, enjoining readers to re-focus analyses of consumption upon the "gut," in order to better
understand how contemporary structures of social inequality are manifested upon the body.[30] The issue editors write that:

> Viscerality [is] a phenomenological index for the logics of desire, con-
> sumption, disgust, health, disease, belonging, and displacement that
> are implicit in colonial and postcolonial relations. Emerging from the
> carnal language of (colonial) excess, viscerality registers those systems
> of meaning that have lodged in the gut, signifying to the incursion of
> violent intentionality into the rhythms of everyday life.[31]

Their assessment offers a powerful intervention for thinking about how
poi's edibility has been classified across time by newcomers to Hawai'i.
Poi's viscous shapelessness, its grey/violet/pink color, and its sour(ing) flavor not only contrasts with normative Western parameters of "good taste"
today, but also articulates nineteenth-century colonialist relationships to
Native foodscapes, which often denied good taste to the "uncivilized."[32]
    Theoretical orientations toward the visceral are key to understanding
how taste politics operate in the space between bodies and terrain because
eating is, at its essence, a reproductive act. For Indigenous peoples, who
know their ancestral homelands by enacting human/nonhuman relations, ingestive connections are crucial elements of placemaking.[33] The
logic then follows, that if settler society is premised, as asserted by Wolfe
and others, upon the "elimination of the native," and that the irreducible
element of settler colonialism is land, then we might understand such
articulations of taste (i.e. whether or not poi is palatable) as a discourse
predicated on larger structures of dispossession both embodied and territorial.[34] I therefore use the subject of poi and aim to extend an analysis
of colonial tastemaking through Native bodies and into the particular
historic (and ongoing) dimensions of settler terrain. Because food is both
edible and agricultural, we must keep one eye carefully trained on its
historical context and the other on the construction of taste in order to
execute a gustatory reading of its cultural meaning. For Hawaiians, who
have experienced the structural dispossession of land and resources, taste
and territory are profoundly co-produced.

—

THE LOGICS OF TERRITORY AND TASTE

Reporting like Twain's on the eating of poi rested upon concrete political impulses. Around the time that *Roughing It* was published as a collection, the American Territory of Hawai'i had just been named. In its wake came a surge of interest among Americans for their "new possession," particularly in regards to its agricultural potential.[35] As the expansion of sugar plantations buoyed its economy, discourses about Hawaiians and their right to land were necessarily mobilized to render them either undeserving or uninterested in agriculture and the capitalist economy. John Roy Musick, in his 1898 book about the American Territory of Hawai'i, explained that,

> the comparative ease with which the Hawaiians on their own land can secure their ordinary food-supply has undoubtedly interfered with their social and industrial advancement. Poi, it is said, has proved the greatest obstacle to the progress of Hawaiians. The ease with which the taro, the vegetable from which poi is made, can be grown, relieves the native from any genuine struggle for life, and unfits him for sustained competition with men from other lands acquainted with hardships.[36]

Musick offers here a powerful example of the interlocking logics of territory and taste through labor, land use, and feeding. In it, the prime agricultural environment afforded by Hawai'i's climate has put the Hawaiian at a political disadvantage: they feed themselves too easily (with Musick apparently unaware of the backbreaking work that kalo cultivation requires). Thus, an argument about agriculture (crops) also portrays poi (food) as a hindrance to the civilizing project, where eating, growing, and political placemaking operate in concert to either affirm or deny one's sovereignty.

The creation of settler taste hierarchies in Hawai'i throughout the nineteenth and early twentieth centuries, in which poi consistently ranked at the bottom, permitted discourses that talked at, around, and alongside Native difference and its problematic persistence. Take, for example, a story entitled, "The Poi Eater's Progress"—a play on the *Pilgrim's Progress*—that circulated in the *Latter-Day Saints' Millennial Star* in 1893. Described as "a queer-looking greyish, sticky compound, resembling paper hanger's

—

paste," one follows an histrionic dialog in the second person that describes a first encounter with poi:

> As you raise it toward your mouth your nose takes cognizance of a sour smell that harmonises perfectly with the appearance of the poi . . . By a sublime effort of will you keep your lips closed over the mouthful, while your companion looks on interestedly, evidently expecting to hear your palate scream with delight . . . The poi is cold and clammy. The poi tastes like stale yeast; it stings your tongue, and an unutterable disgust possesses your soul . . . You can trace its progress through the œsophagus by the horrified shudder that organ gives as the mouthful passes along it; you can hear the villi in your stomach shriek as the frog-like lump makes its appearance among them, and you think you are going to die then and there.[37]

While others around the same time aren't quite as dramatic—some are complimentary enough to call it "not unpleasant"[38]—there formed, nevertheless, a consensus that its texture and its taste were overwhelmingly objectionable.

In other common estimations, poi represented a food of savage sexuality part and parcel to its lack of palatability. Often, disgust for poi's taste compelled descriptions that collapsed together anxieties over "dirty" bodies as both hygienic and copulatory dangers. To continue the passage with which this article opened, Twain's description of Hawaiian poi manufacture continues with an account of its consumption worth quoting in length:

> I think there must be as much of a knack in handling poi as there is in eating with chopsticks. The forefinger is thrust into the mess and stirred quickly round several times and drawn as quickly out, thickly coated, just as if it were poulticed; the head is thrown back, the finger inserted in the mouth and the delicacy stripped off and swallowed— the eye closing gently, meanwhile, in a languid sort of ecstasy. Many a different finger goes into the bowl and many a different kind of dirt and shade and quality of flavor is added to the virtues of its contents . . . All agree that poi will rejuvenate a man who is used up and his vitality almost annihilated by hard drinking.[39]

—

Twain reveals here several layers of the culinary colonial gaze, from texture to body to social practice. What for Kānaka are simple gestures of feeding become, in this depiction, gyrations of pleasure: not one finger, but many fingers, swirl around the bowl before entering a swallowing mouth, head thrown back in "ecstasy." The sexualization of this moment is immediately recognizable (and the titillation of Twain's readers even easier to imagine). This is not a unique characterization of Hawaiians and their poi; in fact, it is a hackneyed example of many common descriptions of Native peoples that came before and after it well into the twentieth century.[40] At the heart of these discourses lay haole anxieties surrounding the productive and reproductive qualities of bodies and foods; that as the very "staff of life," kalo consumption constituted a regenerative act that did not abide settler civility (for bed and table manners alike).

In such descriptions, ideas of queerness emerge literally and metaphorically. "The Poi-Eater's Progress," quoted above, notably identifies queerness as a primary descriptor of the staple food. Twain's allusions to sexual performance furthermore expand nineteenth-century uses of queer (as a word then synonymous with strangeness and eccentricity) to accommodate more recent connotations of the word (in terms of non-normative subjectivities, sexual or otherwise).[41] The collapsing of abjection, taste, and sexuality into a description of poi locates its consumption within a broader historical literature that shows how the language of eating is often employed in the "othering" of racialized subjects because the act of incorporation rests at the very heart of the colonial encounter. To consume, or "eat the other," involves a complex politics of appetite, refusal, expectoration, and insatiety that becomes policed precisely because of the body's permeability: it is a frenzied contact zone rather than a sterile barrier between the civilized and the savage.[42] To taste poi, the non-Native body not only takes in the material queerness of the food, but also the bodily flavors of those with whom the dish is shared. Undoubtedly, moments like this are potent illustrations of the viscerality that Sharon Holland, Marcia Ochoa, and Kyla Wazana Tompkins see as affective indexes of taste and power.[43] Not only that, but their assertion that the metaphorical location of these feelings are anchored in intestines, bowels, innards—areas of the body less visible to normalizing colonial gazes—further classify poi's gustatory queerness.

—

ROOTS OF KNOWLEDGE

Foreigners took a very oral approach to understanding poi, dwelling on mastication, taste, and discourse. But despite these discursive locations, poi is better conceived of as a food of the gut. The corm of the kalo plant, which contains starch granules a tenth the size of those found in the potato, is 98.8 percent digestible.[44] For this reason, it has long been a dietary favorite not only for the healthy, but also the infant and infirm.[45] Scientific studies today continue to recommend poi for its medicinal and healthful properties (even as access to the food became increasingly limited by high retail costs and relatively small production going into the twentieth century) and confirm what Hawai'i's Indigenous people have long been aware of: that the fermented tuber provides an ideal nutritional base to support a large population.[46] However, even as poi's digestibility and probiotic benefits relate the food to late twentieth-century theories of the visceral, it is necessary to articulate its cultural specificity—not only within Hawai'i's settler-colonial history, but also its Indigenous context: as a root of knowledge, genealogy, and sustenance.

The physiological benefits of poi for the gut are merely one facet of its cultural and cosmological importance. It is also a fundamental anchor for knowledge and personhood within Native Hawaiian epistemology. In ʻōlelo Hawaiʻi (Hawaiian language), the word naʻau translates to "intestines, bowels, guts; mind, heart, affections; mood, temper, feelings." Paired with the suffix "ao," the word naʻauao is elaborated to mean, "learned, enlightened, intelligent, wise; learning, knowledge, wisdom, science."[47] This use of language reflects Kānaka orientations toward affect, thinking, and embodiment that are conceptually interlocked. As Manu Aluli Meyer explains in her study of Hawaiian epistemological structures, "to know something is to consider it via your emotions, your mind, and thus Hawaiians point to their stomach region when speaking of something of substance."[48] Viscerality, and both the instinctual and conscious responses to "gut feelings" are constitutive elements of a Hawaiian's very being.[49]

Finally, the symbiotic relationship between eminently digestible poi and the stomach as the epistemic center of Hawaiian identity is genealogic. Kānaka recognize deep ancestral connections to their ʻāina through an origin story at which the kalo plant is central. The story of Hāloa, the common ancestor of all Kānaka Maoli, begins with Papa and Wākea,

---

celestial beings representing the heavens and the earth whose coupling produced the world and everything within it. Multiple versions of this story exist, but in at least one version Papa and Wākea have a daughter named Ho'ohōkūkalani, whom Wākea impregnates twice. The first child, a stillborn, is buried in the ground outside the house. From that site soon grows a kalo plant that Wākea names Hāloa. The second child, also named Hāloa after the plant, becomes the first Hawaiian person, his shared name reinforcing the genealogical ties that Kānaka Maoli have with the kalo root and the land in which it grows, as well as the relationship of mutual care and respect that Kānaka maintain with their food.[50] As scholars have furthermore noted, 'ohana, the word for family, also stems from the kalo plant: 'oha (meaning the kalo corm) is pluralized using the suffix -na in order to illustrate how kalo plants are reproduced from cuttings of older roots and stalks, much like children from parents.[51] These interconnected concepts of food, land, and knowledge serve as the basis for the central argument that I would now like to make: that the perceived inedibility—or queerness—of poi by haole newcomers to the islands is deeply implicated in a history of both cultural marginalization and territorial dispossession.

COLONIAL PLACEMAKING AND SETTLER TASTEMAKING

To think through the meaning of food in relation to normativity, queerness, and indigeneity thereby requires attending to the matter of land. Indeed, it is compelling to ask when and how territory (as opposed to its earlier conception of 'āina) becomes entangled in projects of sustenance and self-determination.[52] Land can also become problematically conflated with the nation-state within settler discourses of ownership and belonging (which, in turn, get refuted, challenged, and flat-out refused as a governing force over those whom it does not equitably serve or have not consented to its power).[53] Territory is, therefore, a complicated term by which to anchor the disenfranchised. Even so, advocating for the importance of Indigenous foodways insistently points to the ecological and cultural importance of growing and cultivating one's own foods—and by extension one's ancestors—for survivance.[54] These material conditions, vital to the continuation of Indigenous societies, are most urgently exemplified by regions like the Pacific, where climate change has shifted the habitability

—

of many islands now bearing the burden of its most immediate effects, with rising water tables, drought, land loss, and a host of other anthropogenically driven threats to food security.[55] And they are further underlined by longer histories of ecological trauma experienced, for example, by Native American Tribes who adapted their foodways to climate changes experienced through forced relocation across a continent.[56] While resilience is a hallmark of Native survival *despite* displacement, material environments undoubtedly remain a key mechanism by which the "logics of elimination" imposed upon Indigenous people persist.

Academic and popular literature emerging from current interest in the local food movement does much to illuminate the indelible and complicated legacies of colonial settlement on placemaking and tastemaking in America. Alternative food practice has turned keenly toward notions of taste and place as interest in civic and ecologically conscious eating grows among America's liberal middle class.[57] In response to concerns over the industrialization and globalization of the American food system, the "local" has emerged as a framework for mitigating rising fuel costs, corporate irresponsibility, and the growing "geographies of nowhere" that (un)mark the American foodscape.[58] However, and particularly in Hawai'i, food miles and community resiliency are not the only drivers of "eating local." Conflated in local food rhetoric is also a discourse about morality and good taste that gives social meaning to what (at least on the surface) appears to be a spatial concern.[59] In other words, collective lived experience through taste, among other things, constructs a territorial politics of food that privileges particular eaters (and makers and growers) over others.

It is also the very reason that kalo cultivation now prominently sits at the center of multiple projects that seek to restore Native Hawaiian self-determination and sovereignty. Today, to grow, pound, and declare poi both healthy and delicious is a political act. One can see these taste politics at play in Hawai'i as food activists argue for increased and legally supported access to Indigenous staple foods. For example, in 2009, O'ahu-based kalo farmer and pa'i 'ai producer Daniel Anthony made news when the Hawai'i Department of Health (DOH) shut down his small commercial distribution due to the "unsanitary" nature of his product. Anthony uses traditional methods to prepare his food, which he then sells to consumers by using a pōhaku and papa ku'i 'ai (both porous materials) in an open-air

—

environment—violations of DOH commercial food regulations.[60] During what ultimately became a cultural standoff between Native Hawaiians and American government officials, the sanitation officer for Anthony's district explained in the wake of his arrest that,

> Mr. Anthony fails to realize that we are not living in ancient times where there were no regulations designed to protect public health. The DOH cannot stand idly by while Mr. Anthony continues to endanger the health of Hawai'i's people under the guise of cultural tradition.[61]

Such a statement elegantly reveals the fraught relationship that food continues to mediate between Indigenous peoples and American citizens in the postcolonial era—anxieties over contamination, indigeneity, and modernity remain staggeringly present within not only public, but also official discourse, about food safety and "cultural tradition."

After nearly two years of debate, a bill passed in the 2011 Hawai'i leg-islative session that legalized the sale of traditionally prepared poi within the State.[62] The process of acquiring an exemption was accompanied by a visible public outcry: the cause received significant press, "Legalize Pa'i 'Ai" bumper stickers proliferated, and activists led by then-University of Hawai'i law student Amy Brinker called to "Indigenize the Law" by rec-ognizing that Western legal frameworks do not adequately accommodate Native needs. Bill 101, known colloquially as "the poi bill," excluded manu-facturers of hand-pounded poi from the DOH's certified food processing establishment requirements under several conditions: first, that pa'i 'ai manufacturers sell carefully labeled batches directly to customers; second, that hand-washing facilities are located at the place of manufacture; and third, that the maker attend a food safety class.[63] These stipulations com-prise an exemption through which the law accommodates foods that resist the disciplinary frameworks of law through their cultural importance (such exemptions had been previously extended to products like honey and sushi).[64] This exemption within the health code now protects traditional pa'i 'ai and poi preparation as long as consumers agree to take on the risks of eating foods deemed "potentially hazardous" under the law.[65]

The efforts of community activists to keep traditionally prepared kalo products in the Hawai'i marketplace has been, by most accounts, a success.

—

Today Anthony distributes his poi and paʻi ʻai through several avenues of sale that range anywhere from the back of his truck parked roadside to regularly stocked display tables in the produce section of Whole Foods Markets in the affluent neighborhoods of Kailua and Mānoa. In addition, the rising profile of Hawaiʻi chefs committed to working with and honoring heritage foods has also expanded kalo's eatership to those who might not relish sour poi, but willingly consume its less fermented counterpart when presented as part of an elevated dining experience. In fact, it is through the rising popularity of paʻi ʻai that kalo has begun a quiet migration away from its historical queerness. Paʻi ʻai is not only sweeter and firmer, but it also offers a friendly pairing with non-Native foods: it can easily be kneaded into pizza "crust" or pan fried like a potato. Even if it isn't (yet) a mainstream food, paʻi ʻai has now taken on cultural capital increasingly celebrated by Natives and settlers alike. And it is here that we might also see the discourses of taste re-emerge to secure kalo's place within a normative framework of cuisine from which it had so long been discounted. In a 2014 interview with Honolulu's *Civil Beat*, Brinker emphasized how, because of its taste, paʻi ʻai offered an ideal platform for Indigenous food advocacy.[66] "There are people who may not like poi but find they love paʻi ʻai, with its mochi-like consistency and milky sweetness," she argued. "When someone with a newfound taste for paʻi ʻai has trouble finding it because there is not enough kalo to meet the demand, the stage is set for more folks to take up farming."[67] In other words, capitalizing on the valued taste of sweetness—rather than more kalo—poi's more typical sourness promised to bridge a return to kalo consumption, cultivation, and Indigenous cultural practice.

CONCLUSION

Today, poi and paʻi ʻai coexist in the contemporary Hawaiʻi foodscape, to be sure, but one has clearly risen in the gastronomic ranks to become one way that eaters can engage with the important Native staple of kalo without coming up against their visceral aversions. New eaters of kalo—particularly paʻi ʻai—think with their mouths, not their stomachs; and they consume a food, rather than enact a genealogical connection. Their enthusiasm for it increases a market demand that promises profitability

—

for farmers and cultural practitioners who, despite any sovereign politics they might have, must also make a living. Nevertheless, this pendulum swing from disgusting to delicious in the eyes of outsiders provides a platform for thinking, ultimately, through what "local" food means for the multiple and overlapping communities who have come to understand Hawaiʻi as home.[68] Recognized as a spatial identity generalizable to alternative food commodity markets, as well as an ethnic identity *particular* to Hawaiʻi's multicultural labor history, the "local-ness" inflected in Hawaiʻi's food movement today suggests that the links between "taste" and "place" are more than just economic concerns. The practice of "eating local" is also an indirect indictment of the structures of dependence imposed by the United States, which sustains tourism- and military-based economies by importing foods at great cost despite Hawaiʻi's potential for diversified agricultural abundance.[69] The politics of kalo have emerged from this historical legacy of gustatory discomfort, where the sour viscosity of poi inflects understandings of its social acceptability. Attention paid to palatability through consistency, flavor, and its emergence through the capitalist market continues to highlight the tensions that remain attached to kalo even as its legal and popular acceptance has secured a favorable place within the complex grammar of Hawaiʻi's local cuisine.

NOTES

1. Twain's emphasis. I use a reprinted version here. Twain, *Roughing It*, 229–30.
2. Readings of Twain as either colonialist or a humorous subversion of the pastoral remain debated, as explained in Sumida, "Reevaluating Mark Twain's Novel of Hawaiʻi." I read his text as examples of what Mary Louise Pratt calls a "contact zone," where deeply subjective understandings of otherness and colonial subjectivity co-constitute, though "often within radically asymmetrical relations of power." Pratt, *Imperial Eyes*, 8. For a good overview of the many ways the Western world envisioned and represented the Pacific, see Driver, *Tropical Visions*. For analyses specific to imperial encounters in Hawaiʻi, see Costa, "Paradisical Discourse"; and Schroeder and Borgerson, "Packaging Paradise."
3. Merry, *Colonizing Hawaiʻi*.
4. Hobart, "Tropical Necessities," 151, 152.
5. These aversions are expressed in historic and contemporary literature, particularly in travel guides. I focus primarily on the nineteenth century in this article, but this carries into the present day. See Friedman's *DK Eyewitness* that describes poi as "definitely an acquired taste," 193.

—

6. The Latin name of the taro, *Colocasia esculenta*, is singular, but it is a highly varied cultivar in Hawai'i. Out of an estimated 300 distinct cultivars by researchers in the early 1900s, University of Hawai'i's College of Tropical Agriculture and Human Resources have identified and preserved 84 distinct types. Cho, Yamakawa, and Hollyer, "Hawaiian Kalo," 4; and Whitney, Bowers, and Takahashi, *Taro Varieties in Hawaii.*

7. Poi production is a labor-intensive process, from wetland kalo cultivation to culinary preparation. For an illustration of how the food has resisted efficient capitalist production, see *Proceedings of the Taro Conference*; and Aikau and Camvel, "Cultural Traditions and Food."

8. Nout, Sarkar, and Beuchat, "Indigenous Fermented Foods," 825.

9. Simonson, Sasaki, and Sakata, *Pupus to da Max*, 117.

10. *Hawaiian Gazette*, "Taro or Kalo."

11. Vincent, *Through and Through the Tropics*, 84.

12. *Pacific Commercial Advertiser*, "Vacation Visit to Hawai'i."

13. See Long, *Culinary Tourism*, which includes a chapter on Hawai'i's many poke festivals; Molz, "Cosmopolitan Mobilities"; and Slocum, "Race in the Study of Food." For Pacific-focused studies, see O'Connor, "The Hawaiian Luau"; Gewertz and Errington, *Cheap Meat*; and Elias, "The Palate of Power."

14. *Travels in the Sandwich and Society Islands* (1856), *Reminisces of Travel in Australia, America, and Egypt* (1883), *Sandwich Island Notes* (1854). I use luau here without its diacritical marks to flag these tourist events as a mere simulacrum of Kānaka Maoli forms of feasting.

15. Of the imported foods to Hawai'i, approximately 81 percent come from the continental United States and 6 percent from other foreign markets. Loke and Leung, "Hawai'i's Food Consumption and Supply Sources."

16. Although archaeological evidence shows that this could sometimes be distributed unevenly. Lincoln and Ladefoged, "Agroecology," 192. The Native Hawaiian population in 1778 has been estimated anywhere between 200,000 or 250,000 to just under 1 million. See Dye, "Population Trends," 2; and Stannard, *Before the Horror*, 32–37. A mere 45 years later, the Hawaiian population had declined to around 135,000, with many succumbing to the spread of foreign disease. Silva, *Aloha Betrayed*, 24.

17. Silva, *Aloha Betrayed*, 48–49. Also Kent, *Hawai'i*; Miike, *Water and the Law*; and Wilcox, *Sugar Water*; Takaki, *Pau Hana*.

18. It is imperative to note here that the Newlands Resolution provided the United States with no legal standing for its occupation of Hawai'i, as explained in Kauanui, *Hawaiian Blood*, 28; and Silva, *Aloha Betrayed*, 160–63.

19. Hitch, *Islands in Transition*, 266; and Wilson, "Hawai'i's $14 Billion Tourism Industry."

20. Fujii and Mark, "The Impact of Alternative Regional Development Strategies," 42; and Gomes, "Farming Finds No Home."

21. Merry, *Colonizing Hawai'i*.

22. Ranked only behind Pima Indians. Shintai, Hughes, Beckham, O'Connor, "Obesity and Cardiovascular Risk Intervention Diet."

23. See Laudan, *The Food of Paradise*; Hiura, *Kau Kau*; and Reddinger, "Eating 'Local.'"

—

24. Tung and Barnes, "Heart Diseases," 110; and Shintai, Hughes, Beckham, and O'Connor, "Obesity and Cardiovascular Risk Intervention Diet," 1647S. The latter study showed that Native Hawaiians placed back on a pre-contact diet (referred to as the "Waianae Diet") experienced marked weight loss and successful adherence rates.

25. Wolfe, "Settler Colonialism."

26. Pukui and Elbert, *Hawaiian Dictionary*, 9.

27. I am building here upon Goeman, "Disrupting a Settler-Colonial Grammar of Place," and Lefebvre's theory of the cultural construction of space in *The Production of Space*.

28. Linnekin, "The *Hui* Lands of Keanae"; Suryanata, "Diversified Agriculture"; Goldberg-Hiller and Silva, "The Botany of Emergence"; and Hobart, "Tropical Necessities."

29. Roy, *Alimentary Tracts*; Spackman, "Leaky"; and Hayes-Conroy and Hayes-Conroy, "Taking Back Taste."

30. Building upon Probyn's *Carnal Appetites*.

31. Holland, Ochoa, and Tompkins, "Introduction," 395.

32. For more on the coloring and valuing of certain cultivars, see Malo, *Hawaiian Antiquities*, footnote 2, 44. The normative Western palate is built, arguably, on the pillars of saltiness, sweetness, and fattiness that emerged from twinned histories of industrialization and Empire. Mintz, *Sweetness and Power*, and, more recently, Moss, *Salt Sugar Fat*.

33. Goldberg-Hiller and Silva, "The Botany of Emergence."

34. Wolfe, "Settler Colonialism," 387–409.

35. This term comes from Musick, *Hawai'i*, published to educate American readers on the benefits of the new territory.

36. Ibid., 67.

37. *Latter-Day Saints' Millennial*, "The Poi Eater's Progress," 376, 377.

38. Sweetser, *One Way Around the World*, 22.

39. Twain, *Roughing It*, 230, 231.

40. On Hawaiian foodways, see Kashay, "Missionaries and Foodways"; on Hawaiians generally, see Imada, *Aloha America*; Merry, *Colonizing Hawai'i*.

41. "queer, adj.1." OED Online. Oxford University Press. December 2015, https://www.oed.com/view/Entry/156236?rskey=cTWUiS&result=2.

42. I borrow this thinking here specifically from Parama Roy's *Alimentary Tracts* (2010) but am also referencing Judith Farquhar's *Appetites* (2002), Kyla Wazana Tompkins's *Racial Indigestion* (2012), and bell hooks's seminal essay "Eating the Other" (1992).

43. Holland, Ochoa, and Tompkins, "Introduction," 395.

44. Cho, Yamakawa, and Hollyer, "Hawaiian Kalo," 2.

45. Malo writes that, "Poi is such an agreeable food that taro is in great demand." *Hawaiian Antiquities*, 42.

46. Brown et al., "The Anti-cancer Effects of Poi." They write that, "Although never officially declared a probiotic, studies conducted in Hawai'i around the 1950s suggested that poi could be useful for the management of infant food allergies and weight gain in failure-to-thrive infants," 767. Also see Brown and Valerie, "The Medicinal Uses of

—

Poi." The "revival" of Hawai'i's taro industry was the subject of a conference in 1965, although, it appears, as a means of capitalizing on agricultural exports to the United States "mainland." *Proceedings of the Taro Conference.*

47. Pukui and Elbert, *Hawaiian Dictionary*, 257.

48. It also connects Kānaka worldviews to the greater Pacific, where embodied knowledge and intellectual knowledge are also indistinct. Meyer, "Native Hawaiian Epistemology," 26.

49. I borrow here from Yee, "The Fragility of Things."

50. This mo'olelo is far more nuanced than I can do justice to in this space. For additional reading, see Malo, *Hawaiian Antiquities*, 238–44; Beckwith, *Hawaiian Mythology*, 293–306; McDougall, *Finding Meaning*, 91–93; and Silva, *Aloha Betrayed*, 101–2.

51. Diaz and Kauanui, "Native Pacific Cultural Studies."

52. The enactment of sovereignty does not *necessarily* require land. Mobility, diaspora, and other contours of home-making are shown to emerge from histories of displacement and are all signals in intersectional identity formation. Tompkins, "Intersections of Race, Gender, and Sexuality."

53. It may be useful, then, to abstract out the notion of land to a more expansive analytic of environment, which has the potential to transcend the boundary-making of nationhood. Here I draw on Simpson, *Mohawk Interruptus.*

54. I borrow this term, which signals active ongoing Indigenous survival, from Vizenor, *Manifest Manners.*

55. Here I refer to overfishing and the ecological strains of commercial agriculture for export. Keener et al., *Climate Change and Pacific Islands.*

56. Whyte, "Back to the Future."

57. Trubek, *Taste of Place*; Weiss, "Making Pigs Local"; and Bell and Valentine, *Consuming Geographies.*

58. In using "geographies of nowhere" I reference Schnell, building upon the work of James Howard Kunstler. "Deliberate Identities," 67.

59. Weiss, in his study of "local" North Carolina pork, helpfully asks: "What do we mean by *place* when we talk about its taste?" Weiss, "Making Pigs Local," 444.

60. Huff, "Health Officials Restrict Poi Pioneer."

61. Ibid.

62. Huff, "State Legalizes Hand-Pounded Poi"; and Cheng, "Got Pa'i'ai?"

63. Hawai'i Senate Bill 101, 2011.

64. Black, "Pounding the Issue."

65. The outcome, largely recognized as a significant victory for both Indigenous rights and food sovereignty within the islands, now buttresses a growing number of organizations that anchor their missions in the perpetuation of Native foodways, including Kāko'o 'Ōiwi, Paepae o He'eia, and Ho'oulu 'Āina. Mikesell, "OK Sought for Traditional Taro."

66. Importantly, kalo cultivation has become central to Indigenous resurgence projects that not only seek to occupy space, but to exercise embodied cultural practice that attends to the spiritual, affective, gustatory, and epistemological dimensions of

—

Native Hawaiian identity. See especially Goodyear-Ka'ōpua, "Rebuilding the Structures that Feed Us."

67. Brinker, "Passage of Poi Bill."

68. Delind, "Of Bodies, Place, and Culture," 123.

69. Teaiwa coins the term "militourism" to signal how the two are interlocking parts of colonial economies, in "Reading Gauguin's Noa Noa."

REFERENCES

Aikau, Hokulani, and Donna Kameha'ikū Camvel. "Cultural Traditions and Food: Kānaka Maoli and the Production of Poi in the He'e'ia Wetland." *Food, Culture, and Society* 19, no. 3 (2016): 539–561.

Beckwith, Martha. *Hawaiian Mythology*. Alexandria, VA: Library of Alexandria, 1970.

Bell, David, and Gill Valentine. *Consuming Geographies: We Are Where We Eat*. London: Routledge, 2013.

Black, Catherine Mariko. "Pounding the Issue." *Honolulu Weekly*, March 9, 2011. https://honoluluweekly.com/cover/2011/03/pounding-the-issue/.

Brinker, Amy. "Passage of Poi Bill a Major Milestone for Hawai'i." *Honolulu Civil Beat*, May 5, 2011. https://www.civilbeat.com/2011/05/10763-passage-of-poi-bill-a-major-milestone-for-hawaii/.

Brown, Amy C., J. E. Reitzenstein, J. Liu, and M. R. Jadus. "The Anti-cancer Effects of Poi (*Colocasia esculenta*) on Colonic Adenocarcinoma Cells *In Vitro*." *Phytotherapy Research* 19 (2005): 767–771.

Brown, Amy C., and Ana Valerie. "The Medicinal Uses of Poi." *Nutrition in Clinical Care* 7, no. 2 (2004): 69–74.

Cheng, Martha. "Got Pa'i'ai? Hand-pounded Pa'i'ai Now Legal." *Honolulu Magazine*, November 29, 2011. https://www.honolulumagazine.com/Honolulu-Magazine/Biting-Commentary/November-2011/Got-pa'i'ai-Hand-pounded-pa'i'ai-now-legal/.

Cho, John J., Roy A. Yamakawa, and James Hollyer. "Hawaiian Kalo, Past and Future." *Sustainable Agriculture* (February 2007): 1–8.

Cooperative Extension Service. *Proceedings of the Taro Conference*. Honolulu: University of Hawai'i, 1967.

Costa, Janeen Arnold. "Paradisical Discourse: A Critical Analysis of Marketing and Consuming Hawai'i." *Consumption Markets and Culture* 1, no. 4 (1998): 303–346.

Delind, Laura B. "Of Bodies, Place, and Culture: Re-situating Local Food." *Journal of Agricultural and Environmental Ethics* 19 (2006): 121–146.

Diaz, Vicente M., and J. Kēhaulani Kauanui, eds. "Native Pacific Cultural Studies on the Edge." Special Issue of *The Contemporary Pacific* 3, no. 2 (2001).

Driver, Felix, ed. *Tropical Visions in an Age of Empire*. Chicago, IL: University of Chicago Press, 2005.

Dye, Tom. "Population Trends in Hawai'i Before 1778." *The Hawaiian Journal of History* 28 (1994): 1–20.

—

Elias, Megan. "The Palate of Power: Americans, Food, and the Philippines after the Spanish-American War." *Material Culture* 46, no. 1 (2014): 44–57.

Farquhar, Judith. *Appetites: Food and Sex in Post-Socialist China*. Durham, NC: Duke University Press, 2002.

Friedman, Bonnie. *DK Eyewitness Travel Guide: Hawai'i*. New York, NY: Penguin, 2013.

Fujii, Edwin T., and James Mark. "The Impact of Alternative Regional Development Strategies on Crime Rates: Tourism vs. Agriculture in Hawai'i." *The Annals of Regional Science* 13, no. 3 (1979): 42–56.

Gewertz, Deborah, and Frederick Errington. *Cheap Meat: Flap Food Nations in the Pacific Highlands*. Berkeley: University of California Press, 2010.

Goeman, Mishuana R. "Disrupting a Settler-Colonial Grammar of Place: The Visual Memoir of Hulleah Tsinhnahjinnie." In *Theorizing Native Studies*, edited by Audra Simpson and Andrea Smith. Durham, NC: Duke University Press, 2014.

Goldberg-Hiller, Jonathan, and Noenoe K. Silva. "The Botany of Emergence: Kanaka Ontology and Biocolonialism in Hawai'i." *Native American and Indigenous Studies* 2, no. 2 (2015): 1–26.

Gomes, Andrew. "Farming Finds No Home on Agricultural Land." *Honolulu Advertiser*, June 12, 2005.

Goodyear-Ka'ōpua, Noelani. "Rebuilding the Structures that Feed Us." In *The Seeds We Planted: Portraits of a Native Hawaiian Charter School*. Minneapolis, MN: University of Minnesota Press, 2013.

Hawai'i Senate Bill 101, 2011. https://e-lobbyist.com/gaits/text/154166.

Hawaiian Gazette. "Taro or Kalo: The Hawaiian Staff of Life." May 2, 1893.

Hayes-Conroy, Allison, and Jessica Hayes-Conroy. "Taking Back Taste: Feminism, Food, and Visceral Politics." *Gender, Place, and Culture* 15, no. 5 (2008): 461–473.

Hitch, Thomas Kemper. *Islands in Transition: The Past, Present, and Future of Hawai'i's Economy*. Honolulu: University of Hawai'i Press, 1992.

Hiura, Arnold. *Kau Kau: Cuisine and Culture in the Hawaiian Islands*. Honolulu: Watermark Publishing, 2009.

Hobart, Hi'ilei Julia. "Tropical Necessities: Ice, Taste, and Territory in Settler Colonial Hawai'i." PhD diss. New York University, 2016.

Holland, Sharon P., Marcia Ochoa, and Kyla Wazana Tompkins. "Introduction: On the Visceral." *GLQ* 20, no. 4 (2014): 391–406.

hooks, bell. "Eating the Other: Desire and Resistance." In *Black Looks: Race and Representation*, 21–39. Boston, MA: South End Press, 1992.

Huff, Daryl. "Health Officials Restrict Poi Pioneer: Supporters of Traditional Poi Challenge Health Department." *KITV Honolulu*, November 23, 2010. https://www.kitv.com/r/25903451/detail.html.

Huff, Daryl. "State Legalizes Hand-Pounded Poi: Governor Signs Bill to Allow Sales of Poi Made Traditional Way." *KITV Honolulu*, November 23, 2010. https://www.kitv.com/r/28275745/detail.html.

Imada, Adria L. *Aloha America: Hula Circuits Through the U.S. Empire*. Durham, NC: Duke University Press, 2012.

—

Kashay, Jennifer Fish. "Missionaries and Foodways in Early 19th-Century Hawaiʻi." *Food and Foodways* 17, no. 3 (2009): 159–180.

Kauanui, J. Kēhaulani. *Hawaiian Blood: Colonialism and the Politics of Sovereignty and Indigeneity.* Durham, NC: Duke University Press, 2008.

Keener, Victoria W., John J. Marra, Melissa L. Finucane, Deanna Spooner, and Margaret H. Smith, eds. *Climate Change and Pacific Islands: Indicators and Impacts—Report for the 2012 Pacific Islands Regional Climate Assessment (PIRCA).* Washington, DC: Island Press, 2012.

Kent, Noel. *Hawaiʻi: Islands Under the Influence.* Honolulu: University of Hawaiʻi Press, 1993.

Latter-Day Saints' Millennial Star. "The Poi-Eater's Progress." 55 (1893, June 5).

Laudan, Rachel. *The Food of Paradise: Exploring Hawaiʻi's Culinary Heritage.* Honolulu: University of Hawaiʻi Press, 1996.

Lefebvre, Henri. *The Production of Space.* Translated by Donald Nicholson-Smith. Oxford: Blackwell, 1991.

Lincoln, Noa, and Thegn Ladefoged. "Agroecology of Pre-contact Hawaiian Dryland Farming: The Spatial Extent, Yield, and Social Impact of Hawaiian Breadfruit Groves in Kona Hawaiʻi." *Journal of Archaeological Science* 49 (2014): 192–202.

Linnekin, Jocelyn. "The *Hui* Lands of Keanae: Hawaiian Land Tenure and the Great Mahele." *The Journal of the Polynesian Society* 92, no. 2 (1983): 169–188.

Loke, Matthew K., and PingSun Leung. "Hawaiʻi's Food Consumption and Supply Sources: Benchmark Estimates and Measurement Issues." *Agricultural and Food Economics* 1, no. 10 (2013). Accessed February 25, 2016. doi:10.1186/2193-7532-1-10.

Long, Lucy, ed. *Culinary Tourism.* Lexington, KY: University Press of Kentucky, 2003.

Malo, David. *Hawaiian Antiquities (Moʻolelo Hawaiʻi).* Honolulu: The Bishop Museum, 1951.

McDougall, Brandy Nalani. *Finding Meaning: Kaona and Contemporary Hawaiian Literature.* Tucson, AZ: University of Arizona Press, 2016.

Merry, Sally Engle. *Colonizing Hawaiʻi: The Cultural Power of Law.* Princeton, NJ: Princeton University Press, 2000.

Meyer, Manu Aluli. "Native Hawaiian Epistemology: Sites of Empowerment and Resistance." *Equity and Excellence in Education* 31, no. 1 (1998): 22–28.

Miike, Lawrence H. *Water and the Law in Hawaiʻi.* Honolulu: University of Hawaiʻi Press, 2004.

Mikesell, Chris. "OK Sought for Traditional Taro." *Honolulu Star-Advertiser*, February 28, 2011.

Mintz, Sidney W. *Sweetness and Power: The Place of Sugar in Modern History.* New York, NY: Penguin, 1986.

Molz, Jennie Germann. "The Cosmopolitan Mobilities of Culinary Tourism." *Space and Culture* 10, no. 1 (2007): 77–93.

Moss, Michael. *Salt Sugar Fat: How the Food Giants Hooked Us.* New York, NY: Random House, 2013.

—

Musick, John Roy. *Hawai'i, Our New Possessions*. New York, NY: Funk and Wagnalls Company, 1898.

Nout, M. J. Robert, Prabir K. Sarkar, and Larry R. Beuchat. "Indigenous Fermented Foods." In *Food Microbiology: Fundamentals and Frontiers*, 3rd ed. Washington, DC: ASM Press, 2007.

O'Connor, Kaori. "The Hawaiian Luau: Food as Tradition, Transgression, Transformation, and Travel." *Food, Culture & Society* 11, no. 2 (2008): 149–172.

Pacific Commercial Advertiser. "Vacation Visit to Hawai'i." January 22, 1906.

Pratt, Mary Louise. *Imperial Eyes: Travel Writing and Transculturation*. London: Routledge, 1992.

Probyn, Elspeth. *Carnal Appetites: FoodSexIdentities*. New York, NY: Routledge, 2000.

Proceedings of the Taro Conference. Honolulu: Cooperative Extension Service, University of Hawai'i, 1965.

Pukui, Mary Kawena, and Samuel H. Elbert. *Hawaiian Dictionary*. Honolulu: University of Hawai'i Press, 1986.

Reddinger, Amy. "Eating 'Local': The Politics of Post-statehood Cookbooks." *Nordic Journal of English Studies* 9, no. 3 (2010): 67–87.

Roy, Parama. *Alimentary Tracts: Appetites, Aversions, and the Postcolonial*. Durham, NC: Duke University Press, 2010.

Schnell, Steven. "Deliberate Identities: Becoming Local in America in a Global Age." *Journal of Cultural Geography* 30, no. 1 (2013): 55–89.

Schroeder, Jonathan E., and Janet L. Borgerson. "Packaging Paradise: Organizing Representations of Hawai'i." In *Against the Grain: Advances in Postcolonial Organization Studies*, edited by Anshuman Prasad, 32–53. Copenhagen: Copenhagen Business School Press, 2012.

Shintai, Terry T., C. K. Hughes, S. Beckham, and H. K. O'Connor. "Obesity and Cardiovascular Risk Intervention Diet Through the Ad Libitum Feeding of Traditional Hawaiian Diet." *American Journal of Clinical Nutrition* 53 (1991): 1647S–1651S.

Silva, Noenoe K. *Aloha Betrayed: Native Hawaiian Resistance to American Colonialism*. Durham, NC: Duke University Press, 2004.

Simonson, Douglas, Pat Sasaki, and Ken Sakata. *Pupus to da Max: The All-Purpose Illustrated Guide to the Food of Hawai'i*. Honolulu: Bess Press, 1986.

Simpson, Audra. *Mohawk Interruptus: Political Life Across the Borders of Settler States*. Durham, NC: Duke University Press, 2014.

Slocum, Rachel. "Race in the Study of Food." *Progress in Human Geography* 35, no. 3 (2011): 303–327.

Spackman, Christy. "Leaky: The Politics of Sensory Infrastructures in the Late Industrial Era." Forthcoming.

Stannard, David E. *Before the Horror: The Population of Hawai'i on the Eve of Western Contact*. Honolulu: Social Science Research Institute, University of Hawai'i, 1989.

Sumida, Stephen H. "Reevaluating Mark Twain's Novel of Hawai'i." *American Literature* 61, no. 4 (1989): 586–609.

———

Suryanata, Krisnawata. "Diversified Agriculture, Land Use, and Agrofood Networks in Hawaiʻi." *Economic Geography* 78, no. 1 (2002): 71–86.

Sweetser, Delight. *One Way Around the World.* Indianapolis, IN: The Bowen-Merrill Company, 1898.

Takaki, Ronald. *Pau Hana: Plantation Life and Labor in Hawaiʻi.* Honolulu: University of Hawaiʻi Press, 1984.

Teaiwa, Teresia. "Reading Gauguin's *Noa Noa* with Epeli Hauʻofa's *Kisses in the Nederends*: Militourism, Feminism, and the 'Polynesian' Body." In *Inside Out: Literature, Cultural Politics, and Identity in the New Pacific,* edited by Vilsoni Hereniko and Rob Wilson, 53–69. Lanham: Rowman & Littlefield, 1999.

Tompkins, Kyla Wazana. "Intersections of Race, Gender, and Sexuality: Queer of Color Critique." In *The Cambridge Companion to American Gay and Lesbian Literature,* edited by Scott Herring, 173–189. London: Cambridge University Press, 2015.

Tompkins, Kyla Wazana. *Racial Indigestion: Eating Bodies in the Nineteenth Century.* New York, NY: New York University Press, 2012.

Trubek, Amy. *Taste of Place: A Cultural Journey into Terroir.* Berkeley: University of California Press, 2006.

Tung, Wei-Chen, and Maureen Barnes. "Heart Diseases Among Native Hawaiians and Pacific Islanders." *Home Health Care Management and Practice* 26, no. 2 (2014): 110–113.

Twain, Mark. *Roughing It.* New York, NY: Harper & Brothers, 1899.

Vincent, Frank, Jr. *Through and Through the Tropics: 30,000 Miles of Travel in Polynesia, Australasia, and India.* 2nd ed. New York, NY: Harper & Brothers, 1882.

Vizenor, Gerald. *Manifest Manners: Narratives on Postindian Survivance.* Hanover: University of Wesleyan Press, 1994.

Weiss, Brad. "Making Pigs Local: Discerning the Sensory Character of Place." *Cultural Anthropology* 26, no. 3 (2011): 371–384.

Whitney, Leo D., F. A. I. Bowers, and M. Takahashi. *Taro Varieties in Hawaii.* Honolulu: Hawaiʻi Agricultural Experiment Station, 1939.

Whyte, Kyle Powys. "Back to the Future: An Introduction to Indigenous Peoples and Climate Injustice." Forthcoming.

Wilcox, Carol. *Sugar Water: Hawaiʻi's Plantation Ditches.* Honolulu: University of Hawaiʻi Press, 1997.

Wilson, Reid. "Hawaiʻi's $14 Billion Tourism Industry Back to Pre-recession Levels." *The Washington Post* GovBeat Blog. September 27, 2013. https://www.washingtonpost.com /blogs/govbeat/wp/2013/09/27/hawaiis-14-billion-tourism-industry-back-to-pre -recession-levels/.

Wolfe, Patrick. "Settler Colonialism and the Elimination of the Native." *Journal of Genocide Research* 8, no. 4 (2006): 387–409.

Yee, Aubrey. "The Fragility of Things and Capacities of the Micro-Political Experiment." *Theory & Event* 18, no. 3 (2015). https://muse.jhu.edu/.

—

URBAN ENVIRONMENTS

INTRODUCTION

Whered when speaking of nature, there is a tendency to think through dichotomies: nature versus culture; mind versus body; or male versus
female. One such enduring division is the urban versus the rural. People
commonly regard urban centers as places apart from nature, marked by
dense human concentration in heavily built environments where pollution
or signs of human invention crowds out the work of nature. Cities and
towns are animated, in this view, by the rush and complexities of modern
life. In comparison, the countryside can be heralded as a more natural,
simpler, and purer space—a refuge, at times, from the excesses, corrup-
tion, and stresses of the city. Further, just as urban and rural environments are often juxtaposed, so too are their inhabitants. Such stereotypes
contrast urban residents, seen as more sophisticated but out of touch with
nature, with rural residents, seen as less cultured but more attuned with
their surrounding environments. Taken together, such notions circulate
reductionist and misguided assumptions of which types of nature and
which groups of people belong in which sorts of landscapes.

Of course, nature defies such clear-cut classifications. Environmental
anthropologists, for example, note the varied and vibrant forms of nature
contained in urban landscapes. Cities often contain niches where forms of

—

nonhuman life flourish, including rivers, lakes, vacant fields, and even the cracks in sidewalks. Some of these forms of urban nature are celebrated, such as charismatic bird species and old-growth trees, while others are less welcomed, such as wild animals or pests and pathogens. Regarding urban and suburban landscapes as sites for nature encourages more creative visions of these spaces as places where residents may connect with more-than-human ecologies. Together with the growing fields of industrial ecology, green design, landscape architecture, and urban food movements, environmental anthropologists are increasingly conducting their research in cities, showing boundaries between the urban and the hinterland to be porous, contested, and dynamic. In this work lively nature comes to be recognized as interwoven with the urban forms often imagined through the removal or containment of nature.

The two articles we have selected for this theme both examine the various ways people articulate and enact imaginations of urban sustainability. In her ethnographic research in Sweden, Cindy Isenhour notes that many ecoconscious Stockholm residents "know" sustainability through relatively narrow parameters based on scientific calculation, green consumerism, and technological efficiencies—a view that often contrasts with ideas of sustainability found outside the city. Despite these differences, Isenhour finds productive points of connection between urban and rural groups regarding their shared global concern for "equality and the fair distribution of environmental risks and benefits" (119). Moving to urban China, Amy Zhang illustrates how biologists and urban planners are embracing the black soldier fly as a more "organic" solution for sustainable waste management. Though promoted as a natural and biological solution for waste, people must still exert much time and care to adapt the black soldier fly to better serve human needs, including the aesthetic demands of hiding the flies from the gaze of urban residents, who desire the "sanitized aesthetic of modern eco-cities" (133).

Collectively, both ethnographies address emerging themes in urban sustainability. With the majority of the earth's human residents currently living in urban areas, there is growing recognition that any long-term sustainability strategies must grapple with cities. Indeed, a growing cohort of scholars and practitioners maintain that cities may prove to be more sustainable than rural areas, as they have the potential to work across

—

more efficient scales for transportation, water use, energy use, and food systems. Even with the growing recognition of the ecological potential of urban landscapes, however, the debate continues over the best methods to realize the vision of the green city. Some people advocate for technological approaches focused on increased efficiency and green consumerism. Others encourage more structural changes to social and economic systems that work within nature's limits and that embrace natural processes, with all their uncertainty and messiness. In all likelihood, crafting sustainable cities will require finding productive points of overlap between these two paths, with the aim of ensuring equal access to ecologically healthy and environmentally just systems for all people, across urban, suburban, and rural landscapes.

DISCUSSION QUESTIONS

1. The case study in Sweden highlights two different pathways often identified for urban sustainability. One focuses on keeping existing structures largely intact but making them "smarter" and more efficient. The other argues that societies need to fundamentally rework their relationships with nature, which requires structural change. What are your opinions of each of these two paths? Do you think there are ways they can work together?

2. In Stockholm, much responsibility for urban sustainability falls to individual consumers. How much responsibility for sustainability do you think should rest on individual decisions? Do you think people can consume their way out of environmental challenges? What do you consider an ideal balance between individual and systemic approaches to sustainability? As a responsible consumer, do you ever feel overwhelmed by making "sustainable" purchasing or lifestyle decisions?

3. Both authors point to ways that urban sustainability projects are also aesthetic projects, concerned with what sustainability should "look like." How do aesthetics factor into sustainability projects in both Sweden and China? Which aspects of nature are visible and invisible in each case? Do you think there are ways to shift popular aesthetics of sustainability, to incorporate messier and less lovely forms of nature? If so, how?

4. What do you learn from these essays about the role government can play in promoting urban sustainability? Have you noticed ways government programs favor particular types of approaches, such as community participation or private-sector partnerships? What potential forms of inclusion and exclusion may these policies lead to, including the access to urban amenities and services? How may city government policies promote a connection to nature among urban residents?

3

HOW THE GRASS BECAME GREENER IN THE CITY

ON URBAN IMAGININGS AND PRACTICES OF SUSTAINABLE LIVING IN SWEDEN

CINDY ISENHOUR

INTRODUCTION

In the sixth century BC, Aesop wrote a now familiar tale of two mice, a country mouse and a city mouse. The city mouse went to visit his friend in the country and was appalled by the rural lifestyle, where mice had only grain to eat. Conditioned by the conveniences of the city, he encouraged his friend to return the visit and experience all the fine things urban life had to offer. The country mouse obliged but, soon after his arrival in the city, was nearly killed when discovered by intolerant humans and hungry dogs. He quickly returned to the country with the retort, "better barley and oats in peace than cheese and figs in fear." Despite the centuries that have passed, the fable still has contemporary resonance. Where hazards are not hungry dogs and angry barkeeps, but rather traffic congestion, energy dependency, pollution, alienation, and crime—urban life continues to present many dangers. Indeed since Aesop's time, some of humanity's biggest challenges

Originally published as Isenhour, C., 2011. How the Grass Became Greener in the City: On Urban Imaginings and Practices of Sustainable Living in Sweden. *City & Society*, Volume 23, Issue 2, pp. 117–134. Reproduced by permission of the American Anthropological Association. Not for sale or further reproduction.

have been associated with cities, from spreading epidemics and deadly water contamination to the destruction of surrounding landscapes and depletion of natural resources.

As urban populations and concerns about global sustainability grow, many have argued that booming cities present great risks for the future. The 2007 State of the World Population noted that cities are "the direct or indirect source of most of the world's resource destruction and pollution" (UN 2007:ii). Despite this, millions of humans are drawn to cities each year by the promise of economic advancement and a better life. Lefebvre (1989) recognized this duality, describing the city as a space akin to a whirlpool, actively streaming together elements of both promise and oppression. Today, approximately half of all the world's citizens live in urban areas (UN 2007). Many, despite the challenges to sustainability posed by urbanization, have come to argue that with technological breakthroughs, compact living, progressive environmental policies, and economies of scale, urban life is increasingly sustainable, perhaps even more sustainable than rural living. Armed with life-cycle analyses, carbon calculators, and a whole cadre of scientific tools, these proponents of urban living argue cities have the potential to be the "fulcrum" of sustainability (Yanarella and Levine 2011).[1]

In the pages to come I tell a tale similar to, if more complicated than, Aesop's. It is also a story about competing claims to a superior lifestyle, but in this case, a sustainable lifestyle. During 14 months of fieldwork in and around Stockholm, Sweden, I spoke with 72 Swedish citizen-consumers living in the country, the city, and in between who, in response to concerns about sustainability, were trying to modify their lifestyles and consumer behaviors.[2] To understand their often contrasting views on sustainability and corresponding actions, I also explored the context of sustainability in Sweden via policy reviews and interviews with 31 representatives of 24 governmental and non-governmental organizations. In this paper I draw upon a small segment of that research to explore how conditions of urban alienation shape the ways that citizen-consumers relate to and act upon information about the environment. I argue that while the dominant urban perspectives shared by politicians and many urban consumer activists have the potential to link citizen-consumers into much larger movements and globalized concerns, they are dependent on expert-generated, highly technical sources of information and therefore risk an exclusion of alternative perspectives and the loss of democratic control over sustainability discourse and policy. These dominant views are contested by others, most notably rural participants, who argue that sustainability hinges on more than improved efficiencies. Despite these differences, however, this research demonstrates that in Sweden even disparate conceptualizations of sustainable living often share a common concern for environmental rights and social justice. Sweden's long history of social democracy and cultural emphasis on equality, even if only in rhetoric, have fostered a concern for intergenerational and global equality among many concerned about sustainability. For many Swedes participating in this research, regardless of where they lived or how they attempted to practice it, sustainable living constituted an effort to use a "fair share of environmental space" so that people in developing nations and future generations could have a fair share as well. While sustainability is certainly an ambiguous and often contested concept, the Swedish case suggests that the "fair share" movement may help to reconcile these tensions, opening pathways for mutual cooperation.

I begin this argument with an examination of dominant urban conceptualizations of sustainable living, linking them to definitions that center on energy efficiency and thus support the idea that urban living is becoming increasingly sustainable. I argue that this conceptualization of sustainability reflects complex global commodity chains and conditions of urban alienation. However, when combined with the contemporary discourses of consumer responsibility, this definition leaves urban citizen-consumers dependent on expert-generated information, risks limiting participation to consumerism, and discounts the importance of civic participation.

THE GREENING OF THE CITY: ON ECOLOGICAL MODERNIZATION AND URBAN ECO-EFFICIENCIES

I begin my tale with Åsa,[3] a 36-year-old communications professional living in the heart of Stockholm. In November of 2007 Åsa answered my call for research participants who had modified their lifestyles in the interest of sustainability. She and her family, she wrote in her email, had recently undertaken a significant change, moving from their suburban villa into an apartment in central Stockholm.

Stockholm was already dark as I walked to Åsa's apartment a few days later for our four o'clock interview. It was relatively easy to find my way to her building, despite the darkness, since she lived just a few blocks from a major transportation hub where the city's highly efficient bus, commuter train, and subway lines intersect. I met Åsa, a petit woman, at her door. With a kind expression, she invited me in and, remarking that she knew I was interested in sustainable consumerism, began showing me around the family's fashionable apartment. She pointed out their new energy efficient appliances in the kitchen, a rug made from recycled fibers in their living room, and a low-flow showerhead in the bath. She was clearly proud of her family's green accomplishments. Åsa's daughter followed us as we made our way around the apartment, presenting a parade of toys along the way. Her son was playing an engrossing video game in his room. Their apartment was fashionable and comfortable, typical for a middle-class, thirty-something Stockholm family. In fact, if Åsa had not pointed out their efficient appliances, showerhead, or "green" rug, it would have been impossible to tell that the family was concerned about the environment or sustainable living more generally. As we sat down in the living room for coffee, I asked Åsa why they decided to move to the city. She responded,

> We felt . . . if we wanted to make a better planet for our kids, we had to change. We started with the sorting (recycling) and the KRAV (organic foods) but then we read about the impact of driving . . . so we knew we had to make bigger changes. We were driving to work everyday, driving the children to *dagis* (preschool) and we had an old villa that was not very efficient. Now we are making a much smaller impact and we are very happy here.

Åsa's comments illustrate a perspective common among ecologically concerned Swedes living in Stockholm—that sustainable living hinges on improving the efficiency of contemporary lifestyles. Åsa's comments also echo statements from Swedish governmental representatives who have frequently expressed the desire to lead the international shift to sustainability (Matti 2009) and have demonstrated their commitment to this goal via significant investments in efficiency improvements. Between 1998 and 2003 Sweden's Local Investment Program dedicated 6.5 billion SEK[4] for the modernization of buildings, infrastructure, and energy systems (Baker and Eckerberg 2007). The city of Stockholm has also invested significant resources to position itself as a modern, sustainable global city. It was, in fact, recently named Europe's first "Green Capital" by the European Commission (2010). From the city's model ecological community, Hammerby Sjöstad, to its district heating, innovative waste system, and congestion tax, the city government has worked progressively to improve resource efficiencies and reduce pollution. Due, in part, to these efforts, some research suggests that Åsa may be correct about the relative environmental impact of urban living in Sweden. According to the city of Stockholm, the city's 1.3 million residents have reduced their energy consumption at greater rates than the balance of Sweden's 9.4 million citizens—by more than 7 percent since the year 2000. Further, Stockholmers release four tons of greenhouse gas per person annually, compared to the national average of 6.5 tons (Stockholmstad 2008:3).[5]

However, until recently the majority of Sweden's efforts to improve efficiencies and reduce emissions have been tied to large technological projects, primarily in urban cores. These projects operated on ecological modernization theory's assumption that ecological crises can be overcome by "technical and procedural innovation" (Adams 2001:110; Spaargaren and Mol 1992). In his report to the UN Johannesburg convention, former Swedish Prime Minister Göran Persson clearly illustrated the acceptance of such thought, writing, "we must be able to produce more with less resources . . . This will require environmentally sounder and more resource efficient solutions" (SNCA 2002:4).

Despite significant gains, these ecological modernization–inspired programs have been heavily critiqued for their technocratic approaches that excluded citizens from efforts to define sustainability, its practice, or appropriate policy (Rowe and Fudge 2003; Baker and Eckerberg 2007; Jörby 2002; Khakee 2002; Feichtinger and Pregernig 2005). Further, it is becoming increasingly apparent that the successes achieved by urban efficiency improvements are being quickly undermined by significant growth in per capita consumption levels (OECD 2004; Alfredsson 2004). As the result of this realization, Swedish sustainability policy has recently transitioned from its focus on large infrastructural solutions to programs centered on consumer responsibility and the construction of sustainable lifestyles

(Matti 2005). Sweden's Environmental Protection Agency (Naturvårdsverket) and Consumer Agency (Konsumentverket) are only two of the many governmental agencies that have designed programs urging Swedes like Åsa to take responsibility for their environmental impacts by improving the efficiencies of their lifestyles.

ON CONSUMER RESPONSIBILITY AND THE CHALLENGES OF "KNOWING" SUSTAINABILITY IN THE CITY

Mainstream environmentalism is well documented among the Swedish citizenry and many Swedes have accepted the call to improve the efficiencies of their lifestyles without question. However—due to the complexity of global markets, urban separation from environmental feedbacks, and the little control that most urbanites have over decisions about the use of productive resources—most urban inhabitants find they have very little personal knowledge upon which to evaluate the "sustainability" of most practices and products. Åsa, like many participants in the study, had a hard time recalling the information she uses to determine which products, services and personal practices are most sustainable. She pays attention to eco-labels and origins in the grocery store, but attributes her rationale for most of the actions she considers sustainable to "common sense." Despite this uncertainty and difficulty tracing the source of her knowledge, Åsa felt sure that her urban lifestyle was more sustainable than those of Swedes living in the suburbs or countryside. She said,

> In the city, I think that people think more . . . they are more informed. Oh my God, now I am really doing a stereotype . . . But when you live like this you save things. When you live in a house by yourself I think you only think about yourself and your own house. You heat the big house and drive yourself everywhere. It is just a different mindset. People who think about these things in the city are people who are well educated.

Åsa's comments illustrate a common sentiment among a subset of the study participants.[6] Twelve research participants expressed negative views about the sustainability of either urban or rural living. While this is certainly not a large number, it emerged as a theme that is difficult to ignore, particularly given that it was unsolicited and unanticipated. Further, the urban assumption that rural residents are uneducated and unable to identify environmental risks or come up with adequate solutions is well documented in international sustainable development discourse (Fairhead and Leach 2003; Neumann 2005; Fratkin and Mearns 2003) and in Sweden where dominant urban discourses on sustainability often discount and exclude rural perspectives (Svensson 2009). My intent in pointing to these competing claims to sustainable lifestyles is certainly not to reify geographical differences. Like so many places, cultural geography is complex in Sweden. Due to relatively late urbanization and a highly mobile population, so called "urban" and "rural" values can be found in both contexts.[7] There is also a great deal of variety in conceptualizations of sustainability among research participants, regardless of where they live. However, it is clear that there is some dispute about the relative sustainability of urban and rural living. It is also clear that many base their claims for the superiority of urban lifestyles on definitions of sustainability focused on energy efficiencies.

Yet Åsa's confidence in the improved sustainability of her urban lifestyle, despite her inability to clearly trace her knowledge about sustainable practice or calculate all the impacts of her lifestyle, raises interesting questions about how citizen-consumers come to know and understand what constitutes sustainable living. The science behind life-cycle analyses is incredibly complex and, given the global and opaque nature of most commodity chains, nearly impossible to determine in a grocery store aisle or when contemplating using an existing but inefficient washing machine or buying a newer model that will reduce the resource costs of future loads but take significant resources to produce.

As such, many Swedes like Åsa rely on advice from the government and environmental organizations as they formulate their strategies for sustainable living. One afternoon, while on my way to a meeting with the leader of Stockholm's Consume Smarter Program (Consumera Smartare), I noticed a brochure about the city's latest environmental program (Stockholmstad 2008). Inside it said,[8]

> Environmentally friendly technologies have brought us a big step on
> the way, and one never stops admiring how many fantastic and good

———

ideas are constantly being born in this field. Technology, however, cannot take care of everything . . . Several of the goals in the environmental program can only be reached if both the city and its inhabitants help.

Several pages later (Stockholmstad 2008:5) the document provided specific examples of what Stockholmers might do to help achieve the program goals. They include:

> Change your car to one that uses less fuel—save money and care
>   about the environment . . .
> Use less laundry detergent—good for your wallet and the environ-
>   ment . . .
> Change your light bulbs to low energy bulbs . . .
> When you buy a freezer, choose one from energy class A and save
>   electricity . . .
> Sort your candleholders as metal . . .
> Use the right amount of pressure in your tires . . .
> Switch off all electrical devices . . .
> Recycle your paper . . .
> Leave your dangerous waste . . .
> Take your bike . . .

These pieces of advice, from the experts in the city's administration, are clearly concentrated on improving the efficiency of contemporary lifestyles and closely mirror the advice given in many other governmental and nongovernmental publications. These dominant views about what constitutes sustainable living do not imply that Swedes need to change their lifestyles, but rather can make them "smarter" and more "efficient" with the use of technologies like energy efficient lightbulbs, hybrid automobiles, and energy-savings appliances. They are certainly practical suggestions that are both easy to implement and can be effective when practiced in aggregate. They also clearly resonate with many Swedes living in the city, like Åsa's family, who want to reduce their impact without compromising their comfort or lifestyle. These strategies are uncontroversial since they do not require structural changes or encroach upon individual choice. However, these efforts encourage the rationalization of contemporary lifestyles, not any sort of critical reflection on the construction of needs or the factors that seem to "ratchet" global consumption levels each year (Shove 2004; Galbraith 2000). Hobson thus argues that "a discourse has been formed that does not threaten consumption as a form of practice but seeks to bind it to forms of knowledge, science, technology and efficiency" (2002:106).

Certainly without such knowledge many research participants experienced significant and stressful ambivalence (Halkier 2001a, 2001b). For people who want to make the right decisions but have little personal information on which to base their actions, simple things like shopping for apples can be stressful. During one occasion, when I was shadow shopping with one of my informants, a 29-year-old student named Johanna, I watched, thoroughly entertained, as she talked her way through the process of choosing an apple at her neighborhood grocery store.

> Okay, so this one (picking up a loose green apple), it says is from Argentina. That is a really long way from here so it takes a lot of energy to come to this store. But it is ecological (organic) and that is important to me because I don't want the chemicals and I don't think it is fair to farmers that grow these things to use chemicals on their land . . . and for their health. These (pointing to a package of four plastic-wrapped apples in a Styrofoam tray) say they are from Sweden but they are not KRAV (organic) and I cannot believe that there are apples on trees anywhere this time of year, even in Skåne (Sweden's southernmost province). Maybe they are not fresh? Can they grow apples indoors? (I replied I didn't know). If so, it is even more horrible because it takes lots of energy to heat these houses. I don't know which one would be better. How can I know? Fuck the apples, I do not take any today.

The call for more sustainable[9] lifestyles among Swedes places increasing responsibility on consumers who are expected to make rational choices at the market. Yet despite this devolution of responsibility, consistent with neoliberal sustainability policy, citizen-consumers have little choice but to rely on external sources of information like labels, life-cycle analyses, and impact projections. Certainly many Swedes rely on governmental advice about sustainable living or industry-sponsored ecolabels designed to give consumers more information about the environmental effects of a given product or service. Indeed, Swedes have been particularly responsive to environmental and social product labels (Micheletti and Stolle 2004; Micheletti and Isenhour 2010). The Nordic Swan is among the most successful regional ecolabels in the world, with 97 percent recognition among Swedish citizens (NCOM 2009), and the organic food label KRAV enjoys more than 98 percent recognition (KRAV 2010).

However, despite the significant support for sustainable consumerism, as a whole Swedes are living far beyond sustainable limits. On average each Swedish citizen has an ecological footprint of approximately seven global hectares and emits 5.6 tons of carbon dioxide every year (Naturvårdsverket 2007). While these levels do not compare to the footprint of the average American citizen (9.5 global hectares and 20–25 tons of carbon dioxide annually), they are far above what is believed to be sustainable (GFN and YUEFI 2009). Further, alternative consumers continue to constitute a small minority of Sweden's population and the market share of organic foods and drinks is less than 5 percent despite rapid growth and significant consumer approval (KRAV 2010). These statistics raise important questions about how much change can be achieved by focusing on increasing the efficiency of contemporary lifestyles and consumer-driven, market-based change. This is not to say that research participants like Åsa and Johanna are making changes to their consumer behaviors in vain. Certainly their efforts are important and should not be discounted. However, contemporary sustainability policies and rhetoric that focus on lifestyle efficiencies place the responsibility for ensuring sustainability on consumers yet solidify the power to define sustainable living with industry and the calculation experts.

Simmel once described modern life as a world of "unrelenting calculations," the product of a monetary economy. In this world, problems are envisioned as a series of mathematical equations to be solved, daily life filled "with weighing, calculating, and enumerating," and qualitative values are reduced to quantitative formulas (1950:411). In the contemporary context of calls for more sustainable living, calculation experts are bestowed with the power to identify and assess risk and to define concepts like sustainability. Yet these "privileged narratives" (Hobson 2002) and the power relations that enable their production are hidden in highly scientific, technical, and managerial discourse. Thus power is located in the institutions that produce scientific discourse (see Allen 2004), including governmental agencies or research institutes dependent on tax revenues and external research funding. Scientists and experts, despite their best intentions, are often tangled in webs of capital and a system with significant interests in sustained economic growth.

Halkier, drawing on her extensive work with consumers in Denmark and throughout the EU, has argued that efforts to make lifestyles more efficient depend on experts and market mechanisms that constitute a "loss of collectivity" and "democratic control" of the sustainability agenda (1999). Certainly by encouraging individuals to participate in the construction of more sustainable cities in their private roles as efficient consumers, these perspectives do not encourage people to act in their public roles as citizens and exclude more radical and politically unpopular ideas related to increased market regulation or degrowth. As such, the dominant sustainability discourse, commonly accepted among many urban participants, has failed to include civil society and therefore potentially sacrificed the potential to achieve more radical changes (Feichtinger and Pregernig 2005).

Further, empirical observations have demonstrated that when Swedes do attempt to actively engage in the sustainability agenda as citizens rather than consumers, experts and politicians often undermine their initiatives "by referring to economic restraints" (Eckerberg and Forsberg 1998:340). The recent focus on more efficient consumption is thus consistent with the contemporary neoliberal policy frame. It does not force the government to impose tougher regulations on industry, or to limit consumer choice. It thus allows the government to maintain its "janus face" as it simultaneously pleases environmentalists by encouraging sustainable lifestyles while satisfying business interests by promoting increased consumption (Sanne 2005). Yet given the conditions of urban living, many citizen-consumers have very little choice but to rely on expert-generated information about sustainable living—information that often prioritizes the rationalization of lifestyles. Given these sources of information, it is no wonder that many urban residents like Åsa and her family claim that the grass is now greener in the city and view their more efficient urban lifestyles with pride.

—

LIMITS OF RATIONALIZATION: QUESTIONING
THE EXPERTS IN THE CITY AND BEYOND

This is not to say that all Swedes, regardless of where they live, readily accept the neoliberal logic of expert-led technological efficiencies or the prescribed duty to rationalize their lifestyles in their private roles as consumers. When asked to list all the things an individual could do to live more sustainably as well as the sustainable practices they personally engage in, the men and women participating in this study exhibited great variability. Some had clearly adopted dominant perspectives linked to technological improvements and greater efficiencies around the home and in the products and services they choose. These participants mentioned things like taking shorter showers, buying "green," "energy efficient," or ecolabeled products, and turning out lights. Others, however, had made more significant lifestyle changes by selling cars, growing their own food, or limiting their consumption of durables to secondhand goods. In fact, 66 percent of the respondents suggested that they were not only trying to use less energy and water or buy products that were better for the environment, but they were also making a significant effort to reduce their consumption of embodied energy by buying fewer things overall.

When exploring this strategy, it soon became apparent that it was based, at least in part, on a generalized distrust of expert-led solutions and technological improvements among some Swedes trying to live more sustainable lives. Jens, a 42-year-old environmental educator living with his wife and two children, for example, took issue with the carbon footprint calculator I had asked him to complete. I had anticipated the challenge, particularly after spending several days completing 16 internet-calculators in an attempt to locate the most comprehensive and culturally appropriate version given the Swedish context. I knew that the version I had chosen had some major weaknesses, but they all did. The calculator I chose was most appropriate for the Swedish context because it gathered information about country cottages, boats, and other factors like district heating and geothermal power, that are often relevant for members of Sweden's privileged well-educated middle-class environmental movement. Jens said about the calculator,

> I think it is basically useless because my wife and I both took the calculator and we had the same, 4.2 tons of CO_2 each year. But that is

---

crazy. We live in the same house but I do not do so much shopping. She (his wife Cara) seems to think that people will not like her if she is not wearing high boots this year and ankle boots next . . . Look at me (gesturing to his wool shirt), I don't care. But she replaces that wardrobe over there every few years. And she'll stand in front of it and say she has nothing to wear. I just don't understand that. And there are always new things around the house . . . And where are they coming from? You know where they are coming from. They are on sale and advertised on the television. They're cheap and probably made in China. What about the energy that it takes to make these things and ship them all over the world? What about the labor? What about the pollution?

For environmentalists like Jens, who question our ability to calculate all environmental and social costs, the precautionary principle, exercised in his case by refraining from consumption, is more reliable. While he can never be sure that carbon calculators are correct or if the new green technologies are actually sustainable, he can be sure that by removing his demand for new products, no additional resources will be used.[10]

And indeed Jens touches on an issue relevant in the Swedish context. Many Swedes are concerned about the environment and the potential for global climate change and have made significant efforts to reduce their direct use of energy, fuel, and water. However, my research suggests that while those interested in sustainability are becoming increasingly aware of embodied energy and resources, the majority has not made this connection, or is unconcerned. Indeed it seems most Swedes do not make the connections between the tangible, material goods they buy and the human labor, natural resources, and energy it took to produce and distribute them. This omission is significant in Sweden where living standards, consumption rates, and environmental impacts are relatively high. Certainly Stockholm is unique in many ways, but as a capital city, it is a hub of commerce in a global economic system, providing widespread access to the world's products and services. Consumer culture is strong and sustained economic growth is a national priority. In 2007 the nation hit an all-time record in spending over the holiday season (DN 2007) and popular holiday presents like clothing, footwear, and recreational equipment all have

—

significant indirect environmental costs (Carlsson-Kanyama et al. 2002). While efficiencies might significantly reduce the environmental costs of many products, sustained increases in per capita consumption often outweigh gains (Throne-Holst et al. 2008; Alfredsson 2004). Further, many scholars have warned of potential rebound effects, or the occurrence of the Jevons Paradox (Greening et al. 2000). For example, even though cars may be more efficient, drivers often rationalize driving more often and farther because of these fuel efficiencies, essentially offsetting any gains. Further, the increasing affordability of energy efficient vehicles drives demand for the resource-extensive production of new cars, regardless of the functionality of existing automobiles or consideration for the use or disposal of functional cars already in existence. Therefore, better fuel efficiency per vehicle is increasingly offset in the short term by replacement production and in the long term by a growing number of cars on the road and miles driven. Rita Erickson writes,

> Reducing direct energy consumption will only partially alleviate energy supply and environmental problems as long as there is no reduction of consumption of material goods and energy intensive services. We need to look at material goods in new ways, to acknowledge the true energy and environmental costs of their manufacture, advertisement, distribution, maintenance, and disposal (1997:168).[11]

Many of the men and women concerned about sustainability who took part in this research questioned dominant sustainability narratives centered on resource efficiencies. Their growing mistrust of technological solutions and life as usual is not surprising given that even highly regarded sources of environmental knowledge are often forced to retract or revise their recommendations. Consider, for example, the biofuels debate. It was only a few years ago that many policy makers thought ethanol would resolve our energy challenges. Not long afterward, it became apparent that the production of some biofuels has serious consequences for food security, deforestation, and climate change. While the Swedish state is aware of these issues, it remains committed to becoming the world's first "oil free" economy and is actively pursuing alternative biofuel technologies. Technology and sustainable policy are constantly evolving but we often find that well-intended new technologies have unintended and sometimes disastrous consequences. Beck (1992) reminds us that knowledge about the environment is always uncertain, particularly because it involves such interwoven and multidirectional chains of causality, stretching across space and time.

Distrust of technological solutions and conceptualizations of sustainability limited to increased efficiencies were shared by many participants, regardless of where they lived. It was interesting, however, that the rural participants were particularly vocal in their mistrust of technological solutions and definitions of sustainability focused on efficiencies. These men and women argued that sustainable living has less to do with the best, most efficient technologies available, and more to do with self-sufficiency and working in cooperation with "nature." One rural participant, Marianne noted,

> Many people talk about technologies that will solve these problems. But it is bullshit. They hope that the technology will save all the problems but it is a matter of changing the system. As I see it, this is the only way but there is great resistance to that. The politicians all want growth, economic growth. I am very much against this technical fundamentalism. We must work according to nature's rules, not our own.

THE ROOTS OF DIFFERENCE: ON URBAN ALIENATION AND VIEWS OF NATURE

As part of this research, I asked all participants questions designed to tease apart exactly what they meant when they spoke about nature and sustainability. There was surprising diversity regardless of location. However, interesting patterns emerged. Stockholmers were much more likely to refer to nature as something "out there," the forests, the mountains, and the streams far away from human influence. Price (1999) has argued that this conceptualization of nature has helped many urbanites to counteract the anonymity, alienation, commercialization, technological control, and complexity of urban lifestyles. But perhaps more important given the recent focus on sustainable consumerism, the conceptualization of nature as "out there" may also help to shelter consumers from the realities of natural resource consumption all around them.

This romantic view of nature has roots dating back to the late 19th century when the rising middle class constructed a vision of nature different than the peasantry or the elite to which they opposed themselves (Frykman and Löfgren 1987). Rather than thinking of nature in a very utilitarian and production-oriented way as the peasantry did, or as something chaotic and wild that must be controlled and colonized as the 17th century elites had, the rising middle class relegated nature to two distinct spheres. On the one hand nature was seen as the rational landscape of industrial production. But on the other, a romantic view of nature associated mountains, forests, and waterways with recreation, contemplation, and romance. Birding and mountaineering clubs became plentiful during this time as urban residents sought to escape the city and get back to nature. It was through this alienation that nature itself became a place apart (Löfgren 1995). The prerequisite for such a romantic view of nature was the withdrawal from a productive and extractive relationship with nature (Frykman and Löfgren 1987:78). Salomonsson writes, "The bourgeois appreciation of nature as a scenic backdrop . . . became widely spread during the course of this century . . . it has since become deeply rooted in the Swedish mentality" (1996:158).

Today, urban separation from productive relationships with natural resources perpetuates this conceptual alienation. As such, many middle-class urban residents continue to hold both romantic and rationalist views of nature. Nature becomes both a place for reflection and relaxation and a resource to be used to fuel development. The rationalist perspective is predominant in the official language of sustainability. Swedish policy documents reflect a weak anthropocentric orientation and a focus on the instrumental value of nature, as natural resources valuable for human development (Matti 2005). In instrumentalism's most extreme form, nature comes to be seen as "bundles of goods and bads to be managed in the name of risk management" (Hobson 2002:98). Technological improvements are seen as necessary to use resources most efficiently and enable future growth, overcoming natural limits. Extreme anthropocentric perspectives are underwritten by the capitalist system which tends to conflate all value with exchange value (Hornborg 1992). Trees, water, and land are viewed as commodities. While Sweden's approach to sustainability is

—

not this extreme and the nation does not prioritize the right to private ownership over the collective right to resources essential for survival, it is certainly common in many nations with capitalist economies and strong neoliberal political orientations.

In contrast, the rural residents participating in this research were united in their insistence that humans are part of nature. No doubt due to their closer engagement with productive resources, they refused to recognize separation between human welfare and the welfare of the entire ecosystem. For them the point of sustainability was not to further rationalize nature, manipulating it through technology for human benefit, but rather to work within nature's limits. These rural participants argued that localized understandings of nature are paramount for sustainability. Nature and sustainability are no doubt contentious terms, generating significant tensions as different social groups stake competing claims to their proper definition. And certainly, urban and rural residents find that their circumstances and geographies give them unique perspectives on both nature and sustainability. Yet, despite these differences and competing claims to a sustainable lifestyle among some urban and rural Swedes, my research suggests that, in the Swedish case, there is ample ground for mutual cooperation and affinity-based activism that spans geographical difference.

CALCULATING POTENTIAL

While rural and urban research participants held different views on nature and sustainability, there was also considerable agreement among those trying to change their lifestyles in response to concerns about sustainability. I was surprised when interviewing people about their motivation for sustainable living, how many responded not only with the anticipated answers about the environment, but with seemingly sincere, well-reasoned, and informed concern for global social and environmental justice. Many participants in rural and urban locales spoke about their actions in terms of reducing their consumption so that people in the developing world could have access to their fair share of world resources. They spoke about their actions in terms of morality, rights, and responsibility. So while many urban participants often spoke about their actions in terms consistent with dominant urban-inspired sustainability discourse (efficiencies and rationalization through technological advancement), their motivations were not necessarily linked to a desire to achieve sustained economic growth. Rather, these research participants were much more concerned with using less so that people in developing parts of the world could use more. Similarly, while rural inhabitants tended to be much more skeptical of ecological modernization efforts and defined sustainable lifestyles in terms of self-sufficiency and cooperation with nature, many of them also expressed deep concern for social equality. Felicia's comments illustrate this perspective:

> I'm not at all worried about me, and I don't think that I'm worried about the future . . . more that we are sitting here and consuming a lot and destroying while people in other parts of the world can't get enough to eat. We are taking their resources and we are making them grow crops that we need instead of food for them. I think that is my biggest concern, but I don't feel any risk to myself.

What is perhaps most interesting given our discussions here, is that regardless of the assumption so common in sustainability policy and discourse, that people are motivated to change their lifestyles by perceptions of immediate and personal risk (Giddens 2009), this research suggests that the Swedes who have made the most progressive lifestyle changes are driven by concerns for equality and the fair distribution of environmental risks and benefits (Isenhour 2010).

Hobson came to a similar conclusion in 2002 arguing that alternative discourses of sustainable consumption and critical social science research suggest that the issue of social justice has more resonance with the public than dominant sustainability discourse centered on the rationalization of lifestyles. This orientation is not surprising in Scandinavia where the Lutheran church and social democracy have resulted in a pervading sense of morality, solidarity, and the need for equality within Nordic culture— at least in rhetoric if not always in practice. Yet for many this sense of solidarity and equality was not confined within the region's geopolitical borders. Swedes place great value on a cosmopolitan mindset. Knowledge of foreign affairs and international travel are, in fact, key symbols of cultural capital in Sweden. Swedes are among the world's most well-traveled

—

citizens (WTO 2010), are highly educated (UN 2005), and have some of the highest levels of newspaper readership in the world. Awareness of and concern for global inequalities are thus heightened in Sweden, although certainly not among all.

Ecological modernization programs have clearly failed to generate significant change, warranting the need for a new approach to sustainability. Feichtinger and Pregernig note,

> critical assessments of global change since 1992 indicate that the prevailing politico-administrative system seems not to be fully capable of implementing the goals of sustainable development in a comprehensive and substantial way. Genuine and far-reaching policy change often requires the status quo to be put in jeopardy (2005:237).

Certainly, the discourse on sustainability that many rural residents share centered on self-sufficiency and a closer connection to natural resources has the potential to counter dominant sustainability narratives. However, as Escobar (2001) writes, local efforts to appeal to the moral sensibility of the powerful rarely work. Further, they fail to address environmental issues on a scale adequate to the task (Allen 2004).

The concept of a "fair share of environmental space" resonates well with Swedes concerned about sustainability, regardless of where they lived or whether they defined sustainability in terms of self-sufficiency or energy efficiency. It thus seems to have potential for challenging contemporary sustainability and democratizing notions of sustainable living. Drawing on an "ethic of care" (Barnett et al. 2005) so meaningful in the Swedish context, the concept has the potential to create networks that extend over both geographical and temporal space and "effectively reduce physical, psychological and cultural distances" (Goodman 2004:906).

While the government's official position and focus on ecological modernization are consistent with the growth-based imperative and the interests of global competitiveness, the Swedish state is not unaware that sustainability hinges on more than improving efficiencies and the protection of the Swedish environment. Jörby argues that many governmental measures "not only aim at reducing impacts in order to improve the environment locally; the local governments try to take on their part of

---

the responsibility for the global environment as well" (2002:239). This language is often difficult to find in official policy documents. While I was in the field, I found very few examples of discourse centered on de-growth in official policy, discourse, and programming. However, more recently— in early 2010—the Swedish Environmental Protection Agency released a report entitled "The Climate Impacts of Swedish Consumption" which moves beyond discussions of emissions reductions in Sweden to examine the total effect of Swedish consumerism in other nations. Thus instead of claiming that Swedes have reduced carbon emissions by nearly 12 percent since 1990 (Naturvårdsverket 2010), the government is now taking an active role investigating and calculating emissions in other lands that can be attributed to Swedish consumer demand. This new focus is not only consistent with the popularity of life-cycle analyses in Sweden, but it also reflects a concern with global equity and responsibility. There are also a few other governmental documents that advocate consuming less so that people in impoverished areas around the world can have more. One document produced by Sweden's Consumer Agency entitled "Environment for Billions" (Konsumentverket 2001) points to research which suggests that wealthy industrialized countries like Sweden would have to reduce consumption by a factor of ten for every human being on the planet to have equal access to the world's resources.

And while a focus on sustainable consumerism and sustainable life-styles imagines individuals in their roles as consumers and thus "neglects any recognition of the motivations of citizens oriented towards rights or social justice" (Berglund and Matti 2006:559), a fair share movement has the potential to reactivate individuals as citizens. My research indicates that many environmentally concerned Swedes do not limit their actions to the market realm. When listing their own sustainable actions, 47 percent of respondents in this study mentioned cooperating with others, 28 percent mentioned citizenship activities including voting, contacting political representatives, and political demonstrations. Others (28 percent) mentioned supporting environmental and social-justice groups and participating in community-based sustainability initiatives. They clearly see their actions as a political exercise and are eager to participate in sustainability initiatives in their roles as citizens, if given the opportunity.

If fair share calculations can not only encourage reduced consumption

—

but also inspire individuals to act in their roles as citizens, there is potential for these calculations to produce more significant change. Escobar argues,

> In constructing networks and glocalities of their own, even . . . in their engagement with dominant networks, social movements might contribute to democratize social relations, contest visions of nature, challenge current techno-scientific hype and even suggest that economies can be organized differently from current neo-liberal dogmas (2001:166).

I suggest that a rights-based discourse can provide a positive source of external pressure in Sweden. Such pressure has the potential to move the sustainability discourse beyond its technocratic, rationalist, and apolitical focus. Further, this human-rights orientation allows us to question the political-economic relations that perpetuate environmental inequality and to push the sustainability discourse towards more participatory solutions. It certainly seems to have promise given that sustainable solutions not only require technical improvements, but also political and economic systems which can remedy power imbalances and ensure that all people, regardless of geography and generation, are able to consume at levels sufficient to meet their basic needs and achieve human dignity.

NOTES

1. Note that these discussions are common on blogs and social media sites. See for example, http://www.gather.com/viewArticle.action?articleId=281474976811916.
2. Because the population of citizen-consumers concerned about sustainability was unknown, I drew upon Haraway's (1991) concept of affinities to identify five organizations working on sustainability. A call for participants was sent to their members and nine to 14 volunteers from each participated in a semi-structured interview for a total of 58. Twelve of these participants and 14 of their family members were also selected to participate in case-study household research which included a review of household expenditures, consumption inventories, and a series of iterative interviews.
3. Åsa's life details have been modified to protect her identity and confidentiality. All research participants have been given pseudonyms.
4. According to OANDA, the average exchange rate for the five-year period between 1998 and 2003 was 8.9 SEK to 1 USD.

———

5. There is some data to suggest that when the impacts of all the products Swedish consumers buy from abroad are considered, these figures are significantly altered (Naturvårdsverket 2010), a point to which I will return momentarily.
6. Fifty of the individual research participants lived in the city or its suburbs and eight lived in the countryside within a two-hour train/bus ride of the city.
7. Seven of the eight rural participants lived in an urban area at some point in their life. Three of them moved to the country once they were financially stable or retired. These participants are also a bit older than the average age for the sample. All eight have deep roots in the environmental movement but several became disillusioned when more significant changes failed to materialize. As such, many of the rural participants now focus on self-sufficiency rather than activism.
8. Translation by Matilda Ardenfors.
9. Note that the concept of sustainable living is vague in practice, often slipping, as if unproblematic, between environmentalism, concerns for social justice or even the assertion of the need for economic growth. In Stockholm, as in many other global cities, the concept is often centered on ecological sustainability, without concern for environmental justice or social sustainability.
10. All households were asked to complete the carbon calculator built by the Swedish Environmental Research Institute (http://www.climate.ivl.se). When Jens calculated his footprint, the calculator did not account for how often one shops. Since then, the calculator has been updated to account for how much one spends annually on items like home furnishings and clothing.
11. Since completing my research, recognition of embodied resources and emissions has improved. In fact, Sweden's Environmental Protection Agency is studying not only emissions in Sweden's borders but also those in other nations driven by Swedish consumption (Naturvårdsverket 2010).

REFERENCES CITED

Adams, W. M.

2001   Green Development: Environment and Sustainability in the Third World. New York: Routledge.

Alfredsson, E. C.

2004   Green Consumption—No Solution for Climate Change. Energy 29:513–524.

Allen, Robert

2004   No Global: The People of Ireland versus the Multinationals. London: Pluto Press.

Baker, Susan, and Katarina Eckerberg, eds.

2007   In Pursuit of Sustainable Development: New Governance Practices at the Sub-National Level in Europe. ECPR Studies in European. Political Science: Routledge.

Barnett, Clive, Paul Cloke, Nick Clarke, and Alice Malpass

2005   Consuming Ethics: Articulating the Subjects and Spaces of Ethical Consumption. Antipode 37:23–45.

Beck, Ulrich

1992   Risk Society: Towards a New Modernity. New Delhi: Sage.

Berglund, Christer, and Simon Matti

2006   Citizen and Consumer: The Dual Role of Individuals in Environmental Policy. Environmental Politics 15(4):550–571.

Carlsson-Kanyama, Annika, Marianne Pipping Ekström, and Helena Shanahan

2002   Urban Households and Consumption Related Resource-Use. *In* Changes in the Other End of the Chain. Butjin et al., eds. Pp. 317–326. The Netherlands: Shaker Publishing.

Dagens Nyheterr (DN)

2007   Julhandeln Mot Nytt Rekord. 8 November.

Eckerberg, Katrina, and Bjorn Forsberg

1998   Implementing Agenda 21 in Local Government: The Swedish Example. Local Environment 3(2):333–348.

Erickson, Rita J.

1997   Paper or Plastic: Energy, Environment and Consumerism in Sweden and America. Westport: Praeger.

Escobar, Arturo

2001   Culture Sites in Places: Reflections on Globalism and Subaltern Strategies of Localization. Political Geography 20:139–174.

European Commission

2010   Green Capital. http://ec.europa.eu/environment/europeangreencapital/index _en.htm. Accessed 26 September 2011.

Fairhead, James, and Melissa Leach

2003   Science, Society and Power: Environmental Knowledge and Policy in West Africa and the Caribbean. Cambridge: Cambridge University Press.

Feichtinger, Judith, and Michael Pregernig

2005   Imagined Citizens and Participation: Local Agenda 21 in Two Communities in Sweden and Australia. Local Environment 10(3):229–242.

Fratkin, Elliot, and Robin Mearns

2003   Sustainability and Pastoral Livelihoods: Lessons from East Africa and Mongolia. Human Organization (62):112–122.

Frykman, Jonas, and Orvar Löfgren

1987   Culture Builders: A Historical Anthropology of Middle-Class Life. New Brunswick: Rutgers University Press.

Galbraith, John Kenneth

2000   The Dependence Effect. *In* The Consumer Society Reader. Juliet Schor and Douglas Holt, eds. Pp. 20–25. New York: New York University Press.

Giddens, Anthony

2009   The Politics of Climate Change. London: Polity.

Global Footprint Network (GFN) and York University Ecological Footprint Initiative (YUEFI)

2009   National Footprint and Biocapacity Accounts, 2009 edition. https://data .footprintnetwork.org. Accessed 10 April 2010.

—

Goodman, Michael K.
2004   Reading Fair Trade: Political Ecological Imaginary and the Moral Economy of
        Fair Trade Foods. Political Geography 23:891–915.
Greening, Lorna A., David L. Greene, and Carmen Difiglio
2000   Energy Efficiency and Consumption—The Rebound Effect—A Survey. Energy
        Policy 28(6/7):389–401.
Halkier, Bente
1999   Consequences of the Politicization of Consumption: The Example of Environ-
        mentally Friendly Consumption Practices. Journal of Environmental Policy and
        Planning 1(1):25–41.
2001a   Consuming Ambivalences: Consumer Handling of Environmentally Related Risks
        in Food. Journal of Consumer Culture 1(2):205–224.
2001b   Routinization or Reflexivity? Consumers and Normative Claims for
        Environmental Consideration. In Ordinary Consumption. Jukka Gronow and
        Alan Warde, eds. Pp. 33–52. London: Routledge.
Haraway, Donna
1991   Simians, Cyborgs and Women: The Reinvention of Nature. New York;
        Routledge.
Hobson, Kirsty
2002   Competing Discourses of Sustainable Consumption: Does the "Rationalization
        of Lifestyles" Make Sense? Environmental Politics 11(2):95–120.
Hornborg, Alf
1992   Machine Fetishism, Value and the Image of Unlimited Good: Towards a
        Thermodynamics of Imperialism. Man (N.S.) 27:1–18.
Isenhour, Cindy
2010   Building Sustainable Societies: Exploring Sustainability Policy and Practice in
        the Age of High Consumption. PhD Dissertation, University of Kentucky.
Jörby, Sofie Adolfsson
2002   Local Agenda 21 in Four Swedish Municipalities: A Tool Towards Sustainability?
        Journal of Environmental Planning and Management 45(2):219–244.
Khakee, Abdul
2002   Assessing Institutional Capital Building in a Local Agenda 21 Process in
        Göteborg. Planning Theory and Practice 3(1):53–68.
Konsumentverket
2001   Miljö för Mljarder: Om Rättvis Konsumption i ett Global Perspektiv.
        Konsumentverket. Stockholm, Sweden.
KRAV
2010   Marknadsrapport 2010. http://www.krav.se/Documents/marknadsrapport2010
        /MarknadsrapportWebb.pdf. Accessed 19 April 2010.
Lefebvre, Henri
1989   The Production of Space. Oxford: Blackwell.
Löfgren, Orvar
1995   Being a Good Swede: National Identity as a Cultural Battleground. In Articulating

———

Hidden Histories. Rayna Rapp and Jane Schneider, eds. Pp. 262–274. Berkeley: University of California Press.

Matti, Simon

2009   Exploring Public Policy Legitimacy: A Study of Belief-System Correspondence in Swedish Environmental Policy. Doctoral thesis Luleå: Luleå Tekniska Universitet.

2005   A Swedish Environmental Norm? Exploring the Normative Foundations of Swedish Environmental Policy. SHARP Working Paper 3, SHARP Research Progamme.

Micheletti, Michele, and Cindy Isenhour

2010   Political Consumerism. *In* Consumer Behavior in the Nordic Context. Karin M. Ekström, ed. Pp. 133–152. Stockholm: Studentlitteratur.

Micheletti, Michele, and Dietlind Stolle

2004   Swedish Political Consumers: Who Are They and Why They Use the Market as an Arena for Politics. *In* Political Consumerism: Motivations, Power and Conditions in the Nordic Countries and Elsewhere. Magnus Boström et al., eds. Pp. 145–164. Proceedings from the 2nd International Seminar on Political Consumerism, Oslo.

Naturvårdsverket (Swedish Environmental Protection Agency)

2010   The Climate Impact of Swedish Consumption. www.naturvardsverket.se. Accessed 20 April 2010.

2007   Allmänheten och klimatförändringen. Electronic document, http://www.naturvardsverket.se. Accessed 23 September 2009.

Neumann, Roderick P.

2005   Making Political Ecology: Human Geography in the Making. New York: Oxford University Press.

Nordic Council of Ministers (NCOM)

2009   The Nordic Swan. www.svanen.nu. Accessed 28 January 2009.

Organization for Economic Co-operation and Development (OECD).

2004   Towards Sustainable Household Consumption: Trends and Policies in OECD Countries. OECD Publishing.

Price, Jennifer

1999   Looking for Nature at the Mall: A Field Guide to the Nature Company. *In* Flight Maps: Adventures with Nature in Modern America. Pp.167–206. New York: Basic Books.

Rowe, Janet, and Colin Fudge

2003   Linking National Sustainable Development Strategy and Local Implementation: A Case Study in Sweden. Local Environment 8(2):120–148.

Salomonsson, Anders

1996   The Swedish Crayfish Party: Rounding Off the Summer with a National Rite. *In* Force of Habit: Exploring Everyday Culture in Sweden. Jonas Frykman and Orvar Löfgren, eds. Pp.151–160. Lund University Press.

Sanne, Christer

2005   The Consumption of Our Discontent. Business Strategies for the Environment 14:315–323.

———

Shove, Elizabeth
2004   Comfort, Cleanliness and Convenience: The Social Organization of Normality. London: Berg.
Simmel, Georg
1950   The Metropolis and Mental Life. *In* The Sociology of Georg Simmel. Kurt H. Wolf, ed. Pp. 409–426. New York: Free Press.
Swedish National Committee for Agenda 21 and Sustainability (SNCA)
2002   From Vision to Action: Sweden's Report to the World Summit on Sustainable Development in Johannesburg 2002. www.ieh.se/agenda21forum/johannesburg _eng.pdf. Accessed 6 March 2005.
Spaargaren, Gert, and Arthur P. J. Mol
1992   Sociology, Environment, and Modernity: Ecological Modernization as a Theory of Social Change. Society and Natural Resources 5:323–344.
Stockholmstad (City of Stockholm)
2008   The City of Stockholm's New Environmental Programme. Stockholm: Stadsledningskontoret.
Svensson, Eva
2009   Consuming Nature-Producing Heritage: Aspects on Conservation, Economical Growth and Community Participation in a Forested, Sparsely Populated Area in Sweden. International Journal of Heritage Studies 15(6):540–559.
Throne-Holst, Harald, Pål Strandbakken, Eivind Stø
2008   Identification of Households' Barriers to Energy Saving Solutions. Management of Environmental Quality: An International Journal 19(1):54–66.
United Nations (UN)
2007   State of the World Population 2007: Unleashing the Potential of Urban Growth. New York: UNFPA.
2005   Human Development Report. Human Development Report 2005. International Cooperation at a Crossroads: Aid, Trade and Security in an Unequal World. New York: UNDP.
World Tourism Organization (WTO)
2010   Factbook and Database. www.world-tourism.org/frameset/frame_statistics.htm. Accessed 4 April 2010.
Yanarella, Ernest J., and Richard S. Levine
2011   The City as Fulcrum of Global Sustainability. New York: Anthem Press.

4

CIRCULARITY AND ENCLOSURES

METABOLIZING WASTE WITH THE BLACK SOLDIER FLY

AMY ZHANG

In the open-air garage, a caretaker dips her spatula into a plastic bin and starts folding over dirt. Under the fluorescent light, the even soil comes to life. Ms. Lin, who grew up in the local agricultural village beside the field laboratory, is carrying out the daily work of fly-raising. Tiny larvae, a lighter shade of brown than the soil, tumble and squirm over one another reaching for the surface. The action subsides after a few minutes, turning the dirt placid again. Curiosity drives me to disturb the peace, so I ask for permission to stir with the spatula. The soil once again rises with excitement. Ms. Lin cheerfully tells me that the larvae feel insecure when exposed and will always burrow to hide. At this stage, the larva's task is to devour the mixture of organic waste—wet vegetable leaves, fish bones, and other kitchen scraps—that she adds to the soil each day. After continuously feeding for about fourteen days, the larva turns into a pupa encased in a hard, dark brown shell. When the pupae are ready to undergo metamorphosis, they will be transferred to a makeshift arboretum. The fully

Originally published as, Zhang, A., 2020. Circularity and Enclosures: Metabolizing Waste with the Black Soldier Fly. *Cultural Anthropology*, 35(1), pp. 74–103. Reproduced by permission of the American Anthropological Association. Not for sale or further reproduction.

—

FIGURE 4.1. A caretaker stirs a tray of larvae in a Guangzhou field research station. Photo by Amy Zhang.

grown pupa will hatch and emerge in its adult form, a large fly with blue translucent wings, and live out the remainder of the week in the garden, to mate and lay eggs before dying.

On this hot and humid evening, I watch as Dr. Wu, the entomologist directing this field laboratory on the edge of Guangzhou, and Ms. Lin, the flies' caretaker,[1] inspect trays of fly larvae undergoing different stages of growth. As part of a broader effort to construct a modern and sustainable waste-management system, Dr. Wu is attempting to raise larvae toward an experimental project to develop the black soldier fly (*Hermetia illucens*) as a biotechnology to speed up the treatment of organic waste. A winged insect that originated in the Americas, the black soldier fly (BSF) is now found in most temperate regions of the world. Over the past twenty years, scientists in China and abroad have experimented with ways to transform the BSF into a living technology for organic waste processing. Their expectations rest on the so-called voracious appetite of the fly larvae to devour organic matter, including municipal food waste, slaughterhouse waste, and animal manure. Unlike other breeds of composting worms that are sensitive to fat content, the BSF is lauded for its ability to break down food waste and consume a "Cantonese diet" high in proteins, fats, and salt. Completing the cycle of regeneration, the full-grown larva is further imagined as a protein-rich food source for agricultural feedstock, or even as a nutrition supplement for humans.

The project captured my attention because it proposed a radically new idea of what counted as a modern solution to waste management in China, a sharp departure from waste-to-energy (WTE) incinerators, the official technology for waste treatment in Guangzhou. Thirty years of urban development and changing consumption and disposal patterns have generated a municipal waste crisis in cities across China. Over the past decade, new policies and programs aimed at environmental remediation have begun to supplement the state's narrow focus on economic development. Since the early 2000s, the Chinese state has pursued a broad range of approaches to waste management guided by the principle of the circular economy (*xunhuan jinji*), which seeks to achieve, above all, "a circular (closed) flow of materials" by using "raw materials and energy through multiple phases" (Yuan, Bi, and Moriguichi 2006, 5). Under the circular economy, all forms of waste material are imagined as potential sources of value generation. In municipal waste management, this approach has most often translated to investing in WTE incinerators and promoting citizen recycling programs. Such government proposals, however, evaded the question of what to do with the organic waste that constitutes more than 50 percent of the city's total municipal waste stream.

Dr. Wu's experiments with the BSF represent a unique attempt at realizing a key principle of the circular economy by targeting organic waste for continuous circulation into novel forms of value. Specifically, his lab's scientific interventions subject the BSF's bodily processes and life cycle—ingestion, excretion, digestion, growth, reproduction, and death—to temporal modifications meant to match the rhythm and scale of human organic waste output. Scientists like Dr. Wu hope to integrate the BSF's metabolism, reimagined as a tool for environmental remediation and capital generation, into the circulation and transformation of

—

human-generated waste to remedy a dysfunctional urban metabolism. They approach the life cycle of the BSF as a natural or lively infrastructural system, one in which nonhuman labor sustains the organic exchange and circulation of matter and energy (White 1996; Carse 2012; Kirksey 2015; Morita 2017; Hetherington 2019).[2] Dr. Wu's experiment with the BSF thus seeks to realize the central principles of the circular economy to develop a new biotechnology through the science of entomology.[3]

In the 1970s, advances in the life sciences coincided with capitalist restructuring to give rise to the so-called biotech revolution, a period of investment in the life sciences (particularly in cellular and molecular biology and genetics) that opened up a new arena for economic growth based on the potential to capitalize on life. Anthropologists introduced the concept of biocapital to interrogate the ways that capitalist political economic structures, such as venture capital or new regimes of outsourcing, shape knowledge production within the technosciences. In the life sciences, the appropriation of biological life processes such as reproduction and growth repeat traditional forms of exploitation and extraction (Franklin and Lock 2003; Sunder Rajan 2006; Roosth 2017),[4] rehearsing a tendency in capitalism to predicate accumulation on the appropriation of the reproductive capacities of life (Vora 2015). In agriculture and food production, for example, scientists and farmers have long imagined animals, plants, and other living substances as producers of value. A range of husbandry practices, including capture, domestication, and breeding, transform a living organism's biological processes into profit-generating mechanisms (Franklin 2007; Landecker 2007; Russell 2010).

Animals and plants are increasingly regarded as effective ecological "workers," their natural proclivities a salve to climate change and ecological crisis (cf. Helmreich 2007; Besky and Blanchette 2018; Hetherington 2019). Consider, for example, how mangroves are used as protection against storm surges (Vaughn 2017), or how an oyster bed is planted to clean up an oil spill (Olson 2018). In keeping with a broader valorization of the assumed lively agency of microbial life in regenerative processes, nature's capacity to facilitate decay or decomposition has increasingly become viewed as fundamental, inevitable, and (therefore) good (Paxson 2013; Jasarevic 2015). Noting that insects and microorganisms facilitate the breakdown of waste, forming lively multispecies assemblages and aggregate on landfills

—

and composting sites (Hird 2013; Reno 2016), scientists like Dr. Wu have shown increasing interest in capturing the latent power or metabolic labor of microorganisms, insects, bacteria, and fungi for environmental restoration. Metabolic labor describes how an animal's vital functions—i.e., growth and reproduction—are targeted to reliably produce value in excess of human inputs (labor and technology) (Beldo 2017; Barua 2018).

Such biotech experiments alter the concept and processes of life itself as bodies and life processes (both human and animal) become new sites of intervention (Haraway 1991; Braun 2007). Metabolic labor is reminiscent of what Jason W. Moore (2015, 54) identifies as capital's repertoire of strategies to appropriate nature's unpaid work and energy for the production of surplus value. Anna Lowenhaupt Tsing (2015, 65), however, points to the specific terms under which capitalism appropriates nature across a range of cultural contexts; diverse, culturally situated logics enable what she calls "salvage capitalism," when capital takes "advantage of value produced without capitalist control." Similarly, ethnographies of biotechnology reveal that a range of cultural logics and imperatives shape the meaning of life. Biocapital manifests in "particular, incongruent manners in different locales," embedded within and enabled by different belief systems and values, such as "salvation" or nationalism (Sunder Rajan 2006, 232). Stefan Helmreich (2008, 474) asks, "Must capital . . . be the sign under which all of today's encounters of the economic with the biological . . . travel"? What alternative economic, cultural, social, and symbolic systems also condition the transformation of biological processes for human purposes?

In an effort to devise a biotechnology to treat organic waste in Chinese cities, scientists are attempting to reconfigure the life cycle of the BSF in accordance with the dominant cultural logics of an ecological, modern vision for waste management. Specifically, my ethnographic work with Dr. Wu reveals how a principle of urban waste management, circularity, and a spatial logic of urban living, enclosures, condition the scientific intervention that promises to harness animal metabolic labor as a biotechnology and a waste infrastructure that can be adapted to the urban ecologies of Guangzhou. In the lab, scientists work to develop optimized breeding techniques to calibrate biological life cycles to the scale and rhythm of urban waste output based on an imagined ideal of how waste might circulate both in the soil and in the city. In an effort to actualize his biotechnology in

—

Chinese cities, Dr. Wu worked persistently to devise an "enclosed" apparatus for adapting his flies to a sanitized urban aesthetic and a now dominant form of urban living. The enclosure, a dominant way of imagining urban space and environmental relations, circumscribes human and nonhuman ecologies and delineates human relations to waste and insects.

As ideologies with broad currency in contemporary China that shape thinking about cities, modernity, and the environment, circularity and enclosure each naturalize a techno-utopian imaginary and render the extraction of human and nonhuman labor invisible. In its ideal form, seen through the lens of circularity and enclosure, the BSF project appears to achieve the ideals of the circular economy as an automated, natural recycling system in which nature's vital capacity becomes endowed with the ability to repair damaged urban ecologies and to sustain the reproduction of urban life. Yet as my ethnographic research in Dr. Wu's laboratory reveals, the practice of aligning animal metabolism with urban metabolism is anything but natural or automatic. Instead, not only does the alignment rely on the constant care for flies by human workers but it also conscripts insects as nonhuman waste workers by reconfiguring their metabolism to urban modes of human living. Moreover, and more surprisingly, efforts to build an automated, self-sustaining, and enclosed biotech apparatus obscure the intimacies that develop between laboring humans and the flies in their care, while the experiments carried out in Dr. Wu's lab generate the potential to forge ecological connections with other forms of life in a moment of mutual vulnerability.

Efforts to realize the logics of circularity and enclosures as manifested in the BSF project illustrate the unacknowledged labor practices, both human and nonhuman, and ecological relations that undergird China's pursuit of a modern approach to waste management. Studies of anthropogenic environments such as industrial sites, burned fields, and the cracks of sidewalks point to the often cosmopolitan, unexpected, and unruly encounters that can take place between humans and nonhumans (Tsing 2015; Stoetzer 2018). Yet the project of integrating the BSF into cities reveals a different relation of cohabitation in China's green urbanism. While humans are keen to capitalize on the biophysical processes of nonhuman life, the sanitized aesthetic of modern eco-cities demands that animal life, particularly insects and pests, be expelled or alternatively contained in enclosures.

—

I begin this article with an account of the development of the circular economy framework for approaching waste management in China, explaining the circular economy's preference for WTE incineration as well as the challenges posed to it by the waste stream in Guangzhou. Next, I juxtapose the genealogy and uses of the concepts of metabolic labor and urban metabolism to understand ecological crisis under capitalism as well as attempts to use biological processes as remediation technologies. Then, turning to the work of the field station, I illustrate ethnographically how, while scientific discourse emphasizes the fly's natural capacity to repair the urban metabolism and to generate value, laboratory experimentations require scientific and care work to erase the seasonal variation in the fly's growth and reproductive cycles to ensure a continuous rhythm of reproduction matched to the tempos and rhythms of urban waste. I then show how Dr. Wu's attempt to realize the principles of the circular economy by creating an enclosed apparatus reflects the aesthetic demands of China's green urbanism. Together, circularity and enclosure, as guiding logics of waste management in Chinese ecological modernization, uphold a fiction of biocapital; they create the illusion that nature generates value and remediates environments without human intervention while mystifying and naturalizing the appropriation of nature and labor in the new green city.

TOWARD AN ECOLOGICAL, MODERN APPROACH TO URBAN WASTE

After two decades of annual double-digit growth, the natural environment in China has borne the heavy cost of the nation's economic miracle. In the early 2000s, China explicitly adopted ecological modernization as an official response to the crisis of environmental degradation. Ecological modernization first emerged as an approach to environmental sustainability in the early 1980s in western European nations such as Denmark and Germany (Mol and Sonnenfeld 2000). Encompassing a wide range of top-down environmental policy and planning tools that marry environmental concerns with economic development, ecological modernization perpetuates a "gospel of eco-efficiency" (Martínez-Alier 2002). Since the early 2000s, China has adopted a strand of ecological modernization theory that emphasizes technological innovation as a model of development that

—

can simultaneously achieve environmental improvement and maintain continued levels of growth (Lei Zhang, Mol, and Sonnenfeld 2007).[5] Waste management constituted one of the strategy's key targets. Early attempts to reform industrial waste management included programs to discover new uses for scraps, the building of eco-industrial parks, and subsidies for the recycling sector (Lei Zhang, Mol, and Sonnenfeld 2007). Unlike more critical approaches to waste that advocate a shift away from capitalist modes of production or a slowdown in consumption, the circular economy as manifested in China is fundamentally fixated on devising technological solutions to discover more efficient uses for waste.

When it comes to municipal waste, the state sanctioned and prescribed the use of WTE incineration as part of the circular economy policy. Marketed as a form of clean and green waste technology, WTE incinerators burn trash to generate electricity, offering an apparent seamless conversion between waste and energy. The central state's support for WTE incineration speaks to a preference for large technological facilities that eliminate the need for complicated schemes to sort waste according to different types of materials. However, as citizens began to raise concerns over toxic emissions released from burning mixed waste without adequate environmental oversight, organized protests against WTE incineration sprung up all over China and became particularly heated in Guangzhou (A. Zhang 2014). Citizens pointed out that large amounts of organic waste posed a critical challenge to waste management strategies in the city. Left unsorted, organic matter, making up more than 50 percent of the municipal stream, creates problems during all phases of waste collection. Vegetable peels and kitchen scraps rot in stairwells and leak during transportation. More important, waste that is heavy in organics lowers the temperature of incinerators, thereby decreasing the efficiency and compromising the safety of burning. The high moisture content of mixed waste in Chinese cities thus undermines the efficacy of the state's decision to rely on WTE incinerators.

In 2013, during the time of my research in Guangzhou, as the city lacked an infrastructure to sustainably process urban organic waste, both the municipal state and citizens (including critics of WTE incinerators as well as waste entrepreneurs) were undertaking initiatives to identify a suitable treatment technology for organics. The most common forms of organic waste treatment used in the Chinese countryside, composting and biogas

—

facilities, had yet to prove adaptable for cities. The Datianshan composting pilot project, an urban composting facility capable of handling more than a hundred tons of organic waste a day, was quickly losing government support as officials sparred over the economic feasibility of scaling up the process (Huang 2013). A food safety scandal over the reuse of gutter oil, where illicit cooking oil collected from sewage drains was reprocessed on a large scale and distributed to restaurants and grocery chains, further generated citizen suspicion over the safety of organic waste reuse (Merrifield 2017).

From dogs in Ottoman Egypt (Mikhail 2013) to critters (rats and flies) today that thrive off of the scraps of human consumption (Benson 2015), organic household waste has long sustained urban animal life. In Chinese cities during the premodern and socialist periods, and even into the early post-reform era, animals living alongside humans constituted an informal organic waste treatment system. Families raised pigs and livestock, and kitchen scraps made up a large part of the animals' diet. On a larger scale, farmers facilitated the integration of urban and rural economies through the practice of collecting hogwash (*shaoshui*), transporting kitchen waste from Guangzhou's restaurants to farms in the countryside to feed livestock. Animal metabolism thus facilitated exchanges between urban and rural economies. In the post-reform period, however, modernization campaigns in Chinese cities targeted hogwash collection as unsanitary, rural, and backward. Agrarian animals and companion insects that once formed an efficient but informal organic waste technology in cities have been all but evicted (Philo 1995). In the BSF project, as I demonstrate below, entomologists endeavor to reintroduce flies to the city in an appropriately modern, technoscientific form. Scientists work to calibrate the metabolic function to erase the seasonal variation of the reproductive cycle of flies, so that the fly reproductive cycle can continuously process human waste.

METABOLIC PROCESS AS LABOR AND
THE CHALLENGE OF URBAN WASTE

The idea of metabolism emerged from efforts to understand interactions between an organism and its environment. First used by biologists to describe "the totality of the biochemical reactions in a living thing" (Fischer-Kowalski 1998, 62), metabolism referred to three types of chemical processes for the circulation and exchange of nutrients and energy: the breakdown of food or nutrients to form new building blocks and energy (catabolism), the building up of tissues (anabolism), and the regulatory mechanisms that govern these intricate systems (Beck, Liem, and Simpson 1991). Among ecologists, metabolism describes biochemical processes not just within a single organism but in interactions on the level of systems, so that metabolic interactions capture the cycling of nutrients between organisms as one animal's waste becomes another's food (Fischer-Kowalski 1998, 63). Natural and social scientists use metabolism to describe nature's capacity for self-regulation. Human ecologists, finally, adopted a homeostatic vision of the cycling of nutrients and energy that ostensibly derived from nature, modeling their understanding of energy and labor exchange between society and environment on "natural interactions" (Rappaport 2000).

Famously, Karl Marx employed the notion of metabolism to conceptualize two processes related to change and transformation between labor and nature: the production of labor power through the exchange of energy between bodies and the environment, and the emergence of an ecological crisis under capitalism. Metabolism (*Stoffwechsel*) is central to Marx's theorization of labor and production, where "concrete" labor refers to the physical activity and metabolic interaction that mediates the exchange of energy between human and nature. Marx viewed the human body as "a site of combustion and exchange" that converted energy into "labor power in the service of more life and capital" (Landecker 2013, 223).[6] For ecological Marxists, capitalism relies on expanding the appropriation of nature's vital processes beyond human bodies (Moore 2015). Animal reproduction and growth represent potential forms of metabolic labor, forces in nature that "capital presupposes but does not itself produce" (Barua 2018). In other words, animal bodies and their metabolic processes constitute "excess" value that capital freely appropriates (Beldo 2017). For instance, the growth and reproductive system of the broiler chicken, bred narrowly and precisely to produce industrial meat (Boyd 2001), constitutes "simultaneously bodily technology and living commodities" (Barua 2018) for the accumulation of capital. Metabolic processes appropriated as labor generate value by "depend[ing] upon non-human vitalities to predictably exceed human inputs to production" (Beldo 2017, 110).

Marxist ecologists use the concept of metabolic rift to describe an environmental crisis that emerged within a capitalist mode of production. Marx interpreted the aggregate of excrement and industrial waste found in cities to be an index of problems created by industrial agriculture (Foster 2000, 163). As John Bellamy Foster (2000) argues, a disjuncture emerged in the nineteenth century as the scale of the production and spatial distribution of agricultural goods disrupted the localized nutrient cycle necessary to replenish soils. In other words, industrial production upset the self-restorative capacity of soil by hindering the return of excrement—endowed with nature's latent power for self-restoration—to the site of production. Urbanization further exacerbated the metabolic rift, increasing the scale of waste aggregated in cities (Foster 2000).

Among urban and industrial ecologists, remediation of the metabolic rift targets waste by reconfiguring linear waste flows toward a closed, circular model. In the field of urban sustainability, urban systems and material flows are constructed in analogy to natural ecosystems; studies of "urban metabolism" render the city a complex and heterogeneous but ultimately ordered system (Tansley 1935; Grimm et al. 2000). The closely related discipline of industrial ecology aims to improve urban metabolism by calculating and engineering material life cycles based on patterns found in the natural world, where one organism's waste constitutes another's food (Frosch and Gallopoulos 1989). The concept of a life cycle expressed in such projects, however, does not capture an attempt simply to mirror nature but to devise interventions to regulate and standardize optimal material flows for human systems. Influenced from the outset by metaphors of feedback loops and energy flows, industrial ecologists conceptualized the life cycle as an essentially technical system to be optimized and perfected.[7]

Chinese policy makers explicitly derived the circular economy from industrial ecology; they similarly target waste and material life cycles as the key to improving urban metabolism. The central aims of the circular economy—"to reduce waste, to transform it into a resource, and to detoxify waste [jianliang hua, ziyuan hua, wuhai hua]"—envision a continuous material circulation to optimize systems of material flows by transforming waste into productive matter (Guang-zhou Renmin Zhengfu Bangongting Mishu Chu [Guangzhou Municipal Government Secretariat] 2015). The circular economy exhibits a high modernist impulse to extend the capacity to govern by accelerating, regularizing, and standardizing nature (Scott 1998). As an alternative to WTE incineration, the BSF and its metabolism are positioned as an advanced biotechnology with the capacity to neutralize toxic, contaminating, and threatening waste material while simultaneously generating surplus value and facilitating the circulation of waste in the city. In Dr. Wu's project, the insect life cycle and its metabolism are presented as a natural biotechnology for realizing a circular vision of waste transformation for cities in which insects and their vital processes are put in service of resolving an urban metabolic rift.

In an effort to realize the mandate of the circular economy, the BSF project draws on the promise of insect metabolism as a self-regulating tool to repair the metabolic rift from urban waste. Yet in doing so, it also appropriates and reconfigures the fly's metabolic nature as an inherent form of labor undergirding the production of value. Metabolic labor, however, as I will demonstrate ethnographically below, should not be read as a description of how biophysical processes produce or constitute value in and of themselves, a tendency Moore (2015, 15) refers to as the "metabolic fetish" of green materialism. Biological capacities are not naturally productive, but "become so only in certain relations" (Helmreich 2008, 474). A repertoire of techniques originating from industrial agriculture have rendered metabolic labor—the "reproductive dimensions of cultural and biological life" (Heller 2001, 406)—a site for intensified production and commodification through domestication, breeding, and novel forms of biological engineering (see also Russell 2010). Experimental practices create, routinize, and normalize systems of labor and exchange, even at the level of cellular reproduction (Landecker 2007). At the same time, an understanding of metabolic function as nature's capacity for self-regulation obscures the ways that scientific work and animal labor are appropriated through laboratory practice to realize a vision of perfect circularity.

PRODUCING CIRCULARITY THROUGH LABORATORY WORK

In 2012–2013, I followed the entomologist Dr. Wu in his then nascent experiments to reintroduce an insect, the BSF, back into cities as a technology for modern urban waste management.[8] Dr. Wu carried out his work with visible enthusiasm for its great potential, even though at the time no one could be sure of the project's success or acceptance by local governments. Two years later, two of Guangzhou's districts, Huadu and Baiyun, were considering deploying the BSF pilot projects as a part of the city's official waste-management infrastructure to treat between two hundred and four hundred tons of organic waste per day (Liang and Cheng 2015). In the summer of 2018, I returned to the field to discover that while the Huadu and Baiyun district governments had shelved their pilot projects, several scientific startups and NGOs in the city were actively running BSF pilot projects to manage organic waste in local communities.

Back in October 2012, I first encountered the BSF project one afternoon during a meeting I attended while working with a local environmental NGO that was conducting research into alternative treatments for organic waste. I sat in a conference room in the Guangdong Entomological Institute, as the institute's director, Dr. Luo, offered the following remarks:

> From the beginning, we've designed the BSF as a technology that is useful for solid organic waste management. There are many advantages [to the BSF] compared with conventional composting technologies. BSF uses an insect to process [waste]. This has a higher efficiency than microorganisms. Why? Because the BSF feeds on solid organic waste. The process of BSF feeding on organic waste is not one of decomposition [*fenjie*], but actually a process of transformation [*zhuanhua*], one of transforming [organic waste] into animal protein. Insect protein is a high value-added resource [*gao fujiaze zhiyuan*]. Microorganisms break down and decompose elements into a more simplified [compound], useful only for composting. By using the BSF to treat kitchen waste, once it matures, we can process it into all kinds of useful products.[9]

Luo's description distinguishes the BSF from other forms of organic waste technology, such as composting and biodigesters, which merely break down waste. Instead, by consuming organic waste, metabolizing and incorporating it into its own body, the BSF is endowed with the capacity to convert organics to a value-added resource, namely, a marketable form of animal protein. In Marxist thought, the value added in a product is typically regarded as the addition of (exploited) human labor. Yet in Luo's framing, the fly's natural metabolic processes and life cycle, supposedly unmediated by human labor, produce a value-added product: animal protein from organic waste. Luo's account echoes what Helmreich (2008, 464) calls the "double fetishism" common to discourses of biotech boosterism. The double fetish allows biological values to appear "in themselves" by representing biological life as the source of value simply because of their origins in living things, and then by erasing the scientific and human labor that goes into creating biovalue in institutional settings such as laboratories. By emphasizing the natural circularity of the fly life cycle, Luo's discourse reiterates the ways that the BSF is envisioned as fulfilling the goals of the circular economy and, as such, naturalizes the vital power of animals as a source of value addition while obscuring human scientific labor that helps generate and enable these capacities. In Dr. Wu's laboratory practice, scientific and care work seeks to align a natural process—an animal's metabolism, its life cycle—with an industrial vision of the circular economy for an optimal, ecological waste regime. In the laboratory, the realization of the vision of circulation hinges on developing strategies to standardize the practice of reproduction, that is, the breeding of fly larvae.[10]

Luo's narrative further obscures the labor of his own researchers, including the repeated attempts and failures of the laboratory experiments focused on the reproductive capacities of the flies that Dr. Wu was devising. The BSF is not only expected to carry out the biological processes of its own life cycle but it must also be made to do so in a standardized and predictable manner so as to process the daily output of a city's organic waste. In effect, the scientific experiments in Dr. Wu's lab are meant to synchronize two life cycles: the reproductive life cycle of flies, and the life cycle of organic waste generated by human activity. The vision informing the BSF project imagines that surplus matter (organic waste) can be turned into a commodifiable surplus population (BSF insects). To realize this vision, the life cycle of the insect—eat, excrete, then die—is rendered interchangeable and interdependent with the flow of materials and nutrients in the city.

Although the BSF project envisions the life cycle of the BSF and the life cycle of organic waste production forming a natural feedback loop, in his laboratory experiments Dr. Wu confronted repeated challenges in

---

automating BSF breeding in a standardized and predictable manner. As Dr. Wu pointed out to me, the key challenge of his system is to devise a method of breeding the BSF that can yield a predictable quantity of flies throughout the changing lighting and temperature conditions of different seasons. Just as attention to the calibration of speed and the nature of circulation proves central to the configuration of production and consumption in late capitalism (Cowen 2014; Duclos, Sánchez Criado, and Nguyen 2017), to be adapted as a biotechnology and a waste infrastructure for cities, the speed and reliable reproduction of fly larvae must complement the predictable rate of human organic waste output.

In his field experimental station, located on a former station owned by the Guangdong Entomological Institute, Dr. Wu and his assistants puzzled over how changing seasons, alternating light quality, humidity, and temperature would alter the timing and rhythm of fly growth and reproduction. The successful reproduction of the BSF required close attention to the condition of the insect at each life stage—egg, larva, pre-pupa, pupa, and adult fly. Each adult BSF will lay up to one thousand eggs that take three days to hatch. The tiny larvae feed continuously for a period of about fourteen days, during which their ability to process waste is at its peak. During this time they grow from a 1-millimeter-long pale golden worm to a dark brown worm with a hardened shell, about 2.5 centimeters long with a mass of 200 milligrams. While the larvae tend to avoid light and will burrow to hide, the fully grown pre-pupa crawls out of its food source to look for a dry, dark location. The pupa will emerge as an adult winged insect. Under optimal lighting and temperature conditions, adult flies mate, and the female lays eggs one day later, completing its life cycle.

Dr. Wu's makeshift workshop had a series of trays and shelving units installed along each wall. The workshop remained humid even as large fans hummed in the background circulating intermittent gusts of warm air between two wire-fence walls. One wall was lined with a series of freshly constructed gray shelving units, with white plastic water pipes running across the horizontal length of the trays. At each stage of their development, the insects require different temperature, moisture, and lighting conditions, so caretakers observe and cater to the specific conditions of each tray. Each tray demarcated a distinct experimental unit that would allow researchers to monitor and make daily alterations to ensure the

—

optimal condition for the reproductive growth and breeding of the flies. The practices in Dr. Wu's lab mirror what scholars have labeled an "infra-stitial" protocol or equipment, one that appears to be routine or boring yet never quite standardized (Kelly and Lezaun 2017).

Along the edges, smeared glue streaks and slight irregularities lent the trays a DIY quality. On the very bottom shelf, in the brown mulch, a few larvae were making their way up the sloped sidings. Dr. Wu told me that he would run water underneath the tray to cool the entire setup in the next batch to ensure better temperature control. At each stage, minute adjustments—more water, moving trays to allow for more air circulation—were made in response to the observed condition of individual batches. Ms. Lin pointed to the pre-pupae in one tray that had made their way from the mulch, their bodies marked by a slight curvature. On the other end of the hall, Lin tipped a watering can into a bed of flat brown soil with BSF larvae hidden beneath to ensure the right amount of moisture.

"This batch is doing extremely well," Lin told me, noting that if the

FIGURE 4.2. The tray system allows minor adjustments to be made to moisture and temperature during each life stage. Photo by Amy Zhang.

---

moisture and temperature control were off, the flies would perish. "When they die, they tend to die in batches," she noted. The loss of not only a single fly but a population of flies is equivalent to a system failure to reliably circulate (waste) and output (energy) in a close-looped system. There was a sadness to her description of the death of the larvae, in contrast to the excitement she displayed when she showed off the squirming worms. She explained to me how the previous fall they had found a tray of dead flies after an especially humid evening. Guangzhou's winter months, with temperatures occasionally dipping below 5°C in January and February, have proven especially difficult for the survival of the larvae. Sometimes rats got into the trays and enjoyed a large feast, hence the cats later seen wandering around the workshop. Whereas in the wild, BSF populations waxed and waned with the changing seasons, in the lab the intimate attentions of an assistant to cultivate and maintain stable conditions enabled the fly population to thrive under varying seasonal conditions.

Guiding me to another series of trays across the workshop, Dr. Wu pointed out that the mulch differs in gradients of darkness depending on

FIGURE 4.3. Newly collected black soldier fly eggs. Photo by Amy Zhang.

—

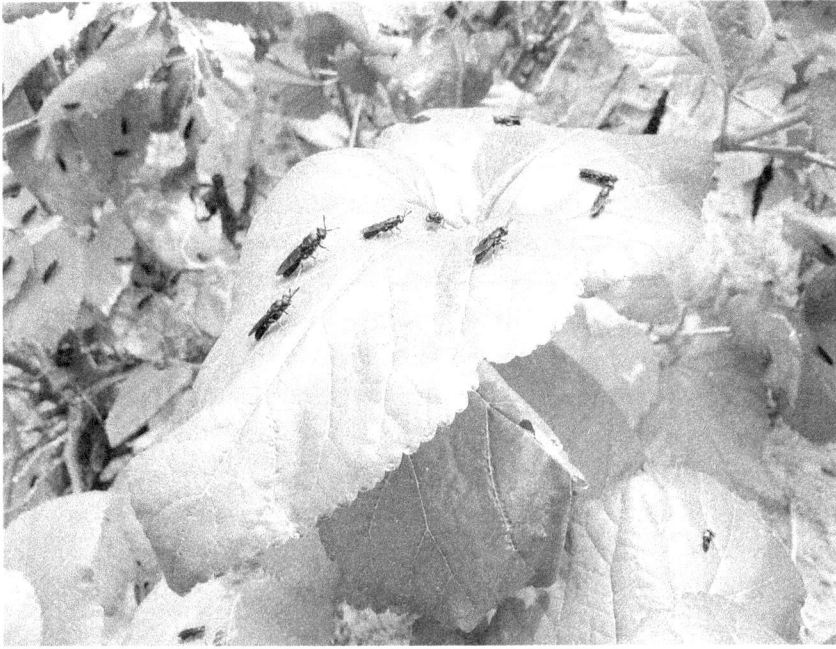

FIGURE 4.4. Adult larvae in the last week of their life cycle resting on leaves in the arboretum. Photo by Amy Zhang.

the age and life stage of the larvae. Laid out on mesh netting over the top of the tray were larvae that had been hand-collected from the garden, which Dr. Wu had constructed behind the garage to house the adult BSF. From a distance, the yellow splatter of the larvae resembled wet pulp, but up close, the squirming, vibrating movement revealed the contours of worms starting to take shape.

In the garden, a sprinkler system periodically sent a stream of mist into the air. Up to six or seven flies could be found resting on green leaves; bushes were dotted with tiny black speckles. Around the bushes, small black figures buzzed and flashed their blue transparent wings. The larger flies were females carrying eggs. They would pass the last week of their life in the tent where they mated, laid eggs, and then died. Unlike household flies that buzz aggressively around humans, the BSF travels at a more relaxed pace, skirting aimlessly in the air, sometimes landing on our shoulders before jetting off. Dr. Wu described the work of raising the BSF to me:

———

I have to control the conditions to ensure that the larva grows up healthy. It's just like raising a child, you shouldn't give it anything dangerous to eat, don't let it go to dangerous places. You make sure that they are full, that the environment is under the best temperature control, and it will grow healthily. Now, these controls are all reliant on human labor, and it requires a lot of experience. Once we're finished, we can use machines / technologies [*shebei*] to control these conditions and they'll be easily passed on.

The minor adjustments made by human laborers to maintain suitable micro-ecologies for insects stand in stark contrast to the vision of an automated system of fly raising, where the production of artificial environmental conditions is meant to be self-sustaining. Instead, the work of raising the BSF reveals a space of dependent cohabitation where new practices of contact and human care and attention prove critical for insect survival. A similar tension between care and control occurs in animal husbandry, where attention to specificities, unpredictability, and embodied practice constitute the human efforts necessary for achieving industrial standardization (Pandian 2008; Singleton 2010; Blanchette 2018). In the BSF project, success in rendering biophysical nature into a reliable infrastructure—mechanized, reliable, and invisible—depends on an intimate relationship between humans and insects. Intimate attention in the lab reveals that techno-utopian dreams of automation and mechanization that eschew the need for labor in the production of value nonetheless rely not merely on human labor but also on forms of care work. In this case, a project to devise an automated breeding machine is conditioned on unacknowledged and willfully obscured physical intimacy and practices of care between humans and insects.

ENCLOSURES OF INSECT REARING AND URBAN LIVING

The practices of intimate attention to insects I witnessed at the field station are ultimately in service of creating a system to mechanize and standardize fly reproduction within an enclosure. The concept of enclosures has been used to describe two developments in capitalism's strategy of appropriating value from nature: the land-enclosure movements that precipitated the

---

FIGURE 4.5. Ms. Lin working in the garden. Photo by Amy Zhang.

agricultural revolution, and an industrial technique in animal husbandry (Franklin 2007).[11] In industrial husbandry, animal enclosures refer to systems of light and temperature regulation devised to increase animals' rate of growth and reproduction with minimal human engagement (Harrison 2013). As a regulated environment for animal breeding and rearing, the enclosure shifts animal biological functions onto an industrial life cycle.

Dr. Wu's desire to build an enclosed apparatus in effect replicates the strategy of enclosures in industrial husbandry. He hopes to engineer a controlled environment for flies to grow and reproduce with minimal human intervention. Next to the trays of fly larvae sits Dr. Wu's first prototype. The structure—roughly seven feet tall, nine feet wide, and eleven feet deep, made of plastic siding, wood, and metal framing, water pipes and metal screws protruding from its sides—is a defunct machine he remains reluctant to discard. Dr. Wu imagined that organic waste and BSF larvae would be fed into the machine, effectively a black box,[12] and that it would output adult larvae ready to hatch. The intermediate life stages of the fly were to have taken place entirely inside the machine, the stages of metamorphosis enclosed and obscured. His hope was that he could one day house his box

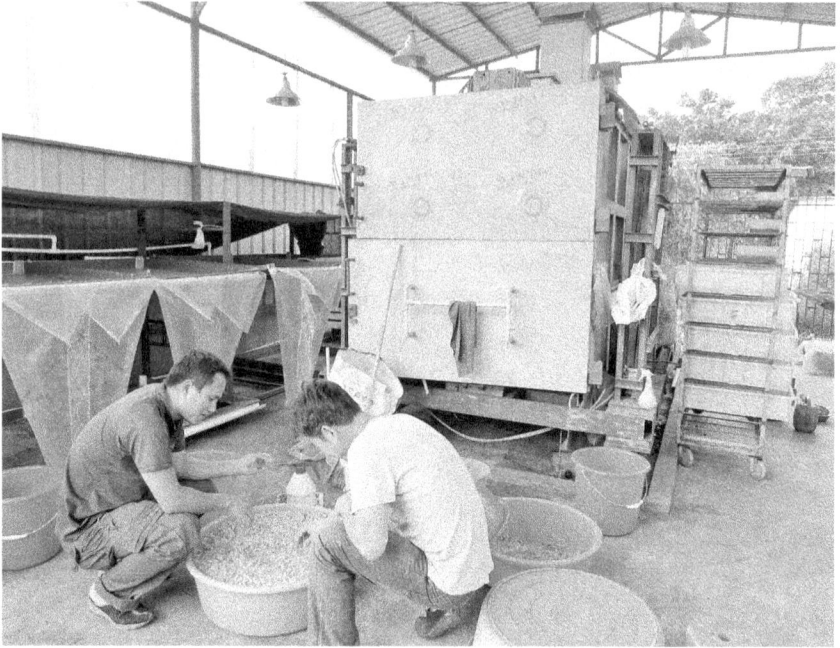

FIGURE 4.6. The enclosed prototype for fly rearing. Photo by Amy Zhang.

in the garden of any urban community, where workers tasked with per-
forming a minimum level of maintenance would periodically service the
machine: adding fly larvae and organic waste and retrieving mature pupae
before they turn into adults, thereby circulating fly larvae and organic
waste like snacks and coins in and out of a vending machine.

The enclosure, however, is not only designed to embody the principles
of industrial husbandry but also, more important, it manifests the aesthetic, spatial, and environmental ideals of an ecological modern method
of urban waste treatment. To turn fly larvae into a waste infrastructure
suitable to the urban high-rises of Guangzhou, Dr. Wu tells me, requires
an enclosed (*fengbishi*) system. Throughout my research in Guangzhou,
municipal planners and officials repeatedly used the term enclosure (*fengbishi*) to describe a spatial and aesthetic characteristic. In the concrete and
sanitized halls of apartment complexes, making waste management modern means making trash imperceptible. Trash is stored in receptacles, hidden in stairwells, separated from the spaces of daily life. Newly designed

fengbishi waste trucks (introduced by the City Management Bureau) enclose waste to conceal odor and the unsightly process of decomposition. Waste labor—whether performed by humans or animals—remains similarly hidden. In windowless basement rooms or utility closets, sanitary workers manually sort recyclables, their labor ensuring the sustainable processing of waste even in the face of failed citizen recycling campaigns (A. Zhang 2019). Dr. Wu's enclosed apparatus similarly shields from view the labor of care that ensures the reproduction of the insect life cycle. In effect, modern waste infrastructure must circulate discard invisibly, while nevertheless ensuring that urban services are delivered regularly and sustainably.

The enclosure is a standardized apparatus that matches an aesthetic order of modern living in contemporary China. In its imagined form, the BSF enclosure echoes the gated housing community (*fengbishi xiaoqu*), a now pervasive spatial form that organizes life in cities. Gated communities manifest a landscape of fear and insecurity (Caldeira 2000; Low 2001). In post-reform China, since the 1990s, enclosed compounds index a desire for a privatized form of living (Tomba 2006). New apartment complexes and suburban compounds offer exclusionary private space through home ownership, the consumption of housing a key means of social distinction (Li Zhang 2010). However, these gated communities also seek to alleviate ecological concerns by reshaping the urban environment according to a sanitized green aesthetic. In newly developed gated communities, aspirations for green living feature prominently. Landscaping and manicured lawns emulate a ruralist ideal (Sze 2015). Gated spaces set apart from the city signify the achievement of a middle-class lifestyle by virtue of being able to extricate oneself from the filthy, crowded, and disorderly elements of urban life. In these new, ostensibly environmentally minded communities, insects and waste, harbingers of disorder and disease, need to be kept at bay. Insect enclosure conceals the cycles of life, growth, metamorphosis, and death, the vital processes of animal life that carry out the labor of ecological remediation but are nevertheless out of step with a desire to create a particular sanitized, green-modernist aesthetic of order.

The enclosed apparatus explicitly enacts a spatial separation between insects, waste, and humans in an urban setting. Dr. Wu knew well that the success of his project depended on overcoming a public revulsion for flies (associated with decomposing waste, filth, and danger) and the

---

broad adoption of a new understanding of the BSF as an ecologically useful insect. To establish a different reputation for the BSF, researchers had to take care that an apparatus generating tens of thousands of fly larvae on an industrial scale did not release unpleasant smells or other discharge that might jeopardize the "environmental quality" of the project. By environmental quality, the team refers both to the apparatus's capacity to meet a series of technical standards for pollution and, more important, to the perpetuation of a spatial order that enacts a politics of concealment for vital processes—reproduction, breakdown, and death—associated with disease, unruliness, and the ungovernability of life.

Prompted by fear of disease and environmental contamination, enclosures circumscribe and control multispecies entanglements that prevent forms of care and identification between humans and insects (Law and Mol 2008; Nading 2014; Blanchette 2015; Kirksey 2015). For example, the control of mosquito populations by public health authorities has been characterized as a form of human labor intended to enact interspecies separation

FIGURE 4.7. A sanitized, green aesthetic is characteristic of many gated communities in China. Photo by Amy Zhang.

and to disentangle relations of cohabitation (Kelly and Lezaun 2014). Sanitation workers target insect breeding grounds (stagnant pools, plants) in the urban landscape and systematically eliminate conditions that facilitate a shared condition of living. In short, biosecurity is founded on a fantasy of "enclos[ing] humans and animals in specific, sterile, and segregated spaces" (Blanchette 2015, 662). In the laboratory, enclosed fly-raising apparatuses entrenched and normalized the capacity to govern the mutability of life through a technical style (Hughes 2012). In the case of urban waste management, enclosures, and the various biological and labor processes they obscure, also facilitate the impression of the achievement of an automated, circular, and ecologically modern vision of waste treatment. In meeting the aesthetic requirements of the modern green city, one that has ejected unruly forms of animal life, the enclosed apparatus further obscures the intimate practices of care and contact between humans and insects that are required to perpetuate the continuous functioning of the circular vision.

INSECT LABOR AND INTIMACY IN THE ECOLOGICALLY MODERN CITY

Gabrielle Hecht (2018) suggests that waste, a material index of the catastrophic effects of humanity's existence on the planet's physical and biochemical systems, constitutes the apotheosis of the Anthropocene. In response to its own pressing waste crisis, the Chinese state has adopted a technocentric approach to ecological modernization. Posed as a solution to the waste crisis forged in an era of acute awareness of ecological decline, Dr. Wu's BSF project revives an older agrarian practice of relying on animals to process human waste, yet in accordance with the principles and demands of an ecologically modern city. In doing so, it attempts to manifest an assumption shared by ecological modernization and green urbanism that the shift toward a clean, automated, green city can be readily achieved through the development of new and better technologies (Halpern 2015; Günel 2019).

Despite such pronouncements, as anthropologists have demonstrated, the fulfillment of the most basic urban provisions, particularly throughout the global South, continue to depend on haphazard practices, improvisation, and existing forms of labor and exploitation (Simone 2004; Anand,

—

Gupta, and Appel 2018; Degani 2018). An ecologically modern approach to waste management in China, as elsewhere, obscures the range and depth of work performed by municipal waste workers and informal laborers whose bodies make possible the movement and transformation of matter (Gidwani and Reddy 2011; Fredericks 2018; Doherty and Brown 2019). In Dr. Wu's laboratory, what is obscured includes not only the behind-the-scenes work performed by assistants like Ms. Lin but also the productive harnessing of insects' metabolic and reproductive activity—as if it, too, were labor. The BSF project, sited at the convergence of biotechnology and China's project of ecological modernization, reveals the fiction of biocapital: the belief that nature itself—absent human intervention, labor, and forms of care work—can generate value and remediate environments. My ethnography of laboratory practice has shown that more complex and nuanced ecological relations between humans and insects are not only obscured but also made possible, even demanded, by efforts to devise biotechnologies to realize green cities in China. And yet, the intimacy between humans and insects required by BSF waste management sits uncomfortably with the expectation that animals be expelled from, or contained and controlled within, modern cities. Here, the apparatus of enclosure, in addition to enabling the BSF biotechnology to capitalize on insects' metabolic and reproductive natures, is designed to fulfill the aesthetic and environmental demand that modern cities be rid of undomesticated animals (e.g., through pest control and by removing agrarian animals and slaughterhouses).

The BSF project thus reflects the contradictory demands of contemporary China's ecological urbanism, concerned with sanitization while increasingly reliant on the biological capacities of nonhumans for environmental remediation. As a hoped-for means to resolve this contradiction, the BSF enclosure's attempts to realize ecological modernization in cities not only aim to produce environmental value, they also condition the terms of multispecies cohabitation for humans and insects. The enclosure enacts an interspecies separation that would seem to foreclose possibilities for "a knot of connection" between humans and insects (Govindrajan 2018, 4).

And yet, in carrying out the daily labor practice of scientific work, we see scientists engage in intimate contact with and care for subjects as uncharismatic as flies. In the shadow of the defunct prototype of the enclosure, I briefly glimpsed the intimate appreciation for the vulnerability

———

and potential of nonhuman life: Dr. Wu, Ms. Lin, and I crouched down around a tray and watched excitedly as the dirt once again turned to life, with hundreds of yellow larvae squirming to the surface.

NOTES

Acknowledgments This article would not have been possible without the generosity of Dr. Wu and his team in Guangzhou. Thanks to Paige West and Mark Moritz for their comments, along with Sarah Besky, Ashley Carse, Nicole Peterson, and Maryann Cairns who read this piece as a part of the 2016 Roy Rappaport Prize Committee. Earlier versions of the work benefited from generous readings and comments of Michael Dove, Dana Graef, Bruce Grant, Susan Greenhalgh, Karen Hébert, Emily Martin, Laura Martin, Andrea Muehlebach, Helen Siu, Shivi Sivaramakrishnan, Mei Zhan, Li Zhang, and Ling Zhang. I am grateful to both the previous and current editorial teams of *Cultural Anthropology* and the anonymous reviewers for their deep engagement and probing questions. Heather Paxson's reiterative edits and incisive comments proved critical for developing the central arguments. D'Arcy Saum read every draft from beginning to end. Versions of the article benefited from the following workshops and presentations: The Environmental History Working Group at Harvard, the Fairbank Center Environments in Asia Lecture series, the Biosocial Network Retreat, and the Center for Urban Environments (University of Toronto Mississauga). Field research was supported by the Wenner-Gren Foundation, the Social Science Research Council, and the National Science Foundation (#1225886).

1. Ms. Lin, the primary caretaker of the BSF experiment, had no formal scientific training, but she was familiar with animal husbandry. Her work at this field station reflects the reliance of scientific research on agricultural labor typical of field-station research in China and elsewhere (see, e.g., Ann H. Kelly and Javier Lezaun [2017] on the reliance on local villagers for mosquito experiments in Africa).

2. I use the terms infrastructure and biotechnology somewhat interchangeably in this article. In Dr. Wu's project, infrastructures and biotechnology are socionatural systems devised to fulfill the infrastructural function of circulation.

3. See Jake Kosek (2010) for an analysis of the scientific engineering of the honeybee and Hugh Raffles (2010) for a history of insects as both a working animal and a companion species in China.

4. Biocapital has been defined as "form(s) of extraction that involves isolating and mobilizing the primary reproductive agency of specific body parts" (Franklin and Lock 2003, 8).

5. See the "China Modernization Report 2007: Study on Ecological Modernization" and the 2008 Circular Economy Law.

6. Ecological Marxists look for concrete labor in sites of metabolic exchange such as agriculture, mining, and fisheries (Howard 2017; Huber 2017).

7. The historical origins and cultural specificities of the concept of the life cycle of things and materials in industrial ecology are rooted not only in biology but also in the principles of machines and information-regulation in cybernetic systems. Key

—

ideas in cybernetics, such as self-regulating nature and energy flows, developed in the decades after the Second World War, precisely when ecology as a discipline was trying to fashion itself after the hard sciences and interested in designing self-regulating machines, such as guided missiles and thermostats (Worster 1994).

8. The systematic annihilation of insects was first promoted by the sanitation campaigns of the 1950s. Public health campaigns regard the elimination of insects and the removal of waste as critical to the production of healthy bodies and the nation (see Rogaski 2002; Bao 2012).

9. All interview extracts are taken from fieldwork conducted in Guangzhou from 2012 to 2014. Pseudonyms are used.

10. In feminist Marxian terms, production and reproduction are alike as processes of the constant exchange of energy through the body, between humans and nature that undergird labor activity. Capital's production of surplus value relies on this appropriation of unpaid labor in the form of domestic work and biological reproduction (Fortunati 1995; Weeks 2011; Moore 2015; Vora 2015).

11. Enclosing animals forms a critical part of the agro-industrial food production that renders biological processes calculable and controllable. For example, climate-controlled housing is used in rearing poultry to achieve "rapid turnover, high density stocking, a high degree of mechanization, a low labor requirement, and efficient conversion of food into saleable products" (Harrison 2013, 35).

12. In science and technology studies, a black box refers to the closing off of the dynamic and contested process in the formation of scientific knowledge and facts (Latour 1987).

REFERENCES

Anand, Nikhil, Akhil Gupta, and Hannah Appel, eds.
2018 *The Promise of Infrastructure*. Durham, N.C.: Duke University Press.
Bao, Maohong
2012 "Environmentalism and Environmental Movements in China since 1949." In *A Companion to Global Environmental History*, edited by J. R. McNeill and Erin Stewart Mauldin, 474–92. Malden, Mass.: Wiley-Blackwell.
Barua, Maan
2018 "Animal Work: Metabolic, Ecological, Affective." Theorizing the Contemporary, *Fieldsights*, July 26. https://culanth.org/fieldsights/animal-work-metabolic-ecological-affective.
Beck, William Samson, Karel F. Liem, and George Gaylord Simpson
1991 *Life: An Introduction to Biology*. 3rd ed. New York: HarperCollins.
Beldo, Les
2017 "Metabolic Labor: Broiler Chickens and the Exploitation of Vitality." *Environmental Humanities* 9, no. 1: 108–28. https://doi.org/10.1215/22011919-3829154.

Benson, Etienne S.

2015   "The Urban Upwelling." *American Historian* November: 40–44.

Besky, Sarah, and Alex Blanchette

2018   "The Naturalization of Work: Theorizing the Contemporary." Theorizing the Contemporary, *Fieldsights*, July 26. https://culanth.org/fieldsights/series/the-naturalization-of-work.

Blanchette, Alex

2015   "Herding Species: Biosecurity, Posthuman Labor, and the American Industrial Pig." *Cultural Anthropology* 30, no. 4: 640–69. https://doi.org/10.14506/ca30.4.09.

2018   "Industrial Meat Production." *Annual Review of Anthropology* 47, no. 1: 185–99. https://doi.org/10.1146/annurev-anthro-102317-050206.

Boyd, William

2001   "Making Meat: Science, Technology, and American Poultry Production." *Technology and Culture* 42, no. 4: 631–64. https://www.jstor.org/stable/25147798.

Braun, Bruce

2007   "Biopolitics and the Molecularization of Life." *Cultural Geographies* 14, no. 1: 6–28. https://doi.org/10.1177%2F1474474007072817.

Caldeira, Teresa P. R.

2000   *City of Walls: Crime, Segregation, and Citizenship in São Paulo*. Berkeley: University of California Press.

Carse, Ashley

2012   "Nature as Infrastructure: Making and Managing the Panama Canal Watershed." *Social Studies of Science* 42, no. 4: 539–63. https://doi. org/10.1177%2F0306312712440166.

Cowen, Deborah

2014   *The Deadly Life of Logistics: Mapping Violence in Global Trade*. Minneapolis: University of Minnesota Press.

Degani, Michael

2018   "Shock Humor: Zaniness and the Freedom of Permanent Improvisation in Urban Tanzania." *Cultural Anthropology* 33, no. 3: 473–98. https://doi.org/10.14506/ca33.3.08.

Doherty, Jacob, and Kate Brown

2019   "Labor Laid Waste: An Introduction to the Special Issue on Waste Work." *International Labor and Working-Class History* 95: 1–17. https://doi.org/10.1017/S0147547919000048.

Duclos, Vincent, Tomás Sánchez Criado, and Vinh-Kim Nguyen

2017   "Speed: An Introduction." *Cultural Anthropology* 32, no. 1: 1–11. https://doi.org/10.14506/ca32.1.01.

Fischer-Kowalski, Marina

1998   "Society's Metabolism: The Intellectual History of Materials Flow Analysis, Part 1, 1860–1970." *Journal of Industrial Ecology* 2, no. 1: 61–78. https://doi.org/10.1162/jiec.1998.2.1.61.

Fortunati, Leopoldina

1995   *The Arcane of Reproduction: Housework, Prostitution, Labor and Capital*. Translated by Hilary Creek. Edited by Jim Fleming. Brooklyn, N.Y.: Autonomedia.

Foster, John Bellamy

2000   *Marx's Ecology: Materialism and Nature*. New York: Monthly Review.

Franklin, Sarah

2007   *Dolly Mixtures: The Remaking of Genealogy*. Durham, N.C.: Duke University Press.

Franklin, Sarah, and Margaret Lock

2003   "Animation and Cessation: The Remaking of Life and Death." In *Remaking Life and Death: Toward an Anthropology of the Biosciences*, edited by Sarah Franklin and Margaret Lock, 3–22. Santa Fe, N.Mex.: School of American Research Press.

Fredericks, Rosalind

2018   *Garbage Citizenship: Vital Infrastructures of Labor in Dakar, Senegal*. Durham, N.C.: Duke University Press.

Frosch, Robert A., and Nicholas E. Gallopoulos

1989   "Strategies for Manufacturing." *Scientific American* 261, no. 3: 144–52. https://doi.org/10.1038/scientificamerican0989-144.

Gidwani, Vinay, and Rajyashree N. Reddy

2011   "The Afterlives of 'Waste': Notes from India for a Minor History of Capitalist Surplus." *Antipode* 43, no.5: 1625–58. https://doi.org/10.1111/j.1467-8330.2011.00902.x.

Govindrajan, Radhika

2018   *Animal Intimacies: Interspecies Relatedness in India's Central Himalayas*. Chicago: University of Chicago Press.

Grimm, Nancy B., J. Morgan Grove, Steward T. A. Pickett, and Charles L. Redman

2000   "Integrated Approaches to Long-Term Studies of Urban Ecological Systems." *BioScience* 50, no. 7: 571–84.

Guangzhou Renmin Zhengfu Bangongting Mishu Chu [Guangzhou Municipal Government Secretariat]

2015   "Guangzhou Shi Shenghuo laji fenlei guanli guiding" [Guangzhou Municipal Waste Recycling Policy]. http://www.nanfanghuanjing.com/c2167.html.

Günel, Gökçe

2019   *Spaceship in the Desert: Energy, Climate Change, and Urban Design in Abu Dhabi*. Durham, N.C.: Duke University Press.

Halpern, Orit

2015   *Beautiful Data: A History of Vision and Reason since 1945*. Durham, N.C.: Duke University Press.

Haraway, Donna J.

1991   *Simians, Cyborgs, and Women: The Reinvention of Nature*. New York: Routledge.

Harrison, Ruth

2013   *Animal Machines*. Wallingford, UK: CABI.

Hecht, Gabrielle

2018   "Interscalar Vehicles for an African Anthropocene: On Waste, Temporality, and

Violence." *Cultural Anthropology* 33, no. 1: 109–41. https://doi.org/10.14506
/ca33.1.05.

Heller, Chaia

2001   "McDonald's, MTV and Monsanto: Resisting Biotechnology in the Age of Infor-
mational Capital." In *Redesigning Life? The Worldwide Challenge to Genetic Engineering*, edited by Brian Tokar, 405–25. New York: Zed Books.

Helmreich, Stefan

2007   "Blue-Green Capital, Biotechnological Circulation and an Oceanic Imaginary:
A Critique of Biopolitical Economy." *BioSocieties* 2, no. 3: 287–302. https://doi.org
/10.1017/S1745855207005753.

2008   "Species of Biocapital." *Science as Culture* 17, no. 4: 463–78. https://doi.org/10.1080
/09505430802519256.

Hetherington, Kregg, ed.

2019   *Infrastructure, Environment, and Life in the Anthropocene.* Durham, N.C.: Duke
University Press.

Hird, Myra J.

2013   "Waste, Landfills, and an Environmental Ethic of Vulnerability." *Ethics and the
Environment* 18, no. 1: 105–24. https://doi.org/10.2979/ethicsenviro.18.1.105.

Howard, Penny McCall

2017   *Environment, Labour and Capitalism at Sea: "Working the Ground" in Scotland.*
Manchester: Manchester University Press.

Huang, Shaohong

2013   "Datianshan xunhuan yuan canchu laji xiangmu tingchan" [Datianshan Project
Halted for Adjustment]. *Southern Daily*, October 28. http://news.ifeng.com
/gundong/detail_2013_10/28/30714222_0.shtml.

Huber, Matthew T.

2017   "Value, Nature, and Labor: A Defense of Marx." *Capitalism Nature Socialism* 28,
no. 1: 39–52. https://doi.org/10.1080/10455752.2016.1271817.

Hughes, Thomas P.

2012   "The Evolution of Large Technological Systems." In *The Social Construction of Tech-
nological Systems: New Directions in the Sociology and History of Technology*, edited by
Wiebe E. Bijker, Thomas P. Hughes, and Trevor Pinch, 45–76. Cambridge, Mass.:
MIT Press.

Jasarevic, Larisa

2015   "The Thing in a Jar: Mushrooms and Ontological Speculations in Post-
Yugoslavia." *Cultural Anthropology* 30, no. 1: 36–64. https://doi.org/10.14506
/ca30.1.04.

Kelly, Ann H., and Javier Lezaun

2014   "Urban Mosquitoes, Situational Publics, and the Pursuit of Interspecies
Separation in Dar Es Salaam." *American Ethnologist* 41, no. 2: 368–83. https://doi
.org/10.1111/amet.12081.

2017   "The Wild Indoors: Room-Spaces of Scientific Inquiry." *Cultural Anthropology* 32,
no. 3: 367–98. https://doi.org/10.14506/ca32.3.06.

———

Kirksey, Eben
2015   *Emergent Ecologies*. Durham, N.C.: Duke University Press.
Kosek, Jake
2010   "Ecologies of Empire: On the New Uses of the Honeybee." *Cultural Anthropology*
        25, no. 4: 650–78. https://doi.org/10.1111/j.1548-1360.2010.01073.x.
Landecker, Hannah
2007   *Culturing Life: How Cells Became Technologies*. Cambridge, Mass.: Harvard
        University Press.
2013   "The Metabolism of Philosophy, in Three Parts." In *Dialectic and Paradox: Configu-*
        rations of the Third in Modernity, edited by Ian Cooper and Bernhard F. Malkmus,
        193–224. Bern, Switz.: Peter Lang.
Latour, Bruno
1987   *Science in Action: How to Follow Scientists and Engineers through Society*. Cambridge,
        Mass: Harvard University Press.
Law, John, and Annemarie Mol
2008   "Globalisation in Practice: On the Politics of Boiling Pigswill." *Geoforum* 39, no. 1:
        133–43. https://doi.org/10.1016/J.GEOFORUM.2006.08.010.
Liang, Yitao, and Guangwei Cheng
2015   "Huadu shuaixian yang heishuimeng shichi laji" [Huadu the First District to
        Experiment with Using the Black Soldier Fly to Eat Waste]. *YangCheng Evening*
        News, May 21. http://news.sina.com.cn/o/2015-05-21/143931859888.shtml.
Low, Setha M.
2001   "The Edge and the Center: Gated Communities and the Discourse of Urban Fear."
        American Anthropologist 103, no. 1: 45–58. https://doi.org/10.1525/aa.2001.103.1.45.
Martínez-Alier, Juan
2002   *The Environmentalism of the Poor: A Study of Ecological Conflicts and Valuation*.
        Cheltenham, UK: Edward Elgar.
Merrifield, Caroline
2017   "Spirit, Monster, Table and Tongue." *Engagement* (blog), Anthropology and
        Environment Society, A Section of the American Anthropological Association.
        October 25. https://aesengagement.wordpress.com/2017/10/25/spirit-monster
        -table-and-tongue/.
Mikhail, Alan
2013   *The Animal in Ottoman Egypt*. Oxford: Oxford University Press.
Mol, Arthur P. J., and David A. Sonnenfeld, eds.
2000   *Ecological Modernisation around the World: Perspectives and Critical Debates*. London:
        Frank Cass.
Moore, Jason W.
2015   *Capitalism in the Web of Life: Ecology and the Accumulation of Capital*. London: Verso.
Morita, Atsuro
2017   "Multispecies Infrastructure: Infrastructural Inversion and Involutionary
        Entanglements in the Chao Phraya Delta, Thailand." *Ethnos* 82, no. 4: 738–57.
        https://doi.org/10.1080/00141844.2015.1119175.

Nading, Alex M.

2014   *Mosquito Trails: Ecology, Health, and the Politics of Entanglement*. Oakland: University of California Press.

Olson, Valerie

2018   "Oysters: System vs. Infrastructure in the U.S. Gulf Coast Restoration Economy." Paper presented at the Annual Meeting of the American Anthropological Association, San Jose, Calif., November 14–18.

Pandian, Anand

2008   "Pastoral Power in the Postcolony: On the Biopolitics of the Criminal Animal in South India." *Cultural Anthropology* 23, no. 1: 85–117. https://doi.org/10.1111/ j.1548 -1360.2008.00004.x.

Paxson, Heather

2013   *The Life of Cheese: Crafting Food and Value in America*. Berkeley: University of California Press.

Philo, Chris

1995   "Animals, Geography, and the City: Notes on Inclusions and Exclusions." *Environment and Planning D: Society and Space* 13, no. 6: 655–81. https://doi.org/10 .1068%2Fd130655.

Raffles, Hugh

2010   *Insectopedia*. New York, NY: Pantheon Books.

Rappaport, Roy A.

2000   *Pigs for the Ancestors: Ritual in the Ecology of a New Guinea People*. Long Grove, Ill.: Waveland Press.

Reno, Joshua O.

2016   *Waste Away: Working and Living with a North American Landfill*. Oakland: University of California Press.

Rogaski, Ruth

2002   "Nature, Annihilation, and Modernity: China's Korean War Germ-Warfare Experience Reconsidered." *Journal of Asian Studies* 61, no. 2: 381–415. http://doi .org/10.2307/2700295.

Roosth, Sophia

2017   *Synthetic: How Life Got Made*. Chicago: University of Chicago Press.

Russell, Edmund

2010   "Can Organisms Be Technology?" In *The Illusory Boundary: Environment and Technology in History*, edited by Martin Reuss and Stephen H. Cutcliffe, 249–62. Charlottesville: University of Virginia Press.

Scott, James C.

1998   *Seeing Like a State: How Certain Schemes to Improve the Human Condition Have Failed*. New Haven, Conn.: Yale University Press.

Simone, AbdouMaliq

2004   *For the City Yet to Come: Changing African Life in Four Cities*. Durham, N.C.: Duke University Press.

Singleton, Vicky

2010   "Good Farming: Control or Care?" In *Care in Practice: On Tinkering in Clinics, Homes and Farms*, edited by Annemarie Mol, Ingunn Moser, and Jeannette Pols, 235–56. Bielefield: Transcript.

Stoetzer, Bettina

2018   "Ruderal Ecologies: Rethinking Nature, Migration, and the Urban Landscape in Berlin." *Cultural Anthropology* 33, no. 2: 295–323. https://doi.org/10.14506/ca33.2.09.

Sunder Rajan, Kaushik

2006   *Biocapital: The Constitution of Postgenomic Life*. Durham, N.C.: Duke University Press.

Sze, Julie

2015   *Fantasy Islands: Chinese Dreams and Ecological Fears in an Age of Climate Crisis*. Oakland: University of California Press.

Tansley, A. G.

1935   "The Use and Abuse of Vegetational Concepts and Terms." *Ecology* 16, no. 3: 284–307. https://doi.org/10.2307/1930070.

Tomba, Luigi

2006   Comments on "Contesting Spatial Modernity in Late-Socialist China" by Zhang Li. *Current Anthropology* 47, no. 3: 480–81. https://doi-org.libproxy.mit.edu/10.1086/503063.

Tsing, Anna Lowenhaupt

2015   *The Mushroom at the End of the World: On the Possibility of Life in Capitalist Ruins*. Princeton, N.J.: Princeton University Press.

Vaughn, Sarah E.

2017   "Disappearing Mangroves: The Epistemic Politics of Climate Adaptation in Guyana." *Cultural Anthropology* 32, no. 2: 242–68. https://doi.org/10.14506/ca32.2.07.

Vora, Kalindi

2015   *Life Support: Biocapital and the New History of Outsourced Labor*. Minneapolis: University of Minnesota Press.

Weeks, Kathi

2011   *The Problem with Work: Feminism, Marxism, Antiwork Politics, and Postwork Imaginaries*. Durham, N.C.: Duke University Press.

White, Richard

1996   *The Organic Machine: The Remaking of the Columbia River*. New York: Hill and Wang.

Worster, Donald

1994   *Nature's Economy: A History of Ecological Ideas*. Cambridge: Cambridge University Press.

Yuan, Zengwei, Jun Bi, and Yuichi Moriguichi

2006   "The Circular Economy: A New Development Strategy in China." *Journal of Industrial Ecology* 10, nos. 1–2: 4–8. https://doi.org/10.1162/108819806775545321.

Zhang, Amy

2014   "Rational Resistance: Homeowner Contention against Waste Incineration in
         Guangzhou." *China Perspectives*, no. 2014/2: 46–52. http://journals.openedition.org
         /chinaperspectives/6458.

2019   "Invisible Labouring Bodies: Waste Work as Infrastructure in China." *Made
         in China Journal* 4, no. 2: 98–102. https://madeinchinajournal.com/2019/07/23
         /invisible-labouring-bodies%EF%BB%BF-waste-work-as-infrastructure-in
         -china/.

Zhang, Lei, Arthur P. J. Mol, and David A. Sonnenfeld

2007   "The Interpretation of Ecological Modernisation in China." *Environmental Politics*
         16, no. 4: 659–68. https://doi.org/10.1080/09644010701419170.

Zhang, Li

2010   *In Search of Paradise: Middle-Class Living in a Chinese Metropolis*. Ithaca, N.Y.:
         Cornell University Press.

—

ENERGY AND ENERGY ALTERNATIVES

INTRODUCTION

As a species, humans stand apart for the ability to harness significant sources of energy from our surroundings—whether from food, fire, water, air, wind, fossil fuels, or nuclear forces. The field of environmental anthropology examines connections between human societies and their sources of energy, across the realms of energy exploration, production, distribution, and waste. Increasingly environmental anthropologists attend to how energy systems exacerbate forms of social inequality, perpetuate disproportionate levels of risk or harm to marginalized groups, and exploit poorer regions of the world for the energy security of rich countries. These topics have led to studies of how energy access and transformation—whether the caloric intake from protein or the availability of hydropower—shape broader patterns in social organization and environmental management.

For anthropologists, therefore, questions of energy often intersect with questions of justice, as members of disenfranchised communities are frequently most affected by the toxic ramifications of energy extraction, pollution, and waste, especially through fossil fuel development. Such discriminatory patterns speak to larger societal forces that have long rested on the exploitation of people and nature for energy procurement, including

---

the systematic violence of slavery, colonialism, and war. Dominant forms of global integration facilitated by coal-powered industrial empires and the rise of petroleum as a form of geopolitical influence have often led to political violence and environmental destruction. Environmental anthropologists have studied these processes across a diversity of sites, including remote villages, energy-extraction zones, industrial corridors, and the higher echelons of energy policy and regulation. More recently, they have studied the intersection of energy innovation and finance capitalism.

Recent work in the anthropology of energy builds from this foundation, while also thinking more broadly about the concept of energy itself. Often intersecting with work in multispecies anthropology, these scholars explore how ideas of energy and relationships with potential energy sources, such as the earth, wind, and sun, are embedded within larger cultural and ecological frameworks of understanding. These differing relationships with energy sources represent particular ontological and epistemological orientations toward nature, which in turn shape how humans are compelled to act toward other animate and inanimate beings. Drawing from political ecology, this research also places locally situated relationships with energy within larger trajectories of political and economic history.

The two articles included in this theme both analyze grassroots energy activism in the United States and discuss how culturally informed ideas of energy in Indigenous and Black communities are inspiring the design of more sustainable and equitable alternative energy systems. In the first piece, Dana Powell and Dálian Long present an ethnographic description of energy activism in the Navajo community of Diné Bikéyah. They note how Navajo energy activists not only oppose harmful extractive energy practices in Indigenous territories but also propose energy alternatives with the potential to "integrate . . . with Diné geologies, philosophies, ethics, and visions for the future" (193). In the second article, Myles Lennon illustrates how questions of energy development are also questions of racial justice and argues that the "ways in which we generate electricity, heat, and fuels have historically denigrated—*de*-mattered—black lives" (213). He describes the formation of new energy alliances between energy-industry experts and antiracist activists—alliances that seek to fundamentally transform energy systems in the United States.

Both pieces show the sustainability implications of ethnographic

—

research that highlights the everyday experiences of energy. They consider energy as not only a thing to be used but also as a relational set of values. As such, energy intersects with questions of power, spirituality, sovereignty, dignity, and justice. For an energy program to be sustainable, then, it must move beyond a strictly financial or technical focus, to also incorporate the more intangible, and personal, aspects of how humans relate to energy systems. Optimistically, both case studies in this section showcase the grassroots enthusiasm and creativity that is being generated toward the goal of transforming energy systems. As Lennon argues, such examples model approaches that empower communities to "orient . . . energy transitions toward deeper intersectional transformations" with the potential to support the sustained well-being of all people and forms of nature (216).

DISCUSSION QUESTIONS

1. Both articles note a variety of ways people define *energy*. What are some examples of these different definitions? How are conceptions of energy informed by culture, politics, spirituality, and history? How do these differences matter when designing energy programs and policies? How would you define the concept of energy?

2. The case studies highlight the potential roles of grassroots energy activism, government-led policies, and the private sector in promoting more sustainable energy alternatives. How may each of these levels contribute to alternative energy solutions? What do you see as areas of potential alliances between these groups? What are potential barriers to collaboration?

3. In his description of grassroots energy activism in Black communities, Lennon argues that "energy is fundamentally a racial matter." What are some examples he uses to illustrate this idea? Do you agree? In addition to racial justice, what other social and environmental movements connect to questions of energy exploration, production, distribution, and waste, including issues of human rights, ecological health, and economic opportunity?

4. In their discussion of Navajo energy politics, the coauthors Dana Powell and Dálian Long discuss their own identities as researchers and note their personal connections to the community. For each author, what

---

was their position in respect to the community? Do you think their positions may have influenced their research or their writing? If so, how? If not, why not? Do you think authors should always include a discussion of their own identity and positionality as it relates to their research? Why or why not?

5. How does the work of environmental anthropologists studying energy provide new ways to think about human relations with nature? Do you see connections between improving energy access and justice and fundamentally rethinking how humans value nature, not merely as a source of materials and energy, but as comprised of entities with their own claims to survive and flourish on this planet?

$\textbf{5}$

LANDSCAPES OF POWER

RENEWABLE ENERGY
ACTIVISM IN DINÉ BIKÉYAH

DANA E. POWELL AND
DÁILAN J. LONG

The rough dirt road to Alice Gilmore's home twists through desert bad-lands of the northeastern Navajo (Diné) Nation, passing the Navajo Coal Mine, gray mountains of coal combustion waste (CCW) and coal seams glittering in the desert sun. These open-air piles of CCW are the leftover deposits from the Four Corners Power Plant, a 2,040-megawatt coal-fired plant twenty miles north on reservation land. As the springtime wind picks up, plumes of silvery ash billow and drift in the direction of Ms. Gilmore's home. This region is called Ram Springs, Burnham, Desert Rock, and Area Four of the Navajo Mine—depending on who is doing the naming. Local Diné people call it Denístsah bit'óh (Ram Springs) for the natural water springs that once nourished large flocks of sheep and goats, even families. Other places, such as Chíí'hagéédí (Place Where Red Sand Is Dug Out), overlap the area and are roots of kinship for local families. The

—

tribal government and the State of New Mexico call the place Burnham, though the tribe recently redrew geopolitical boundaries, generating controversy over where the Burnham community ends and the Nenahnezad community begins. Advocates of a new 1,500-megawatt coal-fired power plant slated for a half mile west of Ms. Gilmore's home refer to this region as Desert Rock, evoking a desolate, uninhabited landscape, lifeless and undeveloped. Finally, the same location is also known as Area Four North, a territorial subdivision delineated by the US Office of Surface Mining in Denver. Looking across the vast desert, such demarcations of place and identity seem absurd. How different people, with their competing interests, have named and imagined this northeastern Navajo landscape is at the heart of an ongoing debate in Navajo land, drawing interest from well beyond the reservation's borders.

The dirt road turns sharply, cutting southwest of the mine and then climbing a small rise up to the Gilmore homestead, an assortment of old weathered structures perched on a hill, treeless and exposed beneath a typically cloudless, sun-soaked, cerulean sky. I pass an old corral made of hand-hewn, rough wooden posts, sheets of tin and discarded truck tires, and a roofless, crumbling house, its sagging sandstone bricks disintegrating back into the ground from which they originated. From this vantage point, the rocky spires of the Jurassic-era Shiprock formation are visible to the west, and the dry riverbeds and stark badlands stretch onward to the east as far as the eye can see. Sunlight reflects off aluminum rooftops of homes in the distance; as in most of the reservation, neighbors dwell far apart for grazing land purposes. Beneath our feet, the dry ground is littered with bones, scraps of plywood, curls of rusted barbwire, shards of broken glass polished smooth by time and the wind, and the glitter of stones: jasper, flakes of quartz and flint. I have come to Ram Springs to join local families and activists in meeting with a group of national journalists who have traveled here to learn about energy development projects affecting Navajo communities.

I arrive early with Mike, an environmental policy specialist, and we wait quietly, scanning the vast horizon, watching for the arrival of the activists and local elders. Soon, Dáilan pulls up in a shiny four-wheel-drive pickup truck; his mother and aunt ride with him in the truck's cab. Dáilan's family resides in Burnham, and they have been resisting the Desert Rock Energy

———

FIGURE 5.1. Alice Gilmore stops to rest at her young sister's gravesite. She has been told by the Diné Power Authority (DPA) that her father long ago signed over all the family's grazing permits to the strip mine. The DPA refuses to show her written records. Her family burial areas, home, and grazing lands will all be destroyed by the new strip mine. Caption and photo by Carlan Tapp.

Project since the tribe proposed it publicly in 2003. Dáilan's mother and aunt are here, along with other older women from the area, to greet the journalists and share their stories for opposing the project. Squinting into the bold midday sun, we unload several metal folding chairs from the truck bed, arrange them for the grandmothers to sit on, and stake the flimsy legs of a tripod flip-chart easel into the hard earth. Dáilan sketches diagrams to illustrate for his elders and the visiting journalists the latest happenings with the proposed Desert Rock project. His mother and aunt sit on the open tailgate and share a thermos of hot coffee. Ms. Gilmore (figure 5.1) welcomes everyone to her home, pulling her thin shawl around her shoulders against the wind, and her daughter translates her words into English: "I want the land to be like it was before, but I know it never will be. Sometimes I really grieve for it. I mourn for it." Softly, almost inaudibly, a mine blast rumbles in the background. Black smoke rises, the ground shudders, and it will be hours before the dust and ash settle.

———

THE EVERYDAY LIFE OF ENERGY DEVELOPMENT

This recent encounter at the Gilmore homestead is part of a much broader, ongoing public, academic, and policy debate over energy development in indigenous territories.[1] Such a debate is entangled in and informed by—as well as informs—national and transnational discussions on sustainability, sovereignty, and the livelihoods of rural communities worldwide. In this chapter, we take up the theme of "Indians and energy" from a perspective that offers a primarily ethnographic analysis of a complex contemporary conjuncture. We draw upon our empirical research and experiences of engagement with the indigenous environmental justice movement in North America as a non-Native ally/anthropologist and a Navajo (Diné) activist and resident of the area in question in this chapter.[2] The work presented here addresses a crucial issue facing indigenous communities across the Americas and beyond: the confluence of lands rich in mineral resources, often expansive rural land bases, economic marginalization, political disempowerment or repression, legacies of disproportionate impacts of fossil fuel development, and, increasingly, intimate experiences with the lived effects of global climate change.[3]

We argue that struggles over energy development taken up by indigenous environmental movements increasingly not only criticize and resist but also generate thoughtful alternatives to the status quo of energy production and extraction, which has been the prevailing mode of operation, in many Native territories. In the case of the complex negotiations that make up the Desert Rock Energy Project controversy, a productive public dialogue has emerged, invigorating debate over the future of energy development for the tribe and the region and producing concrete proposals for renewable energy projects as alternatives to coal-fired electrical power production. This case illustrates how rural, place-based Native communities are responding to the pressures of contemporary energy issues, climate change, fossil fuel extraction, and renewable energy technologies. The significance of these responses reverberates far beyond Navajo land. Renewable energy activism poses an opportunity for new directions in developing sustainable economies, livelihoods, and tribal sovereignty in many locales, with yet undetermined pathways, alliances, and outcomes.[4] Furthermore, we submit that this case demonstrates the intensity of community dialogue on energy issues (voices largely omitted from national and global debates),

—

a discussion grounded in particular energy development proposals and the lives of tribal members at the front lines of these changes.[5]

THE CASE OF DESERT ROCK AND THE POWER OF ALTERNATIVES

Since the passing of the Indian Self-Determination and Education Act of 1975, American Indian tribes have exercised sovereignty by establishing and continually negotiating their own strategies of economic development. For the Navajo Nation, uranium and coal mining have been the primary sources of tribal revenue. After more than two decades of community-based critique and scholarly debates over the effects of uranium "yellow-cake" extraction, radiation exposure, and other contaminants on the health of miners and the environment (see Johnston, Dawson, and Madsen 2010), in 2005 the Navajo Nation passed the Diné Natural Resources Protection Act (DNRPA) to establish a moratorium on uranium mining on the reservation, based on Diné Fundamental Laws. Recently, Navajo Nation president Joe Shirley Jr. issued an official statement that condemned the "genocide" of Navajo people wrought by the Cold War race for nuclear weapons (which require uranium to produce the weapons' plutonium cores). He also endorsed the new book *The Navajo People and Uranium Mining*, which details the suffering and human costs exacted from families by this industry. In press statements and in a publication of his own, President Shirley stood strong against proposals to reopen uranium mines and stressed the need to protect Navajo people from renewing this destructive legacy, which largely serves outside interests of US industry and foreign policy.[6]

The same year that the Diné Natural Resources Protection Act banned uranium mining, the contested Mojave Generating Station in Nevada and its feeder mine on Navajo land, the Black Mesa Coal Mine (operated by Peabody Coal Company), closed under growing pressure from regional environmental groups, both Diné and non-Native. The groups expressed particular concern over the mine's depletion of the N-Aquifer, the primary groundwater source for humans and livestock in the Western Agency of the Navajo reservation. Many of the core groups that pushed for the Black Mesa mine closure have organized themselves into a Navajo-based alliance called the Just Transition Coalition.[7] They are requesting that the regulatory authority (California Public Utilities Commission) mandate the funds received by the utility Southern California Edison from sulfur allowance trading, because of the closure of the Mohave Generating Station, be redistributed directly into renewable energy projects that benefit the Navajo Nation and the Hopi Tribe. Their vision posits an alternative to returning to dependency on local coal resources for livelihoods and tribal revenue.[8] In sum, recent experiences of suffering from uranium extractions have become translated into tribal policy in the form of the DNRPA. And uranium, once the crucial raw material of development for national security, has now become a symbol of historical exploitation and environmental injustice against Navajo people. The moral ambiguity and uncertain investments in coal power, however, remain open and contested matters and serve as a catalyst for the formation of new coalitions and a growing number of proposals for solar and wind power development on tribal lands.[9]

These recent struggles over uranium and coal form an integral part of the background shaping the current politics and debates over the Desert Rock Energy Project (DREP), the latest energy "exploitation" or "opportunity" to emerge on the political and environmental landscape of the Navajo Nation. A microcosm of global debates over climate change, tribal sovereignty, and energy development, DREP is a focal point for examining contemporary concerns over energy development in Indian Country. In 2003 the Houston-based energy company Sithe Global Power partnered with the tribal enterprise, Diné Power Authority, to propose DREP, a 1,500-megawatt, coal-fired power plant as the newest and most expedient means of tribal economic development. The Navajo Nation Council approved the project the same year, and other alliances were established with outside investment firms and entities. Construction of the plant is proposed alongside the tribally initiated Navajo Transmission Project, which would provide the transmission lines and other grid infrastructure necessary to transport electricity from Navajo land to out-of-state utilities, the presumed purchasers of this power. The power plant would cover 600 acres of Navajo land in Burnham (Ram Springs), New Mexico, and would require a 25-square-mile mine expansion of the BHP Billiton Navajo Coal Mine, which operates north of the proposed DREP location. The Four

—

Corners Power Plant and the San Juan Generating Station, two nearby coal plants built in the 1960s, are already significant contributors to poor health and air quality in the Four Corners region.[10] The area is an intense industrial zone categorized as a "national sacrifice area" (along with southern Appalachia and parts of the Great Plains) by the Department of Energy and the Trilateral Commission; exporting power to southwestern cities overrides local public health concerns.[11]

The Desert Rock Energy Project Draft Environmental Impact Statement (DEIS), released in July 2007, notes that the clustering of existing industrial facilities and the necessary supporting infrastructure would "disproportionately impact" local communities.[12] The Desert Rock project would be a significant addition to a region already heavily dependent on coal development, and its projected emissions would amount to putting 2.8 million more vehicles on regional highways per year.[13] Its anticipated annual emissions of 12.7 million tons of carbon dioxide (CO_2), now widely recognized as a major contributor to global warming, are omitted in official discussions of the project. The project proponents' claims of "clean coal" technology coupled with sovereign immunity predominate, thus dismissing DREP's certain contribution to the overall pollution of the Four Corners region and the 15 percent increase in New Mexico's overall CO_2 emissions.[14] Yet, the Navajo Nation administration continues to promote the Desert Rock project as the central hope for tribal economic development, followed closely by the Nation's new Fire Rock Casino outside Gallup, New Mexico, and new tourist attractions in Monument Valley, Arizona. The Desert Rock controversy is unique, however, because its discourse articulates with current transnational debates on indigenous rights, self-governance, and global climate change.

Within the Navajo community, the Desert Rock issue is internally complex and contested, imbued with the experiences of coal and other extractive-industry plant workers, some of whom are now tribal leaders.[15] Many anti-mine and anti-DREP activists have (or had) family members who worked for the Black Mesa Mine or the BHP Billiton Navajo Coal Mine, further complicating the internal dynamics of the movement. These imbrications of a particular family's employment in and resistance to extractive industries form a common theme across Navajo land. Given Dáilan's upbringing as the son and brother of power plant workers, the idea of an additional coal plant at first did not unsettle him and others who live near the two existing coal plants in the area. The environmental pollution of high-impact mining was thought of as "other people's problem," and scenic views of industrial operations were the norm. Many saw the jobs offered by large industries as economic angels, delivering benefits that far outweighed any problems—and the problems themselves were kept quiet, never making the local media. Resonating with events thirty years ago in Burnham (Needham 2010), community people had to take direct action, in the form of a blockade of the proposed site, for their opposition to be taken seriously.

Since the industry's arrival in Navajo land in the early twentieth century, coal mining has become an integral part of Navajo livelihoods and cultural practices, perhaps because extractive industry is systemically embedded in the tribe's economic map as a result of the historical formation of the tribal government. Shortly after oil was discovered on reservation land, federal agencies established the Navajo Nation tribal government in 1924 as a "business council" to enable mineral extraction on reservation lands held in federal trust. Modeled on the federal three-branch system, this new governing structure conflicted with and departed from customary practices of decentralized, regionally based self-governance (Naach'id) and functioned instead to accommodate an emerging US energy paradigm and its attending foreign policy interests.[16] This paradigm of fossil fuel–based extractive industries and uranium mining, in particular, ushered in decades of steady environmental devastation and significant health problems, especially among Navajo mineworkers and plant employees.[17] Such experiences have led many tribal members to mistrust and criticize what they see as a colonized tribal council and its decisions on further fossil fuel development, given the many risks of coal investments.[18]

Like many struggles around development issues, the present controversy over Desert Rock has roots in the Burnham community at least as deep and compressed as the coal beds themselves. Andrew Needham (2010) describes this complex history of energy activism in Burnham, which grew out of the American Indian Movement and a new moment of Navajo nationalism in the 1970s. Whereas Needham found 1970s resisters categorically rejecting energy development, however, we find that many contemporary critics, though rejecting coal development, are promoting

—

alternative forms of energy production. But many tribal members are ambivalent about the unknown cultural and environmental effects of wind and solar installations, and others continue to support coal development primarily for the sake of on-reservation employment. Like the earlier coal gasification plants that were proposed (and eventually defeated through local opposition), the contemporary proponents of Desert Rock also promise employment that will keep Navajo kids "at home," as well as millions of dollars of tribal revenue, which would advance the reservation's standard of living and provide electricity for export to southwestern cities. Unlike the earlier Burnham proposals, however, DREP's advocates laud the possibility of at least partial tribal ownership of the power plant—a move that would realize a dream of former chairman of the Navajo Nation Peter MacDonald, sovereign technologies.[19] Once again, Burnham has become a site of contention over coal-fired power, and community members' 2003–2008 letters to the editor of the *Navajo Times* strike eerie chords of resonance with letters written thirty years before. Current and local expressions of resistance against DREP are part of this long-standing, enduring struggle and Burnham residents' identities as environmental and human rights activists.[20] And just as local opposition in Burnham eventually made pursuing the coal gasification plants in the 1970s "politically impossible" for that administration, current residents and their allies are working to do the same today. This is not a simple case of history repeating itself, however, because the outcomes are unpredictable, the alliances are new, and, more important, the locally based groups are going beyond criticism to propose and demonstrate the use of sun and wind resources as alternative methods of energy development.

The public's mistrust of the Desert Rock Energy Project was palpable and quantifiable at the ten public hearings on the Desert Rock DEIS that occurred on the reservation and in the greater region during the summer of 2007. Across all ten hearings, less than 5 percent of the speakers publicly supported the DREP proposal, and approximately 95 percent of speakers voiced unequivocal opposition. At the end of the DEIS comment period, 54,000 public comments were submitted to the Bureau of Indian Affairs. At one hearing on the reservation, a 74-year-old retired teacher walked purposively to the microphone at the front of the chapter house and expressed her thoughts in a brief statement she introduced as "The Sacrifice of the

Glittering World," alluding to Diné philosophical teachings that the present is a fifth and "glittering" world. Questioning the 1,500 jobs promised by DREP proponents, she spoke of her many years of experience as an educator and warned, "Young people shouldn't be employed in these dangerous, low-level jobs. They need to be educated to think critically. . . . The Nation has chosen to make the Four Corners region a sacrifice area."[21] Subsequent speakers echoed her caution, especially in the discussion of the number and quality of jobs that the plant might provide, arguing that these would be a mere "drop in the bucket" toward improving the tribe's current rates of stifling unemployment and crushing poverty.[22] Furthermore, these speakers argued, the risk to human and animal health and the landscape does not make these few jobs worth pursuing.[23]

ROOTS OF RESISTANCE: COMMUNITY ORGANIZING, BODIES, AND GENDER

The public hearings on the Draft Environmental Impact Statement for the Desert Rock Energy Project garnered local and national media attention, much of which focused on overviews of environmental campaigns, policies, and economics. These stories attracted new allies to the movement but largely overlooked the voices of a diverse spectrum of tribal members and the ways in which specific historical experiences background the present opposition to Desert Rock. In rural communities throughout the Navajo Nation, we find that most individuals do not speak about DREP without referencing a history of injustices and environmental traumas brought on by energy development in recent decades. As part of a broader study, a Burnham resident conducted more than forty qualitative interviews (primarily in the Navajo language) with various project stakeholders, including many Diné people residing around the proposed power plant location.[24] The findings of this three-year ethnographic project demonstrate that the well-being of people and their livestock is the core concern of the local community members opposing DREP. Many of these testimonies point to deep attachments to place, through specific memories and stories, and describe a landscape very much animated and made meaningful by oral histories and place-based knowledge.[25] Many of the testimonies were from elderly area residents—primarily women—who retain the cultural authority in the Diné tradition to make decisions concerning land use and livestock. These elders have witnessed generations of change in their area, including the arrival of the two existing power plants in the 1960s, but remain unconvinced that DREP would satisfy their long-standing desires for household electricity and running water, quality employment for their children, and prosperity overall. Addressing the possibility of being relocated from her land to make way for the power plant, one resident stated:

> I do not wish to move elsewhere. I live right here. This is my birthplace, a place where my father raised us, a place where my father sang his blessing songs and said his prayers for us and his grandchildren. His livelihood still remains. The places he herded sheep are still alive with memories. My life remains here and on the farm where I also live. . . . I lost five of my female cows, and each of them was with an unborn calf during the winter from drinking contaminated water in the mining area. The energy company creates hopes and dreams it does not keep.[26]

Specific attachments to place and to tangible and intangible relationships are iterated with a sense of betrayal. Oral teachings, emplaced memories, and customary know-how become secondary to permits that now define and regulate land ownership.

This particular elder and the woman conducting the interview are part of a much longer history of Navajo women's leadership outside formal political structures, especially in matters related to the health of the land and people. The nonprofit organization Diné Citizens Against Ruining Our Environment (Diné CARE) has been central to much of this work on the reservation, from resisting toxic waste storage facilities, to timber harvesting in the reservation's pine, juniper, and pinon forests.[27] Diné CARE is a reservation-wide, decentralized network of Navajo activists that has been primarily women-led since its inception. In 1987 a toxic waste incinerator proposed for the Navajo chapter of Dilkon, Arizona, spurred this first Navajo grassroots organization to address environmental issues on the reservation. Families and community members mobilized to defeat the incinerator proposal, and their success story traveled, prompting other Native and non-Native communities to seek Diné CARE's support

—

in countering industrial and extractive development projects in the 1990s. Operating as more of a network or web than as a single-site institution, Diné CARE has successfully tackled projects such as the timber harvesting in the Navajo sacred male deity, the Chuska Mountains, bringing about a moratorium on additional harvesting and helping spawn a new generation of activists. Additionally, working with regional and national groups, Diné CARE helped form a five-state coalition that in 2000 helped amend the 1990 Radiation Exposure Compensation Act (RECA), affecting thousands of Navajo (and non-Navajo) uranium miners.

In 2004 Burnham resident and community organizer Sarah Jane White joined with Diné CARE to expose the dangers of the proposed power plant. In response to the tribe's 2003 proposal for DREP, White formed the grassroots group Doodá Desert Rock (No Desert Rock) with the support of Diné CARE.[28] White and Diné CARE's campaign work is geared toward Navajo-centered education about cultural and environmental protection that encourages tribal members to make informed opinions and decisions about energy developments in their communities. White learned of the proposed Desert Rock power plant and translated the issue into the Navajo language for non-English speakers—often with much difficulty, because concepts such as "climate change" and even "coal-fired power plant" (expressed as "giant metal stove") do not translate smoothly or without complex explication. Drawing upon Navajo cultural philosophies and storytelling traditions, White relayed her message to families throughout the vast desert expanse of northwestern New Mexico, traveling door-to-door, following a method of k'é (building relations) and producing knowledge that had already proved central to the success of Diné CARE's campaigns in the 1980s and 1990s. By providing Navajo communities with the resources and support needed to organize at the grassroots level, Diné CARE advances the belief that Diné people are capable of nurturing a sustainable and healthy environment, if provided with solid financial, technical, and spiritual support.[29]

For many Navajo activists, their opposition finds roots in Navajo creation stories, which point to the primary role of women in shaping the lifeways and ethics of the Diné in their ancestral territory. Oral histories, which remain a core method of transmitting these values to new generations, are grounded in stories pertaining to specific locations within a

---

landscape defined by the Diné's four sacred mountains, each one dense with a specific historical knowledge.[30] These four mountains mark the boundaries of Navajo lands (Diné Bikeyah), which are not contiguous with the present-day political boundaries of the reservation. Asdzáá Náádlehe (Changing Woman) is the central Navajo deity, whose teachings and actions form the backbone of Navajo identity, ethics, and ritual. In the story of Navajo genesis, the Navajo people were created from balls of corn pollen and rubbings from the flesh of her own body.[31] Changing Woman formed land and sacred epidermal matter into new, human flesh. Many connect this intimate relationship with an imperative to protect the land against present threats: protection of the land is protection of the embodied self. As ecofeminists and many Native feminists argue, women's bodies are often the first and hardest hit by environmental pollution and ecological degradation, so "everywhere, women [are] the first to protest against environmental destruction."[32] The thickness of these connections between gender, sickness, and environmental activism exceeds the scope of this chapter. It is explored elsewhere in feminist arguments that the health of the environment is materially and metaphorically linked with women's bodies, which are also sites of inscription for racism, colonialism, and other forms of violence.[33]

Historically, Diné society has followed matrilineal kinship arrangements, and Navajo women have organized communities in a manner consistent with power dynamics inherent in a complex clan system first created by Asdzáá Náádlehe. Individuals identify foremost with the clan of their mother, then that of their father and grandparents in the Diné language. Customarily, Navajo elders identify younger generations as "grandchild," "son" or "daughter," "brother" or "sister," which designate clan relationships but do not correspond to the sanguine relations implied in English usage of these same terms. The manifestation of these relationships is essentially at work in Diné grassroots organizing and knowledge formation but is largely absent in the decision-making processes, bureaucratic systems, and planning models in place in tribal governance.[34] As we observed in our work and as many of our (activist and non-activist) consultants articulated, matriarchal patterns and practices are most evident in Navajo communities, whereas patriarchal systems dominate the political, social, and economic practices and agendas of the tribal council.

—

This gendered friction around notions of authorized political leadership is displayed, and rendered more complex, in a recent *Navajo Times* political cartoon depicting US Senator Hillary Clinton (endorsed by the Navajo Nation president Joe Shirley Jr. in her 2008 Democratic Party nomination race against Barack Obama) being encouraged, despite criticism from "Traditionalists . . . [who feel] that a woman should not be a leader."[35] Such support for Clinton, however, contradicts the negative opinions surrounding a Navajo woman's recent bid for the Navajo presidency.

Male privilege, concentrated and reproduced through positions of power, often omits or ignores the ethical and everyday concerns of many Diné (and non-Diné) women about domestic and household economies and a healthful future for the environment and for their children. Many women opposing Desert Rock openly link government policies on energy development and their negative outcomes directly to effects experienced by communities, identifying male decision makers as primarily concerned with the welfare of the political and economic system. The Desert Rock struggle reveals these gendered differences in understanding, analyzing, and acting upon energy development issues, as evidenced by the public hearings, letters to the editor, grassroots leadership, and opinions of key actors involved in this debate.

TECHNOLOGIES OF ATONEMENT: NAVAJO GRASSROOTS PROPOSALS FOR RENEWABLE POWER

Navajo spiritual leaders understand the Diné lifeway to be a daily ceremonial cycle that begins with morning prayer to greet the dawn deities and Father Sun and to request holistic balance with Mother Earth throughout the day.[36] The physical manifestation of one's respect for elements considered natural and sacred is the most appropriate display of homage to the spiritual entities that exist in the Navajo environment—an "environment" that exceeds most conventional imaginaries of "nature." The concept of k'é (relations) is integral to the Diné understanding of "environment," and it is the justification of Navajo resistance to environmental degradation.[37] The Navajo environment is called Nahasdzáán dóó yádílhíl (Mother Earth and Father Sky) and implicitly carries with it an imperative and inherent responsibility to maintain hozhó (beauty and balance) by virtue of the

—

álch'i silá concept (natural pairs face/relate to each other).[38] The epicenter of the bipolar (Earth and Sky) opposites, Nahasdzáán dóó yádílhíl, is tranquility of individual, community, and environment. In this context, toxic pollution violates the spiritual essence of sacred elements such as air and water, creating imbalances in Navajo social, economic, and spiritual life. These imbalances can lead to physical and psychological illnesses manifested in human bodies. Sickness can be healed, however, through atonements and specific ceremonies. As many elders argue, imbalances may be brought on by the violation of various taboos, including engagement with an energy paradigm that does not acknowledge the spiritual landscape central to Diné identities. The Diné environment, in its more expansive definition, has been the site of outside intervention and intrusion at least since the Navajo Long Walk of 1868, when the Diné were displaced from their original homelands through calculated acts of direct and structural violence. Now, through the various technologies of fossil fuel energy development and in collusion with the energy industry, the Navajo government violates its mandate to protect the people, instead participating firsthand in the displacement of constituents from their lands.

Most Diné CARE organizers do not consider themselves "environmentalists" as such, nor do many consider themselves "activists." These slippery categories of identification are used loosely yet are heavily laden, circulating and accruing meaning through a kind of abstract global environmentalism but often taking on specific meanings in particular historic or cultural locations.[39] As Kosek shows, in the cultural politics of nature in northern New Mexico, to be an "environmentalist" is often code for "white" or "outsider" or other specialized and racialized terms of exclusion in an ecologically distinct, ethnically diverse, and historically Native and Hispano region.[40] In this context, it comes as no surprise that many Diné citizens would reject the identification of "environmentalist," despite regional and national media coverage that represents them as such. Cutting across religious, employment, and geographic distinctions, many Diné consider a land-based ethic to be the driving force behind actively seeking to (re)balance many aspects of the Navajo economy and human–nonhuman relationships. In this sense, many activists see their work to protect the land and people as, at its core, work to preserve Navajo cultural identity and knowledge. Emphasizing the intimate links between cultural and

—

environmental survival, Native feminist scholar Andrea Smith argues that "cultural genocide is the result when Native land bases are not protected."[41]

Because Navajo teachings emphasize that the Earth and its natural elements are sacred and active entities, violating certain ethical boundaries (such as removing uranium from the Earth's interior) brings serious repercussions, many of which are so serious as to defy any attempt at atonement. This philosophy is known as the Diné Fundamental Laws (DFL), ethical guidelines for the Diné lifeway, codified and adopted as law in 2005 by the Navajo Nation Council from polyvocal, unwritten transmission through oral histories. Although the Diné Natural Resources Protection Act (DNRPA) of 2005 drew upon the authority of Diné Fundamental Laws to pass a ban on uranium mining, the tribal council takes a contradictory stance on the DFL when discussing Desert Rock.[42] The Diné Policy Institute, a research and policy analysis center located at the tribal college in Tsaile, Arizona, has determined through its collective research that DREP does not comply with the DFL.[43] The application and implementation of these research findings and of the DFL itself, however, remain open and contested matters of intellectual and political debate.[44]

Diné CARE, along with many groups and individuals across the reservation, hopes that development decisions made by and for the Navajo Nation will follow the spirit of the DFL and the pathways of oral teachings that promote forward, critical thinking and planning (nitsahakéés and nahat'a, respectively). This pathway is navigable when all are held accountable to the core concepts of k'é and hozhó and the ethical principles rooted in Diné creation stories. For instance, Jóhonaa'éí, the Sun God, extended solar rays (sháándíín) that impregnated Asdzáá Náádlehe with the Hero Twins, Monster Slayer and Born-for-Water. These sun rays generated the energy needed for the continuation of life and all the Navajo generations and clans that have followed. Oral histories such as this, as well as related understandings of cultural mythologies, receive new meanings through contemporary energy issues and current discourse on sustainable development and climate change. The work to advance renewable energy projects on Navajo lands provides one example of such transformation of meanings. Navajo tribal members understand the controversial legacy of fossil fuel energy development on Navajo lands, but many also envision more sustainable ways of development, ones that comport with the DFL.

—

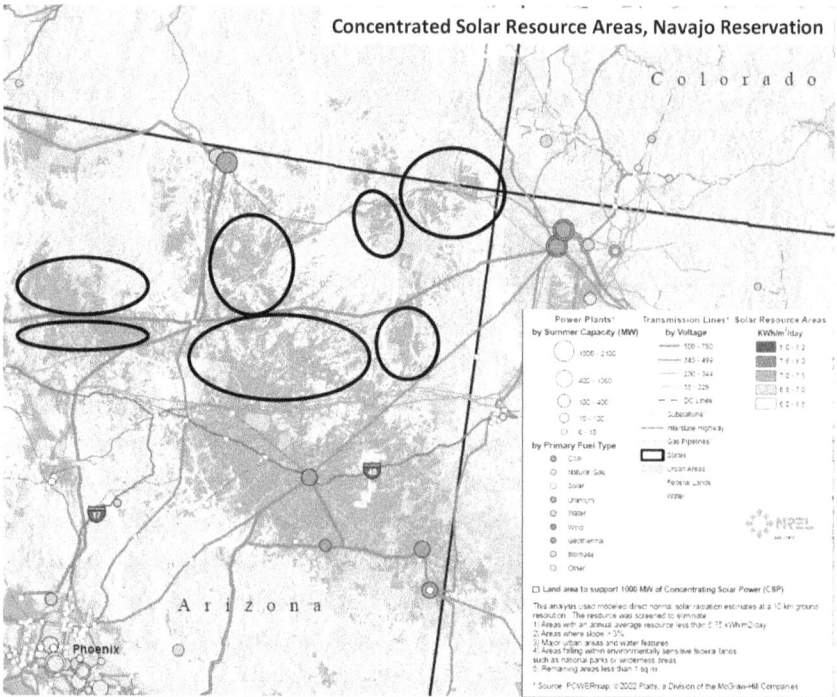

FIGURE 5.2. Navajo solar resources map. Courtesy of National Renewable Energy Laboratory.

Wind and solar resources are plentiful on the reservation, as documented by Department of Energy and National Renewable Energy Laboratory research (figure 5.2). Customary Diné epistemology teaches that the sun and the wind are sacred life-givers, supporting the healthy development of new life when revered and protected from contamination.

In January 2008, Diné CARE, in partnership with the environmental consulting group Ecos Consulting of Durango, Colorado, released a report in response to the Desert Rock proposal and its attending Draft Environmental Impact Statement. The report provides a prescriptive renewable energy analysis and roadmap that conveys customary Navajo understandings of the environment and advances the applicability of such understandings to Navajo energy development. The report, *Energy and Economic Alternatives to Desert Rock*, is tangible proof of Diné tribal members' creative and viable solutions to contemporary problems facing the tribe. In particular, the Navajo Nation is geographically positioned to develop its solar capacity: "The Southwest has solar energy resources that are among the best in the world according to the Solar Energy Industries Association, presenting great opportunities for solar development in the area."[45] "The region's high quality solar resources are evident . . . these available resources are proximate to existing and proposed transmission lines and they dwarf the amount of energy available from excavating and burning Navajo coal over the coming century."[46]

The report reflects a cultural vision historically grounded in Navajo creation stories, philosophy, and DFL. It demonstrates that historic Navajo values are dynamic and flexible and can be applied to and reinvigorated by contemporary technologies. Parabolic troughs, solar dishes and engines, and solar power towers are three systems that would perform well on the Navajo Nation, depending on the materials that make up typical commercial photovoltaic cells. At the time of this writing, renewable energy projects are planned for many areas throughout the Southwest, on and off tribal lands. In March 2008 the German company Schott AG broke ground in Albuquerque, New Mexico, to manufacture solar technology equipment.[47] The Native-owned Sacred Power Corporation continues to install solar systems on both Navajo and Pueblo residential dwellings and on commercial and government buildings in New Mexico and Arizona. On March 14, 2008, the Navajo-Hopi Land Commission of the Navajo Nation asked the US Congress to appropriate funds for a large-scale solar energy project at Paragon Ranch in New Mexico, which would provide power for Navajo families and for export to off-reservation markets.[48]

Wind development is also viable on the Navajo Nation and in the greater Southwest. For example, in December 2007 the Nambé Pueblo partnered with Green Energy Wind to build a 300-megawatt wind farm near Santa Fe, New Mexico.[49] In Diné philosophy, wind (nílch'i) is the breath of life, visible in the whorls on all peoples' fingertips. Its natural movement, harnessed by turbine technology, would produce electrical power on the Navajo Nation for Navajo families and institutions. The report details this research:

> Extensive research on windy lands, utilizing Geographic Information Systems (GIS) has been performed by Sustainable Energy Solutions at NAU (Northern Arizona University), including a report entitled

—

Navajo Wind Energy Development Exclusions: An Analysis of Land Suitable for Wind Energy Development on the Navajo Nation. NAU has found potential Navajo Nation wind capacity within Arizona lands alone at a 70-meter hub height to be over 11,000 MW. Of this, 1,215 MW is particularly high-value Class 4 to Class 7 resource wind. This is total wind capacity on windy land that is also developable, meaning that the lands are not in parks, wetlands, slopes, canyons, etc.[50]

Additional examples of current viable wind projects are the proposed Grey Mountain Wind Farm project near Cameron, Arizona, in the southwestern corner of the Navajo Nation, where anemometers have been collecting wind data for more than a year; the Sunshine Wind Park in eastern Coconino County, Arizona; and the San Juan Mesa Wind Project in east-central New Mexico.

The *Energy and Economic Alternatives to Desert Rock* report found that energy services equivalent to those proposed from Desert Rock could be delivered by a mixture of wind and solar power and natural gas facilities constructed on the Navajo Nation. This, combined with continued growth in utility-funded, energy-efficiency programs in the target power markets of Nevada and Arizona, means that the overall cost of delivered energy would be less than that of Desert Rock. The report finds that renewable energy projects create 80 percent more construction jobs and five times as many long-term operations and maintenance jobs—increased and higher-quality employment being one of the central concerns of the community, nongovernmental organizations, and tribal officials. Moreover, the report finds that solar and wind power can provide greater indirect job creation and more economic multipliers within the regional economy, making the net economic benefits of the renewable energy scenario approximately four times those proposed for Desert Rock.[51] Although the report was initially drafted as a concrete response to the Desert Rock Energy Project proposal during the Environmental Impact Statement process, its analysis is intended to be an energy plan and a vision for the future of the Navajo Nation and the greater region. The technical, traditional, and policy-related knowledge that went into this report is a tool for community-based education on energy development, climate change, and alternative economic possibilities. Culturally specific contextualization and

—

translation into the Diné language make it possible for the report to speak not only to renewable energy experts but also to a wide range of concerned citizens, tribal leaders, larger nongovernmental organizations, and policy researchers.

NATIVE ENVIRONMENTAL JUSTICE: CATALYSTS AND CONNECTIONS

Contemporary debates on the Navajo Nation form a microcosm of struggles in Native communities across North America and around the world. Therefore, the controversy surrounding the Desert Rock Energy Project tells a global story with implications reaching far beyond the geopolitical boundaries of the Navajo Nation. Coal power versus (or in addition to) wind and solar power is an urgent and open question facing "energy-rich" tribes, primarily those western tribes whose lands contain subterranean minerals. Notably, this question is increasingly political in the context of global climate change, emerging global markets for carbon trading, and a growing pan-Indianism evidenced by the newly formed Indigenous Peoples' Caucus and the United Nations Seventh Permanent Forum on Indigenous Peoples. As Garrit Voggesser (2010) details, recent changes in federal energy policy (especially since 2005) and new Department of Energy (DOE) funding sources have created the conditions for renewable energy projects to take hold in Indian Country more rapidly and at larger scales than ever before. In addition to federal funding, a network of grassroots and nonprofit funders are supporting leadership and piloting projects in tribal renewable energy projects.

Despite this complex interplay of enduring challenges, fresh opportunities, and emerging players, the experiences of Native peoples as they relate to the geopolitics of power production remain largely underexamined in environmental justice literature.[52] A full review of the history of environmental justice movements in the United States and related literatures is beyond the scope of this chapter but can be found in interdisciplinary works elsewhere.[53] At stake is the ability to perceive significant historical patterns: the 1987–1989 struggle over the proposed toxic waste dump on the Navajo Nation in Dilkon, Arizona, launched not only Diné CARE but also a national and transnational Native environmental justice

—

movement through the formation of new organizations, new relationships, critical analyses, and energy development campaigns. In this movement, which continues to travel transnationally and articulate (in fact, create) indigenous communities worldwide, the burgeoning question of "green technologies" is not simply economic; it is also deeply cultural, political, spiritual, and social.

As mentioned briefly above, in the late 1980s in Dilkon, Arizona, on the Navajo Nation, the tribe proposed an economic development scheme to build a large-scale medical waste incinerator, treatment, and storage facility in the community. Confronting this proposal as "toxic" and "culturally insensitive" (because of customary Diné perspectives on death and the disposal of bodies), one activist describes how many in the community rejected this proposal. In particular, "the matriarchs in Dilkon came forward, and talked about life in its entirety."[54] News of the successful defeat of the toxic waste treatment facility in the tiny community of Dilkon reached Native and non-Native communities across the country, and in 1990, local activists hosted a gathering called "Protecting Mother Earth." Supporters came from as far away as the Qualla Boundary (Cherokee, North Carolina) and Anishanaabe territory (Minnesota) to camp out for several days and share their experiences and critical analyses of human rights, social justice, and environmental issues in their homelands. This event helped create the Indigenous Environmental Network (IEN), which has continued to hold Protecting Mother Earth gatherings all across the country every other year since 1990. This encounter also spawned movements at multiple and overlapping scales: a reservation-wide/regional movement continues today in the form of community-based organizations from the east to the west of Navajo land, and a national/transnational movement continues today through the work of IEN and other affiliated Native environmental justice organizations. At all levels, these movements focus on the environmental, social, and cultural effects of energy development on Native territories.

At the same time, in the late 1980s an event occurred that implicated the federal government in human rights transgressions against Native communities and helped support the formation of these new, nongovernmental, Native environmental justice organizations. Greenpeace and other groups had been working on uncovering information related to radiation exposure experimentation that occurred during the Cold War period of advances in nuclear technology. In 1994 President Clinton's former energy secretary Hazel O'Leary released previously classified information confirming that the federal government knowingly removed contaminated soil from underground nuclear test sites on Western Shoshone territory (at the United States' Nevada Test Site for nuclear weapons) and buried the material in the rural northwestern Alaska Native community of Point Hope, Alaska, without informing local residents of the risks.[55] This was part of the Atomic Energy Commission's experimental study of the impacts of radioactive fallout on the Arctic environment—and, by extension, on the Arctic's human and nonhuman inhabitants. The US government's intentional deception of the American public in a secret series of toxic experiments was later exposed. This event in Alaska became an organizing force and mobilized many Native and non-Native people to call on the Department of Energy for a cleanup of the Point Hope site. New exposure of nuclear contamination of US populations, the momentum of the antinuclear movement and environmental groups, and the toxic waste treatment facility struggle on the Navajo Nation all helped launch national campaigns such as Honor the Earth and the Indigenous Environmental Network.

For the organization Honor the Earth, confronting and attempting to transform the current paradigm of energy development on tribal lands is about "energy sovereignty" and "energy justice," but of a different kind than has been seen before. This discourse is familiar in that assertions of sovereignty and justice were central to the 1980s mission of the Council of Energy Resource Tribes (CERT) in organizing tribes for greater control over the production and "prudent development" of their energy mineral resources. But Native environmental justice organizations such as Honor the Earth and IEN are distinct in their approaches to technology, calling specifically for investment in wind and solar power to position tribes to lead the country in "green, or at least greener, energy economies."[56]

> Reservations are communities, and the question is, how do you create a sustainable and self-sufficient community? At the same time that we're advocating for this tremendous potential for Native lands to be a hub for renewable energy development that could literally help

power the Nation, we're trying to nurture community capacity, growing intellectual and technical skills, and demonstrating the viability
of a new local energy economy. We are dealing on a grassroots level,
going small turbine to small turbine and solar panel to solar panel
and looking at the benefits of creating renewable energy systems that
foster community.[57]

This vision is being implemented through pilot renewable energy projects, community education, and youth and elder trainings, evidenced by
Honor the Earth's half-dozen ongoing renewable energy projects in diverse
indigenous territories, ranging from a recently installed 65-kilowatt wind
turbine powering the tribal radio station on the Pine Ridge Lakota reservation, to solar heating panel installations for homes and community centers
on the Northern Cheyenne reservation.[58]

Concurrent with this movement's work on alternative energy is work
among tribal governments, energy entrepreneurs, and state agencies. Federal funding sources such as the Department of Energy's Tribal Energy
Program have made more resources available to tribes for research, technical assistance, ongoing educational workshops, and hardware installations
through a proposal and feasibility process.[59] In the private realm, companies such as the Hopi-based NativeSun and part-Diné-owned GeoTechnika
continue to offer renewable energy workshops and hands-on instructional
installations of small-scale systems on residential and community buildings. At a recent training conducted by two of these entrepreneurs (both
women, one Diné) at a Navajo chapter house, the majority of the participants were middle-aged and elderly women from the community who
wanted to find out how they could bring power out to their rural, off-
grid homes and upgrade solar photovoltaic systems installed in the 1980s.
Many of these participants expressed their frustration at having requested
for years without success the extension of electrical power lines to their
homes, despite the transmission lines stretching across their grazing territories within sight of their homes, carrying power to urban settlements.[60]
Small companies such as these often work community by community, in
tandem with tribal and state governments, installing individual systems
and offering technical trainings.

The Navajo Nation is working to strengthen its own renewable energy

---

projects, such as the solar photovoltaic systems installed on homes throughout the Navajo Nation by the tribally owned Navajo Tribal Utility Authority and the large-scale Paragon Ranch Solar Project recently announced by
the Navajo-Hopi Land Commission. Such initiatives—which require collaboration among diverse tribal and nontribal entities—point to the complex networks and unlikely alliances produced through alternative energy
development in Indian Country. The emphasis of this chapter is on the
grassroots, Native environmental justice movements and their small-scale
but big-vision projects, which sometimes (but not always) intersect with
the interests of private entrepreneurs and governmental agencies involved
in renewable energy. The intersections of these diverse networks require
further research and elaboration elsewhere. It remains crucial, however,
to situate the work of these social and environmental justice movements
in the context of other initiatives occurring on tribal land. Their points of
articulation and divergence offer an opportunity to rethink the conventional boundaries and expressions of political action and imagination. In
this instance, we are witnessing the definition of natural resources expand
from the subterranean to the atmospheric, and instead of a collision of the
technological with the spiritual, as we might expect, we see new modes of
integration.[61]

SACRED EPISTEMOLOGIES, GEOLOGIES, AND MODERN TECHNOLOGIES

As mentioned above in the discussion of Diné Fundamental Laws, Native
environmental movements often have their roots in indigenous ontologies and epistemologies—recognitions of particular ways of being in and
knowing the world. As Jennifer Nez Denetdale points out, these ways of
being and knowing are largely transmitted and transformed through Diné
oral history traditions, a practice of knowledge largely overlooked in Eurocentric or dominant narratives of US history.[62] In the Diné worldview, as
one tribal employee put it, Native environmental justice is about a "holistic
approach," which "involves looking beyond the human":

> We are the pollen of offerings made long ago, and so EJ [environ-
> mental justice] includes not just us, but it's about those who are yet to

—

come. The root understanding of our notion of EJ is from the ancestors—their knowledge and teachings. It's from white shell, turquoise,
abalone, and jet . . . it's about "the environment" in the context of
all things. . . . EJ is different in the Native context, first because the
land, or "real estate," is valued differently as reservation and as federal
trust land. Also, EJ is different because of the different, and deeper,
connections to the land held by many Native people. The belief in
Mother Earth and Father Sky and in sites that are sacred is part of
this difference.[63]

Such reflections point to what may be considered an "ontology of difference" among many Native activists and organizations.[64] Distinct and
historically particular relationships to the land and its dramatic geologic
formations, to the past, and to nonhuman others are situated in the context of a neo-colonialism critique and a normative notion of social and
environmental justice. This "ontology of difference" is evident at multiple
scales of the movement, from the Indigenous Environmental Network's
efforts at the climate change summit in Bali, Indonesia, and at ongoing
intertribal gatherings, to Diné CARE's deployment of Diné Fundamental
Laws in its renewable energy advocacy. But this is not a totalizing, complete, or essentialist difference, nor an anti-modernist position. In fact,
Native environmental justice movements overall are not essentially anti-
capitalist, nor do they take capitalism as a uniform, universal enemy (as
do some of their peers in the global justice movement). They are using
their critical difference to call for a novel approach to economic practices
and profit-seeking ventures. In academic, activist, and governance arenas,
many are interrogating the subtle and nuanced meanings of *alternative* and
development:[65]

> The agenda in the US is towards pushing utility-scale, centralized
> renewable-energy systems such as wind and solar, based upon an
> exportation-orientated economic system that views energy produc-
> tion as a commodity. These systems are not sustainable. They only
> prolong large energy structures that view energy production to meet
> an industrial growth system. Without reevaluating what we mean as
> an "alternative energy system," I am concerned we will have wind and

———

solar systems built on the same capitalist model that is depleting the abilities of Mother Earth to meet the needs of an industrialized world. I am an advocate for our Native Nations to develop wind and solar, but most of our tribes have traditional belief systems that must guide us in these forms of development. When we, as Native Nations, create massive wind-power projects, we must have ceremonies to obtain permission to utilize the sacred elements—to harness and process wind and sun into electricity that will be exported off our Native lands into these colonial grid systems that don't directly benefit our people. So how do we, as Diné, or Dakota, or any other Native tribes, reconcile the approach and model of energy development we engage in? We've only begun to ask these questions.[66]

As this suggests, many questions regarding the cultural aspects of energy development remain indeterminate and contested, including—perhaps especially—those concerning renewable energy technologies. The Native environmental justice movement is indeed taking up these difficult questions through its own research and analysis, publications, events, presentations, and organizing work. Diné CARE's *Economic and Energy Alternatives to Desert Rock* report addresses such concerns as it situates its call for renewable energy technologies within a broader cultural framework. But the shift from the Burnham-based coal power activism of the 1970s to the Burnham-based coal power activism of the early 2000s is that no longer does energy development equate to the enemy or a monster; no longer is resistance the reason for the existence of activist identities. Instead, a dynamic analysis and debate are emerging about which specific technologies might integrate (and at what scales) with Diné geologies, philosophies, ethics, and visions for the future.

CONCLUSIONS AND NEW DIRECTIONS

The Desert Rock debate has become a convergence point for concerns over governance, indigeneity, and sovereignty. We see clearly how the experiences of specific places shape how people understand the exploitations and opportunities of energy development. Interestingly, calls for renewable, decentralized power production parallel calls for greater decentralization and autonomy in tribal governance. This turn in Native environmental justice movements toward renewable energy technologies and new practices of democracy indicates a new moment of opportunity, though still precarious and unpredictable.

In Diné Bikeyah, landscapes damaged by uranium and coal mining are the same landscapes that offer possibilities for new forms of power and new partnerships among tribal governments, grassroots activists, federal agencies, energy entrepreneurs, and even industry. Andrew Needham (2010) describes how 1970s activists categorically "objected to energy development itself" and felt that "any participation of the tribe in energy development contradicted the very idea of being Navajo." But nongovernmental organizations, young Diné activists, and tribal government leaders presently are working together on a different approach, seeing renewable energy and a broader "green economy" as hope for a transition toward a renewed reservation economy less dependent on extractive industry and "boom or bust" models. These partnerships are debating energy policies and technologies for the tribe and its local chapters with implications that go beyond local debates to join with academic and policy discussions on the human effects of climate change.[67] Old categories of "modern" and "traditional"—though still rhetorically salient—are insufficient for understanding the ways that cultural practices, Diné epistemologies, and twenty-first-century technoscience are intermingling to form new platforms for analysis and action. Being Navajo, for many of these advocates, is fully commensurate with these new technologies and is practiced through working to redirect "development" for the tribe as a whole. These debates—and the attending installations of large-scale, so-called "appropriate technologies"—remain unsettled. The contested nature of where, when, by whom, and by what means particular renewable energy projects are established raises crucial questions about democracy and participation in any "development" agenda. Likewise, cosmological and ethical considerations of what it means to harness sacred elements such as the wind and sun, which transport energy and creation stories, remain unresolved. Ultimately at stake in these evolving energy-development debates are who controls science, technology, traditional knowledge, and geopolitical space and how this affects opportunities for increased tribal sovereignty in the twenty-first century.

ACKNOWLEDGMENTS

With gratitude, we recognize the funding agencies that have supported our work, helping to make this research possible: Dana acknowledges support from The Wenner-Gren Foundation, the National Science Foundation (grant number 0715346), the Jacobs Fund of the Whatcom Museum, the Royster Society of Fellows, and the Graduate School at the University of North Carolina–Chapel Hill. Dáilan thanks the Tucker Foundation of Dartmouth College and the Olga-Lewin Krauss Fellowship. Both of us are thankful, as well, for the information gathered from the individuals and community-based organizations, which deeply inform this chapter, especially Diné Citizens Against Ruining Our Environment and the San Juan Citizens Alliance.

NOTES

1. In discussions of "development" on indigenous lands, there is a tendency to overlook the experiences, feelings, memories, and creative responses of the people most intimately affected by extractive projects. As a corrective, this chapter aims to foreground the critiques and visions of those communities. At the same time, following recent work in indigenous studies, especially in anthropology, we aim to show how indigeneity in the twenty-first century is formulated in new, unexpected, and unpredictable ways, as shown in de la Cadena and Starn 2007 and Dombrowski 2001. In this case, we suggest that energy development itself is a nexus of changing expressions of indigeneity, in which "modern" technologies of development are not resisted outright but are sites of contestation and shifting cultural meanings.

2. The two authors, a Diné environmental activist and a non-Native cultural anthropologist, collaborated on this piece, each with an acute awareness of his or her own limited and partial position, different background, yet similar engagement, all of which shape the perspectives informing this chapter. Our distinctly different experiences have been streamlined into a "we" voice for the purposes of this chapter, but each of us, in unique ways, is both insider and outsider to the communities and issues described here. Although we speak from our own work and research and not for anyone other than ourselves, we do speak with the voices and experiences of others in mind, others who have been generous enough to teach us.

3. Extensive research and activism across the social sciences document these complex struggles around the world. Some of the best work detailing intersections between indigenous movements and transnational forces, especially those related to extractive industry and activism, can be found in the following: Blaser, Feit, and McRae 2004; Cruikshank 2005; Dove 2006; Gedicks 2001; Grossman 2007; Hodgson 2002; LaDuke 1999, 2006; Nash 2001; Saywer 2004; Tsing 2005; Walsh 2002.

---

4. In the face of global climate change, as Zoltán Grossman (2007:7) shows, emerging projects such as renewable energy technologies may pose new opportunities for strengthening alliances between indigenous and local (nontribal) governments, grassroots movements, and other actors.

5. Our work enters into an ongoing interdisciplinary discussion, in science and technology studies, critical development studies, and globalization studies, in which new theories and practices of critiquing and rethinking "development" are being made, largely through the work of activism and social movements. See Escobar 2008; Hess 2007. See also the work of the Center for Integrating Research and Action (CIRA) at the University of North Carolina–Chapel Hill (http://cira.unc.edu/ [accessed December 2009]).

6. Joe Shirley Jr., "Remembrance to Avoid an Unwanted Fate," statement released in support of the book *Navajos and Uranium Mining* (Brugge, Benally, and Yazzie-Lewis 2007), Navajo Nation, Window Rock, AZ, 2006.

7. At the time of this writing, the Environmental Impact Statement on the Black Mesa Mine has been reopened, raising the possibility that Peabody Coal Company may be permitted to resume mining at Black Mesa.

8. Enei Begaye of the Black Mesa Water Coalition, personal communication July 6, 2008. Spearheading this network of nongovernmental organizations are the Black Mesa Water Coalition, Sierra Club, Grand Canyon Trust, and To Nizhoni Ani. For more information, see http://www.blackmesawatercoalition.org/justTransition.html (accessed December 2009). For more background on energy development at Black Mesa, see Begaye 2006.

9. For examples of renewable energy work on tribal lands being done beyond Navajo territory, see the work of the Intertribal Council on Utility Policy, Honor the Earth, and the Sacred Power Corporation.

10. The air emissions of greatest concern are sulfates, nitrates, carbon monoxide, mercury, fine particulate matter, and large particulate matter, as detailed in the "Health-care Costs" section of the report. Ecos Consulting, *Energy and Economic Alternatives to the Desert Rock Energy Project*, Report for Diné CARE, Durango, CO, January 12, 2008, pp. 12–21.

11. For more on the notion of "geographies of sacrifice," see Kuletz 1998; on the Trilateral Commission's decision, see Sklar 1980:243.

12. URS Corporation, *Draft Environmental Impact Statement on the Desert Rock Energy Project*, prepared for the US Department of the Interior and the US Bureau of Indian Affairs, 2007, chapter 5, p. 30.

13. Paul Sheldon, Senior Manager, Policy and Research Programs, Ecos Consulting, personal communication March 25, 2008.

14. Sue Major Holmes, "Richardson Questions Desert Rock," *The Durango Herald*, July 28, 2007.

15. We use *Navajo community* and *Navajo Tribe* as shorthand for this heterogeneous, diverse, and dynamic population. Far from being a bounded group of people, a

singular or stable entity, the Navajo community is diasporic, globally networked, and internally differentiated in many ways.

16. David Wilkins (2003:84–85) writes, "The [Navajo Nation] council was largely a creature of the Secretary of the Interior and certainly not an organization organizing powers of self-government."

17. For further discussions of the impacts of uranium mining and the Navajo peoples' production to fuel the nuclear age, see Brugge, Benally, and Yazzie-Lewis 2007; Eichstaedt 1994.

18. Ward Churchill (1993:264) terms large numbers of uranium mines within reservation boundaries "radioactive colonization," stating that "90 percent of mining that occurred was on or adjacent to Indian lands."

19. The current proposal, at the time of this writing, stands at 10–25 percent tribal ownership of the plant.

20. Dorothy Holland addresses the complex intersection of historical, "enduring struggles" and contemporary formations of new activist identities in Holland and Lave 2001 and in Holland 2003.

21. Diné elder, DEIS public hearing, Shiprock Chapter House, Shiprock, New Mexico, July 12, 2007.

22. As detailed by Indian Country Extension, with data taken from the 2000 US Census, "according to the Navajo Nation's 2000–2001 Comprehensive Economic Development Strategy, the nation's unemployment rate is 44 percent, the median family income is $11,885, and the per capita income is $6,217. Over 56 percent of Navajos live below the poverty level, the highest poverty rate in the U.S., even among American Indians" (http://www.indiancountryextension.org/extension.php?=6 [accessed December 2009]).

23. The full record of public comments such as these is on public record with the US Department of Interior, Bureau of Indian Affairs.

24. Sarah Jane White, personal communication September 24, 2007. Burnham Native and elder Sarah Jane White initiated grassroots resistance to the proposed Desert Rock Energy Project while still holding office as a chapter official in 2003–2004, shortly after the tribe proposed the plant. Over the course of three years (2005–2008), White went door-to-door in her own community to interview local residents. The findings of her research are included in Ecos Consulting (see note 10), appendix A.

25. For related discussions on the intersections among stories, oral histories, language, and place-based knowledge, see Basso 1996; Escobar 1998, 2001. Specific to the Navajo context, see Kelley and Francis 1994.

26. Ecos Consulting (see note 10), appendix A, Stakeholder #1.

27. In this chapter, we focus on the work of Diné CARE because it has been the primary locus of the research and practice informing our collaborative project. Other grassroots initiatives in Navajo land are also working on the Desert Rock issue, focusing more broadly on environmental, social justice, and energy development issues (see,

———

for instance, the work of Doodá Desert Rock, the Black Mesa Water Coalition, To Nizhoni Ani, and C Aquifer for Diné).

28. For additional background on the early stages of Navajo grassroots resistance to the Desert Rock Energy Project, as well as related gender dynamics, see Long 2007.

29. For a more detailed discussion on the background, campaigns, philosophies, and experiences of Diné CARE from the 1980s through mid-1990s, especially pertaining to the campaign against the timber industry in the reservation's Chuska Mountains, see Sherry 2002:24.

30. For more on this notion of storied landscapes and the dynamism of nonhuman others in shaping Native identities, knowledges, and histories, see Cruikshank 2005.

31. Scarberry 1981.

32. Mies and Shiva 1993:2–3.

33. The Hóózhójí Ceremony (Blessing Way Ceremony) was performed on Asdzáá Nádlééhi, and this ceremony is the backbone of all Diné ceremonies.

34. See Krauss 1996:257.

35. Ahasteen cartoon, *Navajo Times*, February 14, 2008.

36. There are multiple and diverging religious and spiritual practices and orientations among Navajo people, including "traditionalists" (or the Corn Pollen Way), the Native American Church and Roadmen, Catholicism, various strains of Protestantism, and, more recently, charismatic fundamentalist Christianity practiced in summer tent revivals and new churches. Medicine men and women are the "Navajo spiritual leaders" overtly referred to in this discussion because many Diné people consider them to be the locus of "Navajo culture and tradition," even if the same people engage in other religious practices. Many spiritual leaders in the newer traditions, however, may share similar principles relating to the "environment." More research is necessary to explore the current conjuncture of religious diversity and environmental ethics.

37. The concept of k'é is used not only by activists to ground their work but also by Diné policy analysts and researchers working on similar concerns. See the recent working papers of the Diné Policy Institute, including Curley 2007.

38. Roger Begay, Bicultural Training Manager, Peace Making Program, Judicial Branch of the Navajo Nation, offered this concept to explain the Diné offerings, ceremonies, and prayers to rectify human "wrongdoings" to the environment. Begay notes that the Navajo deities did not give the Diné "knowledge to mine uranium, coal, and oil"; therefore, proper conduct ("putting things in place") and accordance with Fundamental Laws will help "put things into perspective within the universe" (Roger Begay, personal communication December 13, 2007).

39. For more on the transnational circulation of environmental identities, especially as they pertain to indigenous groups in Asia, see Tsing 2005.

40. Kosek 2006.

41. Smith 2005:122.

42. Moreover, there is a dissonance in the council's codified use of DFL and Navajo

—

popular understanding of DFL based on k'é. As previously mentioned, orality of DFL in Navajo communities shapes popular knowledge formation and is understood to be articulated in the context of decision making, accountability, and the future to come. The council, however, uses DFL to guard its prior decisions on coal development

43. For the full DPI report, see Benally and Curley 2007.

44. Alex et al. 2008.

45. Dr. Frederick H. Morse, "Central Station Solar Electricity: Concentrating Solar Power," cited in Ecos Consulting (see note 10 above), 50.

46. Ibid.

47. Associated Press, "Albuquerque Attracts German Solar Plant," *Santa Fe New Mexican*, March 3, 2008.

48. "Navajo Hopi Land Commission Asks Congress to Fund Proposed Solar Energy Initiative at Paragon Ranch," press release, Navajo Nation Washington Office, March 14, 2008.

49. Staci Matlock, "Nambé Pueblo Plans Wind Farm, Proposed Facility Would Be State's Largest," *Santa Fe New Mexican*, December 19, 2007, http://www.santafenewmexican .com/Local%20News/Pueblo_plans_wind_farm (accessed December 2009).

50. Ecos Consulting (see note 10), 47.

51. Ibid., Executive Summary.

52. Here, we follow the argument set forth in Hooks and Smith 2004.

53. See, for instance, Bullard 1990; Doretta E. Taylor, *Race, Class, Gender, and American Environmentalism*, US Department of Agriculture, Forest Service, Pacific Northwest Research Station PNW-GTR-534, 2002.

54. Earl Tulley, Diné CARE founding member, personal communication February 15, 2008.

55. See Peschek 1997.

56. Staff member of a leading national Native environmental organization, personal communication March 4, 2008.

57. Ibid.

58. Honor the Earth has partnered with engineers and nonprofit organizations such as the Intertribal Council on Utility Policy, as well as tribal governments, on numerous other projects: for example, the first Native-owned-and-operated wind turbine in the United States, installed on the Rosebud Lakota reservation in South Dakota; solar photovoltaic installations on the reservation of the Skull Valley Band of Goshutes in Utah; and solar power on the Dann Ranch in Western Shoshone territory in Nevada. Additional collaborative projects with Southwest tribes are underway.

59. See the US Department of Energy's Web site, http://apps1.eere.energy.gov /tribalenergy/ (accessed December 2009).

60. The Navajo Tribal Utility Authority recognizes the ongoing challenges and costs of rural electrification, noting that it costs approximately $20,000–$25,000 per mile (and more, depending on the terrain) to bring transmission lines to rural home-steads (NTUA employee, personal communication June 17, 2008).

61. Much of the "resistance theory" literature posits indigenous communities as inherently resistant to technology or to "development" as such. We are working around this reductive polarity, highlighting instead the more complex and subtler considerations at work among tribal governments and communities, who face particularly difficult dilemmas of balancing economic well-being with environmental and public health.

62. See Denetdale's (2007:17–50) critique of conventional renditions of Diné history and her advancement of a methodology for decolonizing narratives of the past.

63. Earl Tulley, personal communication March 18, 2008.

64. For a discussion of this "ontology of difference" as expressed through Navajo environmental activism, see Powell and Curley 2009.

65. For a more extensive deconstruction of capitalism as a unifying global force, coming from community-based movements working on establishing alternative economic practices and new economic subjectivities, see Gibson-Graham 2006.

66. Tom Goldtooth, Director, Indigenous Environmental Network, personal communication June 12, 2006.

67. We argue that this work is both a form of producing knowledge and a form of politics that exceeds conventional definitions of political action often set forth in political science and social movements studies. As argued elsewhere, this creates a kind of intellectual and political "knowledge-practice" that engages, mobilizes, and informs university-based knowledge production. For further discussion of this concept of "knowledge-practice" in social movements, see Casas-Cortés, Osterweil, and Powell 2008.

REFERENCES

Alex, Nikki, Moroni Benally, Andrew Curley, Amber Crotty, and James Singer
2008 Navajo Nation Constitutional Feasibility and Government Reform Project. White Paper. Tsaile, AZ. Diné Policy Institute.

Basso, Keith H.
1996 Wisdom Sits in Places: Landscape and Language among the Western Apache. Albuquerque: University of New Mexico Press.

Begaye, Enei
2006 The Black Mesa Controversy. Cultural Studies Quarterly 29:29–31.

Benally, Moroni, and Andrew Curley
2007 Comments on the Desert Rock Energy Project, Draft Environmental Impact Statement. July. Tsaile, AZ: Diné Policy Institute.

Blaser, Mario, Harvey A. Feit, and Glenn McRae
2004 Introduction. *In* In the Way of Development: Indigenous Peoples, Life Projects and Globalization. London: Zed Books.

Brugge, Doug, Timothy Benally, and Esther Yazzie-Lewis, eds.
2007 The Navajo People and Uranium Mining. Albuquerque: University of New Mexico Press.

Bullard, Robert D.

1990 Dumping in Dixie: Race, Class, and Environmental Quality. Boulder: Westview Press.

Casas-Cortés, María Isabel, Michal Osterweil, and Dana E. Powell

2008 Blurring Boundaries: Recognizing Knowledge-Practices in the Study of Social Movements. Anthropological Quarterly 81 (1): 17–58.

Churchill, Ward

1993 Struggle for the Land: Indigenous Resistance to Genocide, Ecocide, and Expropriation in Contemporary North America. Monroe, ME: Common Courage.

Cruikshank, Julie

2005 Do Glaciers Listen? Local Knowledge, Colonial Encounters, and Social Imagination. Vancouver: University of British Columbia Press.

Curley, Andrew

2007 Uranium, Coal and the Logic for Non-withdrawal: The Use of Traditional Principles in Natural Resources Policy and Governance on the Navajo Nation. Tsaile, AZ: Diné Policy Institute.

de la Cadena, Marisol, and Orin Starn, eds.

2007 Indigenous Experience Today. Vol. 2. Oxford and New York: Berg.

Denetdale, Jennifer Nez

2007 Reclaiming Diné History: The Legacies of Navajo Chief Manuelito and Juanita. Albuquerque: University of New Mexico Press.

Dombrowski, Kirk

2001 Against Culture: Development, Politics, and Religion in Indian Alaska. Lincoln and London: University of Nebraska Press.

Dove, Michael R.

2006 Indigenous People and Environmental Politics. Annual Review of Anthropology 35:191–208.

Eichstaedt, Peter H.

1994 If You Poison Us: Uranium and Native Americans. Santa Fe, NM: Red Crane Books.

Escobar, Arturo

1998 Whose Knowledge, Whose Nature? Biodiversity, Conservation, and the Political Ecology of Social Movements. Journal of Political Ecology 5:53–82.

2001 Culture Sits in Places: Reflections on Globalism and Subaltern Strategies of Localization. Political Geography 20:139–174.

2008 Places and Regions in the Age of Globality: Social Movements and Biodiversity Conservation in the Colombian Pacific. Durham, NC: Duke University Press.

Gedicks, Al

2001 Resource Rebels: Native Challenges to Mining and Oil Corporations. Cambridge, MA: South End Press.

Gibson-Graham, Julie Katherine

2006 A Postcapitalist Politics. Minneapolis: University of Minnesota Press.

Grossman, Zoltán

2007 Possible Climate Change Responses for a United League of Indigenous Nations.

———

Report of the Northwest Indian Applied Research Institute. Olympia, WA: The Evergreen State College.

Hess, David J.

2007   Alternative Pathways in Science and Industry: Activism, Innovation, and the Environment in an Era of Globalization. Cambridge, MA: MIT Press.

Hodgson, Dorothy L.

2002   Introduction: Comparative Perspectives on the Indigenous Rights Movement in Africa and the Americas. American Anthropologist 104:1037–1049.

Holland, Dorothy

2003   Multiple Identities in Practice: On the Dilemmas of Being a Hunter and an Environmentalist in the USA. Focaal—European Journal of Anthropology 42:23–41.

Holland, Dorothy, and Jean Lave

2001   "History in Person: An Introduction." In Enduring Struggles: Contentious Practice, Intimate Identities. Dorothy Holland and Jean Lave, eds., 1–32. Santa Fe, NM: School of American Research Press.

Hooks, Gregory, and Chad L. Smith

2004   The Treadmill of Destruction: National Sacrifice Areas and Native Americans. American Sociological Review 69:558–575.

Johnston, Barbara Rose, Susan Dawson, and Gary Madsen

2010   Uranium Mining and Milling: Navajo Experiences in the American Southwest. In Indians and Energy: Exploitation and Opportunity in the American Southwest. Sherry L. Smith and Brian Frehner, eds., 111–164. Santa Fe, NM: School for Advanced Research Press.

Kelley, Klara Bonsack, and Harris Francis

1994   Navajo Sacred Places. Bloomington and Indianapolis, IN: Indiana University Press.

Kosek, Jake

2006   Understories: The Political Life of Forests in Northern New Mexico. Durham, NC: Duke University Press.

Krauss, Celene

1996   Women of Color on the Front Line. In Unequal Protection: Environmental Justice and Communities of Color. Robert D. Bullard, ed., 256–271. San Francisco: Sierra Club Books. First published in 1994 by Random House.

Kuletz Valerie

1998   The Tainted Desert Environmental and Social Ruin in the American West. New York: Routledge.

LaDuke, Winona

1999   All Our Relations: Native Struggles for Land and Life. Cambridge, MA: South End Press.

2006   Recovering the Sacred: The Power of Naming and Claiming. Cambridge, MA: South End Press.

Long, Dáilan J.

2007   Diyin Nohookáá Diné nihi'doo'nii: We Are Called the Holy Earth-Surface-People;

———

Navajo Resistance to Cultural Genocide, Environmental Injustice, and the Desert Rock Energy Project. Master's thesis, Dartmouth College.

Mies, Maria, and Vandana Shiva

1993   Ecofeminism. London and New York: Zed Books.

Nash, June C.

2001   Mayan Visions: The Quest for Autonomy in an Age of Globalization. New York: Routledge.

Needham, Andrew

2010   "A Piece of the Action": Navajo Nationalism, Energy Development, and Metropolitan Inequality. *In* Indians and Energy: Exploitation and Opportunity in the American Southwest. Sherry L. Smith and Brian Frehner, eds., 203–220. Santa Fe, NM: School for Advanced Research Press.

Peschek, Joseph

1997   National Security Tales and the End of the Cold War. *In* Tales of the State: Narrative in Contemporary US Politics and Public Policy. Sanford F. Schram and Philip T. Neisser, eds., 212–222. New York: Rowman and Littlefield.

Powell, Dana E., and Andrew Curley

2009   K'e, Hozhó, and Non-governmental Politics on the Navajo Nation: Ontologies of Difference Manifest in Environmental Activism. E-Journal of the World Anthropologies Network (January):4.

Sawyer, Susana

2004   Crude Chronicles: Indigenous Politics, Multinational Oil, and Neoliberalisn in Ecuador. Durham, NC: Duke University Press.

Scarberry, Susan J.

1981   Land into Flesh: Images of Intimacy. Frontiers: A Journal of Women Studies 6 (3): 24–28.

Sherry, John William

2002   Land, Wind, and Hard Words: A Story of Navajo Activism. Albuquerque: University of New Mexico Press.

Sklar, Holly, ed.

1980   Trilateralism: The Trilateral Commission and Elite Planning for World Management. Boston: South End Press.

Smith, Andrea

2005   Conquest: Sexual Violence and American Indian Genocide. Cambridge, MA: South End Press.

Tsing, Anna Lowenhaupt

2005   Friction: An Ethnography of Global Connection. Princeton, NJ, and Oxford: Princeton University Press.

Voggesser, Garrit

2010   The Evolution of Federal Energy Policy for Tribal Lands and the Renewable Energy Future. *In* In Indians and Energy: Exploitation and Opportunity in the American Southwest. Sherry L. Smith and Brian Frehner, eds., 55–88. Santa Fe, NM: School for Advanced Research Press.

———

Walsh, Catherine E.
2002   The (Re)articulation of Political Subjectivities and Colonial Difference in
        Ecuador: Reflections on Capitalism and the Geopolitics of Knowledge. Nepantla:
        Views from South 3:61–97.
Wilkins, David E.
2003   The Navajo Political Experience. Lanham, MD: Rowman and Littlefield.

6

DECOLONIZING ENERGY

BLACK LIVES MATTER AND TECHNOSCIENTIFIC EXPERTISE AMID SOLAR TRANSITIONS

MYLES LENNON

1. INTRODUCTION

Let me introduce you to two dissimilar figures with unlikely parallels. John, a self-described "energy expert," is the white male CEO of a multinational renewable energy technology firm in Manhattan's Financial District—a company predominantly staffed by white male engineers. Janelle, in contrast, is a public housing resident, a young Black Lives Matter activist without a college degree, and a volunteer at an environmental justice organization in a working-class black community on the other side of Manhattan.

Last year John steered one of his weekly company meetings away from their quotidian discussions on energy monitoring software to a topic that had never been discussed in their board room: the matter of black lives. As dozens of engineers looked on with muted surprise but nods of approval, John lamented two high profile murders of black men by the police and expressed support for the Black Lives Matter protests that had sprouted up

Originally published as, Lennon, M., 2017. Decolonizing Energy: Black Lives Matter and Technoscientific Expertise amid Solar Transitions. *Energy Research and Social Science*, *30*, pp. 18–27. Reprinted with permission by Elsevier, all rights reserved.

in response to the murders, calling on his company to address structural violence against marginalized Americans.

A week after John's intervention, Janelle similarly steered a conversation with her colleagues in a surprising direction. But instead of preaching to a corporate office, Janelle sat among a sea of black faces in a church at a meeting of a grassroots campaign to empower working-class people of color to produce their own electricity through solar panels. The meeting initially focused on racial disparities in renewable energy access, but Janelle wanted to discuss something else. Citing an expert report, she proposed that the campaign should champion anaerobic digestion, a technically complex renewable energy production process. While this suggestion wasn't the typical contribution from someone who fit her underprivileged profile, the room followed her lead; a spirited conversation ensued on anaerobic digestion's pros and cons.

We can locate parallel discursive shifts in John's and Janelle's conversational detours in spite of their contrasting positionalities. Whereas John amplified intersectional antiracist ideas in a predominantly white, corporate, technocratic space, Janelle brought attention to a technocratic tool in a predominantly black, antiracist, intersectionally minded space.

My ethnographic research at grassroots "energy democracy" campaigns and private renewable energy companies in New York City and the San Francisco Bay Area suggest that these conversational detours bespeak the broader convergence of technoscientific expertise and antiracist activism in the industrialized energy sector. I found that traditional white-collar energy experts have embraced a holistic, intersectional ethos at odds with the dispassionate corporate technocratic outlook characteristic of traditional energy labs and corporations [67]. At the same time, antiracist activists have enfolded technocratic energy issues (such as feed-in tariffs and net metering) into their intersectional agenda, increasingly situating themselves in the technical spaces that produce industrialized electricity, heat, and fuels.

In this paper I argue that renewable energy technologies and the antiracist metaphysics of the Black Lives Matter movement have operated as a material-discursive[1] node enabling these coterminous shifts, simultaneously infusing activist spaces with a technoscientific outlook and attuning energy experts to ethical matters beyond society's "energy needs." This

—

"node" is not a concrete entity; it is a conceptual paradigm gesturing to the intersections of material technologies that aim to decentralize the grid and activist discourses that aim to decentralize social governance. I argue that this node is not simply reconfiguring the sociopolitical dynamics of the industrialized energy sector; it is also challenging understandings of what energy fundamentally is in the late-modern U.S., bridging the conceptual gap between mechanized modern electricity and relational forms of non-industrialized energy.

I call on energy activists and scholars to deepen this reconceptualization by drawing from the metaphysics of the Black Lives Matter (BLM) movement. Amid burgeoning efforts across the U.S. to "democratize" energy, I contend that BLM presents a heuristic through which we can more radically decolonize energy. Highlighting the historical imbrications of slavery and industrialized energy generation, I argue that the colonial apparatus transformed energy—the ability to change matter—into a commoditized form that made certain lives not matter. This framework suggests that pervasive understandings of energy—not simply regimes of generating energy—reify ontological hierarchies and their attendant structural inequalities. As such, I call for intersectional work that challenges dominant conceptions of energy as a "thing" that one can have, instead conceiving of energy in terms of vital relationality, that is, the interdependent ties between all forms of matter. By reimagining energy, unleashing it from its colonial context, we can begin to disentangle the systems through which we change matter from the systems through which certain lives are made to not matter. This reconceptualization, in turn, can link together John's call for intersectional reflection and Janelle's call to be heard in a technical register by collapsing the categorical boundaries between "objective" kilowatts and personal ontological concerns—between Black political praxis and "racially unmarked" technoscientific knowledge.

2. BIG-E/LITTLE-E ENERGY KNOWLEDGE

While energy is often mistakenly characterized as "prediscursive"[2]—an apolitical biophysical phenomenon governed by the laws of thermodynamics, existing irrespective of human culture—in fact it is inextricably entangled with our values and symbolic categories [3]. Far from a concrete entity, energy is an abstraction [4] that different societies give shape to through disparate discourses and practices.

Scholars often contend that social groups conceptualize energy as either: a mechanized, quantifiable phenomenon generated by and capable of being deployed anywhere with industrial technology; or a context-specific force of life, embedded in relations between different beings and attuned to all living matter. For instance, Rupp ([5]: 80) distinguishes between "formalist models" for understanding energy as a "quantifiable" infrastructural force and "substantivist models" for understanding energy as a "qualitative force that is socially embedded and mediated by people's relationships with each other and with the conditions of their daily lives." Similarly, Berry ([6]: 83) "distinguish[es] between two kinds of energy: that which is made available by living things and that which is made available by machines." The "living" kind of energy is characterized by "mutual relationship[s]" between humans and other forms of life such as soil ([6]: 87), whereas machines "come between us and life," severing such relationships ([6]: 91).

Lohmann's distinction between "Big-E 'Energy'" and "little-e 'energies'" aptly captures this dichotomous framework:

> The abstract concept of "energy" that states and scientists use today—call it Energy with a capital "E"—has largely been a creation of fossil-fuelled industrial capitalism. Coexisting with the abstract Energy are much older, multiple, vernacular, mutually-incommensurable "energies" associated with various subsistence purposes, together with indigenous conceptions of energy flows that bear little resemblance to the kilojoule-quantified interchanges of Energy . . . Lower case "energies" remain entangled with particular times—seasons, the daily cycle of light, the months it takes to grow crops . . . —and particular places—rivers where mills can be built, forests from which wood can be cut, latitudes where trade winds blow . . . [Inversely] Big-E Energy can be accumulated and deployed . . . anywhere regardless of the local environment . . . ([45]: 26)

Big-E and little-e conceptualizations of energy are often marked by race, gender, class, and geography. Highly educated white male "energy experts" overwhelmingly shape Big-E Energy conceptually [67], defining this industrialized force through white-collar consulting [7], economics [8], government policy [9], the development industry [10], and laboratories ([67]). Tethered to large institutions invested in the fossil fuel or nuclear industries, these experts produce knowledge grounded in simplistic understandings of energy based on statistical abstractions [11,12]. Energy experts often appear so entrenched in their narrow technical apparatus that they lack any firm understanding of the social context and environmental ramifications of the Big-E systems they promote [13,14].

Ethnographic literature on energy suggests that these experts mark their knowledge as a currency of elite social status, reinforcing systems of hierarchy through paternalistic narratives of poor communities of color [15] or dismissals of women's knowledge on the grounds that it is "inferior and non-scientific" ([16]: 59). In contrast, this literature affiliates little-e energies with off-the-grid indigenous communities, such as Alaska Natives who have "a conception of energy as a manifestation of moral relationships among animals, people, and land" ([17]: 105) or swidden farmers in rural South America who value what Gudeman calls "vital energy"— a "biosocial flow" that "gives vitality" to all living beings and "makes and mediates social relationships from near kin to distant strangers" ([38]: 57).

At the same time, communities of color in the Global North have traditionally had limited involvement in energy knowledge production. While they have been disproportionately impacted by industrialized energy production [18,19] and have mobilized against the inequitable siting of power plants, oil refineries, and fossil fueled infrastructures [18,20], they have historically played a limited role in cultivating hegemonic understandings of energy as a quantifiable force that can improve society and in the institutions tasked with materializing this teleological schema. As knowledge is the basis of biopolitical regimes [21], it is no coincidence that communities of color are routinely shut out from planning the energy infrastructures grounded in such Big-E discourses [19].

3. RECONCEPTUALIZING ENERGY

My ethnographic research at five renewable energy companies and four grassroots environmental justice organizations in New York City and the San Francisco Bay Area suggests that renewable energy technologies have converged with intersectional activism to reconfigure the racial and class character of Big-E Energy, destabilizing the Big-E/little-e dichotomy.

Dan, one of my main interlocutors, exemplifies these conceptual shifts. As a white male electricity expert with an advanced degree in engineering and an upper-level position at an international firm focused on rural electrification vis-à-vis solar and wind power, Dan appears to be the paradigmatic Big-E technocrat described above. But his worldview diverges considerably from that of the technocratic trope. He explains, "Energy is a force—I know that sounds like a physics definition but I mean it in a more metaphysical way. I think of energy as vitality—the vitality of people, communities and societies . . . [to] change the world around them—and it can be physical but it could be more emotional, social." In linking energy to vitality, social forces, communality, and metaphysics, he sounds nothing like the fossil fuel intelligentsia in Nader's work; his conceptualization of energy bears greater resemblance to that of the swidden farmers in Gudeman's account of "vital energy" in rural household economies ([38]: 57). Dan is well aware that his "personal" understanding of energy does not conform to industry discourse, which, in his words, is "more like gigajoules or dot dot dot of a standard metric." Put simply, Dan conceptualizes energy through a little-e lens that he contrasts with his industry's Big-E bias.

But in exploring his day-to-day practice it becomes apparent that his little-e outlook and Big-E context cohere in ways that destabilize this rather simple binary. Dan directly engages with energy as a mechanized phenomenon, designing the specifications of systems that generate industrialized electricity through a centralized grid. Yet he does so with the recognition that renewable electricity and grid connectivity collectively represent just one approach to generating energy—that people have the power to transform matter beyond the scope of top-down energy policies. While his work is officially focused on ramping up renewable electricity deployment, he does not approach it with giga-joule-generation as his end goal. Instead, he intentionally directs this work so that it is integrated into community-driven approaches to livelihood and well-being. This primarily entails painstakingly documenting community "listening sessions" so as to capture local understandings of the "good life" and partnering with local organizations to integrate renewable energy systems into endogenous governance initiatives, focusing specifically on how Big-E Energy can foster

---

greater communal cohesion, and not simply quantifiable power. While one can problematize an engineer's efforts to "listen" to "the community," the point here is that for Dan, Big-E systems must be designed in service of locally defined metaphysical conditions, enfolding subjective understandings of "life" into technologies often characterized by their objective dimensions. His practice is informed by an understanding of energy that bridges the gap between the physical and metaphysical, calculability and vitality, the technical and the emotional—approaching Big-E systems as but one means of materializing a little-e cosmology.[2]

Most of the other renewable energy experts I spoke to echoed this syncretic understanding of energy, acknowledging that the oft-mechanized phenomenon that their work focuses on is not only discernible through gigajoules—that at times energy can be attributed to something as subjective as human emotions. Several explicitly gestured to ecocentric concepts to problematize parochially mechanical understandings of energy. "Energy is a living breathing organism that needs to be attended to just like everything else," explained a renewable electricity financing expert, challenging a Cartesian outlook that denigrates energy to the status of a non-human thing. Similarly, an energy engineer critiqued the energy sector on the grounds that it tries "to oppose weather conditions" instead of embracing the flows and whims of the biosphere. Many of these self-identified energy experts were at a loss for words when asked to define energy, knowing full well that the physics textbook conception of it was inadequate.

This notion that energy is more than a Newtonian force, that it exists outside of a technoscientific telos, undergirds these technocrats' encounters with race. John demonstrated this in his impassioned call to his company to address structural violence against black communities:

> There's a lot of inequality in this country and the way people get treated based on the color of their skin or their gender or their sexual orientation is just wrong, and the stuff that's happening with the police is more than wrong, it's really horrifying . . . For those of us who have experiences and identities of power and privilege—whether that's through race or gender or class or education—we need to create spaces and opportunities for us to come together and have conversation, and talk about our stories and share our thoughts, and our

—

hopes, and fears . . . we need to think about how our actions and our words might be hurting certain communities . . . If our company's in the business of making the world a better place, then we can't ignore these issues.

Notably, this call to action subtly invoked the company's expertise; this firm prides itself on using its technical knowledge and technology to "mak[e] the world a better place." They put a premium on deploying solar in marginalized communities, they support grassroots "climate justice" campaigns, and they do scientific research in service of climate policy. The CEO's imperative to address racial injustice and foster dialogue about police brutality was, in his mind, part and parcel of the company's broader work to improve society through technology and to leverage renewable energy toward holistic social change. He proceeded to call another all-staff meeting to discuss how the company should address institutionalized racism, a gesture that drew an affirmative response from the engineers and software specialists unaccustomed to intersectional ruminations in the boardroom. Much like this firm, the other renewable energy companies I explored were staffed and led predominantly by white men, yet they also shared a vision for a broad-based energy transition that addresses long-standing sociopolitical inequities.

In short, many experts in the renewable energy field both conceptualize energy and approach their work in ways that differentiate them from traditional fossil fuel and nuclear technocrats. Without completely abandoning instrumentalist epistemologies, these experts additionally cultivate a little-e orientation to Big-E infrastructures and situate industrialized energy in broader sociopolitical contexts like structural racism.

The advent of renewables has also dramatically broadened the field of actors who explicitly define their work in relation to industrialized energy. In recent years, people of color and other marginalized groups have reflexively positioned themselves in the domain of Big-E discourse and policy, redefining a field traditionally dominated by STEM-credentialed white men. This positioning is most salient in the grassroots efforts for "energy democracy" led by communities of color and labor unions. "Energy democracy means that community residents [as opposed to credentialed experts] are innovators, planners, and decision-makers on how to use and

—

create energy that is local and renewable" (Center for Social Inclusion [22]: www.centerforsocialinclusion.org). As a vision for decentralizing Big-E systems toward racial and economic justice, energy democracy envisages the equitable deployment of renewable energy technologies to empower communities traditionally burdened by fossil fuels. In this way, energy democracy advocates reimagine industrialized energy as a potential means of upending systems of institutional oppression, creating unlikely linkages between intersectional activism and the technocratic realm of electricity grids and markets. This convergence is particularly notable when it involves the fiercely grassroots Black Lives Matter (BLM) movement. As "an ideological and political intervention in a world where Black lives are systematically and intentionally targeted for demise," (Black Lives Matter [23]: www.blacklivesmatter.com) BLM, on the surface, makes strange bedfellows with industrialized energy regimes.

Jacqui Patterson, a black environmental justice activist, fleshed-out this unlikely linkage in a webinar presentation organized by the Energy Foundation entitled "Energy Democracy, #BlackLivesMatter, and the NAACP Advocacy Agenda." Citing the demographics of coal mining casualties, black children's asthma morbidity rates, and black communities' disproportionate vulnerability to anthropogenic climate change, Patterson argued that the ways in which we generate electricity, heat, and fuels have historically denigrated—*de*-mattered—black lives ([24]: www.naacp.org). She then offered an unconventional antidote to this structural violence: net metering, a billing mechanism for accelerating investment in renewable energy technologies. She contended that net metering has the potential to empower black people to generate "community wealth" and "control . . . an aggressively paced transition from a fossil fuel based energy economy, to one that protects . . . the health and wellbeing of [their] communities" by enabling them to sell excess electricity produced by locally owned energy technologies back to the grid [24]. In this schema, the bottom-up deployment of technological alternatives to fossil fuels through net metering is an integral component of intersectional work affirming black lives, as it counters hegemonic regimes of energy generation that disproportionately cause blacks' bodily harm and enables them to secure their own livelihoods.

Patterson's vision is compelling, yet it offers a somewhat unusual hypothesis: that a financial instrument intended to expand an energy

—

market has the potential to work in service of a radical, decentralized political movement affirming the fundamental value of black lives. While financial instruments have long played a role in proposals to build prosperity for marginalized social groups [25], seldom are they touted as a piece of a broad intersectional puzzle predicated on transgressive principles such as "loving engagement," and "unapologetically Black" (Black Lives Matter [23]: www.blacklivesmatter.com). In fact, radical movements traditionally reject mechanisms for capital accumulation, characterizing such mechanisms as antithetical to their collectivist and often anti-capitalist projects [26].

That said, the unlikely intersections of radical movements and capitalized technology do not suggest that antiracist activism situated in the politics of energy is necessarily technocratic or top-down. Several BLM activists demonstrated this when they chained themselves together and occupied a runway at a London airport, catalyzing the cancelation of all flights. This disruptive action aimed to highlight the ways in which black lives are unequally impacted by fossil fuel energy production, conceptualizing oil-driven climate change as "a racist crisis" [27].

This sense that energy is fundamentally a racial matter animates energy democracy campaigns for the equitable deployment of solar technologies, although this may not be apparent at first glance. A meeting of one such campaign facilitated by a racial justice nonprofit organization and a solar energy specialist in a low-income co-op in New York City focused on the financing and logistics of solar panel installation—decisively technical matters—through a wonky PowerPoint with data on kilowatt hours that made only passing references to race. But several community members directly engaged with this work through the lens of BLM. "As historically discriminated-against groups, we haven't had the infrastructure—government hasn't chosen to develop clean infrastructure in our communities—in the same ways government hasn't been accountable to black lives," explained Shirley, a black activist, in laying out her rationale for taking part in the campaign. "BLM and energy democracy share similar goals," she added. By situating energy infrastructure in a broader trajectory of racist governmental neglect, and by linking the liberatory objectives of BLM with the technological imperatives of the energy democracy movement, Shirley suggests that a technical endeavor to secure solar financing for black communities can be a strategy for addressing the statist de-mattering of black lives. Power figures prominently in this analysis. Shirley's not simply suggesting that solar infrastructure can benefit black communities; she's explicitly arguing that it can counteract institutional oppression.

Debar, a black graduate student also in attendance, took this analysis a step further.

> "Black Lives Matter is not just about racist cops killing black men. It's about recognizing that systems of power have targeted us for demise and doing everything in our power to stop it . . . So when we talk about solar panels here, when we talk about renewable energy, we're not talking about lowering our energy bills, we're not talking about making our homes greener or whatever. We're talking about taking power back, controlling our own power systems . . . We gotta fight on multiple fronts; in my mind, solar energy is just one of many paths to liberation."

Debar, here, endows industrialized energy delivered through renewable technologies with racially transgressive potential, radically differentiating it from traditional Big-E frameworks. BLM is the conceptual filter that demarcates industrialized energy in Debar's and Shirley's statements, embedding it in both systems of institutional oppression and broad-based struggles for social change. Through the heuristic of "black lives," energy appears as a tool of racialized power and a potential means for decentralizing such power, impelling these black activists to take part in expert-led meetings on energy technology, a matter that they knew little about.

This heuristic is salient to other BLM interventions in the realm of industrialized energy. For instance, in public protests and demonstrations in support of energy democracy, activists chant and hold signs with the quintessential BLM phrase "I can't breathe," a reference to the last words of Eric Garner—a black man who was choked to death by white police officers—to connect the incidence of fossil fuel pollution and asthma in black communities with police brutality and the systematic de-mattering of black lives. The name of a BLM activist's blog, "Black Lungs Matter," echoes this intersectional orientation to energy. Along these lines, one BLM activist I interviewed evoked the long historical trajectory of antiracist activism

—

in the U.S. by reconceptualizing Big-E Energy as "a civil rights issue" on the grounds that fossil fuel production disproportionately impacts marginalized communities and, more crucially, that "the very folks who are trying to strip our voting rights are the same folks who are trying to make sure there's no regulation so they can continue to pollute with impunity," arguing that these two forms of legal maneuvering are "very interconnected because they know if we had voting rights we could fight for cleaner energy." A prominent activist's think-piece, "#BlackLivesMatter Advancing Energy Democracy," evokes BLM to call for bottom-up action toward a racially inclusive renewable energy industry. In these testimonies, BLM and its underlying intersectional ethos reconceptualize Big-E Energy as a matter of racial justice. Through this reconceptualization, black activists mobilize their communities to participate in energy democracy campaigns and consciously situate their lives in prominent discourses of "energy."

To summarize, both energy experts and antiracist activists have begun to reimagine Big-E Energy in different but complementary ways. The experts have enfolded the sorts of social justice matters and ecocentric knowledge traditionally anathema to the energy industry into their work. At the same time, the activists have leveraged the technical tools and energy technologies traditionally affiliated with such experts in service of an antiracist vision. These shifts have reconfigured prominent discourses of industrialized energy, situating it in narratives where progress is not solely understood through quantitative metrics and where transformations of matter aren't unmarked by race. The next section will explore the catalysts of these shifts to elucidate how we can orient our energy transitions toward deeper intersectional transformations.

4. INTERSECTIONAL SOLAR

My research suggests that the physical technologies we have at our disposal and the political currents governing our imaginary collectively produce our understandings of what energy is and our vision for what to do with it. Specifically, I found that the physical properties of renewable energy technologies and the intersectional ethos foundational to BLM operate as a material-discursive node, enabling marginalized actors to transform the energy industry.

To unpack this claim, we can follow Boyer ([28]: 325), who locates political agency in the materiality of energy generation systems to suggest that "modern power" is bounded in the resources and technologies through which we produce and distribute electricity, heat, and fuels. This "energopower," as he frames it, in turn shapes how we understand and subsequently situate ourselves vis-à-vis energy. For example, as Özden-Schilling [29] shows, the material-temporal properties of electricity infrastructures—the ways they instantaneously transmit large quantities of energy that must be proactively managed in order to keep the grid running—legitimate and reconfigure the capitalistic discourse of "supply and demand." This discourse, in turn, shapes energy experts' understanding of electricity and their own conception of their positionality at the helm of Big-E infrastructures; their job, as they see it, is to match electricity's supply and demand. Put simply, the confluence of material conditions and hegemonic discourses demarcates the vocational contours of subjects who reflexively situate their work in relation to energy.

This sort of material-discursive power was palpable at the energy democracy campaign meetings where I met Shirley and Debar. Local black activists regularly gestured to and mentioned the sun at these meetings, which were held at the height of summer. Specifically, they remarked on the sun's steady presence and force, and its proximity to their roofs—verifying its power based on their lived experience beneath its rays. As a solar energy expert explained the technical components of photovoltaic electricity systems with a PowerPoint, characterizing the local potential for solar power in terms of kilowatt-hours, participants corroborated these expert assessments by evoking their own embodied understanding of the sun: its abundant character in their neighborhoods and the ways it illuminates their homes during the day. "It gets real sunny on my block, I can barely see the TV in the morning [because it's so sunny], so we can damn sure power this whole community ourselves without you, Con Edison [the utility company]," remarked an elderly woman with no prior experience in the energy sector. "I see these yuppies out here sunbathing on they new balconies," lamented a local man, referring to his gentrifying neighborhood, "why can't we use that sun power to power our own 'hood?" Whereas the unmarked, fortress-like, fossil fueled electricity power stations dotting the city's poorest communities appear indiscernible and inaccessible—their barbed wire uninviting, their machinery hidden—the sun's beams and blinding properties seemed, at these meetings, to suggest something unalienated and comprehensible. Everyone in the room knew well how the solar system's central body beat down on treeless concrete at summer's apogee.

As these conversations shifted to the community's energy democracy plan, it was precisely this verifiable potential that legitimated their campaign's lofty goals for aggregating solar installations over a short period of time. While no community members at these meetings identified themselves as "energy experts," the idea that they, a low-income community of color with no technical experience with electricity, could develop and implement a plan to ramp up the deployment of an energy technocommodity, was partially made possible by their lived experience with the sun—by its presence as a discernible force of light and power.

This presence, though, did not solely empower the community to participate in the realm of industrialized energy. As explored above, an intersectional politics that connects environmental degradation with structural racism—at times through the heuristic of black lives—has oriented many black activists to the energy democracy movement. In other words, intersectionality is foundational to many black activists' engagement with industrialized energy. "[R]ather than a principle with a fixed set of subjects or applications, intersectionality is flexible in its applicability" ([30]: 91), and, as such, operates as a malleable analytic capable of tying together structural oppression and technocratic matters such as net metering. As a decentralized movement, BLM is similarly flexible, operating, simultaneously, as an outgrowth of intersectional activism, a catalyst for intersectional activism, and a metaphysical framework for reconfiguring intersectional activisms including energy transition advocacy. This flexibility is evinced by the BLM Policy Platform which connects fossil fuel divestment and reinvestment in community-controlled renewable energy technologies with a diverse array of intersecting social justice agendas to empower black people (M4BL Platform [31]: https://policy.m4bl.org). In this way, intersectionality and the physical properties of renewable energy operate less as political catalysts in isolation and instead as a material-discursive node enabling activists from marginalized groups to envision, plan, and mobilize for a future where black communities control and are empowered by industrialized energy systems—where democratically operated Big-E infrastructures serve as the material bedrock of a more equitable society. In other words, the materiality of solar and the intersectionality of BLM (and other social justice movements) collectively demarcate a unique ontological space where oppressed people can position themselves as agential stakeholders in industrialized energy regimes that have traditionally been unconcerned with the matter of black lives. Furthermore, the potential of solar technologies to decentralize the electricity grid—to enable communities to own and generate their electricity—makes it particularly amenable to an intersectional movement critical of centralized state authority. In other words, solar's material capacity to transform the grid coheres smoothly with BLM's vision for communal self-determination (as opposed to top-down governance)—and this cohesion, in turn, orients black activists to spaces focused on energy. In highlighting technology and intersectionality, I'm not suggesting that other entities such as government incentives or the semiotics of "the clean energy market" are not also entangled in such a material-discursive node. Instead, I wish to foreground the formative material-discursive conditions of black activist participation in the industrialized energy sector. The node, as I conceive it, decentralizes agency, locating black activists' power not simply in their own initiative but rather in the confluence of technologies and ideologies that they proactively encounter, enable, and co-constitute.

This material-discursive node is perhaps most legible in renewable energy planning workshops convened by public-private partnerships. Energy bureaucrats or urban planners typically facilitate these workshops, which are held in professional offices and lecture halls. While the formal agendas of these workshops often include "community solar" and "low- and moderate-income communities," white energy professionals, businesses, and technocrats overwhelmingly focus these meetings on tax credits, market growth, and financial tools. However, several black energy democracy activists took part in a few of the meetings I attended, and while they were registered participants—not protestors—they disrupted these meetings' technocratic affect, wearing bright T-shirts instead of standard business attire, offering impassioned spiels on a "community-led energy transition" for "blacks and other minority groups," citing statistics on local low-income residential buildings ripe for solar investment, demanding that local government prioritize the "victims of environmental racism" in piloting community solar programs, excoriating high-rise gentrifying residential development with the potential to block poorer homes' exposure to the sun, and offering a glossy future-oriented rendering of solar-saturated residential homes in their neighborhoods. These performances conjured a vision predicated on both an ethic that marginalized communities matter and the biospheric and technological conditions of solar—a material-discursive node. The material capacity of solar to decentralize the grid and its compatibility with an intersectional discourse that celebrates decentralized authority collectively empowered marginalized laypeople to participate actively in a space with all of the symbolic trappings of white-collar technocracy.

These sorts of performances have fundamentally altered the semiotic landscape of industrialized energy, reconfiguring how experts frame Big-E systems. For instance, New York State's 2002 energy plan, a technocratic government document, focused predominantly on the State's strategy for ensuring a stable supply of energy primarily from fossil fuels; it only tangentially mentioned low-income communities of color in relation to equitable power plant siting. In 2015, conversely, the State's energy plan prominently lauded the potential of renewable energy to strengthen low-income communities of color, making the case for community-driven electricity programs like shared solar—ideas that are directly attributable to the advocacy of intersectional activists in statewide policy proceedings, working groups, and other expert spaces where they shifted public discourse (as evinced by the aforementioned workshops). Put simply, the confluence of renewable energy technologies and intersectional activism has altered how State bureaucrats frame and approach energy, enabling a form of antiracist governmentality where communities of color are empowered to manage their own energy futures.

This sort of intersectional reconceptualization of industrialized energy in expert-driven spaces was on plain display when John reconvened his staff to explicitly discuss structural racism. In a meandering conversation, staff reflected on the BLM protests that were sprouting up in cities across the country and how the company can improve its professional interactions with communities of color to expand their solar installations in low- and moderate-income residential buildings—a muddled discourse on race that emerged from John's contention that ameliorating injustice must be a part of the company's commitment to "making the world a better place." While engineers in traditional technocratic settings "may come across as apolitical or clued out about contemporary issues outside of technology" ([32]: 41), the engineers at this meeting employed an explicitly political lens to contextualize their work in the broader workings of society. Here, too, the material-discursive node was operative. As discussed, the company views its clean energy technologies as a vehicle toward social progress. The ways in which solar ostensibly improves the environment—its material capacity to "reduce greenhouse gas emissions"—are enmeshed in broader understandings of societal improvement—of improving public heath, reducing energy bills, and strengthening affordable housing via energy upgrades. The company's energy experts evoked this web of meanings to amplify an antiracist politics atypical of Financial District firms. For instance, one employee contended that "it's very easy for us to criticize the cops . . . but systems of oppression work together and the same stuff that's leading to horrific police killings of innocent black men and women is the same system of oppression that's causing gentrification, yet we don't acknowledge that we have a part to play in gentrification by installing solar for a lot of nasty building owners." She then called on the company to focus solar installations on rent-stabilized low-income housing to combat gentrification. We see here that intersectional activists' antiracist discourses and rooftop solar panels interactively engender a corporate imaginary where liberal white experts can help install a better future in service of marginalized communities through the socially conscious deployment of industrialized energy.

In sum, the intersectional ethos foundational to movements like BLM and the material dimensions of solar have created new spaces for antiracist activists to take part in the traditionally technocratic realm of industrialized energy, endowing renewable technologies with the capacity to support intersectional change. Implicit to this work is a proposition that industrialized energy can work in service of broader efforts to make black lives matter. The next section will consider this proposition, calling for a deeper reconceptualization of energy in ways that better tend to structural oppression through energy democracy activism.

---

5. "ENERGY" MATTERS

While antiracist activists endow solar panels with the capacity to upend the fossil fueled order that de-matters black lives, a close look at the solar industry destabilizes this conceptualization. Far from a "clean" technology, most solar panels are manufactured with no environmental or public health regulation in poor Global South communities, exposing the people of color who work solar factory assembly lines and live in factory-adjacent homes to a host of deleterious toxins and pollutants that severely compromise their health and well-being [33]. Put simply, solar production de-matters Global South communities, evincing the ways in which "toxins participate vividly in the racial mattering of locations [and] humans" ([34]: 10). This, in turn, problematizes any effort to make black lives matter by democratically provisioning renewable energy technologies. Much like the black activists fighting environmental injustices in the U.S., Chinese activists in recent years have mobilized to shut down the corrosive solar manufacturing plants which have poisoned their bodies and environment [35]—mobilizations that are entirely disconnected from the U.S. energy democracy movement. Furthermore, one of the largest solar manufacturing companies contracts production out to a prison labor program that pays prisoners well below the minimum wage [36]—their product situated squarely in a racist penal system that de-matters black lives [37]. While solar installation jobs are touted as a means of building prosperity in communities ravaged by the prison industrial complex—the basis of an alternative economy affirming the value of the black lives that have been deemed expendable by the police state—that same violent system continues to exploit those lives in the production of technologies that foreground the utopic energy democracy vision. Finally, this vision pays little attention to the thirty-year lifespan of solar panels and their inevitable decommissioning—a development that will likely contribute to the e-waste crisis [68] already hampering the low-income communities that disproportionately house waste management infrastructures. For these reasons, the struggle to democratize industrialized energy in ways that support black lives must not uncritically rely on the expansion of solar technology markets that de-matter multiple marginalized groups.

While it is important to address these problems through codified labor standards, technological innovations, and supply chain oversight, such interventions cannot de-link industrialized energy from material-discursive regimes of racialized de-mattering. Instead, the Big-E conception of energy that undergirds energy democracy campaigns is rooted in a broader semiotics of racial hierarchy. To understand why, let's revisit that Big-E conception.

Although energy democracy activists vociferously argue that energy development clearly has racial implications—that, for instance, power plants are disproportionately sited in low-income communities of color—the inherent properties of energy as they understand them are entirely non-racialized. These activists conceptualize energy as a physical force that can be created without regard for social categories like race. Although this conception largely emerged from an epistemological milieu centered on electrons, circuitry, and the power of machinery, it also took shape through racial subjugation—the de-mattering of black lives. In other words, our capacity to conceive of energy as a commoditizable force is contingent on systems that denigrate people of color—a premise I will now elaborate.

In both the Big-E and little-e frameworks, energy implies or is related to a change in matter; from the vital forces pulsing through human bodies laboring in lowland fields [38] to the industrialized force catalyzing economic growth in energy experts' models [14], energy moves, transforms, or acts on matter. These understandings of energy are rooted in and mirror the most basic definitions of energy in physics, that is, the capacity to elicit or cause change in matter [39]. As a "capacity" or a "potential," energy "is not a concrete entity" [40]—not a thing that one can own. Along these lines, "energy is superhuman in the sense that humans cannot create it. They can only refine or convert it" ([6]: 81). Importantly, this process of converting energy—of eliciting changes in matter—also demarcates who and what matters in the metaphysical sense—who or what demands our reverence and concern. Put simply, our capacity to change matter marks our sense of what matters.

To illustrate this, we can consider what mattered to human societies prior to industrialized energy in the broad historical epoch that Goudsblom [40] calls the "fire regime." For about 250,000 years, humans primarily harnessed energy through the domestication of fire [40]. Whereas humans once sustained their lives by exclusively harnessing energy through the intake of food, resembling all species in this respect, fire-based innovations

—

gradually set humans apart, making us the only species to elicit changes in matter through the use of fuels [40]. The fire regime catalyzed a range of cultural forms and representational practices, as humans adopted religious beliefs, prayers, spiritual communities, and sacred holidays to reify and worship the divine forces that they believed maintained the flames that fueled their livelihoods [41]. The fire regime, in other words, generated intricate belief systems and normative values, demarcating matters of importance. Put differently, the uniquely human ability to elicit changes in matter through fuels created entire infrastructures of mattering—sociocultural systems that assigned value and importance to certain matters of survival and livelihood.

While preindustrial fire worshipping societies are not a monolith, we can glean from their totality a basic facet of fuel-driven existence: our representational practices and semiotic structures cannot be extricated from the practices through which humans elicit changes in matter. Well before the emergence of the English word "energy" in the sixteenth century, many human societies did not "distinguish between the natural and the spiritual" properties of transformations of matter—did not, for instance, separate fire's divine character from its biospheric impacts—"because the prescientific concept of energy did not bear a primary reference to physical operations" ([42]: 18). Furthermore, when we consider the first formal definition of energy in English—"force or vigor of expression" [43]—we see that the word has frequently been understood not merely in terms of its physical properties but also its capacity to convey meaning. Thus, energy is not simply an objective phenomenon; it is instead a material-discursive force—its materiality inseparable from the values it mediates.

The epistemological transformations generated by Cartesianism and the technological innovations made possible by Newtonian physics and rationalist metaphysics worked to separate the discursive realm (and its tropes of mattering) from the ability to elicit changes in matter. With the proliferation of propositions separating "mind" from "matter" and scholarship contending that the universe operates according to immutable laws, a new understanding of energy took shape, that is "the power of 'doing work' possessed at any instant by a body or system of bodies" [43]. In other words, the concept of energy came to emphasize the physical potentiality intrinsic to material forms, suggesting that this potentiality exists without

—

semiotic mediation. We can partially locate this conceptual separation of the material from the discursive—physical matter from subjective mattering—in the industrial technologies through which we harness energy. As Marx argues, industrial technologies enabled humans to elicit changes in matter in ways that were "entirely emancipated from the restraints of human strength" ([44]: 499), generating understandings of energy as a force not embedded in humans' material relations with vegetation, seasonal rhythms, and the biospheric phenomena on which our lives depend, but instead as the mechanistic output of technological processes untethered to local context, communities, or customs [45]. In this way, industrial technologies endowed the process of energy generation with a mechanistic affect that appears disconnected from the discursive space through which we demarcate what matters to us.

However, a quick historical scan of the Big-E Energy apparatus makes clear that discursive mattering was always instrumental to industrialized transformations of matter. While such a scan often begins with the steam engine, the light bulb, or other fossil fuel technologies, none of these mechanical innovations points to the origins of industrialized energy. Instead, the first industrial-scale energy infrastructure was the Trans-Atlantic Slave Trade—the foundational apparatus in the de-mattering of black lives. I will now trace the roots of this energy infrastructure to elucidate the racialized nature of industrialized changes in matter.

6. SLAVERY AND INDUSTRIALIZED ENERGY

The Trans-Atlantic Slave Trade commoditized human beings by violently disciplining them to elicit profitable changes in matter through commercialized land transformations. In this way, it was an unprecedented energy generation regime providing colonial societies with a mechanized infrastructure that enabled them to efficiently produce commodities and consolidate wealth.

Of course, this "peculiar institution" was not the first system of human enslavement to power societies. Before fossil fuels, "civilization ran on a two-cycle engine: the energy of solar-fed crops and the energy of slaves. Shackled human muscle built, powered, and emboldened empires from Mesopotamia to Mexico" ([46]: 17–18). But the Trans-Atlantic version of

———

this energy infrastructure was unique in its reliance on financial capital and racial difference—its denigration of Africans and their descendants through regimes of commodification in pursuit of monetary profit. In the U.S., this racialized, capitalized system cohered through the expansion of colonial plantations, vast spaces of commercial activity "owned" by a privileged planter class who sought to ramp-up production of the era's foremost commodities, tobacco and cotton, in the seventeenth and eighteenth centuries [47]. Their profit maximization imperatives necessitated an infrastructure through which they could efficiently acquire land and labor, and exploit multiple forms of life—soil, plants, human bodies—to transform matter into capitalized goods. Racial difference formed the bedrock of this infrastructure, as the planter class propagated a discourse of "savages" to legitimize the murder of Native peoples on the grounds that they were ontologically inferior, facilitating the violent privatization of the land these peoples inhabited to expand the plantation system [48]. In other words, a social hierarchy that posited that Native peoples were racially inferior to Euro-American colonialists foregrounded the physical infrastructure used to efficiently extract the sun's energy in the drive for surplus value. The American plantation—a material landscape organized in ways that maximized the profitable transformation of matter—could not exist without a violent symbolic order that distinguished between the human race (white people) and savages (Native people).

The planter class then expanded this racial caste system to forcefully and inexpensively grow the labor force they needed to cultivate their new property. By designating Africans as a "savage" race, more boorish and barbaric than the red-skinned peoples, they magnified the racial symbolic order to generate and legitimize a complex system of chattel slavery [48]. Importantly, this expansion of the symbolic order was predicated on skin color—blackness—as it appeared to be the most legible physical marker of ontological difference and thereby the most convenient means of "subjugat[ing] the 'foreign'" ([49]: 70). In these ways, the industrialized transformation of matter was predicated on making black lives not matter.

In crudely tracing the well-known origins of American slavery, I wish to emphasize that the racial caste system that undergirded this peculiar energy infrastructure did not simply denigrate Africans and Natives; it concomitantly denigrated non-humans. In other words, white colonialists

—

legitimized the murder, dispossession, and enslavement of the people who unwittingly constituted the "black" and "red" races on the grounds that these races were inferior to the human race [48]. The industrial-scale extraction of energy from slaves was rooted in their ontological status as less-than-human. In this way, the production of industrialized energy reified the Cartesian divide between the human and non-human. Put differently, the notion that energy is a "thing" which humans can produce—a quantifiable force untethered to interbeing relationality or subjective meaning—emerged from the notion that some humans matter more than other humans. In other words, contemporary understandings of energy took shape at the intersections of racial alterity and anthropocentric dualism.

Colonial history further illustrates this proposition. Whereas Native peoples in North America cultivated animistic ontologies and emphasized "reciprocity" between humans and their biophysical environs ([50]: 80), the first European colonists viewed their newly discovered land as "hideous and desolate wilderness" and "savage," ontologically inferior to Puritan patriarchs whose God called for the forceful "subjugation" of nature ([51]: 100–101). Note that the term used to denigrate nature—savage—was the same term used to dehumanize Native and African peoples; in these schemas, the human is both superior and a white man. This colonialist outlook was part and parcel of a broader Cartesian epistemology that took shape in the sixteenth and seventeenth centuries conceptualizing humans as "masters" of nature and endowing man with a divine right to, in the words of Francis Bacon, "establish and extend the power and dominion of the human race itself over the universe" ([51]: 127). This metaphysical hierarchy paralleled the racialized subjugation of African slaves, comparably (although not identically) relegating nature and Negroes to the realm of the domitable.

This colonialist anthropocentrism was grounded in a "philosophy of nature based on particles of inert, dead matter moved by external forces . . . [that] could be exploited for human progress" ([51]: 127), enabling humans to affix monetary prices onto the trees, water, and soil that they transformed in the conversion of energy toward their own ends. It was also foundational to "emergent substance dualism," which posited that all substance can be classified as either matter—that which can be spatially

—

extended—or mind—that which thinks—creating an ontological division between the mind and body that posited the latter as a machine "that operated according to mechanical laws" in contradistinction to the cognitive agency of the human brain ([51]: 199). In this context, a new understanding of energy emerged in the early nineteenth century through the discipline of physics. As discussed, "energy" originally denoted "vigour of expression," a concept linked to cognitive processes, but came to mean "the power of 'doing work' possessed at any instant by a body or system of bodies" [43], a concept which situated energy in a physical realm distinct from the mind.

This new definition is indicative of the broader epistemological context of colonial society and its intersecting ontological propositions. The notion that the human race is superior to non-human savagery—whether "savagery" takes the form of wilderness or Native and black people—is inseparable from the notion that the human mind is superior to matter, that it is capable of discerning and controlling matter through the cognitive processes of science, and that the capacity to elicit changes in matter—that which we refer to as energy—is a physical potentiality realized through labor (i.e., "work") and discrete from the domain of the mind. In this schema, energy is isolated in mechanistic corporeality, a physical realm connected broadly to matter beneath the mental capacities of the human—capacities which distinguish white men from non-human savagery. As a concept denoting bodily work, energy's corporeal character cannot be separated from the toiling African slaves whose labor constituted the nascent country's commercialized transformations of matter and whose bodies were marked as black to make them not matter. In other words, industrialized energy—mechanized work that fuels commercial society—was traditionally rooted in an anthropocentric white supremacy that debased matter, nature, and non-white bodies in intersecting ways, de-mattering black lives in the process.

With the abolition of slavery, fossil fuels replaced slaves as the main industrialized means of transforming matter, marking the first major energy transition in the U.S. Yet throughout this transition, the symbolic order that enabled colonial society to denigrate black lives in the interest of exploiting nature proved resilient. In other words, the racial and class-based hierarchies that privileged white property owners—the exemplary masters of nature—over landless laborers, and all white lives over non-white lives stayed firmly intact in the post-emancipation period [52], as the Industrial Revolution ignited the ascendance of fossil fuels. The combustion engine, the electricity grid, and the assembly line—all fruits of this ascendance—created new opportunities for the wealthy white men who controlled them to transform matter in ways that further mechanized black bodies in the pursuit of profit and more fully enmeshed this white supremacist order in the subjugation of a growing multiracial proletariat and non-human forms of life. From the relegation of former black slaves and their descendants to the "least desirable jobs" on coal-powered assembly lines ([53]: 35) to the exploitation of poor Chinese immigrants through the development of the first coal-powered transportation system, the railroad [54]; from the swelling ranks of infirm, indigent black and white coal miners [55], to the proliferation of racist policies that pitted the white working masses against non-whites for control over the wealth created by this industrialized system (such as redlining [56] and the Chinese Exclusion Act [54]), the transition to fossil fuels institutionalized racial hierarchies in ways that intersected with regimes of capitalist exploitation. At the same time, these regimes caused unprecedented ecological degradation [57], magnifying the "dominance" of white men over nature—the anthropocentric hierarchy that had been institutionalized through the colonial apparatus. In these ways, black and brown lives retained their ontological kinship with non-human nature: inferior, exploited—de-mattered.

Furthermore, fossil fuel technologies had profound ramifications for how we understand energy. By replacing the activities and eroding the skills that humans traditionally used to sustain their lives, these technologies made energy appear not as a capacity that we can convert but as a thing that can be grown and "accumulated in stockpiles" ([6]: 82), a market without biophysical limitations, or an object which humans can have and reproduce—much like a slave whose being is understood in terms of their owner's profits and their labor's bodily reproduction. Our alienation as energy consumers from the forms of human and non-human exploitation that enable us to, for instance, flip a light switch [58], mirrors the obfuscation at the root of our former slave-based energy system, which hid the trauma of enslavement beneath the veneer of the cotton commodity [59]. In other words, "energy," in its fossil fueled form, resembles the wilderness and enslaved bodies through which it once predominantly circulated: a lifeless thing in the debased realm of matter (as opposed to mind).

All of these interconnected developments propagated a much broader and more sophisticated energy generation system which disproportionately impacts the health and welfare of low-income communities of color in the U.S.—communities which house a disproportionate share of power plants, oil refineries, and highways, and whose members pay a disproportionate share of their income on energy [60]. We can talk endlessly about fossil fuels' deleterious impacts on communities of color, but the point here is that our commercialized infrastructure for transforming matter—which includes solar panels on low-income buildings—has always taken shape through structures of meaning and materiality that deem certain lives expendable. While it would be reductive to claim that industrialized energy creates ontological equivalences between inert commodities, human laborers, and biospheric matter, we can say that it operates as a central mechanism in the unstable, ongoing material-discursive practice of de-mattering certain forms of life along racist, anthropocentric ontological spectrums.

7. DECOLONIZING ENERGY

If industrialized transformations of matter are contingent on black bodies not mattering, perhaps the energy democracy movement must begin to forge new relationships with matter. Perhaps, as we organize to aggregate solar installations in low-income communities of color or advocate for net metering policies, we can also tend to the forms of energy that lack industrial transmission lines, approaching it as something other than the electrical output of solar technologies.

The little-e conception of energy is helpful in this regard. It locates the capacity to change matter in the relational ties between people, plants, animals, other biospheric forms, and even the modern technologies which we are inextricably composed of [61]—not in a product which one can have and grow. As suggested above, the materiality of solar technologies has begun to orient modern actors to this relational energy in spaces saturated with Big-E systems, generating a greater engagement with the sun's biophysical properties among marginalized people who never previously interacted so consciously with solar radiation. Similarly, for many of the renewable energy experts discussed above, the industrialized systems that they develop, monitor, and monetize are not simply mechanical entities for efficiently delivering an immutable commodity; they are also vital forces integral to the workings of an ecosystem, a source of livelihood that keeps humans in harmony with the biosphere. As such, the advent of renewables presents an opportunity to further reconceptualize Big-E systems in terms of this relational energy, connecting us to lives obfuscated by industrialized transformations of matter.

Large-scale renewable energy projects in Native American communities are instructive toward this end. While these communities deploy renewable energy technologies to tap the abundance of sun and wind on their lands, they do so by nourishing their long-standing relations with biospheric elements and through their cultural practices to mediate ancestral ties such as "morning prayer to greet . . . Father Sun and to request holistic balance with Mother Earth" ([62]: 243). In so doing, they consciously work to eschew the alienating, exploitative trajectories of industrialized energy. By amplifying their vital relations with biospheric matter vis-à-vis Big-E infrastructure, they transform solar and wind systems from strictly biopolitical technologies to what Powell calls "technologies of existence" ([63]: 128)—infrastructures through which they generate "enjoyable" ways of being and cultivate lively relationships to local space ([63]: 126). Navajo activist Tom Goldtooth explains:

> . . . utility-scale, centralized renewable-energy systems such as wind and solar, based upon an exportation-orientated economic system that views energy production as a commodity . . . are not sustainable . . . Without reevaluating what we mean as an "alternative energy system," I am concerned we will have wind and solar systems built on the same capitalist model that is depleting . . . Mother Earth . . . I am an advocate for our Native Nations to develop wind and solar, but most of our tribes have traditional belief systems that must guide us in these forms of development. When we, as Native Nations, create massive wind-power projects, we must have ceremonies to obtain permission to utilize the sacred elements—to harness and process wind and sun into electricity that will be exported off our Native lands into these colonial grid systems that don't directly benefit our people.

In calling for relations with biospheric forces and linking electrical grids with the colonial project, Goldtooth pushes us beyond efforts to democratize the solar industry. Instead he offers insights for decolonizing energy, that is, disentangling it from the historically intersecting colonizations of brown bodies and non-human nature. Decolonization operates on the grounds that it is "inadequate to merely include people of color in untransformed institutions" and that "a comprehensive *unsettling* of colonial logics and institutions" is necessary to bring about change ([64]: 205). Toward this end, an energy democracy movement that connects marginalized people with other vital forms can challenge the anthropocentrism of industrialized energy—its privileging of humans over the ecosystems from which it emerges—destabilizing the symbolic conditions which positioned white humans over savagery and de-mattered black lives.

Hartman [65] provides a blueprint for decolonizing energy in recounting her experience as an American black woman grappling with her African ancestry and the legacy of slavery in Ghana when the country encountered prolonged electricity disruptions. Unprepared for navigating the world at night without the lifeblood of electricity, she relied on a flashlight while the Ghanaians around her made due in the darkness. "I . . . feared [my flashlight] was the equivalent of the pith helmet worn by colonial administrators. Illuminating the world seemed like an act of violence, when everyone else was willing to fare in darkness" ([65]: 174). It's telling that Hartman affiliates her small source of modern energy with the colonial apparatus, indexing the ways in which energy production often de-matter black lives. She continues:

> My flashlight was a defense not against dark, dark Africa but against my own compromised sight . . . I had been in Ghana nearly half a year and I barely understood the world around me . . . But over the course of weeks, I began to experience a kind of relief when the lights went out . . . The darkness provided a welcome retreat from my failure and, to my surprise, the threshold to a world I had failed to notice. I became . . . adjusted to a city without lights . . . As I made my way through streets . . . the people hidden from view and the things I had failed to notice now bumped into me in the night. . . .

—

She goes on to describe a pair of trysting lovers on a soccer field, "a night soil man" carrying waste over his head, "ordinary flies darting above the sewers," a seamstress who she knows slumbering outside with her daughter, and countless other forms of life that she grew attuned to beneath the canopy of the nighttime, relating to these physical forms—seeing in them the subtleties of existence—in ways electricity had previously precluded ([65]: 175–176). In other words, the lack of industrialized energy impelled Hartman to *re*-encounter matter, making many of the lives that had once seemed immaterial to her begin to matter. In her efforts to confront the legacy of an energy system that had enslaved her ancestors and de-mattered black lives, those lives came to matter only when the failures of modern electricity demanded a new engagement with materiality. Importantly, this did not entail a full-fledged abnegation of modern forms of energy. To the contrary, she depended on her flashlight to illuminate that which she previously had not seen. Indeed, transgressive encounters with matter do not necessitate Luddism. We can utilize modern technologies to transform matter in ways that facilitate lived connections, striking a balance between industrialized and relational energies predicated on the proposition that black lives matter.

As black activists and marginalized groups carve their own space in the Big-E realm, striking this balance becomes all the more imperative. We can foster relational energy in an industrialized context on multiple levels. On a transnational level, black energy democracy activists can cultivate relations with Global South activists protesting the exploitative conditions of solar panel production; on a local level, we can follow Hartman's lead and cultivate relations with our immediate environs by attenuating our dependence on industrialized energy, looking for traces of life when we loosen our grip on electricity, heat, and fuels; on a bodily level, we can follow BLM's energy transition agenda and cultivate relationships with the land that sustains us—the biospheric matter from which many blacks were displaced in the fossil fuel revolution—recognizing that food is both an "energy" issue and a matter of black livelihood; on an interpersonal level, when we convene meetings to discuss the sobering technical matter of energy technology, we can cultivate relations with one another's bodies and voices through jokes, song, and dance, "free[ing] up" the joyful,

—

vibrant "energy flows [that] can get blocked in our bodies" as a result of patriarchy, poverty, racism, and other intersecting oppressions ([66]: 117); and on a technological level, we can continue to prioritize the development of decentralized energy systems such as microgrids and shared solar— systems, in other words, that connect neighbors together, empowering us to collectively own and operate the mechanized transformations of matter that are integral to modern existence. The totality of these endeavors can disrupt the forms of systematic alienation through which (neo-)colonial powers de-matter myriad beings. While the transition from a slave-based energy system to a fossil fuel-based energy system did not affirm the value of black lives, the transition to renewables presents new opportunities toward this end.

In this paper I have argued that renewable energy technologies and intersectional ideologies have collectively enabled marginalized groups to participate in and shape the technocratic energy sector, reconfiguring dominant understandings of energy and generating new political imaginaries from the grassroots to the corporate boardroom. The heuristic of "black lives" has played an important role in this reconfiguration, injecting a crucial antiracist metaphysics into discourses of industrialized energy. This heuristic has the potential to open up new conceptual space with regard to energy, elucidating the limitations of renewable alternatives like solar and connecting us with the forms of life de-mattered by Big-E transformations of matter. When we consciously harness the energy that flows among traditionally overlooked lives, we transform the regimes of mattering that predicate industrialized energy, calling attention to the ontological value of that which we're distally connected to through the grid. And in these moments, we incrementally dim the hierarchical metaphysics that relegated black lives to the fleshy fuel of our first commercial-scale transformations of matter—a metaphysics still operative in the placement of black communities by coal-fired power plants or the relegation of U.S. prisoners to assembly lines producing solar panels. Instead these lives begin to matter, impelling us to reconsider the systems through which we transform matter.

NOTES

1. Karen Barad [1] coined the phrase "material-discursive" to refer to the co-constitutive nature of meaning and materiality. Drawing from quantum physics, Barad troubles the Cartesian distinction between "things" and "words," contending that the boundaries between objects and subjects are not self-evident and are instead made legible through ongoing "intra-actions" between myriad physical properties and metaphysical values—material-discursive practices. "Intra-action," here, destabilizes individualist metaphysics by suggesting that no entity is a discrete "thing" with finite ontological boundaries—that all objects, subjects, and ideas are entangled and therefore constantly "intra-acting."

2. Whether his projects actually succeed in adhering to a little-e ethos or substantially differ from traditional large-scale electrification projects are matters that merit serious investigation.

REFERENCES

1. K. Barad, Meeting the Universe Halfway: Quantum Physics and the Entanglement of Matter and Meaning, Duke University Press, Durham, NC, 2007.
2. J. Butler, Gender Trouble: Feminism and the Subversion of Identity, Routledge, London, UK, 1990.
3. S. Strauss, S. Rupp, T. Love, Powerlines: cultures of energy in the twenty-first century, Cultures of Energy: Power, Practices, Technologies, Left Coast Press Inc., Walnut Creek, CA, 2013.
4. J. Burgess, M. Nye, Rematerializing energy use through transparent monitoring systems, Energy Policy 36 (2008) 4454–4459.
5. S. Rupp, Considering energy: $E = mc^2$ = (magic culture)^2, Cultures of Energy: Power, Practices, Technologies, Left Coast Press Inc., Walnut Creek, CA, 2013.
6. W. Berry, The Unsettling of America: Culture and Agriculture, Sierra Club Books, San Francisco, CA, 1986.
7. A. Mason, M. Stoilkova, Corporeality of consultant expertise in arctic natural gas development, J. North. Stud. 6 (2) (2012) 83–96.
8. M. Thompson, Among the energy tribes: a cultural framework for the analysis and design of energy policy, Policy Sci. 17 (3) (1984) 321–339.
9. A. Hudgins, A. Poole, Framing fracking: private property, common resources, and regimes of governance, J. Polit. Ecol. 21 (2014) 304–319.
10. L. Lohmann, Carbon trading, climate justice and the production of ignorance: ten examples, Development 51 (2008) 359–365.
11. L. Bank, Basic energy needs and multiple fuel use: some reflections on energy policy and social theory, Domestic Use of Electrical Energy Conference 1999 (1999).
12. J. Tatum, Energy Possibilities: Rethinking Alternatives and the Choice-Making Process, SUNY Press, Albany, 1995.
13. H. Norrström, Sustainable and balanced energy efficiency and preservation in our built heritage, Sustainability 5 (6) (2013) 2623–2643.

---

14. L. Nader, The harder path—shifting gears, The Energy Reader, Wiley-Blackwell, Oxford, 2010.
15. L. Nader, N. Milleron, Dimensions of the 'people problem' in energy research and 'the factual basis of dispersed energy futures', Energy 4 (1979) 953–967.
16. E. Cecelski, Re-thinking gender and energy: old and new directions, ENERGIA/EASE Discussion Paper, Energy, Environment & Development (EED), 2004.
17. C. Chapman, Multinatural resources: ontologies of energy and the politics of inevitability in Alaska, Cultures of Energy: Power, Practices, Technologies, Left Coast Press Inc., Walnut Creek, CA, 2013.
18. R. D. Bullard, Dumping in Dixie: Race, Class and Environmental Quality, Westview Press, Boulder, CO, 2000.
19. Gwen Ottinger, The winds of change: environmental justice in energy transitions, Sci. Cult. 22 (2) (2013) 222–229.
20. J. T. Roberts, M. M. Toffolon-Weiss, Chronicles from the Environmental Justice Frontline, Cambridge University Press, Cambridge, 2001.
21. M. Foucault, The Birth of Biopolitics: Lectures at the Collège de France, 1978–1979, Picador, New York, NY, 2010.
22. Center for Social Inclusion, Energy Democracy. Retrieved September 10, 2016, from http://www.centerforsocialinclusion.org/ideas/energy-democracy//.
23. Black Lives Matter, Guiding Principles. Retrieved March 20, 2016, from http://blacklivesmatter.com/guiding-principles//.
24. J. Patterson, Energy Democracy, #Blacklivesmatter, and the NAACP Advocacy Agenda, (2015) May 29, Retrieved March 20, 2016, from http://www.naacp.org/blog/entry/energy-democracy-blacklivesmatter-and-the-naacp-advocacy-agenda.
25. Muhammad Yunus, Banker to the Poor: The Story of the Grameen Bank, Aurum Press, London, UK, 2013.
26. M. Bray, Translating Anarchy: The Anarchism of Occupy Wall Street, Zero Books, 2013.
27. A. W. Kelbert, Climate Change Is a Racist Crisis, The Guardian, 2016 Retrieved on February 1, 2017, from https://www.theguardian.com/commentisfree/2016/sep/06/climate-change-racist-crisis-london-city-airport-black-lives-matter.
28. D. Boyer, Energopower: an introduction, Anthropol. Q. 87 (2) (2014) 309–333.
29. C. Özden-Schilling, Economy electric, Cult. Anthropol. 30 (4) (2015) 578–588.
30. V. May, Pursuing Intersectionality, Unsettling Dominant Imaginaries, Routledge, New York, NY, 2015.
31. M4BL Policy, Invest-Divest, (2016) Retrieved August 20, 2016, from https://policy.m4bl.org/invest-divest/.
32. D. Riley, Engineering and Social Justice, Morgan and Claypool Publishing, San Rafael, CA, 2008.
33. O. Zehner, Green Illusions: The Dirty Secrets of Clean Energy and the Future of Environmentalism, University of Nebraska Press, Lincoln, 2012.
34. M. Y. Chen, Animacies: Biopolitics, Racial Mattering, and Queer Affect, Duke University Press, Durham, NC, 2012.

———

35. BBC News, China Solar Panel Factory Shut After Protests, (2011) September 19, Retrieved April 1, 2016, from http://www.bbc.com/news/world-asia-pacific-14968605.

36. N. Groom, INSIGHT-Prison Labor Helps U.S. Solar Company Manufacture at Home, Reuters, 2015 June 10, Retrieved on April 2, 2016, from http://www.reuters.com/article/solar-prison-suniva-idUSL1N0YP17Y20150610.

37. M. Alexander, The New Jim Crow: Mass Incarceration in the Age of Colorblindness, The New Press, New York, NY, 2010.

38. S. Gudeman, Vital energy: the current of relations, Soc. Anal. 56 (1) (2012) 57–73.

39. C. H. Stone, A neglected topic in chemistry teaching, Sch. Sci. Math. 35 (8) (1935) 795–798.

40. J. Goudsblom, Energy and civilisation, Hum. Fig. 1 (2012) 1.

41. S. Pyne, Fire: A Brief History, University of Washington Press, Seattle, WA, 2001.

42. B. Clarke, From Energy to Information: Representation in Science and Technology, Art, and Literature, Stanford University Press, Palo Alto, CA, 2002.

43. Oxford English Dictionary, Oxford English Dictionary, Third edition, Oxford University Press, Oxford, 2010.

44. K. Marx, Capital: Volume I, Penguin Classics, London, 1990.

45. L. Lohmann, Energy Alternatives: Surveying the Territory, The Corner House, UK, 2013.

46. A. Nikiforuk, The Energy of Slaves: Oil and the New Servitude, Greystone Books, Vancouver, 2014.

47. S. L. Malcomson, One Drop of Blood: The American Misadventure of Race, Farrar, Straus and Giroux, New York, NY, 2000.

48. S. P. Harvey, Ideas of Race in Early America, Oxford Research Encyclopedia of American History, 2016 Retrieved from http://americanhistory.oxfordre.com/view/10.1093/acrefore/9780199329175.001.0001/acrefore-9780199329175-e-262?print=pdf.

49. H. Spillers, Mama's baby, papa's maybe: an American Grammar Book, Diacritics 17 (2) (1987) 65–81.

50. W. LaDuke, The Winona LaDuke Reader: A Collection of Essential Writings, MBI Publishing, Minneapolis, MN, 2002.

51. C. Merchant, Ecological Revolutions: Nature, Gender, and Science in New England, University of North Carolina Press, Chapel Hill, NC, 1989.

52. B. J. Fields, K. E. Fields, Racecraft: The Soul of Inequality in American Life, Verso, New York, NY, 2012.

53. S. R. Crew, The great migration of Afro-Americans, 1915–40, Mon. Labor Rev. 110 (3) (1987) 34–36.

54. T. E. Boswell, A split labor market analysis of discrimination against Chinese immigrants, 1850–1882, Am. Sociol. Rev. 51 (3) (1986) 352–371.

55. R. L. Lewis, Black Coal Miners in America: Race, Class, and Community Conflict, 1780–1980, University Press of Kentucky, Lexington, 1987.

56. S. E. Tolnay, K. D. Crowder, R. M. Adelman, Race, regional origin, and residence in northern cities at the beginning of the great migration, Am. Sociol. Rev. 67 (3) (2002) 456–475.

———

57. Vitousek, et al., Human domination of earth's ecosystems, Science 277 (5325) (1997) 494–499.
58. M. Degani, et al., Conversation 1: theorizing energy and culture, Cultures of Energy: Power, Practices, Technologies, Left Coast Press Inc., Walnut Creek, CA, 2013.
59. L. B. Glickman, Buy for the sake of the slave: abolitionism and the origins of American Consumer Activism, Am. Q. 56 (4) (2004) 889–912.
60. B. Bovarnick, D. Banks, State Policies to Increase Low-Income Communities' Access to Solar Power, Center for American Progress, 2014 Accessed on March 10, 2016, at https://cdn.americanprogress.org/wp-content/uploads/2014/09/LowIncomeSolar -brief.pdf.
61. D. Haraway, Simians, Cyborgs, and Women: The Reinvention of Nature, Routledge, 1991.
62. D. Powell, D. Long, Landscapes of power: renewable energy activism in Diné Bikéyah, Indians & Energy: Exploitation and Opportunity in the American Southwest, School of Advanced Research Press, Santa Fe, 2010.
63. D. Powell, Technologies of existence: the indigenous environmental justice movement, Development 49 (3) (2006) 125–132.
64. J. Rosa, Y. Bonilla, Deprovincializing Trump, decolonizing diversity, and unsettling anthropology, Am. Ethnol. 44 (2) (2017) 201–208.
65. S. Hartman, Lose Your Mother: A Journey Along the Atlantic Slave Route, Farrar, Straus and Giroux, New York, NY, 2007.
66. A. M. Cox, Shapeshifters: Black Girls and the Choreography of Citizenship, Duke University Press, Durham, NC, 2015.
67. Laura Nader, The politics of energy: toward a bottom-up approach, Radcliffe Q. 67 (1981) 5–6.
68. D. Mulvaney, et al., Toward a Just and Sustainable Solar Energy Industry, Silicon Valley Toxics Coalition, 2009.

NONHUMAN
LIFE

INTRODUCTION

Humans share the earth with animals, plants, and a great diversity of other entities across land, water, and air. At its core, environmental anthropology considers the ways people navigate relationships with other-than-human species. Indeed, the previous three themes of this reader can be read, in part, as a meditation on how people situate themselves within, apart, and against the nonhuman components of nature. These bonds can be considered through specific species, such as cows or elephants, or across particular environments, including deserts, swamps, and forests. Anthropologists point to the incredible range such relations with nonhuman life can take, from those predicated on violence and extraction, to ones based on mutual respect and care.

Regardless of its focus, the majority of foundational work in environmental anthropology bestows a privileged ontological position to humans when theorizing human-nature relationships, whereby human forms of knowledge, experience, and action are established as the baseline for identifying productive action and thought. In comparison, animals, plants, trees, and other nonhuman entities are more likely to be considered inactive targets for intervention, or as passive vessels for the absorption of human meaning and value. Recently, emerging work in multispecies ethnography has taken a more-than-human perspective on the entanglements of nature, decentering this predominantly human view. This scholarship, at times referred to as the "ontological turn," takes seriously other, nonhuman ways of knowing, experiencing, and being in the world. It asks how animals, plants, and other facets of the environment act upon humans and how they may form generative communities of their own. Some scholars also consider the forms of consciousness and agency contained in entities often assumed to lack such traits.

In this theme, we have selected two recent articles in environmental anthropology that take a multispecies approach to understanding the relationships between humans and nature. Together they interrogate two of the main categories of nonhuman nature: plants and animals. In each of their ethnographies, the authors attend to the complex lifeworlds of nonhumans, while not losing sight of the entrenched forms of power contained within human historical, political, and economic systems. It is within this nexus of human and nonhuman forces that the everyday relations of nature emerge.

In the first article, Radhika Govindrajan draws from a legacy of work in environmental anthropology on the relationships between people and domesticated animals, crafting a careful ethnography of the ways that goats come to stand in for humans in the context of animal sacrifice in the Central Himalayan region of India. She notes the twinned relationships of violence and care that shape the interspecies engagement between households in villages of the Indian Himalaya and the goats that are so integral to their lives and livelihoods. In the second article, John Charles Ryan takes us from animals to plants. As he notes, plants are commonly regarded in Northern thought as passive, sessile, and silent automatons lacking a brain, as accessories or backdrops to human affairs. Ryan, drawing from scholarship in the emerging field of human-plant studies (HPS), asks us to instead imagine plants as "agentive, autonomous, and intelligent subjects" (284) that are active collaborators in the production of material and cultural landscapes.

Taken together, the two authors draw connections between the ethnographic sensibilities of multispecies studies and broader sustainability

---

concerns. To various degrees, each author shifts the burden of proof prevalent in much Northern thought, moving from assuming nonhuman entities such as plants and animals have little or no capacity for agency, to assuming that these species may, in fact, represent alternative forms of intelligence and consciousness. Such a shift, in turn, necessitates that people reconsider existing frameworks for environmental ethics, including what constitutes forms of cruelty and of care toward nonhuman beings. It encourages a fundamental rearrangement of human and nonhuman power dynamics, whereby humans are not unquestioned masters of nature but rather "plain citizens" within it (Leopold [1949] 1989). This humbler view opens space for sustainability initiatives that are more mindful of the plurality, creativity, and beauty that constitutes nature, across all forms of life.

DISCUSSION QUESTIONS

1. One challenge of multispecies anthropology is developing appropriate research methods. Even if anthropologists try to decenter human perspectives, their work is necessarily filtered through human senses, language, and knowledge. What methods do the authors in this section use to observe and analyze nonhuman perspectives? What do you see as the strengths and weaknesses of these methods? Can you propose additional ways to investigate nature that consider nonhuman forms of experience and agency?

2. The authors point to different forms of power that nonhuman beings may exercise. Yet humans often have more power compared to nonhumans, exerting considerable force over plants, animals, and landscapes. In your opinion, how do analyses of power factor into understanding multispecies relationships? What are the possibilities and limits to nonhuman forms of power?

3. The authors each argue that rethinking the consciousness, agency, and selfhood of other species leads to a reexamination of environmental ethics—one based on care and reciprocity. Do you agree? What are the potential benefits and challenges of conferring legal rights to entities such as animals, rivers, and even nature? Do you see connections

—

between new understandings of multispecies relationships and questions of sustainability?

WORK CITED

Leopold, Aldo. (1949) 1989. *A Sand County Almanac, and Sketches Here and There*. Oxford: Oxford University Press.

———

7

"THE GOAT THAT DIED FOR FAMILY"

ANIMAL SACRIFICE AND INTERSPECIES KINSHIP IN INDIA'S CENTRAL HIMALAYAS

RADHIKA GOVINDRAJAN

In the summer of 2013, a series of cloudbursts, floods, and landslides struck India's Central Himalayan state of Uttarakhand, causing thousands of deaths and devastating homes and entire villages. A few weeks after the rains abated, people flocked to temples across the region to seek an explanation for the destruction from their *devi-devta* (local goddesses and gods). At a temple dedicated to the local Hindu deity Golu in the eastern part of the state, I struck up a conversation with Devidutt, an elderly man accompanied by several members of his family.[1] With them was a goat intended for sacrifice, nibbling at the garland of roses that hung loosely around his neck. Everyone around us was trying to make sense of the devastation of the last few weeks, and so were we. I agreed with Devidutt that the recent boom in construction had weakened the mountains, and he nodded when I reviewed the theories of climate change circulating in the Indian press.

But, he said dismissively, such talk was mere speculation. There was

---

Originally published as, Govindrajan, R., 2015. "The Goat That Died for Family": Animal Sacrifice and Interspecies Kinship in India's Central Himalayas. *American Ethnologist*, 42(3), pp. 504–19. Reprinted with permission from John Wiley & Sons, all rights reserved.

—

another, undeniable, explanation for the destruction, and it had nothing to do with construction or climate change. "I saw on television that there are hundreds of corpses floating in the Ganga," he said wearily. "What else could it be but a sign that our deities are angry?" When I asked what might have ignited this divine rage, he told me that, in the olden days, deities took human sacrifices until they were finally persuaded to accept animals instead. But in 2011, an Uttarakhand High Court ruling, in response to numerous petitions from animal rights organizations, announced that only animals whose meat was subsequently consumed could be sacrificed in temples. Devidutt suggested that this ruling had scared some people into abandoning sacrifice, which, in turn, had angered the deities. Thus, he concluded, the monsoonal fury of the last few weeks was divine revenge. The gods had resumed taking human sacrifice and would continue to do so until animal sacrifice was offered to them again.

Devidutt's daughter-in-law, Neetu, spoke up. "Even this goat knows the gods are upset," she said to me, gesturing at the animal that stood beside us. The old man nodded. He related how, for the last two weeks, every time he had taken the family's goats out to graze, this particular goat had gone missing. The first time it happened, Devidutt had been afraid that the goat had strayed into a neighbor's field, but he had found him kneeling outside a little village shrine dedicated to Golu, as if he were praying. The same thing happened for several days in succession. "In the mountains," he observed, "animals have a special relationship with *devi-devta*. This goat is a devotee of *Golu devta*. This is a *devbhumi* (land of the gods), and animals play their own part in maintaining its sacred power. The disaster happened because the gods were unhappy. The goat recognized that and was telling me to do my duty and sacrifice him to Golu."

I was intrigued by this explanation of the goat's behavior and asked how the family knew that the animal was telling them it was time for him to be sacrificed.[2] Neetu responded first, saying,

> It's like this . . . we raise them from birth. That's how we know what they want . . . Do this [she pulled the goat's ear] and they go down instead of up . . . when they nudge you here [gesturing to her hip] you know they want water. They cannot speak, but they have a language . . . that's how we know. You feel *mamta* (maternal love) for them as

—

you do for your children. Nobody asks a mother how she knows that her infant is crying because it is hungry. You just know because you gave birth to it and raised it. We may not give birth [to these animals], but we raise them like mothers. They consider us mothers too. That's how we knew the goat was telling us it was time to give *puja* (a devotional offering) . . . Of course, it saddens us when our animals die. But in the olden times we would sacrifice our children, no? This is another form of that. These goats die for their family.

It would be easy to dismiss Neetu's perspective as a self-serving response to claims that sacrifice causes unconscionable suffering for sentient beings. After all, one could point out, the comparison between children and goats is limited, as people do not kill their children. The question of asymmetrical power is urgent, and I return to it below. But to read Neetu's and Devidutt's words as disingenuous would prevent us from exploring the world of possibilities they open up for explaining the complex processes through which human and nonhuman animals come to be constituted as kindred subjects in relation to one another and to the gods in this mountain landscape.

What if, instead, we were to take these emic categories of experience as the starting point of analysis? What might adopting the perspective of Neetu and Devidutt reveal about sacrifice as a practice of intimacy between humans and nonhumans? Sacrifice is generally understood in terms of a set of ritual images, narratives, and acts that renew social relations through the displacement of societal conflict onto a scapegoat (Bloch 1992; Durkheim 2001; Frazer 1912; Girard 1977; Lambek 2007). Some theorists suggest that the basic principle of ritual sacrifice is substitution, the use of a surrogate victim for the original other (Doniger and Smith 1989; Hubert and Mauss 1981; Lévi-Strauss 1966). What makes this substitution possible, they assert, is the "theoretical identification of the sacrificer and the victim" (Doniger 1988:99). But in what material and affective contexts does this theoretical identification between human and nonhuman emerge? Is it possible to trace, through thick ethnographic description, how an animal becomes an appropriate stand-in for a human victim in a sacrifice? What insights can the field that has variously been described as "multispecies ethnography" (Kirksey and Helmreich 2010), "interspecies" anthropology

—

(Livingston and Puar 2011), and the "anthropology of life" (Kohn 2007) offer one of anthropology's oldest and most enduring concerns—sacrifice—and vice versa?

An interspecies approach to the study of ritual animal sacrifice illuminates how the identification of human with nonhuman animal in sacrificial contexts is enabled by a sense of shared kinship fostered through the embodied experience of everyday entanglement in relations of care, attention, and subjection. These proximate intimacies, based in no small part on the embodied language that Neetu described sharing with her animals, create a realm of affective and relational kinship between human and nonhuman animals. Neetu invoked this kindred mutuality in her use of the term *mamta* to describe her feelings for her goats and their response to her maternal care. Ritual sacrifice acquires power and meaning through its grounding in precisely this world of kinship between human and animal.

Casting an interspecies lens on sacrifice, then, illustrates how this phenomenon is animated by a sense of interspecies kinship sustained by embodied and relational practices of intimate care. But what can an affective theory of sacrifice offer multispecies anthropology? I contend that animal sacrifice in Uttarakhand is itself constitutive of interspecies kin relations. When grappling with ethical dilemmas about the value of different lives and who has power over death, many villagers turn to the register of kinship to describe how sacrifice deepens the bonds of relatedness between them and the animals they offer to the gods. They speak of this ritual practice as the closing of a circle of kinship, a moment that cements the connection of individual goats to their human families. By dying in place of a human family member, some women said, goats repay the care they receive, much as children in the past consented to their sacrifice for the sake of the family. This (re)making of interspecies kinship is, no doubt, violent, but the role of sacrifice in establishing and strengthening connections and kin relations between human and nonhuman animals is undeniable. Interspecies kinship, thus, both crafts and is crafted by sacrificial acts.

To explore the creative possibilities and ethical dilemmas that arise in framing the act of sacrifice as one of interspecies kinship, I turn first to an examination of the material and affective conditions in which kin solidarity emerges between disparate beings, focusing on the intersection

---

of care and violence as a productive site for the creation of these bonds. I then address a question that is crucial to scholarship on sacrifice—the circumstances that allow for the identification of animal with human and the consequent substitution of the former for the latter as a ritual offering—by examining ideas of animal agency and selfhood. Following this discussion, I ethnographically trace how a sense of interspecies kinship emerges across two interconnected social realms in the mountain villages of Uttarakhand: firstly, in the shared status of humans and nonhuman animals as self-aware and reflexive subjects of powerful local deities who demand sacrifice from their followers and, secondly, through embodied practices of domestication that produce a sense of interspecies mutuality, what humans often cast in terms of *mamta*, or maternal love. Finally, in light of the experience of my ethnographic subjects, whose lives are intimately entangled with other lives in ways that bring questions of relation and ethics to the fore, I ask if sacrifice can be dismissed as an act of killing that frees the sacrificer from any obligation to relate to the sacrificial victim as one who also has life.

CARE AND VIOLENCE: THE CONDITIONS OF KIN SOLIDARITY

The idea that sacrificial animals share a bond of kinship with those who sacrifice them is not new to anthropology. In his work on early Semitic sacrifice, William Robertson Smith (1927) proposes that the original sacrificial animal was akin to a totemic animal, believed to be holy by those who sacrificed it.[3] Through their communal consumption of sacrificial meat, human worshippers not only emphasized their blood relationship to the sacrificial animal and the god but also reaffirmed their blood bonds with one another. Sigmund Freud, summarizing Smith's work, writes that in prepastoral societies "the sacrificial animal was treated like one of kin; the sacrificing community, its god, and the sacrificial animal were of the same blood, and the members of a clan" (1998:117).[4] While this work opens up a space for thinking about the kindred dimensions of sacrifice, the sense of interspecies kinship at work in Uttarakhand is closer to what Emile Durkheim describes for the Gewwe Gal tribespeople of New South Wales, who believed "that each person has within him an affinity for the spirit

—

of some bird, beast or reptile. It is not that the individual is thought to be descended from that animal, but that a kinship is thought to exist between the spirit that animates the man and the spirit of the animal" (2001:192).

Though attentive to how kinship between humans, animals, and gods is crucial to the creation of sacrificial meaning and power, Smith, Freud, and Durkheim do not say much about what it is that leads to this kinship. What, then, are the conditions of possibility in which a sense of interspecies kinship arises? What historical and contemporary structures shape affective attachments and disavowals? In the villages of the Central Himalayas, the kinship of spirit between human and animal is fostered by practices of domestication that rely on the embodied participation of one being in the life of another. It is through the everyday process of going "in and out of each other's minds and bodies," to borrow Maurice Bloch's (2012) evocative turn of phrase, that humans and animals come to be constituted as kin. Whether communicating with one another through a language of the body that requires understanding what a touch signals or quite literally entering the other's body, as I once observed a woman doing when she helped her goat give birth by gently pulling the kid out of the womb, the "intercorporeal" nature of care, which I consider in more depth below, is the condition of possibility for the slow emergence of kin solidarity between human and nonhuman animal (Ingold 2011; Al-Mohammad and Peluso 2012).

However, these relational, embodied entanglements that I call "kinship" are forged not only through practices of embodied care but also in the crucible of embodied violence. The spectacular act of violence that lies at the very heart of sacrifice in Uttarakhand—the beheading of the sacrificial animal—is as crucial to the constitution of a sense of kinship between human sacrificer and animal victim as is the everyday process of attending to and caring for that animal. What messy ethics emerge, then, from the complicated imbrications of care and violence that characterize these entwined human and animal lives? Many in the mountains are critical of animal sacrifice, whether animal rights groups who decry the cruelty of sacrifice, Hindu reform organizations who believe the practice is un-Hindu, or young *paharis* who are keen to abandon practices that, to them, reek of "tradition."[5] These critics would be skeptical of the claim that interspecies kinship and love shape the act of sacrifice. They would perhaps argue that the undeniable violence of sacrifice—the cries of the

---

animals in their last moments, the spasming of headless torsos, the gush of blood and guts—must force an engagement with animal death and human responsibility for it.

Some people who look to negotiate this ethical quagmire find ways to decenter death and violence by speculating about the possibility of life after death, a popular node for the relation of human to nonhuman in South Asia. In the course of a conversation in 2011, a young man named Bansi asked me if I remembered a particular scene from the Kumauni movie *Balivedna* (Sacrificial Pangs; see Bali Vedna Part 1.DAT 2013; Bali Vedna Part 2.DAT 2013), a stinging critique of animal sacrifice that we had watched together. The scene he referred to involved a conversation about animal souls between a temple priest and a village headman, on the one side, and, on the other side, a youth shattered by the sacrifice of his favorite goat. The priest and the headman, arguing with the youth about the importance of sacrifice, assert that sacrificial death, unlike ordinary forms of death, releases animal souls from the cycle of rebirth and guarantees their happiness.

Bansi recounted how, watching *Balivedna*, he was reminded of a particularly rambunctious goat he used to take out grazing as a child. The goat led him down paths he had never followed before, and he recalled those afternoons of exploration with pleasure. He lowered his voice as he told me about how the goat was eventually sacrificed, leaving him bereft. "I liked that scene in the movie a lot," he said after a few moments of silence.

> I remember how much I cried when that goat was sacrificed. I didn't take the animals to graze for days until my father slapped me hard across my face and told me I had to go. But what the headman said made me happy. I realized if I really loved that goat then I should be happy that his soul was *mukt* (released), not sad that he died. He died as *puja*, not at the butcher's. Our deities will look after him. Thanks to that . . . he might have been reborn as a human, who knows?

The obvious comfort Bansi derived from the thought that the goat's soul might have been liberated from the cycle of rebirth as a result of local deities' pleasure with the sacrifice, an idea ridiculed in the film, speaks to how difficult it is for those who live in intimate proximity with companion animals to come to terms with their deaths. While the intimacy Bansi recalled so poignantly does not stand outside power, it is a vivid reminder that human relationships with nonhumans are characterized by a plenitude of affect that complicates any convenient dualism between love and death, distress and pride, veneration and consumption.[6] To invoke John Berger, a peasant can become fond of her goat and still be happy to watch him die a sacrificial death.[7] Indeed, any attempt to explore the complex relationships between humans and nonhumans will be poorer for not taking into account how, in the interstices of power and violence, spaces for love, care, and mutuality flourish.

SACRIFICE AS AN INTERSPECIES RELATIONSHIP: MATERIALIZING SACRIFICIAL MATTER

Anthropological writing on sacrifice conceives of it as involving three participating beings, objects, or domains: one who gives, one who receives, and one who is given or sacrificed (Carter 2003:4).[8] In *Sacrifice: Its Nature and Functions*, Henri Hubert and Marcel Mauss (1981) define sacrifice in terms of the root *sacré*, that which "makes sacred." They conceptualize sacrifice as a "religious act which, through the consecration of a victim, modifies the condition of the moral person who accomplishes it" (Hubert and Mauss 1981:13). For them, the sacrificial victim serves as a link between the sacred and the profane; its consecration goes beyond it to sacralize the person who makes the offering. Other scholars have suggested that the purpose of the sacrificial victim is not so much to link sacred and profane as to ransom the life of an original human victim. The human who sacrifices an animal is, in effect, "ransoming" him- or herself from death at the altar of the gods. It is this "sleight of hand," this game of "displacement and replacement," that distinguishes sacrifice from other forms of death, that redeems it from criminality (Doniger and Smith 1989:189).

For the most part, this body of work emphasizes the symbolic significance of the sacrificial victim at the expense of a serious consideration of how sacrificial bodies and objects are lively "material-semiotic" beings (Haraway 2008:4). The question of why a particular animal or flower or vegetable is chosen as a substitute for a human victim is treated as a semiotic one: the ideal victim is as symbolically close to human as possible. One

reason for this emphasis on semiotics at the expense of materiality, especially in the Vedic South Asian context, could be a reliance on sacrificial
myths and texts, which, as Wendy Doniger notes, treat substitution not as
a historical question but as one relating to "the nature of ritual symbolism,
explaining how it is that plants or mantras stand for animals, and animals
for humans, in the sacrifice" (2009:153).

Such systems of classification that allowed nonhumans to symbolically
stand in for humans in sacrifice struck Claude Lévi-Strauss as "wanting in
good sense" because they "adopt a conception of the natural series which is
false from the objective point of view for . . . it represents it as continuous"
(1966:227–228). However, these continuities between human and nonhuman, which might seem inconsistent from an "objective point of view,"
make more sense if we locate the production of semiotic meaning firmly in
the world of lived interactions between different beings. To fully appreciate
sacrificial substitution, in other words, these myths and rituals must be
situated in a broader world of historical embodied entanglements between
human and nonhuman, where animals are simultaneously good to eat,
"good to think" (Lévi-Strauss), and good to "live with" (Haraway 2008).
Sacrificial animals, furthermore, must be recognized as more than just sacrificial matter. Sacrificial identification is not with the "idea" of animals,
as E. E. Evans-Pritchard (1953:185) declared in his work on Nuer sacrifice,
but with lively corporeal animals who act "as quasi agents or forces with
trajectories, propensities, or tendencies of their own" (Bennett 2010:ix).[9]

Indeed, the "consequential materiality" of animals is a crucial component in people's understanding of them as kin (Kosek 2006:23). The extension of kin relations to nonhumans is not a human projection of cultural
meaning onto a fetish but a recognition that emerges from complex and
constitutive lived relationships with individual animals who engage, exasperate, and enchant the humans whose lives are entangled with theirs.
A variety of nonhuman animals traverse the rural landscape of the Central
Himalayas. Goats, leopards, buffaloes, birds, wild boars, cows, monkeys,
and bears are among the many animals with whom humans share this
landscape. The actions of these nonhuman animals often exceed people's
expectations of them, animating social processes and relationships in
unexpected ways. While their agency, like that of humans, does not stand
in any easy relationship to what social theorists might acknowledge as

—

intention, mountain villagers argue that many animals act with precisely what the former think of as perceptible intention.[10] This imputation of intentional agency to animals is not restricted to livestock companions. Elsewhere I discuss how monkeys, especially translocated macaques from the plains, are spoken of as creatures who deliberately trouble humans, throwing clean washing in the dirt, stealing food they do not eat, and scaring people just for their own amusement (Govindrajan 2015). Similarly, women in the mountains often speak in excited whispers about male bears who desire human women, sometimes kidnapping and having sex with them. These desires are not ascribed to instinct but are framed as intentional acts of interspecies love and sex. It is to these willful, intentional nonhuman actors that humans extend the ties of kinship.

The recognition of animals as agents shapes the perception that people and animals are related in another way—they are both selves. I use the term *self* to capture people's belief that animals, like humans, are relatively reflexive creatures with an awareness of being in a world that they inhabit with humans, other nonhumans, and the divine.[11] This Kumauni (and South Asian) understanding of selfhood is not restricted to an autonomous, singular human body but is "mutable, multidimensional, nonlinear . . . a moving part among other moving parts" (Smith 2006:xvi).[12] Two clarifications are in order here. Firstly, this shared sense of selfhood is hierarchical: Nonhumans are believed to possess a less-developed sense of self than humans possess. Secondly, not all kinds of animals are thought to possess selfhood in the same way or to the same degree. The intimate, embodied proximities of everyday life allow humans to attribute what can be called "selfhood" to livestock in a way that they do not to wild animals. However, despite these gradations, even wild animals can be reflexive beings with a "point of view" (Kohn 2007). For instance, some villagers said that leopards are such fervent devotees of *devis* that they know if a person has sullied a temple by transgressing rules of purity and pollution. Even if the transgression was inadvertent, I was told, leopards will sit in front of the temple in the middle of the day, terrorizing people until a purification ceremony is carried out.[13]

This understanding of selfhood as going beyond a human individual is consistent with notions of the self in Indic thought.[14] Popular notions of the self and self-representation in South Asia are hybrid, contingent, and

—

relational.[15] Indeed, as William Sax points out, "Hindu thought . . . anticipates postmodern and poststructuralist 'deconstructions' of the person/ self in the sense that it accords no ontological primacy to the phenomenal 'person' or 'individual', regarding it as a mere appearance, the temporary effect of a variety of underlying causes" (2002:11). Further, the significance of complex notions of selfhood is not restricted to ethnographic contexts alone. In his work on possession in South Asia, for instance, Frederick M. Smith notes that Vedic texts such as the Satapatha Brahmana insist on a "self that is constitutive of an intimate interplay between human, divine, and sacrificial bodies" (2006:9).

In Uttarakhand, the idea that animals are reflexive and self-aware beings both shapes and is shaped by the sacrificial substitution of animal for human. While this perception emerges organically from the everyday unfolding of lives, it acquires deeper significance in the context of people's belief that animals share a meaningful relation with local deities. People believe that the actions of mountain deities affect not just their own lives but also the lives of animals, bringing human and nonhuman together in a shared bond of supplication to the divine. Sometimes, villagers told me, the moods and experiences of deities are reflected in and mediated through the behavior of animals. A sudden spike in wild boar incursions into cultivated fields, for instance, could be a sign that the gods are upset. In other words, the experiences of deities and animals are thought to converge in certain moments, revealing an affective connection between them. Animals can act in ways that depend on and reflect divine preoccupations. As far as villagers are concerned, then, the selfhood of animals is constituted not only in relation to people but also in relation to the gods. It is to this world of entanglements between human, animal, and the divine that I now move.

"GODS EXPECT THE LIFE OF A DEVOTEE": HUMAN–ANIMAL KINSHIP IN A SACRED GEOGRAPHY

In popular discourse, Uttarakhand is often called a "devbhumi," a land of gods. Vishnu and Shiva, Yamuna and Ganga, the "textual deities" of Hinduism (Babb 1975) who are called "bhagwan" to distinguish them from local devi-devta, reside in some of Hinduism's holiest shrines in the

Himalayas. However, it is not just the high gods residing in the Himalayas who make this land a devbhumi but hundreds of local deities as well, who live alongside humans and nonhumans and are an integral part of their everyday lives (Berreman 1963; Sax 2009). Indeed, the presence of thousands of humble shrines dedicated to these deities ensure that this is truly a "sacred geography," a "living landscape in which mountains, rivers and forests are elaborately linked to the stories of the gods" (Eck 2012:5). These deities are perceived as agents, corporeal residents of the Hindu world who are "existentially coeval" with humans and make decisions that affect human lives (Chakrabarty 2007:16; cf. Sax 2009; Singh 2011).

Blood sacrifice is an important part of the worship of these deities. During festivals, hundreds of animals are sacrificed over the course of one day, but a smaller number of animals are also sacrificed most weeks of the year. A portion of the sacrificial meat is given to the officiating priest who acts as the representative of the deity, and the rest is consumed by the immediate family and relatives who provide the animal. Most of the animal sacrifices I observed during the course of my fieldwork, whether in large temples or at more humble shrines in villages, involved goats. Goats are raised primarily for sacrifice and meat in this region, and it is common for people to earmark certain animals for sacrifice. The ubiquity of goats, and their consequential (over)representation in sacrifice, has been aided over the last few years by government rural development policies that encourage goat keeping as a source of livelihood.[16]

The practice of sacrifice has become the subject of (renewed) debate over the last decade, forcing people to evaluate and explain their relationship with local deities and the animals they sacrifice. Part of the unease over sacrifice comes from the growing influence of the pan-Indian gods of Hinduism, who have increasingly taken their place alongside local devi-devta in mountain homes. High gods have always traveled through this landscape with pilgrims and migrants, but they have become more prominent in the last few decades through television and other forms of media. Their interlocutors, whether traveling ascetics or gurus who preach from Sanskrit texts on television, argue that blood sacrifice has no place in the "traditional" Hinduism dominated by the divinities of the Sanskrit tradition.

Animal rights organizations share in the disapproval of sacrifice. Since

2009, many such groups have called for a ban on animal sacrifice in Uttarakhand on the grounds that it is cruel and has no ritual significance in Hinduism.[17] Alliances with Hindu religious reform organizations who claim that Vedic texts contain no references to animal sacrifice have played an important part in buttressing the assertion that sacrifice is not religiously sanctioned and, further, that it deviates from the love of nature and pacifism that these groups believe are the hallmark of Hinduism.

In 2011, the Uttarakhand High Court ruled on a public interest litigation (PIL) brought before it by an animal rights group that has been vocal in its opposition to sacrifice over the last decade. The petition demanded a complete ban on animal sacrifice in the region. Instead, the High Court announced that any animal sacrificed had to be consumed by the sacrificers. In addition, animals could no longer be sacrificed in the open courtyards of temples but only in closed sheds set aside for the purpose. This ruling was interpreted by animal rights groups as amounting to a total ban, and they visited temples across the region to let people know that sacrifice was illegal. As a result, while everyday forms of sacrifice went on unhindered, the number of animals brought to temples on festival days declined. It was this ruling and its effects that Devidutt referred to the day I met him, his daughter-in-law, and the kneeling goat.

What the monsoon proved to Devidutt and many others was that local deities, the devi-devta of the mountains, were still the most powerful forces to be reckoned with. The destruction was seen as visible proof of their shakti, their sacred power, and as a warning to their devotees, both human and nonhuman, not to ignore them. Even those ambivalent about sacrifice, who believed that it was barbaric and backward, were forced to acknowledge that the gods were demanding their due. Lakshman, a man who had not sacrificed an animal in years, sacrificed one of his family's goats a few days after the cloudbursts. Explaining his actions, he said,

> Such things [monsoons] are held in check by sacrifice. People like me stopped giving sacrifice because of the court order and so this is happening. The gods are taking their sacrifice like this, and all their devotees are suffering. Do you think animals are suffering any less? Thousands of goats and cows are lying dead in rivers and gorges. This is a disaster for everybody.

———

He echoed a common refrain at the time. Many people worried about how to placate the gods, who were seemingly angry with everyone. As far as Neetu and Devidutt were concerned, even the kneeling goat seemed to recognize their anger and the need for conciliation. But the belief that animals are meaningful participants in this regional cosmology and subject to the dominion of deities predates and extends beyond the monsoon of 2013. People in the mountains think that animals are capable of talking, listening, and responding to deities, much like they themselves, and this belief plays an important part in their perception of animals as social beings with reflexivity and self-awareness.

The ability of animals to relate to and communicate with deities and humans alike is a crucial link in the sacrificial chain and is often considered a necessary condition for sacrifice to successfully appease the gods. In 2010, I joined a family of paharis on a trip to a powerful temple dedicated to the devi Ma Kalika, where they sacrificed eight goats. After the family had consumed a small portion of the meat as *prasad* (blessed offerings), an argument broke out between Neema, the matriarch of the family, and her nephew, Girish, who was visiting from the United States and had refused to eat the meat. Girish wanted to know why his aunt had not sacrificed flowers or coconuts instead of goats. "This is barbaric," he said to her bluntly in front of assembled family. "The gods would be as happy, if not happier, with flowers or coconuts." His aunt snorted derisively. In the old days, the gods would eat human sacrifice, she explained, ostensibly for my benefit but really for her nephew. The gods relented when an old widow with only one child begged for mercy. In exchange, she promised to sacrifice something that was precious to her, the animals she had raised just like children. "Coconuts aren't precious," Neema said to her nephew. "There's no loss when you give devi-devta coconuts. But giving an animal is like giving a person. A life is given in place of a life."

An elderly uncle-in-law of Neema's entered the fray by observing that "gods expect the life of a *bhakt* (devotee) because it tells them how much *bhakti* (devotion) they can command. A coconut isn't a devotee, an animal is." While this argument did not carry much weight with Girish, others in the room were impressed by the clarity of his statement. The sacrificial substitution of an animal's life for a human's life made sense in a way that substituting a coconut did not. A coconut is unlike a goat because

—

a coconut does not have the capacity to pray that a goat, like humans, is believed to possess. For Neema's uncle, and for a number of other mountain people, this lack of ability to relate to the gods as a self-aware being defeats any claim that the coconut might have to a sense of self.

The idea that goats are self-aware, subjective beings is especially powerful during that moment in the sacrificial process when they are thought by humans to consent to their own sacrifice. On the day of sacrifice, goats are first blessed by the priest of the temple dedicated to whichever deity is receiving the sacrifice. The goats' foreheads are anointed with a paste of vermillion and turmeric. A drop of water is then touched to the mouth of each goat, inducting him into the *gotra* (lineage group) of the family dedicating him to the deity.[18] A priest at the Ma Kalika temple in Kumaun explained to me that by being inducted into a family's gotra, a goat takes a *samkalp*, a vow to complete a particular religious task. In essence, the priest continued, the goat takes a vow to sacrifice himself to a deity on behalf of the family of which he is now part. This samkalp is completed when the goat is asked for his final consent to sacrifice. A sticky mixture of rice and water is sprinkled on his back to make him shake his body (Figure 7.1). If he shakes, it is read as a sign that he has consented to the sacrifice and the deity has accepted it (Figure 7.2). He is then whisked off to the sacrificer's shed to be beheaded, and his meat is subsequently distributed among family and friends. If he does not shake, he cannot be sacrificed that day since he is believed to have withheld consent and the deity is thought to have refused to accept his sacrifice.

When I asked the priest why some animals refuse to "consent," he thought for a while before responding. "Some people bring animals for sacrifice without any feeling of piety or devotion. Just to display their wealth . . . But animals are . . . true bhakts. If they feel that the person who's offering them to the god doesn't understand the real meaning of a sacrifice . . . doesn't have true devotion and gratitude in their heart, then they refuse to consent." From this perspective, the ability of sacrificial goats to publicly authenticate the sincerity and devotion required of humans for a successful sacrifice derives from the fact that they are part of a "reflexive ensemble" composed of humans, animals, and the divine (Kockelmann 2011:440). As far as the priest was concerned, only animals with a measure of reflexive self-awareness can understand and consent to their death in

FIGURE 7.1. A mixture of rice and water is sprinkled on the backs of sacrificial goats to make them visibly perform what people understand to be consent by shaking their bodies. Photo by Radhika Govindrajan, March 2011, Ma Kalika temple at Gangolihaat, Uttarakhand.

FIGURE 7.2. A woman pays obeisance to her goat, who has just shaken his body and is about to be taken to the sacrificial shed. Photo by Radhika Govindrajan, March 2011, Ma Kalika temple at Gangolihaat, Uttarakhand.

the same way that humans understood the necessity of their sacrifice and consented to it in the past. Here, the "identification" that must precede sacrificial substitution is between reflexive and self-aware kindred subjects.

This understanding of particular animals as kindred reflexive beings does not always extend to the level of species. Mountain villagers share a sense of kinship with mountain animals. The subjectivity of these particular animals, like that of the humans they live alongside, emerges from their entanglement in a web of interconnections with the deities of the devbhumi. Dinesh, a migrant from the mountains, told me how his elder brother, with whom he shared a house in Delhi, had once decided to sacrifice a goat to Golu devta. Not having the time to make a trip to the mountains, he asked the family priest to come to Delhi and oversee the ritual. But the goat, a big male the brothers had bought at the market in Delhi, refused to shake. They kept soaking it with water, but the goat just stood there. "And my elder brother is a devout man," Dinesh said. "Unlike me, he even observes rules of purity and pollution." Finally, it was the priest who suggested that they send for a goat from the mountains. A month later, after some expense, the goat was secured and promptly consented to the sacrifice. The problem with the first goat, Dinesh explained, was that animals in the plains simply did not have the same power that mountain animals did. "Why would that poor goat shake when he didn't have any connection with Golu devta?" Dinesh's friend, who was listening to us discuss the episode, was initially dubious of this reasoning but eventually started nodding vigorously. "Yes, there's something there. Things are just different in a devbhumi. The people are different, the animals are different." In this case, the web of relatedness through which humans and animals become subjective, self-aware beings derives its strength from being rooted in a particular sacred geography that is infused with the sacred power of local deities.

THE LOVE OF A MOTHER: DOMESTICATION, LOVE, AND DOMINATION

Mutual subjection to powerful local deities is not the only factor that creates the potential for human–animal relatedness. The intimate embodied proximities of everyday life open up a realm thick with the possibility of kinship between humans and nonhumans. This domain of affective kinship is at once "actively material" and "irreducibly discursive" (Raffles 2002:8). Nowhere is this discursive materiality more evident than in the embodied language that humans and animals use to communicate with one another. This "language of mutual response" (Haraway 2008) spoken through the body is crucial to the creation and maintenance of this affective realm. The kin relationship that Neetu described sharing with her goats was, for her, grounded in the fact that not only could she touch her goats to communicate what she wanted from them but they could also touch her to signal desires and fears of their own. These embodied forms of communication reveal that the "becoming" of human and nonhuman is a process of "becoming with" and "becoming together" (Haraway 2008:208, 244; cf. Parrenãs 2012; Smuts 2007).

In rural Uttarakhand, this process of becoming is one in which *mamta*, maternal love, plays an important role. The term *mamta* is culturally understood in Uttarakhand, and in India more generally, to describe the emotion a mother feels toward her child. In mountain villages, people's use of this term in referring to their livestock companions speaks to the redoing of kinship through the extension of familial relations to nonhumans (cf. Cormier 2013; Franklin and McKinnon 2001; Haraway 2008). A surprising number of men, especially of an older generation, who are involved in the daily care of animals also use the term despite its feminine markings (Figure 7.3). The mamta that paharis describe feeling for their animals is spontaneous and unplanned; they say it "just happens" (*ho jati hai*), much as a mother feels mamta for a child. The comparison with children is apt since it captures the everyday exasperations and annoyances that are such an integral part of raising both animals and children.

An incident that occurred one summer day in 2011 drove this similarity home for me. I was accompanying my friend Kusum and her herd of ten goats down a narrow village path lined on either side with stinging nettles and fruit trees. One little white goat with brown spots had climbed up a small tree and was making quick work of its leaves. Before Kusum could fling a stone at it, an elderly farmer appeared on the other side of the low stone wall that bordered the path and proceeded to scold Kusum loudly for not controlling her animals.

The week prior to this unexpected meeting, Kusum's goats had ravaged

—

FIGURE 7.3. A man holds aloft a goat that he says treats him like a mother. Some men, especially of an older generation, use the term *mamta*, "maternal love," to describe how they feel about the goats they raise. Photo by Radhika Govindrajan, July 2012, Nainital District, Uttarakhand.

a wheat field belonging to the farmer, whose name was Narinder Bisht. Kusum's younger children had been with the goats that day but had fallen asleep while watching them. The goats promptly wandered into nearby fields and set to work, where they were caught in the act by Narinder. He tied them to a post and sat next to them, waiting to scold the children when they appeared to collect their goats. Unfortunately for him, he too made the mistake of falling asleep, whereupon the children, who had been watching him from a distance, quietly untied the goats and took them home, flushed with triumph at having escaped a scolding. Having caught Kusum now, Bisht let loose, giving her an earful about her "thieving children" and "poisonous goats."

That evening, Kusum told her husband what had transpired. "It's these goats," she said at the end, "always the root of conflict. *Dusht* (wicked) animals." "Goats and children," her husband grumbled, casting an eye on their two girls, who were watching television instead of doing their homework. "They're both so troublesome. What can you do?"

Like Kusum's husband, other farmers often draw comparisons between raising children and raising goats. They emphasize similarities especially when talking about what exasperating animals goats are, about their willfulness and tendency to run away when no one is watching them. "You have to scold both children and goats," a woman told me once, laughing as I struggled ineffectually to coax a goat away from a patch of garlic. "If you had children or goats, you would know this. They don't understand anything without a beating." She threw a stone at the goat, and it moved off lazily as if to prove her point.

The similarity between raising goats and taking care of children was frequently invoked when women tried to explain the emotional attachment they felt to their animals (Figure 7.4). Bhagwati, a woman who was pitied and admired for raising four young children, seven goats, and three cows all at the same time, told me that getting her animals ready to go out and graze was much like getting her children ready for school in the morning. She would get to the cowshed by five every morning, where the animals were awake and waiting for her. She would give them dried grass before sitting down to milk the cows. The goats, she said, would frolic around her, nuzzling and butting her from every side as she focused on milking. "They're silly," she laughed. "They want attention all the time. It reminds me so much of my younger children, who get jealous when I'm getting the older children ready for school. They keep running around me demanding that I focus on them. It's annoying but also endearing."

The daily ritual of raising both children and animals and watching them grow at the same time creates strong bonds of affection between caregiver and care receiver. "Just as you feel maternal love for your children, it's like that with the animals you raise," Bhagwati said to me once, trying to put into words the bond she felt with her animals. Animals respond to this mamta much as children do, making it clear that this feeling of kinship is not a human projection onto unresponsive animals but a mutually enriching relationship. One woman became famous for being accompanied by a goat kid at all times. Even if she tethered him to a post in the cowshed, he would escape and follow her. On one such occasion, during a *bhajan* (devotional singing meet) at the temple, the kid curled up next to the woman, causing everyone to break into gales of laughter. The woman could not keep the smile off her face when she joked that the kid was her youngest child, one that still had not cut the umbilical cord. Indeed, many kids who are abandoned by their own mothers turn to their human "mothers" for milk, seeking them out among all the other members of the household. The bond between them looks, sounds, and feels like kinship on both sides.

The idea that livestock animals can demonstrate a need for human care, thus fostering a sense of mutual kinship, was reinforced for me by a conversation with an old man who spent most of his days taking the family's goats out to graze. One day he told me his goats reminded him of his grandchildren. "Sometimes they ignore you even when you call them until your throat is hoarse. They're very good at ignoring you when they want to. But sometimes, like when their father or mother butts them, they come running to you for comfort." One night, he recounted, somebody was careless enough to leave the door to the animal shed unlocked. A little after midnight, the sound of frantic bleating and thudding hooves woke everyone in the family up. "I think it was a jungle cat," he said, "that must have been trying to carry off one of the kids." The feline escaped when members of the household ran toward the shed banging pots and pans. One of the kids had puncture wounds in her neck, but no serious harm had been done. The family tied the kid up next to her mother, but she kept bleating. "Finally, I had to go out to the shed," the old man said. When he untied the kid, she ran toward him and huddled in the curve of his waist. Her hair was still standing on end and she was trembling uncontrollably. The old man murmured words of comfort to her until the trembling stopped, but she would not stay quiet without him. Every time he tried to leave, she would bleat nervously, and all the other goats would join in. "I just stayed there until morning," he recalled softly. "You see, she's used to being with me. My presence reassures her. I'm like her mother. She needed me more than she needed her own mother that night."

I was surprised by the man's use of the term mother, but it was a good reminder that the task of raising children and animals is still something that women normally do. The idiom of parental affection for children is very much a maternal idiom, probably a reflection that, in the mountains, women do much of the care work associated with raising children. The lack of a word for paternal love is evidence that the language of caregiving is a gendered one and that men who provide care assume female roles. This gendered language extends to caring for animals since women in

FIGURE 7.4. A kid tugs at the saree of the woman who fed her after her mother refused to give her milk. Photo by Radhika Govindrajan, 2011, Nainital District, Uttarakhand

this region do most of the work associated with raising livestock. Their tasks include cleaning out the cowshed in the mornings, cutting leaves and grass for fodder in the mornings and evenings, making hay to spread on the floor of the cowshed throughout the postmonsoon season, and taking animals out to graze on an everyday basis. Animal-related work is women's work.[19]

The intimate, embodied proximities described above, which are the source of mutual kinship binding human and nonhuman animals, play an important part in making sacrifice feel "real." On a festival day in 2010, when hundreds of goats had been sacrificed at a devi temple, I sat down next to a young woman with red-rimmed eyes and tear-stained cheeks. Concerned about her state, I asked what was wrong. She explained that her family had sacrificed a goat that morning, one of three goats she had raised herself. "I'll feel terrible tomorrow," she said with a wry smile. "The cowshed will be so empty. But this is real sacrifice." When I asked her what she meant by "real sacrifice," she responded with a question of her own. Did I know that the gods used to demand human sacrifice? I nodded. In those days, she continued, children used to die to save their parents; they went willingly to their death so that everyone else could be safe.

> Today things are different in some ways. Nobody sacrifices children anymore, we sacrifice animals. But in some ways it's not that different. When you live with animals and raise them, they are like your children. And when they shake [to consent], you feel that sense of pride in knowing that your children will die willingly to repay the mamta they receive. That's a real sacrifice, when you offer a goat you love almost as much as your child, and he repays your love by dying.

The young woman's words, whose sentiment I heard repeated by many others over the course of fieldwork, are a vivid reminder that animal sacrifice is rooted in a realm of affective sociality characterized by the mingling of domination, domestication, and love (cf. Tsing 2012). But the sense of pride that mingled with her sadness when the goat shook to indicate what the young woman read as consent illuminates something else about the nature of sacrifice: it is not just predicated on a sense of interspecies kinship but is also constitutive of it. For the young woman, the goat's sacrificial death

—

cemented her belief that she and the animal were united by a kin relationship. As she understood the situation, the goat had repaid the maternal love with which she had raised him by agreeing to die on behalf of his human family. Sacrifice is, no doubt, a violent making and affirmation of interspecies kinship. But, then, all relations of intimate proximity, to some degree, are inflected by power. Nor can the complex coexistence of love, guilt, pride, and death in ethnographic sacrificial contexts be captured by the idea that the logic of sacrifice entails no obligation or responsibility to any living being other than the human (Haraway 2008).

Recognizing that sacrifice rests on and fosters a complex copresence of human and nonhuman subjects entangled in embodied and mutual kinship relations with one another is particularly crucial in a South Asian context where, increasingly, *ahimsa* (nonviolence) and, by extension, vegetarianism, is idealized as the only acceptable Hindu mode of relating to nonhuman animals (Ghassem-Fachandi 2012).[20] Rituals like animal sacrifice are under attack by animal rights activists and Hindu reform organizations as "corruptions" of Hindu practice as a result of influences from other religions, particularly Islam.[21] Much is at stake politically in acknowledging the diversity of human relationships with animals and reclaiming sacrifice as part of Hindu practice. Recognizing that acts of sacrifice can be acts of interspecies kinship, characterized by responsibility and domination, guilt and relief, and love and death opens up a world in which it is possible to trace a multiplicity of forms of being and becoming.

CONCLUSION

I asked at the outset of this article what the field of interspecies ethnography and the anthropology of religious sacrifice can offer each other. In response, I have argued that the literature on sacrifice in anthropology and religious studies has, for the most part, emphasized the symbolic nature of the relationship between sacrificer and sacrificial victim and focused less on the affective, corporeal dimensions of their engagements. Drawing on the ethnographic context of the Central Himalayas, I argued that sacrifice in Uttarakhand derives meaning and power from its location in a realm of interspecies kinship that is embodied and relational. The intimate proximities of humans and animals that are the hallmark of domestication are

—

facilitated by an embodied language of mutual response, a language that allows humans and animals to "speak" without words. Further, this kinship is predicated on Kumauni villagers' understanding of the animals they tend to and sacrifice as subjective beings with reflexive self-awareness. It is this sense of embodied relatedness, with its hierarchies and incompleteness, that gives meaning to sacrificial substitution.

But what can the understanding of sacrifice as an act of interspecies kinship offer the field of human–animal studies? The answer is not immediately apparent. Scholars like Donna Haraway, while optimistic about the potential for "shared suffering" in complex copresences characterized by the relative unfreedom of animals and by "nonsymmetrical suffering and death" (2008:77), argue that the idiom of sacrifice forces it outside this realm of complex mutuality. The "solace of Sacrifice," a guilt-free form of killing, cannot capture the contingent and complex nature of inequality between two beings who "have face" (Haraway 2008:76). Following Jacques Derrida, Haraway contends that the logic of sacrifice works only because "there is a whole world of those who can be killed, because finally they are only something, not somebody, close enough to 'being' in order to be a model, substitute, sufficiently self-similar and so nourishing food, but not close enough to compel response" (2008:79).

Where does this leave us, then, on the question of what an interspecies theory of sacrifice can offer the field of multispecies ethnography? Let us put aside the idea that the logic of sacrifice is transcendental and pure, a claim that is complicated by the related literature, which notes that sacrificial idioms and practices are contingent on their location in particular ethnographic times and places. What of Haraway's more serious claim that sacrifice turns the animal as somebody into the animal as something that is not close enough to command a response from the human? The complex sacrificial practices and relationships at work in Uttarakhand, far from bearing out this understanding, open up a world rich with the possibility of mutual response and recognition. The sacrificial animal is not something but a recognizably self-aware and responsive being with whom humans share affective, intimate proximities. People's awareness that the animal killed in ritual sacrifice dies for them and in place of them both fosters and validates the affective bonds of what I have described as an interspecies kinship. Nor is the solace of sacrificial death uncomplicated

———

for these people who are intimately entangled with animals who not only have face but also voice and feeling. For Bansi, the young man who talked about his distress at the sacrifice of his goat companion, solace came only many years after the animal's death and was sparked by the hope that the abrupt and violent cessation of an interspecies friendship would be made up for by the liberation of the goat's soul. With the same sense of uncertain hope, I close with a reminder that isolating the violence of sacrifice from its companion constituents—love, guilt, grief, and devotion—would be to do fundamental injustice to the complexity of the interspecies encounter it entails. To reject the possibility that the kneeling goat might be something other than a scapegoat would mean rejecting an invitation to enter this world of entanglements and the promise it holds not just for those living in it but also for those who aspire to more ethical relationships with nonhumans.

ACKNOWLEDGMENTS

This article is based on fieldwork carried out over 18 months between 2010 and 2011 and over subsequent visits in 2012 and 2013. I thank the people in Uttarakhand who graciously permitted me into their homes and lives. My fieldwork was generously supported by the American Institute of Indian Studies, the Macmillan Center for International and Area Studies, the Program in Agrarian Studies at Yale, and the South Asian Studies Council at Yale. This article has benefited over the years from conversations with and comments from K. Sivaramakrishnan, James Scott, Helen Siu, William Kelly, Kamari Clarke, Sara Shneiderman, Juno Parreñas, Jake Kosek, Joshua Rubin, Sahana Ghosh, Nancy Abelmann, Andrew Orta, Hayder Al-Mohammad, Tariq Omar Ali, and Jayadev Athreya. I am grateful to the reviewers for their thoughtful and generous comments and to Angelique Hauregud and Linda Forman for their meticulous reading, which has greatly improved this piece.

NOTES

1. Uttarakhand is split into two divisions (mandals), Garhwal in the west and Kumaon in the east, where I carried out research for this project. The two regions are culturally and linguistically distinct even though they are politically unified, and, more

———

significantly, Garhwali and Kumauni people see each other as somewhat distinct (Berreman 1963; Sax 2002). For an account of the mass regional movement that led to the creation of the state as a new political entity in the Indian union in 2000, see Mawdsley 1998.

2. I use the male pronoun to refer to sacrificial goats since only males are selected as ritual offerings.

3. The holiness of the animal, Smith argued, was reflected in the fact that its life could not be taken by any one individual but only through the consent and participation of all the members of the clan.

4. Some scholars have questioned whether the sacrificial victim Smith described was as totemic as he claimed (see, e.g., Evans-Pritchard 1953; Lévi-Strauss 1966).

5. *Pahari* literally means "of the mountains," from the word *pahar* (mountains), and is generally used to refer to the non-Tibetan, Indo-European-language-speaking Hindus who inhabit the lower elevations of the Himalayas in north India and throughout Nepal. This region comprises what the anthropologist Gerald Berreman calls a "cultural area" (1960:774). While the term pahari is often used derogatorily by plains people to index cultural backwardness, it is the term that mountain people use most often to signal their distinct cultural identity.

6. In recent years, social theorists have devoted a great deal of attention to affect. Brian Massumi (2002) uses the term to describe an embodied intensity that is distinguished from emotion and language. For him, affect is asocial but not presocial. It pertains to matter and is usually thought of as emergent and dynamic. Exposing the concept of affect to critical scrutiny, William Mazzarella notes that contemporary theory puts in place a binary between immediacy and mediation that obscures how the latter "is at once perhaps the most fundamental and productive principle of all social life precisely because it is necessarily incomplete, unstable and provisional" (2009:302). With his observation in mind, I think it worth noting that the affective relations between people and animals in Uttarakhand are not presubjective or prelinguistic but mediated through an intercorporeal language between bodies that are inextricably material and discursive. For more on affect, see Parreñas 2012, Rutherford 2012, and Stewart 2007.

7. Berger writes that "a peasant becomes fond of his pig and is glad to salt away its pork. What is significant . . . and is so difficult for the urban stranger to understand, is that the two statements in that sentence are connected by an and and not by a but" (1980:7).

8. A rich body of philosophical work addresses the psychological, semiotic, ethical, and gendered dimensions of sacrifice and the sacred. Given this article's ethnographic focus, however, I do not focus on this body of work. See Keenan 2005 and Carter 2003 for reviews of this literature.

9. In his work on sacrificial rituals among the Nuer, Evans-Pritchard (1953) is careful to situate the relationship between sacrificer and sacrificial victim in the broader context of social life. He observes that sacrificial equivalence, the idea that two beings are of the same order and can therefore be substituted for one another in sacrifice,

———

had always been between a man and an ox. This equivalence, Evans-Pritchard insists, can be understood only in terms of the broader identification of the Nuer with their cattle in daily life. The use of ox names for men, the place of oxen in rituals of initiation, the value attached to cattle for their milk and as bridewealth are all emblematic of the identification of men with cattle in sacrifices. The significance of cattle in sacrifice was thus inseparable from their material and symbolic prominence in Nuer social and economic worlds. Despite his focus on the embodied, affective relationships that the Nuer shared with their cattle, ultimately, for Evans-Pritchard, it was not the particular "ox of initiation" but, rather, the "idea of oxen" with which people identified. He writes, "Any ox will therefore serve the purpose, or, indeed, no ox at all—only the memory, or rather the idea, of an ox" (Evans-Pritchard 1953:185).

10. In an essay on what interspecies ethnography can learn from indigenous standpoints, Kim Tallbear (2011) points out that recent scholarly interest in human relationships with nonhumans and the power of nonhumans to shape human political, social, and cultural words echoes, in some ways, an "American Indian metaphysic." However, she argues, this work falls short of taking indigenous standpoints seriously in its insistence on framing indigenous peoples' understandings of animals they live with as metaphor rather than reality. Following from that, to separate the question of animal agency from that of intention does not quite capture the radical nature of mountain villagers' insistence that animals are thoughtful and conscious beings who act in considered and intentional ways.

11. Conceptions of self and person are tricky to define, as several scholars have noted, leading to inconsistent and problematic understandings of what exactly selfhood entails (Sax 2009; Smith 2006). The only certainty is that one can say nothing certain about the "universality or the absolute cultural relativity of notions of self, personhood, individual, and the like" (Sax 2009:7).

12. For more on the self in a South Asian context, see Ewing 1990, Sax 2002, and Smith 2006.

13. In an article on state efforts to control a man-eating leopard in neighboring Garhwal, Nayanika Mathur notes that villagers believed the leopard was a devotee of "the Hindu god Shiva, given his circumambulation of the town's Shiva temple" (2014:163).

14. Human recognition of the personhood and selfhood of animals is not restricted to the South Asian context. The theory of Amazonian multinaturalism and monoculturalism put forth by Eduardo Viveiros de Castro (2004) points to the modalities through which many Amazonians recognize the personhood of nonhumans. Similarly, Eduardo Kohn notes that for the Amazonian Runa, "all beings, and not just humans, engage with the world and each other as selves—that is as beings that have a point of view" (2013:4).

15. This is not to suggest a dichotomy between East and West, with the West represented by individual persons and the East represented by relational persons. As Sarah Lamb points out, "a focus on relationality does not mean that no notion or experience of individuality or individual autonomy exists" (1997:282).

16. Goats were not the only animals sacrificed. Chickens were, on occasion, offered to

———

a malevolent spirit named Masan, who is worshipped near bodies of water around midnight. Women are not allowed to attend these nocturnal rituals for fear they might be possessed by malignant spirits. I never saw chickens sacrificed at large temples but only at smaller shrines on a few occasions. One reason chickens were not commonly sacrificed in the villages where I conducted fieldwork is that only a handful of families raised them. One had to travel some distance to procure a live chicken, whereas goats were always in ready supply and could be acquired either from one's own sheds or, at a pinch, from a neighbor. People also spoke of having sacrificed buffaloes in the past, especially to goddesses as part of the reenactment of the killing of the buffalo demon, Mahisasura. However, by the time I started fieldwork in the region, it was rare for people to sacrifice buffaloes, for reasons related to the recent legal controversy over animal sacrifice. People claimed that a sacrificial buffalo was thrown off a cliff after its death; its meat, unlike that of a goat, was never consumed because of its ritual impurity, although upper-caste villagers gossiped about the supposed fondness of lower-caste villagers for buffalo meat and claimed that its consumption reinforced the latter's inferior status (cf. Sax 1991). Much more could be said about people's relationships with buffaloes and chickens, but I restrict my focus here to relationships with goats, who dominated the sacrificial arena in my ethnographic experience.

17. Groups seeking a ban on religious sacrifice must make this argument since the constitution of India allows religious groups freedom to profess and propagate their religion.

18. The term *gotra* refers to a group that includes all persons who trace descent in an unbroken male line from a common male ancestor.

19. The gendered natue of people's relationships with domestic animals, and the ways in which the trope of mamta reinscribes and normalizes forms of gendered labor, is a fascinating and important topic and one that deserves closer attention than I can give it in this article. For further reading on the gendered dimensions of care, see Haraway 2003, Parrenãs 2012, and Freccero 2011.

20. In his work on anti-Muslim pogroms in the Hindu-dominated Indian state of Gujarat, Parvis Ghassem-Fachandi makes the important point that ahimsa began as a "protective technique against the effects of the necessary violence" in the ritual of sacrifice (2012:12). However, contemporary forms of Hindu nationalism in the state, while advocating ahimsa toward the animal victims of sacrifice, have replaced the original animal victim of religious sacrifice with a Muslim victim. During the Gujarat pogrom of 2001, Ghassem-Fachandi notes, "people invoked the symbolic technologies of killing and sacrifice" in their attempts to exterminate Muslims and create a united Hindu community (2012:12).

21. The disassociation of sacrifice and meat eating from Hinduism has, as Ghassem-Fachandi (2010:161) points out, deeply disturbing implications. In Gujarat, Hindu agents of violence were able to argue that they were simply doing to Muslims what Muslims were identified as doing—slaughtering animals and consuming meat.

REFERENCES

Al-Mohammad, Hayder, and Daniela Peluso

2012   Ethics and the "Rough Ground" of the Everyday: The Overlappings of Life in Postinvasion Iraq. HAU: Journal of Ethnographic Theory 2(2):42–58.

Babb, Lawrence

1975   The Divine Hierarchy: Popular Hinduism in Central India. New York: Columbia University Press.

Bali Vedna Part 1.DAT

2013   YouTube video, 1:16:58, published by "bceeri." June 12, 2013. https://www.youtube.com/watch?v L6VknTUFK˙w, accessed May 15, 2015.

Bali Vedna Part 2.DAT

2013   YouTube video, 1:11:09, published by "bceeri." June 12, 2013. https://www.youtube.com/watch?v 5t˙dJBn6cp4, accessed May 15, 2015.

Bennett, Jane

2010   Vibrant Matter: A Political Ecology of Things. Durham, NC: Duke University Press.

Berger, John

1980   About Looking. New York: Pantheon Books.

Berreman, Gerald

1960   Cultural Variability and Drift in the Himalayan Hills. American Anthropologist 62(5):774–794.

1963   Hindus of the Himalayas: Ethnography and Change. Oxford: Oxford University Press.

Bloch, Maurice

1992   Prey into Hunter: The Politics of Religious Experience. Cambridge: Cambridge University Press

2012   In and Out of Each Other's Bodies: Theory of Mind, Evolution, Truth, and the Nature of the Social. Boulder, CO: Paradigm.

Carter, Jeffrey

2003   Understanding Religious Sacrifice: A Reader. London: Bloomsbury Academic Press.

Chakrabarty, Dipesh

2007   Provincializing Europe: Postcolonial Thought and Historical Difference. Princeton: Princeton University Press.

Cormier, Loretta

2013   Kinship with Monkeys: The Guaja Foragers of Eastern Amazonia. New York: Columbia University Press.

Doniger, Wendy

1988   Other People's Myths: The Cave of Echoes. Chicago: University of Chicago Press.

2009   The Hindus: An Alternative History. New York: Penguin Press.

Doniger, Wendy, and Brian Smith

1989   Sacrifice and Substitution: Ritual Mystification and Mythical Demystification. Numen 36(2):189–224.

———

Durkheim, Emile
2001   The Elementary Forms of Religious Life. Carol Cosman, trans. New York: Oxford University Press.
Eck, Diana
2012   India: A Sacred Geography. New York: Harmony Books.
Evans-Pritchard, E. E.
1953   The Sacrificial Role of Cattle among the Nuer. Africa: Journal of the International African Institute 23(3):181–198.
Ewing, Katherine
1990   The Illusion of Wholeness: Culture, Self, and the Experience of Inconsistency. Ethos 18(3):251–278.
Franklin, Sarah, and Susan McKinnon
2001   Relative Values: Reconfiguring Kinship Study. Durham, NC: Duke University Press.
Frazer, J. G.
1912 [1854]   The Golden Bough: A Study in Magic and Religion. London: Macmillan.
Freccero, Carla
2011   Carnivorous Virility; or Becoming-Dog. Social Text 29 (1106):177–195.
Freud, Sigmund
1998 [1918]   Totem and Taboo. A. A. Brill, trans. New York: Dover.
Ghassem-Fachandi, Parvis
2010   Ahimsa, Identification and Sacrifice in the Gujarat Pogrom. Social Anthropology/Anthropologie Social 18(2):155–175.
2012   Pogrom in Gujarat: Hindu Nationalism and Anti-Muslim Violence in India. Princeton: Princeton University Press.
Girard, Rene
1977   Violence and the Sacred. Baltimore: Johns Hopkins University Press.
Govindrajan, Radhika
2015   Monkey Business: Macaque Translocation and the Politics of Belonging in India's Central Himalayas. Comparative Study of South Asia, Africa and the Middle East 35(2):246–262.
Haraway, Donna J.
2003   The Companion Species Manifesto: Dogs, People, and Significant Otherness. Chicago: Prickly Paradigm Press.
2008   When Species Meet. Minneapolis: University of Minnesota Press.
Hubert, Henri, and Marcel Mauss
1981 [1864]   Sacrifice: Its Nature and Function. W. D. Halls, trans. Chicago: University of Chicago Press.
Ingold, Tim
2011   Being Alive: Essays on Movement, Knowledge and Description. London: Routledge.
Keenan, Dennis King
2005   The Question of Sacrifice. Bloomington: Indiana University Press.

Kirksey, Eben S., and Stefan Helmreich
2010   The Emergence of Multispecies Ethnography. Cultural Anthropology
        25(4):545–576.
Knight, John
2005   Animals in Person: Cultural Perspectives on Human-Animal Intimacies. London:
        Bloomsbury Academic Press.
Kockelmann, Paul
2011   A Mayan Ontology of Poultry: Selfhood, Affect, Animals and Ethnography.
        Language in Society 40:427–454.
Kohn, Eduardo
2007   How Dogs Dream: Amazonian Natures and the Politics of Transspecies Engage-
        ment. American Ethnologist 34(1):3–24.
2013   How Forests Think: Toward an Anthropology beyond the Human. Berkeley:
        University of California Press.
Kosek, Jake
2006   Understories: The Political Life of Forests in Northern New Mexico. Durham, NC:
        Duke University Press.
Lamb, Sarah
1997   The Making and Unmaking of Persons: Notes on Aging and Gender in North
        India. Ethos 25(3):279–302.
Lambek, Michael
2007   Sacrifice and the Problem of Beginning: Meditations from Sakalava Mythopraxis.
        Journal of the Royal Anthropological Institute 13:19–38.
Lévi-Strauss, Claude
1966 [1962]   The Savage Mind. Chicago: University of Chicago Press
Livingston, Julie, and Jasbir Puar
2011   Interspecies. Social Text 29(1 106):3–14.
Massumi, Brian
2002   Parables for the Virtual: Movement, Affect, Sensation. Durham, NC: Duke
        University Press.
Mathur, Nayanika
2014   The Reign of Terror of the Big Cat: Bureaucracy and the Mediation of Social
        Time in the Indian Himalayas. Journal of the Royal Anthropological Institute
        20(1):148–165.
Mawdsley, Emma
1998   After Chipko: From Environment to Region in Uttaranchal. Journal of Peasant
        Studies 25(4):36–54.
Mazzarella, William
2009   Affect: What Is It Good For? In Enchantments of Modernity: Empire, Nation,
        Globalization. Saurabh Dube, ed. Pp. 291–309. London: Routledge.
Parreñas, Rheana "Juno" Salazar
2012   Producing Affect: Transnational Voluntarism in a Malaysian Orangutan
        Rehabilitation Center. American Ethnologist 39(4): 672–687.

Raffles, Hugh

2002   In Amazonia: A Natural History. Princeton: Princeton University Press.

Rutherford, Danilyn

2012   Commentary: What Affect Produces. American Ethnologist 39(4):688–691.

Sax, William

1991   Mountain Goddess: Gender and Politics in a Himalayan Pilgrimage. New York: Oxford University Press.

2002   Dancing the Self: Personhood and Performance in the Pandav Lila of Garhwal. New York: Oxford University Press.

2009   God of Justice: Ritual Healing and Social Justice in the Central Himalayas. New York: Oxford University Press.

Singh, Bhrigupati

2011   Agonistic Intimacy and Moral Aspiration in Popular Hinduism: A Study in the Political Theology of the Neighbor. American Ethnologist 38(3):430–450.

Smith, Fred

2006   The Self Possessed: Deity and Spirit Possession in South Asian Literature and Civilization. New York: Columbia University Press.

Smith, William Robertson

1927 [1889]   Lectures on the Religion of the Semites: First Series. London: A. and C. Black.

Smuts, Barbara

2007   Embodied Communication in Non-Human Animals. In Human Development in the Twenty-First Century. Alan Fogel, Barbara J. King, and Stuart G. Shanker, eds. Pp. 136–146. Cambridge: Cambridge University Press.

Stewart, Kathleen

2007   Ordinary Affects. Durham, NC: Duke University Press.

Tallbear, Kim

2011   Why Interspecies Thinking Needs Indigenous Standpoints. Fieldsights— Theorizing the Contemporary, Cultural Anthropology Online, April 24. http://www.culanth.org/fieldsights/260-why-interspecies-thinking-needs-indigenous-standpoints, accessed May 5, 2015.

Tsing, Anna

2012   Unruly Edges: Mushrooms as Companion Species. Environmental Humanities 1:141–154.

Viveiros de Castro, Eduardo

2004   Exchanging Perspectives: The Transformation of Objects into Subjects in Amerindian Ontologies. Common Knowledge 10(3):463–184.

———

8

PASSIVE FLORA?

RECONSIDERING NATURE'S AGENCY
THROUGH HUMAN-PLANT STUDIES

JOHN CHARLES RYAN

1. INTRODUCTION

What else than the living organism allows one to see and sense true time?
For a plant, a form is equivalent to an age—form is linked to size. Time
is inextricably and correlatively tied to its life. A year is a node, a layer,
a body separated from its surroundings and annexed, added onto, raised,
directed, appointed, placed, built upon.

—FRENCH POET AND PHILOSOPHER PAUL VALÉRY [1]

As agents of healing, sources of food and fiber, objects of ornamentation, symbols of inspiration, and images of beauty, plants have been integrally connected for ages to human societies worldwide [2]. As the ethnobotanists Michael Balick and Paul Cox assert in *Plants, People, and Culture: The Science of Ethnobotany*, "the very course of human culture has been deeply influenced by plants, particularly plants that have been used by indigenous peoples around the world" [3]. Economic, aesthetic, and

---

Originally published as Ryan, J. C., 2012. Passive Flora? Reconsidering Nature's Agency through Human-Plant Studies (HPS). *Societies*, 2 (3), pp. 101–21. Reprinted with permission from John Charles Ryan.

———

medicinal values are only a few of many associated with plants, both in Indigenous and non-Indigenous societies. Cultivated plants, in particular, have had multiple aesthetic purposes throughout history. In seventeenth-century Holland, for example, the fervid love of flowers galvanized the social and economic furor over tulips known as "tulipmania" [4]. In Australia, according to herbalist and botanical researcher Cheryll Williams, "few truly appreciate the immense contribution that our native plants have already made to our welfare—nor their extraordinary future potential and the need for their conservation" [5].

As the study of people, plants, and values, ethnobotany has been positioned traditionally in the social sciences as an interdiscipline linking botany and anthropology with an emphasis on Indigenous uses of plants [6,7]. Economic botany focuses on the material role of plants across societies as foods, fibers, and objects of commerce. As defined by G. E. Wickens, economic botany is "the study of plants, fungi, algae and bacteria that directly or indirectly, positively or adversely affect man [sic], his livestock, and the maintenance of the environment. The effects may be domestic, commercial, environmental, or purely aesthetic; their use may belong to the past, the present or the future" ([8], p. 2). In contrast, medical botany examines specifically the influence of plant medicines on human well-being [9]. However, in addition to ethno-, economic, and medical botany, there are recent noteworthy developments in the discipline of geography as "human-plant geographies" [10,11]; philosophy and theology as "philosophical botany" [12]; critical theory and literary studies as "critical plant studies" [13]; and cultural studies and transdisciplinarity as "cultural botany" [14].

By and large, utilitarianism is one of the dominant social values associated with plants: as food, fodder, fiber, and medicine; as substances or active ingredients; as the raw material of the natural world acted upon by the social world in a myriad of ways. Non-utilitarian social values associated with plants include aesthetic (e.g., the planting of kangaroo paws at botanical gardens or the use of herbs, such as parsley, as a soup garnish); symbolic (e.g., the use of trees and wheat in heraldry or the long-standing association between roses and love); linguistic and metaphorical (e.g., expressions such as "solid as an oak" and "flexible as a willow"); nationalistic (e.g., the wattle on the Coat of Arms of Australia, as shown in Figure

—

8.1); and cosmological and mythological (e.g., the Norse *Yggdrasil* or Tree of Life). For instance, plant creatures figure prominently in J. R. R. Tolkien's Middle-earth fantasy writings, including *The Hobbit*, *The Lord of the Rings*, and *The Silmarillion*. For example, in *The Lord of the Rings*, Frodo Baggins is put under a spell of sleep by the wise Old Man Willow. Other plants in the Tolkien legendarium are represented as embodiments of humans, often with magical or healing capabilities [15].

However, in contemporary thought, the view of plants as active and intentional beings is mostly limited to fantasy, mythological, and children's literature. Admittedly, such myth-based associations between plants and human life, prosperity, and death do not provide an adequate basis for establishing plant intelligences, although these kinds of myths do affirm the cultural relevance of plants across diverse societies. However, human-plant geographies, critical plant studies, philosophical botany, and cultural botany, as four significant developments in the way in which plants are regarded and researched socially and culturally, offer a way forward for contemporary perceptions of plants. These four approaches to plants differ markedly from ethno-, economic, and medical botany in their renewed conceptualization of plants as autonomous, agentic beings, rather than as mute materials or mere messages. In *Environmental Culture*, the Australian environmental philosopher Val Plumwood proposes a new model for thinking about and studying the non-human world, one which would regard nature as an *agent in*—rather than an *object for*—the production of knowledge and socioecological practices. The paradigm envisioned by Plumwood points to an ethics of dialogue between a researcher and an autonomous subject of research. Plumwood's approach would necessitate "sensitive listening and attentive observation [and] an open stance that has not already closed itself off by stereotyping the other that is studied in reductionist terms as mindless and voiceless" ([16], p. 56).

As Plumwood's argument goes, a dialogical model of knowledge-making is a response to the subject-object hierarchies—promulgated by conventional science-based research including ethno-, economic, and medical botany—between a disengaged knower and a passive known (or a yet-to-be-known). Identifying this subject-subject knowledge paradigm as "an uncompleted task for modernist science," Plumwood posits an urgent ecological and intellectual need to "recast the nature-devaluing aspect of

—

FIGURE 8.1. The Coat of Arms of Australia is the recognized symbol of the country. Initially granted to Australia by King Edward VII in 1908, this version was granted in 1912 by King George V. The Coat consists of major floral and faunal symbols of Australian nationhood, including the Golden Wattle (*Acacia pycnantha*) on which the kangaroo and emu are posed. This is one example of the symbolic use of plants to represent national identity. (Image source: WikiMedia Commons)

rationalism" ([16], p. 55). According to Plumwood, an ethical science— evolving from a reconceptualization of the subject of research—would at the same time help to redress the hyper-separation between the humanities and the sciences, thus bringing forward an "ecological humanities" ([16], pp. 50–56; [17–21]).

Plumwood's call is perhaps nowhere more relevant than to the study of plants—organisms conventionally regarded as automatons; as voice-less objects worked over by animate agents such as animals; as mindless constituents of the biosphere or landscape; and as mere material for physical and aesthetic consumption [11,12,22–24]. As Matthew Hall argues trenchantly in *Plants as Persons: A Philosophical Botany* (2011), plants are regarded ordinarily in scientific and social scientific discourses as passive, and are assumed to lack intelligence, consciousness, and behavior—those qualities defining animality [12,25–27]. As living beings, plants continually transact with their socioecological milieus, as the histories of agriculture, horticulture, silviculture, and biological invasions attest. Indeed, plants constitute certain social practices and customs as well as the ethics surrounding them. However, the agency of plants and their particular intelligences have yet to figure fully into the study of social practices and knowledge production. As suggested above, ethnobotany and its affiliates are dominated by a view of plants as food, fodder, fibers, and medicines. Of course, societies *act upon* plants: as weeds to expunge, as forests to harvest, as crops to trade, as seeds to plant, as ornamentals to accompany, as backdrops to ongoing social dramas. Houle asserts that the "backgrounding of herbality—indeed of ecology—is directly linked to the foregrounding of animality. It is a gestalt operation" [28]. While plants are more active and autopoietic than they have been depicted as in literature, art, and science, there are obvious fundamental differences between plants and animals—especially in terms of mobility, psychology, and emotions—that ought to be recognized. However, as recent research in the plant sciences argues, the differences between plants and creatures normally regarded as sentient are neither as profound as previously thought nor as substantial as purported for maintaining the predominant attitude towards plants as disposable materials, ecological automatons, or static backdrops to human desires.

What if we were to consider how plants *act upon* us, contributing to the co-generation of our cultural practices, values, perceptions, relations, artifacts, and all else through their volitions in the *umwelt* of which all living beings are part? The outlandishness of the question belies a deeply engrained assumption that, of course, plants do not produce *anything* but are shrewdly used by intelligent beings to produce the things of culture. The apparent foolishness of the question reaffirms the socially and scientifically indoctrinated position—the anthropocentric and zoocentric assumption—that plants cannot bear agency because they do not have brains. In his popular account of the reciprocality between plants and people, *The Botany of Desire: A Plant's-Eye View of the World*, Michael Pollan comments on the language used to describe human-vegetal relationships: "Even our grammar makes the terms of this relationship perfectly clear: *I choose the plants, I pull the weeds, I harvest the crops.* We divide the world into subjects and objects, and here in the garden, as in nature generally, we humans are the subjects" ([29], p. xiv). I extend Pollan's argument that, rather than a condition of people *acting upon* plants, it is more productive to consider global phenomena, such as agriculture, horticulture, and silviculture, as co-generated by people and plants in a shared *umwelt* reflecting a non-individuated, non-zoocentric form of intelligence.

The observation that people assimilate plants to social practices and customs reflects only one side of the reciprocality that characterizes human-vegetal relationships; it entails only the single condition of humans *acting* upon plants, or in Pollan's words, "I choose the plants, I pull the weeds." Human-plant studies (HPS) would consider the obverse condition as well, that of plants *acting upon* humans to co-generate our milieus of sustenance, the places in which our everyday lives run their courses. The recognition of this dual aspect of the human-vegetal dynamic lays the groundwork for the more contentious discussion of intelligence(s). However, considered to lack intelligence and volition, plants have been construed as inactive objects—decorative, aesthetic, and utilitarian (see Figure 8.2). As some theorists argue, the narrow ascription of intelligence to animals can be attributed to "brain chauvinism," the assumption that thinking, volition, and communication are the qualities of "brained" organisms ([30], pp. 6–11). As Hall and Hallé argue, this zoocentric bias predicates intelligence on animal definitions ([12]; [25], p. 29). Indeed, the study of flora, across the humanities, social sciences, and biological sciences, reflects the assumption that plants are *acted upon* constituents—rather than *acting* partners—in socioecological networks. As a consequence, the notion that plants could possess ethical standing—as an outcome of their autonomy as demonstrated by recent scientific insights—is "downright silly" according to a recent article in *Nature* ([31], p. 824).

The object-making discourses intrinsic to the humanities, social sciences, and biological sciences devalue the agencies of plants. In light of this, it is imperative to interrogate our social, cultural, and scientific assumptions about the botanical world. Despite their marginalized and passive position in Western worldviews, plants constitute more than 99% of the earth's biomass ([32], p. 463). Plant physiologist Anthony Trewavas, a prominent proponent of floristic intelligence, observes the capacity of plants for adaptive behavior; they "possess a fine ability to adjust and

PASSIFLORA LAURIFOLIA LINN DC

FIGURE 8.2. *Passiflora laurifolia* by Francisco Manuel Blanco (1880–1883). A species in the family Passifloraceae, *Passiflora laurifolia* is also known as Jamaican honeysuckle. An invasive plant in many parts of the world, it is native to Central and South America. Although often visually captivating, botanical illustration tends to communicate to a viewer only one phase in the life cycle of a plant and often neglects to depict the complex biological and cultural environments of which the plant is part. Representations such as these tend to fix living beings in space and time, reinforcing the perception of plants as static objects or "passive flora." (Image source: WikiMedia Commons)

optimally exploit the local environment" ([24], p. 16). Moreover, a recent body of writings characterizes plants as agentive, autonomous, and intelligent subjects and considers the wide-ranging implications of research into plant intelligence and consciousness, pioneered most notably by Charles Darwin in the nineteenth century [12,26,27,33–35].

The aim of this article is to collect these embryonic pieces of theory, science, and historical exegesis—scattered across the humanities, social sciences, and biological sciences—under the heading of HPS, an interdisciplinary research framework which would regard plants as intelligent, conscious, and capable subjects, rather than mechanical accessories—as "passive flora." Building upon the conceptual positions of environmental philosopher Val Plumwood, anthropologist Deborah Bird Rose, philosopher and botanist Matthew Hall, and plant scientists such as Anthony Trewavas, as well as the precedent of human-animal studies (HAS), the basis for the ongoing development of human-plant studies through various frameworks will be posited. The implication of this framework is the reconsideration of plants in all forms of research, including the role of plants in society and their representations in the humanities. I will address the following keystones of human-plant studies: (1) plants are intelligent and volitional organisms; (2) plants are integral to socioecological networks and practices; (3) plant intelligences are viable exemplars for societies, cultures, and communities; (4) the roles of plants in society are best articulated through interdisciplinary research that considers art, literature, philosophy, Indigenous knowledges, and science; (5) the HPS framework will complement existing paradigms of ethnobotany and its affiliates.

2. THE PARADOX OF ACTIVE ANIMALS AND PASSIVE PLANTS

Although biologically alive, plants have been conceptualized as unthinking assemblies which only react when acted upon. Indeed, many of the dominant cultural metaphors for passivity are botanical. For example, to plant one's feet; to set down roots; and to be vegetative imply a limited capacity for movement and intelligence. A "vegetable" is someone trapped in a mindless state—verging on death—without the ability to reason or feel. Trewavas asks rhetorically, "Do plants exhibit intelligent behaviour?

—

The use of the term 'vegetable' to describe unthinking or brain-dead human beings perhaps indicates the general attitude" ([24], p. 1).

In the same regard, geographers Russell Hitchings and Verity Jones note a paradox. Although represented as passive elements of the environment, plants are also the quintessence of dynamic nature, epitomizing the ancient notion *physis*: "Vegetation is something passive in contemporary understanding: to be in a vegetative state is to be without mind. Yet the root meaning of the word 'vegetative' is associated with activity and enlivened animation" ([11], p. 15). Indeed, the late fourteenth-century word "vegetative" suggested "endowed with the power of growth" but it has been associated pathologically with brain death only since 1893 [36].

The assumption that intelligence is an attribute of animals and that plants are "mindless and voiceless" ([16], p. 56; [37]) is not endemic to the social or biological sciences. In works of art, plants are often cast as passive objects of aesthetics; wildflowers in particular have widespread popularity—though limited agency and intelligence—in many forms of art and literature [38] (see Figures 8.1 and 8.2). D. H. Lawrence and Mollie Skinner's depiction of the Western Australian red gum or marri (*Corymbia callophylla*) in *The Boy in the Bush* (1924) presents one example: "Red gum everywhere! Fringed leaves dappling, the glowing new sun coming through, the large, feathery, honey-sweet blossoms flowering in clumps, the hard, rough-marked, red-bronze trunks rising like pillars of burnt copper" ([39], pp. 92–93). The passage depicts living trees in static terms of color and form to create aesthetic objects—"pillars of burnt copper."

While recent scholarly work in literary criticism and animal studies has produced "zoocriticism" to research the linkages between animals, literature, and culture [40], an analogous humanities-based field has yet to emerge for plants. (And would it be called *phytocriticism?*) How are the humanities and social sciences to couple new scientific understandings of flora to the criticism and creation of art, literature, and social practices involving plants? How can the humanities and social sciences help to resolve a widespread societal perspective "that regards plants basically as automatons" ([24], p. 2)?

As a tentative response to these questions, I offer some background. In critical theory, which has affected greatly the course of contemporary humanities and social sciences, the rhizome (of plants) has become a

—

FIGURE 8.3. The Mangles Kangaroo Paw (*Anigozanthos manglesii*) is the floral emblem of Western Australia and has adapted to its environment through a vigorous rhizomal system that enables the plant to endure extreme climatic fluctuations including drought and fire. The interest in the rhizome, as a potent intellectual metaphor in critical theory and postmodernism, is well-suited to the Mangles Kangaroo Paw, an enduring expression of environmental beauty and resilience in Western Australia. (Image source: Author)

significant metaphor for lateral thinking that cross-cuts subject-object binarisms (see Figure 8.3). For Deleuze and Guattari, the rhizome encapsulates postmodern yearnings because it "has no beginning or end; it is always in the middle, between things, interbeing, intermezzo. The tree is filiation, but the rhizome is alliance, uniquely alliance" ([41], p. 27). The rhizome counters the growth-focused "arborescent" tropes of modernity by "burrowing through substance, fragmenting into simultaneous sprouts, moving with a certain stealth, powerful in its dispersion" ([42], p. 87).

The rhizome signifies the broad, subtly perceptible time scales over which plants evolve and exist. Valéry intimates this with his statement "time is inextricably and correlatively tied to [a plant's] life" ([1], p. 107). Carl Jung, as well, commented that "life has always seemed to me like a plant that lives on its rhizome. Its true life is invisible, hidden in the rhizome. The part that appears above ground only lasts a single summer . . . What we see is the blossom, which passes. The rhizome remains" ([43], p. 37). In contrast to animals, plants exhibit liminal temporality—an interbeing, *intermezzo*—between immediately mobile mammality and relatively immobile geology. The difference of time scales, observes Trewavas, "frequently makes plants *seem unmoving*" ([24], p. 1, italics added).

Research into plant communication and behavior—which counters the notion of "passive flora"—commenced in North America in the early 1980s ([28], p. 98). This scientific research increasingly characterizes plants as autonomous agentic beings. The notion of intelligent plant behavior, however, can be traced back to Charles Darwin. In *The Power of Movements in Plants* (1880), Darwin and his son Francis described the embryonic root or the plant radicle as a brain:

> It is hardly an exaggeration to say that the tip . . . acts like the brain of one of the lower animals; the brain being seated within the anterior end of the body, receiving impressions from the sense organs, and directing the several movements. ([44], p. 573)

Charles Darwin and his son noted that the root tips perceived environmental stimuli and responded in particular to touch, moisture, gravity, and light. Furthermore, the radicle could discriminate between stimuli by selecting a growth response that would most benefit the whole plant. Plant

—

scientist Peter Barlow writes "the complete set of tips endows the plant with a collective brain, diffused over a large area, gathering, as the root system grows and develops, information important for plant nutrition and survival" ([34], p. 39). Rather than mechanical tropic movement towards stimuli as in phototropism or geotropism, the radicle exhibits "root nutation," which for Darwin described the volition of the radicle brain, signified by its discriminatory ability. The plant brain is located diffusely in its "circumnutating root," a system which can identify self and non-self roots, further suggesting the idea of volition, intention, and self-directedness in plants ([34], p. 48).

Drawing from the observations of the Darwins, plant neurobiology has recently been established as a discipline within the plant sciences. The premise of plant neurobiology is that plants are intelligent organisms, endowed with the capacity to learn, to communicate, and to make key decisions regarding their survival in the face of particular environmental constraints. Research increasingly confirms that plants use a variety of volatile compounds to thwart insects and other predators, but also to communicate with other plants within an ecosystem ([33], p. 21). In fact, the immobility of plants relative to animals has generated a battery of adaptive strategies deployed as deliberate survival choices. These strategies, moreover, include the capacity for remembering environmental stressors and factoring these memories into future decisions [45]. Trewavas defines plant intelligence as "adaptively variable growth and development during the lifetime of the individual" ([24], p. 1). He characterizes the particular intelligence of plants as "mindless mastery" to intimate that plant intelligence exists without a central brain or mind, but rather as a diffuse system of intelligence located loosely in the roots (and signified by the phenomenon of root nutation, as mentioned above) [27]. An extensive review of current research in plant intelligence is out of the scope of the present discussion, but can be found in key works such as *Communication in Plants: Neuronal Aspects of Plant Life* (editors Baluška, Mancuso, and Volkmann). However, the argument that plant intelligence is located in the roots reflects a zoocentric gravitas amongst plant physiologists to seek a brain analogue in plants or, in other words, a single organ or physical repository of intelligence governing the volitions of the whole organism. The kind of botanical intelligence I advocate is, indeed, diffuse, but is not the property of certain

—

plant tissue located in discrete anatomical regions and manifested through pheromonal mechanisms. Drawing from biosemiotics, I will look towards the *umwelt* of the plant in defining intelligent behavior in relation to the condition of reciprocality with people and environment. It is only through this form of intelligence that plants have adapted to their environmental constraints over remarkable expanses of space and time.

Only recently have social and cultural studies of plants considered the scientific advances of the last thirty years. Of significance is Matthew Hall's *Plants as Persons* (2011) [12]. After tracing the notion of plant "personhood," or the moral consideration of plants in social practices, in various traditions from Christianity to Neopaganism, Hall synthesizes scientific research in plant sensation, movement, signaling, communication, intelligence, and learning to build a well-grounded, interdisciplinary argument for the reconsideration of plants ([12], pp. 137–156). As Hall argues elsewhere, the implications of intelligence (here used to include the capacity for sensation, signaling, learning, and communication) are far-reaching; plants are "sensitive, active, self-governing organisms" ([22], p. 173), "intentional, intelligent agents which actively try to maintain and perpetuate their own existence" ([12], p. 156). Similarly, Trewavas pinpoints a turning point "sweeping away the detritus of passivity, replacing it with an exciting dynamic—the investigation of plant intelligence" [27]. The intelligence and self-directedness of plants could catalyze a comparable revolution in the way in which we study environment and society.

Moreover, the intelligence of plants manifests in their transactions with other organisms as part of self-governing socioecological systems, or what Hoffmeyer calls in the context of biosemiotics "this infinite swarm of swarming swarms" or the "inner semiosphere," relating individual bodies and physiologies to the collective intelligences produced by multiple individuals working in symphony over durations of time in expanses of space ([46], p. 125). Hoffmeyer defines the semiosphere as:

> Like the atmosphere, the hydrosphere, and the biosphere. It penetrates to every corner of these outer spheres, incorporating all forms of communication: sounds, smells, movements, colors, shapes, electrical fields, thermal radiation, waves of all kinds, chemical signals, touching, and so on. In short, signs of life. ([46], p. vii)

As part of the semiosphere, plants can be seen to demonstrate highly integrated forms of intelligent behavior without exhibiting brain physiology analogous to animals. Not only is the biological model of intelligence predicated on zoological rather than botanical definitions, it further assumes a strongly individuated organism with the capacity to exploit its environment and manipulate other species in the Darwinian sense of survival fitness. It is most optimal, then, to regard the particular intelligence of plants as a dual mode comprising individual expression—the volition, behavior, and adaptation of herbs, shrubs, and trees on the level of single organisms—coupled with the manifestation of these same traits collectively by communities and populations of plants in ecosystems. The consideration of this acutely expressed dual mode of plant intelligence can liberate HPS from the erroneous assumption that, in order to argue for intelligence in the botanical world, researchers only need to identify the "brain-like" or neuronal features of plant anatomy. Recent plant research shows that, not only have neuronal molecules been identified in plants, but also that some of the same neurobiological processes in animal brains are present in plants.

In countering the notion of plants as passive and somewhat fixed objects of science and culture that lack brains, botanical research across disciplines could consider principles of process and their implications for human understandings of plants as non-passive, as agentic and active participants in socioecological systems. The plant morphologist Rolf Sattler identifies how stasis—stillness, inertia, synchronicity—figures into contemporary understandings of plants. He transfigures the binary between stasis and dynamism by characterizing plant structures themselves as processes in perpetual action rather than fixed material manifestations:

> Structure tends to be considered static, whereas process is dynamic. If we mistake the map for the territory, we conclude that plants consist of structures within which processes occur. On closer inspection we learn, however, that what appears static is in fact also dynamic. ([47], p. 451)

Extending Sattler's ideas here, one could say that plants inhabit the world dynamically and liminally at the margins between being and

—

becoming; stasis and process; synchronicity and diachronicity; and visual representation and bodily experience. Sustained sensory awareness of flora in a place implies that the "map"—the static appearance of the greenness of plants in botanical imagery, for example—is not the "territory"—the place of bodily interaction, the social milieu where people transact with plants in multiple, commonplace ways. In contrast to an atomistic philosophy of nature as an aggregation of stable things, a process perspective elicits "temporality, historicity, change, and passage as fundamental facts" ([48], p. 3). Rather than biochemical extracts or anatomized parts, plants can be defined by their connectivities to dynamic events and other mutable beings. As plants change before our senses, so too do our bodies and social practices in relation to the plants. Process as a guiding principle in botanical research taps into the capacity of plants for complex and dynamic behaviors independent of the zoocentric model of intelligence.

Positively for the view of plants as agentic and autopoietic, Hoffmeyer's interpretation of biosemiotics rests on the assertion that "living creatures are self-referential, they have a history, they react selectively to their surroundings, and they participate in the evolutionary incorporation of the present in the future" ([46], p. 51). Hoffmeyer argues for "a theory on organisms as subjects" and, in doing so, stresses the importance of Jakob von Uexküll's *umwelt* or lifeworld theory. The *umwelt* is where interpenetration between an organism and its environment happens as

> The conquest of vital aspects of events and phenomena in the world around [the creature], inasmuch as these aspects are continually being turned—by way of the senses—into an integral part of the creature. The *umwelt* is the representation of the surrounding world within the creature. ([46], p. 58)

Importantly, the *umwelt* "allows the creature to become a part of the semiotic network found in that particular ecosystem" ([46], p. 58), including the sounds, smells, and sensations of the environment as these stimuli impact reciprocally upon individual organisms and intelligent systems. A population of living things inherently dwells in a "semiotic niche" ([46], p. 59). Significantly, biosemiotics, according to Hoffmeyer, permits interpretations of intelligence independent of zoocentric models. Biosemiotics:

—

Releases the genie of reason from the well-guarded bottle which we
know as the human brain and accords it an immanent position in
the natural history fairy tale. This move enables us to unite the two
separate spheres: Cultural history runs parallel to natural history; at
one time they were one and the same. ([46], p. 95)

Notably, Hoffmeyer describes "swarm intelligence," implying that "rather
than the brain being pre-programmed to produce intelligence, intelligence
seems to swarm out of it" ([46], p. 114). Insofar as the model can get past
the location of intelligence in a brain, Hoffmeyer's biosemiotics appears
to offer a way through the predominant paradigm of animal intelligence
that has proved the basis for judging, and subsequently dismissing, plant
intelligence: "Only animals have nervous systems and brains; these have
never been found in plants—and from the dawn of evolution their purpose
has been to control bodily actions, behavior" ([46], p. 47). On the diffuse
intelligence of plants, Marder comments:

Each plant in its singularity is a collective being, a loose and disor-
ganized assemblage, and, hence, a community of plants that do not
comprise a unified whole, do not constitute either an individual or
an organism. In vegetal beings, life is de-centered—not, as some
might think, concentrated in the vital 'organ', the root, but dispersed and disseminated throughout the body of plant communities.
([49], p. 29)

3. HUMAN-PLANT STUDIES: ADDRESSING
THE QUESTION OF THE PLANT

Drawing from intellectual currents such as biosemiotics, which reconfigures the separation between nature and culture, HPS would become
the site for the revolution—an interdisciplinary framework that would
suffuse the arts, humanities, and social sciences with scientific awareness
of plants as intelligent beings, as outlined in the previous section. In an
issue of the journal *Antennae* titled "Why Look at Plants?" Giovanni Aloi
asks provocatively:

———

> Would there be productive opportunities in attempting to understand plants from different perspectives, just as the field of human-animal studies has proved possible with animals? What contributions to our understanding of animals could a focus on plants make? Could we even envisage that, in the near future, we may have a field of human-plant studies? ([50], pp. 3–4)

A precedent for HPS exists in HAS, focusing on animals and human-animal relations and differing to the anthropological subdisciplines ethnobiology and ethnozoology. Armstrong and Simmons identify "the cultural, philosophical, economic and social means by which humans and animals interact" as central to HAS research ([51], p. 1). In similar terms, Shapiro and DeMello note the "question of the animal" that has been at the centre of HAS since its inception in the early 1990s: "Why do we think about animals in the ways that we do?" ([52], p. 311). A corresponding question would guide human-plant studies: "Why do we think about plants in the ways that we do?"

Definitions of HAS emphasize its interdisciplinarity, akin to other "studies" with radical political origins—environmental, women's, and cultural, for instance ([52], p. 6). HAS is "a rapidly growing interdisciplinary field that examines the complex and multidimensional relationships between humans and other animals. [It comprises] psychology, sociology, anthropology, political science, history, literary criticism and other disciplines in the humanities" [53]. HARN, the Human-Animal Research Network, characterizes HAS as critical of the history of "human" and "animal." HAS addresses, for example, "why some animals have protective legislation and others do not; why some of us eat particular animals but not others; why being 'an animal' is akin to denigration, and what cruelty to animals says 'about us'" [54].

As a common subject of analysis, animals and the question of animality and society define HAS. The field addresses the "lack of scholarly attention given to nonhuman animals and to the relationships between human and nonhuman" ([52], p. 2). HAS investigates human relations to animals and the experiences of animals as autonomous creatures, not merely as "cultural artifacts, symbols, models, or commodities in a largely

---

human-centred world" ([55], p. 332). According to recent HAS theorists, in order to make progress as a scholarly field, HAS will need to identify "ways of understanding animals and human-animal relations that are not constrained by traditional disciplinary boundaries and methods" ([56], p. 3).

The strength of HAS is its receptivity to scientific perspectives—biology, zoology, and ethology in particular—without its possible constriction by empirical methods solely ([56], p. 3). Freeman and Leane advocate a transition within HAS from multidisciplinarity—in which disciplines comingle without significant integration of knowledges and methods—to interdisciplinarity where "scientists, social scientists, and scholars in the humanities collaborate intellectually" ([57], p. 4). The steady growth of human-animal studies in universities and scholarly journals suggests the timeliness of these approaches to the question of the animal ([52], p. 3). An April 2012 article in *The Washington Post* concludes that HAS is in transition from a fringe activist movement to an increasingly established scholarly field [58].

Extending the HAS precedent, HPS would redress the lack of scholarly focus given to plant intelligences, as well as secular or sacred human-plant interactions. Comprising more than 99% of the earth's biomass [32], plants are integral to culture, society, literature, and art—not only ecology and scientific awareness. As an example, in the biodiverse South-West of Western Australia, botanical imagery proliferates in visual culture—contemporary wildflower photography [59]; endemic symbols of statehood [60] (see Figure 8.2); and the works of botanical artists [61–63]. HPS would identify innovative ways of understanding plants and people-plant relations. It would do so through knowledge of empirical advances but without the limitations of disciplinary parameters, as HAS strives to do with increasing recognition and influence. HPS would engage an interdisciplinary dialogue with botany, conservation biology, forestry, agronomy, horticulture, sociology, cultural studies, medical herbalism, ethnobotany, and landscape architecture, for example.

In light of advances in scientific understandings, HPS would regard the autonomy of plants and their bearing in social practices—not merely their relevance as cultural symbols or aesthetic accessories. The further negotiation of the moral standing of plants would also be included within HPS [12,22,64,65]. What constitutes cruelty to herbs, shrubs, and trees? What does the unbridled overuse of flora for human physical and aesthetic

—

consumption say "about us?" How should we reconsider plant and human interactions through the prism of recent advances in conceptualizing plants? Moreover, HPS would re-examine kinship and connectivity between plants and society, including the paradigm of plants as teachers [66]. In Fremantle, Western Australia in 1833, to offer a colonial example again from the biodiverse corner of Australia, the Austrian botanist Baron Charles von Hügel remarked in his journal "I could not wait to get out into Nature, into my *kindred* world of plants, which had so often held my gaze when bowed down by deep sorrow" ([67], p. 23, italics added). A feeling of kindredness, reflected here by von Hügel, implies that plants are much more than inert backdrops to human affairs, as Matthew Hall, Anthony Trewavas, and other scholars in various fields have already argued in convincing detail.

4. THE WEST AUSTRALIAN CHRISTMAS TREE THROUGH A HUMAN-PLANT STUDIES LENS

In order to glimpse how the HPS framework can be applied to actual plants, I offer a brief example comprising traditional Indigenous Australian Dreaming knowledges and contemporary scientific understandings. According to ethnobotanist Philip Clarke, "the 'Dreaming' is an Aboriginal English term used to embrace indigenous religious beliefs about the Creation and the laying down of Aboriginal Law" ([7], p. 23). Agency in the botanical world is perhaps best exemplified through the Aboriginal concept of Dreaming plants, which facilitate strong, long-standing ontological links between plants and people. Sacred plants are often recognized as ancestral beings themselves or as deeply implicated with the spiritual passage of human beings to the after world. As Clarke goes on to explain, "even when plants do not represent the actual Ancestors, they may be seen as having been involved with Dreaming activities in the Creation" ([7], pp. 23–24). Some plants have clear utilitarian roles as foods, fibers, and medicines in Aboriginal societies (and have thus been used intelligently and sustainably by those societies). Others have *perceived* agency as Creation beings actively contributing to the generation of cultural beliefs, practices, and traditions; and/or *actual* agency in their resilient modes of adaptation to the socioecological landscapes of which

---

they are part. Indeed, some plants are known as powerful, sacred, and vital plants to Aboriginal societies: agentic, autonomous, and volitional Creation beings, qualities of the botanical world that have only recently been corroborated by plant science. A prominent example is the West Australian Christmas Tree—known as *mudjar* in the Aboriginal Australian language Nyoongar and *Nuytsia floribunda* to scientists—which is endemic to the South-West corner of Western Australia. The plant has numerous significant ecocultural meanings [68]. Modern botanical science classifies *Nuytsia* as a mistletoe endemic to the South-West region. As a root and rhizome hemi-parasite, the plant parasitizes a number of hosts but also has the ability to make its own food through photosynthesis [69]. The parasitizing rootlets coming off the main roots of the *Nuytsia* are so tenacious that they have been known to burrow into underground utility lines.

In the 1930s, the ethnographer Daisy Bates noted the close associations between Nyoongar (or Bibbulmun) spirituality and the Christmas Tree:

> The tree-*Moojarr*, or *Moodurt* . . . was to the Bibbulmun [Nyoongar] the 'Kaanya Tree' 'the tree of the souls of the newly dead'. From time immemorial the soul of every Bibbulmun rested on the branches of this tree on leaving its mortal body for its heavenly home, *Kurannup*, the home of the Bibbulmun dead which lay beyond the western sea. ([70], p. 86)

Nuytsia facilitated the passage of souls to the after world, but as Bates claimed, the tree was feared and avoided. Other early ethnographers recorded the use of *Nuytsia* as food, water, and decoration, suggesting that within the South-West, there have been variable spiritual beliefs and cultural practices surrounding the tree [71].

The colonial diarist and settler George Fletcher Moore described the Christmas Tree as "*Mut-yal*, s.-*Nuytsia floribunda*; colonially, cabbage-tree. The only loranthus or parasite that grows by itself. Another anomaly in this land of contradictions. It bears a splendid orange flower" ([72], p. 80). As the world's largest parasitic plant, the Christmas Tree epitomized the baffling growth habits of New World species in the eyes of European botanists. It represented the departure of the Australian landscape from Old

FIGURE 8.4. Marianne North's "Study of the West Australian Flame-tree or Fire-tree" (1880). *Nuytsia floribunda*, or the West Australian Christmas Tree, is represented here as a European elm with a fluted canopy and fairly symmetrical overall form. Human-plant studies, as a framework for researching *Nuytsia* and other plants, would invoke interdisciplinary perspectives on the species in question, while also exploring the agency of plants in contributing to the formation and cohesion of human societies and cultural practices: Indigenous, colonial, and post-colonial. (Image source: Reproduced with the kind permission of the Director and the Board of Trustees, Royal Botanic Gardens, Kew)

World norms. Even the name "Christmas Tree," flowering in yellow as it does in the heat of the late spring and early summer months of November and December, runs contrary to the image of the evergreen Christmas tree brought indoors from the cold and deep snow of the English countryside.

Early European colonists to Western Australia reported mixed admiration and disdain for *Nuytsia*. The tree in flower was first recorded by the crew of Dutch explorer Pieter Nuyts's vessel Gulden Zeepaard in 1627 [71]. *Nuytsia* was assigned as its scientific name in 1831 by the botanist Robert Brown and the tree was referred to as "Fire Tree" ([73], p. xxxix) amongst the colonists. In the journals of Western Australian surveyors Alfred Hillman and Septimus Roe, *Nuytsia* indicated infertile country and was described disparagingly as part of the intolerable scrubbiness of the landscape [68]. In 1880, peripatetic artist Marianne North painted "Study of the West Australian Flame-tree or Fire-tree," now part of the botanical art collection at Kew Gardens in England. However, the tree depicted in the painting appears more like a European elm tree with its pleasant vase-like form than most Christmas Trees found in the Western Australian wild (see Figure 8.4).

For some Aboriginal Australian people, the Christmas Tree is considered a sacred, Dreaming plant linked to the souls of the deceased. The writings of early settlers and ethnographers point to some of the spiritual beliefs and material practices surrounding Nuytsia. In the 1930s, Bates reported the view of Nuytsia as a home for disembodied spirits when she wrote that the Nyoongar people "did not fear the tree; they loved it, but held it sacred for its spiritual memories. The souls of all their forbears had rested on the spirit tree on their way to Kurannup" ([70], p. 153). However, writing in the 1880s, diarist and settler Ethel Hassell reported the use of Nuytsia root as a candy:

> They gave me one of the roots to taste, telling me it was called mungah. The outer skin was pale yellow but easily stripped off leaving a most brittle centre tasting very like sugar candy. ([74], p. 26)

A ghoulish creature called a gnolum, in the form of a very tall, very thin man, enticed boys away by offering them the roots of the mungah tree ([74], p. 65). In traditional Nyoongar thought, the mungah tree is literally ensouled, bearing the spirits of the deceased and facilitating their passage to the next life. The tree is not simply the passive material or medium for the forging of cultural artifacts or practices. Indeed, the sacred tree is acted upon as a sugar candy eaten or as decoration worn for ceremonial purposes. However, in the tree's capacity to liaise with the spiritual world, to invoke fear and respect, and to associate with other-worldly figures, it manifests some degree of agency synchronized to the active processes of its social, spiritual, and ecological milieu—its broader umwelt. Hence, human-plant studies reflects on Indigenous knowledges of plants in conjunction with scientific and Western cultural knowledges to identify points of commonality and cross-pollination.

———

5. RECONSIDERING THE ROLE OF PLANTS IN SOCIETY THROUGH HPS

What intellectual niche would human-plant studies serve and what can recent developments in the humanities and ecocultural theory contribute? For an answer, I return to environmental philosopher Val Plumwood's *Environmental Culture*. HPS would need to reconstitute subject-object and disciplinary dichotomies that posit plants as passive and the study of plants as empirical only. To this effect, Plumwood advocates an "ecologically-integrated humanities knowledge field" ([16], p. 51). For Plumwood, the "ecological humanities" bridge "the great split . . . between nature (science) on the one hand and culture (philosophy and the humanities, cultural studies) on the other" ([16], p. 51). In Plumwood's view, plant research, most commonly associated with the sciences (botany) or social sciences (anthropology and ethnobotany), is restricted to "the sphere of the 'objective' . . . where the subject/object constructions reign supreme" ([16], p. 52).

Echoing Plumwood, anthropologist Deborah Bird Rose and historian Libby Robin argue that the ecological humanities bridge dichotomies intrinsic to Western thinking about nature through an "ontology of connectivity" [21]. Canonical works in the ecological humanities, such as Carolyn Merchant's *The Death of Nature*, portray nature as "an *active partner* rather than *passive accessory* in the unfolding of human communities" ([75], p. 183, italics added). Through the premise of connectivity between plants and society, HPS would provide a framework for conceptualizing plants as active partners in knowledge production and cultural practices, "as social beings with agentive efficacy" ([66], p. 554). HPS would investigate plants and everyday human-plant interactions—for example, South African botanical species in Western Australia (see Figure 8.5) towards a reconsideration of "planthood." Hence, HPS would align closely with the theoretical advances of the ecological humanities, as well as the methodological precedents of ecocriticism [40]; ecocultural studies [17]; human-animal studies [55]; human-plant geographies [10,11]; multispecies ethnography [66]; and biosemiotics [46,76].

Importantly, this framework would look towards Indigenous knowledges in reconceptualizing these divides [7,77]. Intrinsic to Aboriginal Australian relations to non-human beings, kinship (involving totemism and custodianship) expresses a "connectivity ontology" between plants and

FIGURE 8.5. Exotic *Gladiola* spp. plants alongside a railway line near Bunbury, Western Australia. Termed "invasive" and "opportunistic," weeds often exhibit adaptive group behaviors that enable them to establish vigorous populations around the world. Should weeds like this beautiful *Gladiola* be known as obnoxious pests or intelligent colonizers? (Image source: Author)

people ([7], p. 58; [21]). Philosopher Mary Graham outlines two axioms of Aboriginal philosophy: (a) the land is the law and (b) you are not alone in the world, the former signifying that "meaning comes from land" and the latter, "a kinship system which extends into land." The stories of different clans describe "Creator Beings," including plant beings, that enabled sleeping "proto-humans to become fully human" [77].

The interdisciplinary focus of HPS would bring about novel research approaches—steeped in ancient ontologies—in which plants and human-plant interactions and social relations might be better understood. HPS would conceptualize botanical intelligence broadly as a syncretic quality emerging from intelligent systems and encompassing the potentiality for plants to become "persons," as central to particular Indigenous worldviews. Most crucially for the development of human-plant studies is the differentiation between botanical intelligence—plants *acting upon* people to co-orchestrate cultural beliefs and practices in the *umwelt* of living organisms—and the intelligent use of plants—people *acting upon* plants in utilitarian and potentially exploitative ways that posit "intelligent" animals against "passive" plants. The ecological humanities afford a strong basis for this further articulation of human-plant studies. Above all else—as Hall, Plumwood, Rose, and Robin suggest—HPS implies an ethics of research involving care and connectivity with plants. Such dialogical approaches—to be advanced further within HPS—regard nature as an agent in knowledge formation and "articulate ethical and social engagement with respect for what is studied" ([16], pp. 55–56). Extending the animal and society precedent, human-plant studies would interrogate the history of "human" and "plant" (and their association in Western ontology), the latter laden with connotations of passivity and the former with presuppositions of intelligence. This call for interdisciplinarity posits plants, their intelligences, and their social and cultural relations as productive areas for research to be explored further from a myriad of perspectives. As Marder asks, "and what would it mean to write and think in a vegetal—if not a vegetative—state, having left one's head behind or walking on one's head? What is the outcome of our approximating the locus of vegetal being?" ([13], p. 474).

ACKNOWLEDGMENTS

The author is indebted to the Centre for Research in Entertainment, Arts, Technology, Education and Communications (CREATEC) and the School of Communications and Arts at Edith Cowan University (Australia) for their support during this research. He also thanks the three anonymous referees whose suggestions greatly enhanced the article. The author finally wishes to acknowledge that the concepts and general argument underpinning this article borrow extensively from the recent work of Australian environmental philosopher Matthew Hall and his landmark publication *Plants as Persons: A Philosophical Botany* (2011).

REFERENCES AND NOTES

1. Paul Valéry quoted in Hallé, F. *In Praise of Plants*; Timber Press: Portland, OR, USA, 2002; p. 107.
2. Goody, J. *The Culture of Flowers*; Cambridge University Press: Cambridge, UK, 1993.

—

3. Balick, M.; Cox, P. Preface. In *Plants, People, and Culture: The Science of Ethnobotany*; Scientific American Library: New York, NY, USA, 1996; p. vii.

4. Goldgar, A. *Tulipmania: Money, Honor, and Knowledge in the Dutch Golden Age*; University of Chicago Press: Chicago, IL, USA, 2007.

5. Williams, C. *Medicinal Plants in Australia: Bush Pharmacy*; Rosenberg Publishing: Dural Delivery Centre, NSW, Australia, 2010; Volume 1, p. 8.

6. Balick, M.; Cox, P. *Plants, People, and Culture: The Science of Ethnobotany*; Scientific American Library: New York, NY, USA, 1996.

7. Clarke, P. *Aboriginal People and Their Plants*; Rosenberg Publishing: Dural Delivery Centre, NSW, Australia, 2011.

8. Wickens, G. E. Economic botany. In *Economic Botany: Principles and Practices*; Wickens, G. E., Ed.; Kluwer Academic Publishers: Dordrecht, The Netherlands, 2001.

9. Lewis, W.; Elvin-Lewis, M. *Medical Botany: Plants Affecting Human Health*, 2nd ed.; Wiley: New York, NY, USA, 2003.

10. Head, L.; Atchison, J. Cultural ecology: Emerging human-plant geographies. *Progr. Hum. Geogr.* 2009, *33*, 236–245.

11. Hitchings, R.; Jones, V. Living with plants and the exploration of botanical encounter in human geography research. *Ethics Place Environ.* 2004, *7*, 3–18.

12. Hall, M. *Plants as Persons: A Philosophical Botany*; SUNY Press: Albany, NY, USA, 2011.

13. Marder, M. Vegetal anti-metaphysics: Learning from plants. *Continent. Philos. Rev.* 2011, *44*, 469–489.

14. Ryan, J. Cultural botany: Towards a model of transdisciplinary, embodied and poetic research into plants. *Nat. Cult.* 2011, *6*, 123–148.

15. Hazell, D. *The Plants of Middle-Earth: Botany and Sub-creation*; Kent State University Press: Kent, OH, USA, 2007.

16. Plumwood, V. *Environmental Culture: The Ecological Crisis of Reason*; Routledge: London, UK, 2002.

17. Conley, V. Eco-subjects. In *Rethinking Technologies*; Conley, V., Ed.; University of Minnesota Press: Minneapolis, MN, USA, 1993; pp. 77–91.

18. Giblett, R. *People and Places of Nature and Culture*; Intellect Press: Bristol, UK, 2011.

19. Griffiths, T. The humanities and an environmentally sustainable Australia. *Australian Humanities Review* 2007, *43*, available online: http://www.australian humanitiesreview.org/archive/Issue-December-2007/EcoHumanities/EcoGriffiths .html (accessed on 1 May 2012).

20. Haraway, D. *When Species Meet*; University of Minnesota Press: Minneapolis, MN, USA, 2008.

21. Rose, D.; Robin, L. The ecological humanities in action: An invitation. *Australian Humanities Review* 2004, *31–32*, available online: http://www.australianhumanities review.org/archive/Issue-April-2004/rose.html (accessed on 1 May 2012).

22. Hall, M. Plant autonomy and human-plant ethics. *Environ. Ethics* 2009, *31*, 169–181.

23. Ryan, J. 'Plants that perform for you'? From floral aesthetics to floraesthesis in the Southwest of Western Australia. *Aust. Humanit. Rev.* 2009, *47*, 117–140. Available

—

online: http://www.australianhumanitiesreview.org/archive/Issue-November-2009
/ryan.html (accessed on 1 May 2012).

24. Trewavas, A. Aspects of plant intelligence. *Ann. Bot.* 2003, *92*, 1–20.

25. Hallé, F. *In Praise of Plants*; Timber Press: Portland, OR, USA, 2002.

26. Trewavas, A. The green plant as an intelligent organism. In *Communication in Plants: Neuronal Aspects of Plant Life*; Baluška, F., Mancuso, S., Volkmann, D., Eds.; Springer-Verlag: Berlin, Germany, 2006; pp. 1–18.

27. Trewavas, A. Mindless mastery. *Nature* 2002, *415*, 841.

28. Houle, K. Animal, vegetable, mineral: Ethics as extension or becoming? The case of becoming-plant. *JCAS* 2011, *1/2*, 89–116.

29. Pollan, M. *The Botany of Desire: A Plant's-Eye View of the World*; Random House: New York, NY, USA, 2002.

30. Vertosick, F. *The Genius Within: Discovering the Intelligence of Every Living Thing*; Harcourt: New York, NY, USA, 2002.

31. Editorial. Open to interpretation. *Nature* 2008, *453*.

32. Breckle, S. *Walter's Vegetation of the Earth: The Ecological Systems of the Geo-Biosphere*, 4th ed.; Springer-Verlag: Berlin, Germany, 2002.

33. Baluška, F.; Volkmann, D.; Hlavacka, A.; Mancuso, S.; Barlow, P. Neurobiological view of plants and their body plan. In *Communication in Plants: Neuronal Aspects of Plant Life*; Baluška, F., Mancuso, S., Volkmann, D., Eds.; Springer-Verlag: Berlin, Germany, 2006; pp. 19–35.

34. Barlow, P. Charles Darwin and the plant root apex: Closing a gap in living systems theory as applied to plants. In *Communication in Plants: Neuronal Aspects of Plant Life*; Baluška, F., Mancuso, S., Volkmann, D., Eds.; Springer-Verlag: Berlin, Germany, 2006; pp. 37–51.

35. Karban, R. Plant behaviour and communication. *Ecol. Lett.* 2008, *11*, 727–739.

36. Harper, D. Vegetative. *Online Etymological Dictionary* 2012. Available online: http://www.etymonline.com/index.php?term=vegetative (accessed on 1 May 2012).

37. See also page 84 in Marder, M. Plant-soul: The elusive meanings of vegetative life. *Environ. Philos.* 2011, *8*, 83–89.

38. Ryan, J. Plants as objects: Challenges for an aesthetics of flora. *Philos. Stud.* 2011, *1*, 222–236.

39. Lawrence, D. H.; Skinner, M. *The Boy in the Bush*; Eggert, P., Ed.; Cambridge University Press: Cambridge, UK, 2002.

40. Huggan, G.; Tiffin, H. *Postcolonial Ecocriticism: Literature, Animals, Environment*; Routledge: New York, NY, USA, 2010; pp. 133–202.

41. Deleuze, G.; Guattari, F. *A Thousand Plateaus: Capitalism and Schizophrenia*; Massumi, B., trans.; Continuum: London, UK, 2004.

42. Kaplan, C. *Questions of Travel: Postmodern Discourses of Displacement*; Duke University Press: Durham, NC, USA, 1996.

43. Jung, C. *The Earth Has a Soul: The Nature Writings of C. G. Jung*; North Atlantic Books: Berkeley, CA, USA, 2002.

44. Darwin, C.; Darwin, F. *The Power of Movements in Plants*; Murray: London, UK, 1880.

45. Goh, C.; Nam, H.; Park, Y. Stress memory in plants: A negative regulation of stomatal response and transient induction of rd22 gene to light in abscisic acid-entrained *Arabidopsis* plants. *Plant J.* 2003, *36*, 240–255.

46. Hoffmeyer, J. *Signs of Meaning in the Universe*; Haveland, B., trans. Indiana University Press: Bloomington and Indianapolis, IN, USA, 1996.

47. Sattler, R. Homology, homeosis, and process morphology in plants. *Homology: The Hierarchical Basis of Comparative Biology*; Hall, B., Ed.; Academic Press: San Diego, CA, USA, 1994.

48. Rescher, N. *Process Philosophy: A Survey of Basic Issues*; University of Pittsburgh Press: Pittsburgh, PA, USA, 2000.

49. Marder, M. Resist like a plant! On the vegetal life of political movements. *Peace Stud. J.* 2012, *5*, 24–32.

50. Aloi, G. Editorial. *Antennae* 2011, *17*.

51. Armstrong, P.; Simmons, L. Beastiary: An introduction. *Knowing Animals*; Simmons, L., Armstrong, P., Eds.; Brill: Leiden, The Netherlands, 2007.

52. Shapiro, K.; DeMello, M. The state of human-animal studies. *Soc. Anim.* 2010, *18*, 2–17.

53. Animals and Society Institute, Inc. Human–Animal Studies. Available online: http://www.animalsandsociety.org/pages/human-animal-studies (accessed on 1 May 2012).

54. The University of Sydney. HARN: About us. HARN: Human Animal Research Network 2012. Available online: http://sydney.edu.au/arts/research/harn/about/index.shtml (accessed on 1 May 2012).

55. Shapiro, K. Editor's introduction: The state of human-animal studies: Solid, at the margin! *Soc. Anim.* 2002, *10*, 331–337.

56. Potts, A.; Armstrong, P. Hybrid vigor: Interbreeding cultural studies and human-animal studies. In *Teaching the Animal: Human-Animal Studies Across the Disciplines*; DeMello, M., Ed.; Lantern Books: Brooklyn, NY, USA, 2010.

57. Freeman, C.; Leane, E. Introduction. In *Considering Animals: Contemporary Studies in Human-Animal Relations*; Freeman, C., Leane, E., Watt, Y., Eds.; Ashgate: Surrey, UK, 2011.

58. Joseph, M. The growing field of animal studies. *The Washington Post* 2012. Available online: http://www.washingtonpost.com/lifestyle/magazine/the-growing-field-of-animal-studies/2012/04/10/gIQA9AvjCT_gallery.html (accessed on 1 May 2012).

59. Breeden, S.; Breeden, K. *Wildflower Country: Discovering Biodiversity in Australia's Southwest*; Fremantle Press: Fremantle, Australia, 2010.

60. Hopper, S. *Kangaroo Paws and Catspaws: A Natural History and Field Guide*; Department of Conservation and Land Management: Como, Australia, 1993.

61. Nikulinsky, P.; Hopper, S. *Life on the Rocks: The Art of Survival*; Fremantle Press: Fremantle, Australia, 1999;

62. Nikulinsky, P.; Hopper, S. *Soul of the Desert*; Fremantle Press: Fremantle, Australia, 2005.

63. Pelloe, E. *Wildflowers of Western Australia*; C. J. De Garis: Melbourne, Australia, 1921.

64. Kohák, E. Speaking to trees. *Crit. Rev.* 1993, *6*, 371–388.

---

65. Stone, C. *Should Trees Have Standing? Law, Morality, and the Environment*, 3rd ed.; Oxford University Press: New York, NY, USA, 2010.

66. Kirksey, S.; Helmreich, S. The emergence of multispecies ethnography. *Cult. Anthropol.* 2010, *25*, 545–576.

67. Von Hügel, B. *New Holland Journal: November 1833–October 1834*; Clark, D., trans. Melbourne University Press at the Miegunyah Press in Association with the State Library of New South Wales: Melbourne, Australia, 1994.

68. Hopper, S. Nuytsia floribunda. *Curtis's Botanical Magazine* 2010, *26*, 333–368.

69. Paczkowska, G.; Chapman, A. *The Western Australian Flora: A Descriptive Catalogue*; Wildflower Society of Western Australia, Inc., the Western Australian Herbarium, CALM and the Botanic Gardens & Parks Authority: Perth, Australia, 2000.

70. Bates, D. *Aboriginal Perth Bibbulmun Biographies and Legends*; Bridge, S., Ed.; Hesperian Press: Victoria Park, Australia, 1992.

71. Cunningham, I. *The Land of Flowers: An Australian Environment on the Brink*; Otford Press: Caringbah, Australia, 2005.

72. Moore, G. *Diary of Ten Years Eventful Life of an Early Settler in Western Australia*; University of Western Australia Press: Nedlands, Australia, 1884.

73. Lindley, J. *A Sketch of the Vegetation of the Swan River Colony*; James Ridgway: London, UK, 1840.

74. Hassell, E. *My Dusky Friends*; C. W. Hassell: Dalkeith, Australia, 1975.

75. Eckersley, R. The death of nature and the birth of the ecological humanities. *Organ. Environ.* 1998, *11*, 183–185.

76. Hoffmeyer, J. *Biosemiotics: An Examination into the Signs of Life and the Life of Signs*; Favareau, D., Ed.; Hoffmeyer, J., Favareau, D., trans.; University of Scranton Press: Scranton, PA, USA, 2008.

77. Graham, M. Some thoughts about the philosophical underpinnings of Aboriginal worldviews. *Aust. Humanit. Rev.* 2008, 45. Available online: http://www.australian humanitiesreview.org/archive/Issue-November-2008/graham.html (accessed on 1 May 2012).

CLIMATE, LANDSCAPE, AND IDENTITY

INTRODUCTION

I n considering human relationships with nature, landscapes offer a useful category to think through. Broadly speaking, landscapes represent
terrains of connectivity, taken across space and time. We may speak of
urban landscapes, agrarian landscapes, geological landscapes, infrastructural landscapes, or even political landscapes. In this section, we consider
how everyday readings of local landscapes help to ground more abstract
concepts, including the effects of global climate change and questions
of identity and human rights. Both authors in this section draw from
ethnographic methods to examine the meanings, memories, and forms
of knowledge contained in seemingly mundane aspects of landscapes—
whether they be grains of sand, plastic buckets, or parking lots.

One increasingly urgent and abstract question that people across the
world are grappling with is how to understand and address global climate
change, which is altering relationships of nature on a planetary scale.
Spurred by the escalating scope and scale of climatic events such as floods
and droughts, many governments are finally instituting more forceful
measures to manage the drivers of climate change, which have long been
linked to human activities, including fossil fuel use; carbon dioxide emissions; and the widespread degradation of forests, grasslands, shorelines,

oceans, and soil. Even with increased attention to the escalating effects of climate change, however, proposed policy solutions inevitably seem too modest in scope to significantly address the challenges ahead. Indeed, one formidable obstacle to addressing climate change is its sheer magnitude, which can seem to dwarf any one individual's experiences, ideas, or capacity to advocate for positive change. Understanding and addressing climate change therefore requires bringing together large-scale planetary trends with exploring how individuals experience environmental changes in their daily lives.

Environmental anthropology considers both global and local perspectives of climate change, as it amplifies the narratives of farmers, families, city residents, social leaders, climate scientists, policy makers, and other individuals who are seeing the effects of climate change firsthand. For example, Sarah E. Vaughn notes the experiences of residents of Georgetown, Guyana, who are working with a Red Cross climate adaptation program designed to help households prepare for increased flood risk due to climate change. She examines the everyday politics of environmental knowledge production, noting how the project ultimately presents people with "a model for reimagining the ordinary," as mundane objects such as rags, bleach, and water filters have become central in navigating climate adaptation programs (314).

The power of local landscapes to help individuals articulate and confront large-scale social and ecological challenges is also seen in the second article of this section, in which Vanessa Agard-Jones considers two coastal beaches on the Caribbean island of Martinique. Agard-Jones connects these beach landscapes to the complex legacies of colonialism, discrimination, and ecological degradation on the island. She examines the ways that these landscapes of sand and sea shape human notions of self and memory, especially regarding relations of same-sex intimacy and desire. Crafting an ethnography that foregrounds the ephemeral traces that human experiences leave on landscapes, she considers how sand becomes "a repository both of feeling and of experience, of affect and of history" (336).

Collectively, the two pieces highlight how ethnographic research contributes to sustainability work. Environmental anthropology presents a nuanced picture of how people experience environmental and social change, whether through the slow violence of colonial legacies or the

---

devasting rush of floods and storms. Circulating stories of how environmental and social change becomes embedded in everyday life underscores that achieving sustainability goals requires more than collecting data and formulating models. It also requires observing how changes in cultural and ecological climates prompt shifts in consciousness, as people begin to perceive, value, and navigate the world around them in different ways. Ethnography underscores the relevance to sustainability programs of understanding who people trust, how they learn, who they love, and what they aspire to achieve. Through such insights, environmental anthropology not only confronts the formidable environmental and social challenges we currently face but also identifies potential avenues for hope and healing for people and for all forms of nature.

DISCUSSION QUESTIONS

1. What are some connections that the authors show between the large-scale dynamics of environmental change and the day-to-day experiences of individuals? Have you noticed ways climate change has altered your own experiences of daily life or your relationship with your local environment? Do you think understanding how climate change influences the everyday aspects of people's lives can help us devise better strategies to address climate-related challenges? If so, how?

2. What are some ways that the authors connect material components of local landscapes with individual memories? Can you think of specific places that connect to meaningful memories in your life? In what ways are landscapes suited to hold meanings and memories for individuals? What may be some of their limitations?

3. Both articles point to ways that people learn to "live with" the consequences of environmental change, social discrimination, or both. For each of these case studies, what does living with such dynamics entail? Which groups in each community do you think would have an easier time living with social and environmental challenges, and which groups would likely suffer more severe costs? More generally, how may climate change or social injustices exacerbate disparities across society? Why does addressing these inequities matter in the quest for sustainability?

———

9

IMAGINING THE ORDINARY IN PARTICIPATORY CLIMATE ADAPTATION

SARAH E. VAUGHN

I. INTRODUCTION

In 2009 I met with Margaret at her home in Sophia, a former squatter town on the fringe of Guyana's capital city, Georgetown.[1] "I have to get some glasses," she explained while walking to a kitchen cabinet. She collected the glasses and then made her way to the stove to boil water to clean them. I sat a few feet away next to a window staring at a plastic vat in her backyard. Placed on a wooden platform, it appeared to levitate above surrounding weeds and a kitchen garden. Connected to it were two drain pipes that ran from the house's roof to channel rainwater. "How often do you go to the vat for water?" I asked. "It depends: who's coming over, when it rains, what I'm cooking . . ."

Margaret worries about flood waters damaging the vat's platform. The vat has to be monitored at odd moments in the course of the day, week, month, and year, especially during the wet season. She is vigilant, just like other Sophia residents. Even Red Cross staff visited after a disastrous

—

flood in 2005 and warned of more if not worse flooding due to climate change. She grew accustomed to these warnings, with Red Cross staff holding training workshops about water safety and plastering signs throughout Sophia that read "Evacuation Route." "I use it [the vat] only if the sky isn't too gray or the rain too heavy," she noted as she poured soda into our glasses. If the sky was gray and the rain heavy, she disinfected water with bleach and filtered it with a rag. Intuition is both a necessity and pleasure in itself. It spreads fast, even without the help of expert clarification.

Margaret's vat informs her everyday routine and commitments to the Guyana Red Cross. Vats along with rags and bleach used to filter water are ordinary things, insofar as they can be found in most Guyanese households. Margaret is dependent on them and so realizes that climate-related flooding is not a disruption but rather is embedded in and informs everyday activities. In this article, I examine the ways Red Cross training shapes people's understandings of the ordinary. For Margaret, the ordinary is experienced through talk, rumors, claims, and discourses about climate adaptation. But as she suggests, even though the Guyana Red Cross has provided warnings to Sophia residents about intense flooding, she still lives in uncertainty about how her life will be impacted by it.

Between December 2004 and February 2005, multiple storms resulted in over 60 inches of rain along Guyana's Atlantic coastal plain (Blommestein et al. 2005). The storms were unprecedented compared to engineers' records that estimated seven inches as the average monthly rainfall. The storms resulted in extensive flooding across the coastal geopolitical regions 3, 4, and 5 where 62% of the nation's population resides (roughly 520,000 people). Timing the release of water from the coast's main dam, called the East Demerara Water Conservancy (EDWC), into canals was crucial. If water was released when the tide was high, Georgetown would have been inundated with water from not only the EDWC but also the sea. Engineers devised a plan that allowed them to release water into a nearby river. While this strategy saved Georgetown in this instance, it further exacerbated flooding in rural communities.

After the 2005 disaster, engineers worked with World Bank consultants to create flood models. Scenarios were bleak, whether from a rising tide or abnormal rainfall events; the EDWC was in need of a major overhaul in design to withstand future flooding (Kirby et al. 2006). The flood models offered more than a prognosis of climate change's impacts on Guyanese coastal drainage. They convinced the state that its "top down" approach to flood control was limited, if not piecemeal. In turn, a number of different state agencies requested that local nongovernmental agencies (NGOs) help establish community-based or participatory climate adaptation programs. The Red Cross took the lead with one of four pilot programs in Sophia. Between 2009 and 2010, Red Cross workers trained Sophia residents in vulnerability capacity assessment (VCA). Conceived of in the early 1990s to educate densely populated urban communities about environmental risks, the VCA is the core methodology of the International Red Cross Federation's volunteer network. Its primary activity includes people participating in focus groups and household surveys about vulnerability in the places they live. A mix of preparedness, relief, and coping strategies, Sophia's VCA centered on teaching residents how to use household water management equipment, or vats, septic tanks, and water filtration kits.

In a neighborhood of roughly 36,000 people, five male and fifteen female adults regularly participated in Sophia's VCA training for a year. They volunteered to participate as VCA trainees after the Red Cross staff contacted the head of Sophia's community center. Already members of a community awareness group, the VCA trainees described themselves not only as "community advocates" but also as familiar with drainage issues that affected Sophia. They had various occupational and class backgrounds. Some were unemployed while others held multiple jobs as electricians, vendors, caretakers, political activists, teachers, and low-level government employees. This diversity influenced the knowledge exchanged about flooding as well as expectations about the purpose of water management equipment. Training was led by a rotating group of five staff from the Guyana Red Cross, who for the most part had very different daily realities from those of VCA trainees. Their home life, work, and leisure were shaped by Georgetown's middle-class environs, although some did have experience as first responders in 2005. The VCA thus intended to chart a knowledge network beyond a preoccupation with disaster and its root causes. In particular, VCA trainees and Red Cross workers worried that repeated episodes of intense flooding could create conditions for exposure to contaminating water in Sophia. The water management equipment, in this respect, was important not only because

—

of its function. It was also a symbolic resource for remapping lived connections between expertise and accountability.

Instead of a focus on disaster, the VCA helps Sophia residents pay attention to how vulnerability manifests and unfolds in everyday life. This emphasis on process rather than event suggests that climate change has become an impasse to achieving or making a good life for one's self. Ongoing crisis and a sense of living with climate insecurity thus take shape not only around infrastructures but also within scenes of a working day, familial duties, and social obligations. Following cultural theorist Lauren Berlant, in this article I track "crisis ordinariness," or the activities, narratives, and technologies people rely on in the everyday to live with systematic crisis while learning to preserve optimism for the future (Berlant 2011, 81). Crisis ordinariness is often triggered by traumatic events such as disasters, but it is a condition that also incites uncertainty about the relationship between ways of knowing and intuition. Thus, while Berlant uses the concept to track the distorting effects and the "precarity" (see note) that neoliberal capitalism has brought the everyday in Euro-America, I find it useful for analyzing participatory climate adaptation in two ways (Berlant 2011, 196–198).[2]

First, crisis ordinariness provides a framework to track participatory climate adaptation projects' affective and sensorial impacts on populations across space and time. Second, as a condition marked by broader processes of neoliberalism, an analysis that is sensitive to crisis ordinariness reveals the uneven—and at times contradictory—economic, political, scientific, and social activities that undergird participatory climate adaptation. Specifically, I argue that participatory climate adaptation can be understood as not simply a mode of governance, but as a model for reimagining the ordinary.

I spent 15 months between August 2009 and November 2010 conducting in-depth interviews and observing VCA trainees in Sophia. I participated in Red Cross workshops as well as social gatherings led by organizers of Sophia's community center. This article is based on 30 interviews conducted during these workshops and training. In its first section, I argue that the VCA creates an epistemic space that refracts debates about crisis ordinariness into the domain of the household. I then examine Guyana's broader sociohistorical context of postcolonial development and the 2005

—

disaster, to show the shift in narratives about the ordinary related to participatory climate adaptation.

The following two sections offer an analysis of how the VCA's water filtration kit undergirds the production of household vulnerability surveys. It is a document important for what the Red Cross calls ensuring the VCA's "expansion" across communities. I show that despite the stated intent of the survey, it provides only guidelines for how Sophia residents should use water filtration kits. In other words, the survey is a type of document geared toward representing an aspiration for adaptation rather than a description of it in practice. I suggest that this gap between imaginary and practice is generative of broader discussions about crisis ordinariness as an analytic for climate adaptation scholarship, and the residual spaces for politics it can incite in the everyday.

2. THE ORDINARINESS OF VULNERABILITY

This article follows in the lineage of critical anthropological and geographical scholarship that examines vulnerability to environmental risks as a complex historical experience (Hoffman and Oliver-Smith 2002, Bankoff et al. 2013). I contribute to this literature by examining the ordinary— a common-sense assumption about the "constancy of life" (Dumm 1999, 1)—as it shapes participatory climate adaptation projects. At the same time, I explore the ethics of such projects, as vulnerability transforms the sociomaterial arrangements of the ordinary.

Guyana is particularly vulnerable to climate change, with 300,000 people, or roughly 30% of the population, residing in the coastal capital city Georgetown. Some areas are between 2 and 6 feet below sea level, bounded by a seawall and an intricate grid of canals that drain rainwater and groundwater into the Atlantic Ocean. With the proximity of the sea, a torrential biannual wet season, and the sodden realities of cascading rivers, flooding is a constant threat. Georgetown's grid dates back to the eighteenth century when the French, Dutch, and later the British settled the area as a colonial trading hub to service nearby sugar plantations. The city's canals were built on an autonomous grid, other than the Lamaha Canal, which engineers designed in the 1830s to connect Georgetown to the EDWC for a potable water supply.

The national and municipal governments have developed an elaborate, if inconsistent, system for dredging canals. This system is exemplified by the milling crowds and the compulsory work of foremen, which can become cumbersome along Georgetown's narrow and many unpaved roads. Days before a forecasted storm, foremen stall traffic with their excavators and block roadways with mounds of debris. Indeed, the drainage grid has historically constituted security and a space for imagining the everyday (Rodney 1981).

Its function, however, is dependent on much more than dredging. In recent decades, Georgetown has experienced an increase in informal housing (Edwards et al. 2005). This expansion is overwhelmingly supported by a remittance economy, with migrants renting multiple units within a building to relatives or close acquaintances (Corbin and Aragon 2014). With only 50 miles of canals to support Georgetown and its surrounding environs such as Sophia, the city is overcrowded and drainage overtaxed by garbage and piecemeal road development. It is a situation that many engineers and planners argue contributed to the city's extensive flooding in 2005. Settlement in Georgetown has therefore been associated with costs for maintaining drainage to reproduce kin relations and less so the speculative logics of real estate capital, as has been argued of other flood-prone global Southern Hemisphere ("global South") cities (Ranganathan 2015). And this fact has not escaped the attention of the Guyana Red Cross.

Through exercises in water management equipment and household vulnerability surveys, the VCA does not simply reflect the biopolitical expectation that the household is where flood hazards should be mitigated. It is also a technique for developing skepticism about the world and its related technological, ecological, and sociopolitical pressures (Cavell 1994). I show that VCA trainees' decision-making about such activities—including how to create water filtration kits or a flood emergency contact list—prompts an unlearning of their dependence on the drainage grid. The VCA produces forms of expertise that cut across affective, public/private, and epistemic divides.

Scholars in the anthropology of climate change have analyzed this dynamic in other contexts. Their studies illustrate that participatory climate adaptation projects are based on the assumption that "resilience" to climate change is built into livelihood systems (Crate 2011; see also Watts

2014). National and international governmental aid is coordinated from the bottom up, with an appreciation that communication about climate adaptation has a human and not solely a numerical dimension (Lazrus 2012). To this extent, decisions about, say, water allocation or flood embankment design are negotiations about the competing value of global and local knowledge to survival (Broad and Orlove 2007, Mathur 2015). This emphasis on scale counters a certain sort of teleology, revealing that even if participatory climate adaptation projects seek to curb climatic impacts, vulnerability shapes daily life in unexpected ways (Puri 2015). But while these studies demonstrate that daily life is a source of inspiration for participatory climate adaptation, scholars tend to assume that its knowledge practices are separate from this realm.

In contrast, I show that narratives about daily life, or the ordinary, are an important outcome of participatory climate adaptation projects. In the case of the VCA, trainees not only develop trust in water management technologies to protect them from contaminated flood waters. These technologies help them become hypervigilant of corporeal routines, such as walking or bathing, to identify (un)familiar patterns in the surrounding environment. In such instances, clogged canals or broken bridges are things that "pose a set of quandaries" to movement, sensorium, and cognition (Barad 2011, 21). VCA exercises, in turn, become key scenarios where trainees develop a collective awareness of vulnerability despite their various personal life histories and situations of privilege. I suggest that participatory climate adaptation projects construct the ordinary as an "intersecting space where many forces and histories circulate" for navigating what is overwhelming (Berlant 2011, 21). In other words, participatory climate adaptation is derived from a mobile skill set, or translocal expertise that VCA trainees can apply anywhere in the event a flood displaces them from Sophia.

It is no surprise, then, that VCA trainees interpret the Red Cross as helping them achieve a good life, even if in the present they experience what feel like intractable flood hazards. Achieving a good life, Lauren Berlant argues, is dependent on how people make the most of an "environment" that repeatedly causes them trouble. She writes, "An environment can absorb how time ordinarily passes, how forgettable most events are, and how people's ordinary preservations fluctuate in patterns of undramatic attachment and identification" (Berlant 2011, 100). Like Berlant, I track why the environment helps people make sense of temporality. I empha-size, however, that for many VCA trainees the environment is not only an index of time but a resource for judging when and how ethics materialize across space. They are not content living with derelict drainage even with continued assistance from the Red Cross. Yet, with every new flood hazard encountered through training, they learn to "live off the grid" and create networks of care that circumvent those of the state.

In this respect, participatory climate adaptation projects work in con-cert with processes of neoliberal development and engineering sciences that have made drainage an unsustainable reality in Guyana. At the same time, VCA trainees actively recognize the strategic essentialisms and poli-tics on which participatory climate adaptation is often grounded or cri-tiqued. They do not forget those stories about climate change that resist grand narratives of catastrophe (Stengers 2015). As a staunch refusal to separate climate data from other ways of knowing, the VCA amounts to an effort to represent, organize, and manage crisis ordinariness.

3. ORDINARY EVENTS

The Guyanese state has long been invested in shaping its citizens as modern subjects with the requisite sensibilities for flood control. Most notably, the postindependence state adopted a party doctrine of coopera-tive socialism in 1974, deeming "self-sufficiency" a necessary factor for the nation's development. What followed was a state-sponsored campaign called "Feed, Clothe, and House the Nation" that had ambitions to rep-licate Julius Nyerere's experiment with cooperatives in Tanzania (Peake 2005). Residents functioned as members of Neighborhood Democratic Councils (NDCs) responsible for maintaining infrastructure (e.g., canals and roads) and reporting their status to state agencies. However, the sense of political possibility opened up by NDCs was tempered by concomitant debt crises and electoral fraud. The 1970s and early 1980s bore witness to the withdrawal of International Monetary Fund (IMF) recognition in 1982 and the channeling of resources away from social services to political party financing (Thomas 1984). In particular, drainage was poorly maintained, as urban planning became dependent on filling canals to create roads to accommodate nascent public housing. These experiences of neglect led

—

many Georgetown residents to abide by, rather than flout, state-sustained ideologies of self-sufficiency.

Elements of this ideology did not dissipate with Guyana's transition from socialism to a liberal market and democracy in the late 1980s. These reforms were targeted through a structural adjustment policy called the Economic Recovery Program (ERP). Its objectives were twofold: to find external sources to fund development projects and to reschedule unpaid debt to the IMF, World Bank, and other foreign creditors. While the president implemented a variety of tax schemes through the ERP, the program also focused on reducing the number of state agencies. To fill the technical vacuum, IMF-sponsored development projects required that people other than state officials (i.e., grassroots actors) had to play an active role in project implementation (Ifill 2000). Similar to other postsocialist and postcolonial societies, structural adjustment policies in Guyana created fissures between the "complex techniques" citizens devised to survive the everyday and their experiences of "participation" in development projects (Thomas 1984, 176).

Mark Pelling, for instance, argues that the Guyanese government and national institutions responsible for coordinating urban flood control and infrastructure rehabilitation

> . . . [held] back from projecting participation as empowerment and [implied] that local residents [had] most to contribute as labor (self-help) and in maintenance (management) of resources, rather than in problem identification and project management roles; and that they [continued] to be beneficiaries of external support rather than equal partners with professional agency staff. (Pelling 1998, 476)

Additionally, many Georgetown residents could not gain state approval for new canals because funding agencies feared that those projects would overlap with the "responsibilities" of ongoing housing renewal programs (Pelling 1998, 478). In turn, households responded individually to flood hazards and on the other, large-scale drainage improvements were dependent on development projects (482). While Pelling argues that these competing flood responses were in tension with Georgetown residents' ideals about empowerment, wet season rainfall counts remained rather predictable. Between 1990 and 2004, there was only one significant flood in Georgetown, and that event was attributed not to rainfall but to a sea-wall breach (Pelling 1999). Hence, state agencies and the Red Cross were "active in providing relief aid, but [there was] no established coordinating unit for disaster preparedness" in Georgetown (Pelling 1999, 252).[3]

This lack of coordination was most telling during the 2005 disaster. The storms that contributed to the disaster were not associated with the biannual wet season, but rather with weather systems that usually affect the southern part of Guyana. The multiple storms caused record water levels in the EDWC (59 ft. GD), which worsened downstream conditions in the Georgetown section of the Lamaha Canal. Flooding reached four to five feet in the city, with residents stranded in their homes or shelters for a period of one to three weeks. Given that the state was ill prepared to respond to the vulnerabilities of both the EDWC and polity, civic and United Nations organizations provided assistance to affected populations. In real time, these organizations conducted surveys about the household resources affected populations used to cope. Alissa Trotz (2010) argues that, as a result, information about the disaster's impacts on households went underrepresented in government reports. Part of the shock of the disaster was that the state, even weeks into the event, could not provide basic information about how flood waters could affect daily routines, such as access to public transportation. In many respects, the disaster created an arena for the consolidation of a public discourse about participation alongside the mobilization of a new social imaginary about the ordinary.

This postdisaster social imaginary posited the ordinary as circumscribed less by the geography of the drainage grid than the "humble" water management equipment that circumvent it. By 2009, the Guyana Red Cross positioned itself as the main architect of this geography, proceeding with a program in participatory climate adaptation that emphasized VCAs. The program built on the report "Background document for the preparedness of climate change," completed by 23 other Red Cross National Societies in Latin America, the Caribbean, Africa, and Asia. The report details the efforts of national societies to use Intergovernmental Panel on Climate Change data to spur greater collaboration between state agencies and local communities. Even "without full scientific analyses on climate projections," Red Cross engagements offer an abiding appeal of immediacy (IFRC 2009,

5). "Humanitarianism in a changing climate," the report argues, is rooted in identifying climatic risks that will affect technologies and resources used for programs such as the VCA (p. 1). As climate change increasingly frames humanitarian sentiment, it provides a ready measure—easily quantified and statistically represented—for negotiating the terms of participation. As Guyana Red Cross workers note in the report, successful climate adaptation is the "expansion of VCA" methods across communities as much as disaster relief (p. 9).

The 2005 disaster made evident that the relation between climate-related flooding and vulnerability are not mapped neatly onto divisions between public and private. Both domains, so it appeared, needed to adapt to climate change. The intensity of the storm eroded people's confidence in the EDWC at the same time that conceptions of self-sufficiency become yardsticks for judging survival, and not simply the viability of NDCs. This process of judgment is in stark contrast to the observations scholars have made of other climate-related disasters, such as Hurricane Katrina. They argue that the failure of infrastructure disrupts normalized understandings of public/private responsibility for goods and services (Somers 2008). This focus on political transaction, however, reinforces the idea that participatory climate adaptation will have obvious civic outcomes and a design that can supersede the environment at hand. Instead, I emphasize that participatory climate adaptation requires a politics beyond rights claims, shifting to one that reaffirms the pragmatics of everyday survival. The VCA is thus a tacit reminder of the threat climate change poses to Guyana and that discourses about participation shape a broader experience of crisis ordinariness.

For this reason I caution against viewing participatory climate adaptation as a mere ideological effect of neoliberal development. Analyses that appeal to this teleology assign historical finality where many climate vulnerable populations seek to assert practical solutions for living with hazards (Chakrabarty 2012). Indeed, discovering practical solutions to hazards is not only a preoccupation of those living in postdisaster or marginalized global South contexts. Bruce Braun describes parallel sensibilities in England where climate adaptation involves a "profanation" of technologies, such as fuel gauges and electric cars, to "modulate natural processes" in the everyday (Braun 2014, 60). But technologically bounded representations

—

of the ordinary are not the only possible register through which participatory climate adaptation is made legible. I use the remainder of this article to further detail participatory climate adaptation as it is directed toward various activities for maintaining crisis ordinariness.

4. WORLD MAKING

Sophia was founded by squatters during Guyana's transition out of socialism in the late 1980s. The settlement is located on mostly swampland and abandoned plantations, with pockets of land suitable for rice cultivation. It has since thrived, attracting rural migrants from all over the country who have successfully integrated small-scale farming (e.g., mostly leafy greens and sheep and cattle herding) on vacant lands. Unlike other working poor neighborhoods in Georgetown, access to cultivatable land has contributed to Sophia's racial and ethnic diversity. With over 7,000 households, it has a majority Black (60%) population but with a significant number of people identifying as East Indian (15%), Mixed Race (12%), Amerindian (10%), and Other (3%) (Marks 2014, 5). Since the early 2000s, state agencies have surveyed land and formalized the process for leasehold registration. Public services including garbage collection and canal dredging remain inconsistent, while many areas are drained by makeshift trenches that residents have planned and dug. To this extent, vulnerability in Sophia is contoured by poverty and insecure land tenure but the flood dynamics parallel those of greater Georgetown.[4]

One afternoon in 2009 I sat with Steven on the balcony of the community center in Sophia looking at photographs. They were black and white and printed on typing paper. The reflected glare of the sun blurred the images of murky trench water and debris. One by one, he pulled photographs from his manila folder exclaiming, "I just didn't have enough film to catch everything." A few weeks prior, he rode through B Field looking for eroded canal embankments. His pictures resembled the aerial photographs of compromised flood infrastructures taken by engineers during the 2005 disaster. Late to the scene, Steven and the engineers were witnesses who did not know when the disturbance began or would end. Steven boasted about how meticulous he was, but admitted that his photographs only depicted part of the story. He reminded me, "I didn't get into people's yards.

—

I don't know what they do [to stop floods]." Steven surmised that Sophia residents' yards, and by extension their homes, are much more complex sites for a range of intimacies with flooding and its containment.

These intimacies were often the topic of discussion at VCA training. At the community center, Red Cross workers focused a number of meetings on teaching VCA trainees how to assemble and use do-it-yourself water filtration kits. Filled with things that are found in most Georgetown households, the water filtration kits include towels, chlorine bleach, and bottles. VCA trainees have to be careful not to contaminate the bottles and towels when collecting water from across vats, wells, buckets, and faucets to boil. Likewise, VCA trainees have to be vigilant even after initial collection of water and monitor their bodies for exposure to dysentery, cholera, or leptospirosis, a zoonosis transmitted through water or soil contaminated by animal urine. Puddles in yards increase the possibility of exposure even after floods. Red Cross workers suggested not only that each household in Sophia should have a water filtration kit, but also that VCA trainees should agree to hold periodic tutorials at the community center. As part of a routinized procedure, the water filtration kits provide guidelines for how to respond to health risks whatever the conditions of a particular household (Redfield 2013).

What is important here is not that VCA training is tied to ideals about acts of volunteerism. These ideals are shot through with a mix of cynicism and aspiration, sentiments that informed many VCA trainees' interest in the Red Cross in the first place. Instead, the training reflects an attention to the endurance, as opposed to the destruction, of things in daily life (Stewart 2005). It is a kind of attention that "arises in the effort to know what is happening or to be part of it, [and] the exciting presence of traces, remainders, and excesses" (Stewart 2005, 1015). While the water filtration kits provide a routinized procedure, they also call VCA trainees' attention to moments of impact between bodies and floods that are far from straightforward or causal.

The water filtration kits, while intended to be very standardized and mobile technology, also depend on how VCA trainees are hailed by others, who might experience flood-related loss, damage, or injury in different ways. VCA trainees struggled to talk about these experiences when they developed household vulnerability surveys. They brainstormed a number

—

of questions for the survey: Does your family have a water filtration kit? How high were the last flood waters in your home? Do you have an evacuation route? They also developed an appendix for the surveys that included a space for each respondent to list the responsibilities of family members, neighbors, and local state agencies in the event of a flood. As VCA trainees brainstormed, a Red Cross worker interjected to help. He explained: "This is bottom-up We never know exactly what to expect, but you can come together to help bring out the best in each other." With a successful track record managing other community-based environmental programs, this Red Cross worker was well rehearsed in making participatory decision-making appear self-evident. He encouraged VCA trainees to share testimonials about floods and their use of water filtration kits. One VCA trainee noted:

> We don't want to have to keep each other company [at meetings] . . . And I say we deal with this [kit] now and get this over so that when something really big happens again we need everyone to understand that we need to be sufficient. I don't have all the information . . . this is why we need training. We all need to know where flooding happens . . . To know that even if we take care of everything, some water will still come in your yard.

This VCA trainee recognizes that he has some understanding about drainage on his property but very little understanding of its dynamics throughout greater Sophia. In these terms, he does not know in advance of a flood how the water filtration kit will help him. He can only guess. His testimonial dramatizes the plural uses of water filtration kits, while creating a metanarrative about the common occurrence of flood hazards in Sophia.

Testimonials, in other words, served multiple purposes for training in water filtration. On the one hand, they facilitated discussion about the kind of material evidence trainees can find and gather in their daily lives to monitor water supplies. On the other, testimonials triggered conversations about the rather open-ended dynamics of caring for things and bodies that climate change demands. As an activity, testimonials remind us that crisis ordinariness depends on people withholding judgment about the future (Berlant 2011, 51–96).

In particular, a number of VCA trainees talked about leptospirosis to emphasize the deep sense of nervousness they have come to attribute to water contamination. While there were just over 40 cases of infection, alongside drowning and dehydration, leptospirosis caused 19 of the 33 disaster-related deaths in 2005. There were no cases reported in Sophia, which means that livestock owners in Sophia who used their bottom flats to herd sheep and cattle had figured out a method of survival.

The tense mix of human and nonhuman bodies registered in exchange. Some passed on health officials' warnings to not handle livestock carcasses and to keep them as far away from the interior of the house as possible to limit the spread of infection. Others started a relief system, where people volunteered to go to a shelter or a hospital in Georgetown to retrieve drugs (prophylactic drugs such as doxycycline) to pass along to family, neighbors, and friends. VCA trainees admitted, however, that based on their 2005 disaster experience, they had not developed a good sense for infection and often attributed their nausea, headaches, or fever to other diseases. Just about every bodily ailment they have come to associate with leptospirosis. But they discovered that concentrating on how much rain saturates the ground is their best chance at diagnosis.

Another VCA trainee emphasized this point about diagnosis when he suggested that intense flooding challenges reason:

> I'm trying to provoke a thought about what to do with different levels of water. Say it's like two feet of water, right away you gotta think of health, the latrine, you know . . . Say you begin with five or three feet [of water], but again, what's the difference? You have to now move because it's beyond, you know, bearable. But wherever you go, you are still exposed to a health risk. That's the thing; we know that 90% of our septic tanks aren't constructed the way they need for safety. But with the flood it compromises both, the person and the infrastructure. The kits are helpful, to a point I guess. But I still feel that with a septic tank I am safer than without . . .

This VCA trainee has become less confident in drainage and so even more reliant on water filtration kits. He references the three- and five-foot water levels experienced during the 2005 disaster as his new norm for living

—

comfortably with floods. Yet, he also notes that flood hazards related to leptospirosis and "faulty" septic tanks are difficult to discern no matter a flood's water level. As a knowledge practice, testimonials shape the powerful tension between what can be known and what remains unspeakable about the impacts of a changing climate on the ordinary.

Not only do these testimonials address complex experiences of displacement in daily life brought about by structural inequalities and crises. Trainees also detail the ways in which these experiences shape intuition about climate-related flooding. In these testimonials floods are described as a porous mix of affective, epistemological, technological, and bodily processes.

Mark Carey and colleagues have described parallel concerns about glaciology knowledge and climate change. Shaped by a cultural framework embedded in daily life of not only science but humble forms of water management equipment, glaciology knowledge represents "ice itself as an element of change and . . . as a [thing that is] part of society" (Carey et al. 2016, 1). Given the prominent place of glaciers in the global discourse about climate change, Carey suggests that the term "cryoscapes" is one way to describe the relations between people and ice. A similar dynamic is at play for VCA trainees in Guyana, where "floodscapes" mediate ethical decisions about what counts as a water filtration kit and the kinds of knowledge it shapes about the unpredictability of daily life impacted by climate change. The testimonials reinforce the idea that crisis ordinariness cannot be contained through ridged training or for that matter witnessing. At times the reality of this mundane fact can cease to be significant or burst into VCA trainees' lives and demand that it cannot be ignored.

5. ACCOMMODATING EXPERTS

A few weeks into their efforts, VCA trainees completed pilot surveys of households in an area of Sophia known as North Field. Deemed to be on the fringes of Sophia's fertile lands, North Field postdates Sophia's era of informal squatting (c. 1999). More homes are built on surveyed plots but it is located in a catchment near the outfalls of the Atlantic. Despite the lack of census data, it is rumored to be a higher income East Indian and Mixed Race area, albeit with numerous female-headed households.

My interlocutors expressed intrigue about the data they would collect. The mere presence of these households complicated their collective awareness of vulnerability. These households are more economically secure but inhabit a space that is more flood-prone than the rest of Sophia. VCA trainees recognized that floods do not care who lives where, but that it was their responsibility to create alliances between vulnerable bodies and spaces.

Data collection for the surveys was not easy. For the survey, Sophia's VCA trainees were joined by staff from other Caribbean Red Cross branches looking to complete their volunteer certification. The irony was not lost on VCA trainees who were instructed by Guyana's Red Cross staff to act as "cultural ambassadors" for the day. It is worth noting that many of the VCA trainees did not view these foreigners as intruders or as an affront to their work, but as needed labor for the tall task of surveying. They surmised that the surveys would tell them something more general about how floods might vary across space. The surveys circulated as a genre that became "delaminated from its location in someone's story or some locale's irreducibly local history" (Berlant 2011, 12). This means that the surveys were not merely constituted by speech acts, such as brainstorming exercises and testimonials performed at prior meetings. Their time surveying North Field was also an embodied practice that created the terms for the surveys' circulation.

Take for instance the ditches, weeds, and fire ant hills, both harbingers and impasses, that surrounded the entryways of many homes. VCA trainees learned how to slow their gait and brush insects off their bodies to avoid being injured by these obstacles. While most North Field residents ventured from their homes to their yards to greet VCA trainees, some shouted their answers from windows, and a few simply did not venture out to meet them on public roads. The obstacles VCA trainees faced dramatized that each survey was differently constructed by entanglements between humans and flood hazards.

Data collection was not limited by the boundary between the home and the public road. It was performed within domestic spaces as well. A woman by the name of Renee spoke in extensive detail about cement blocks she used to protect the house's foundation from flood waters. She insisted that while she felt high above the water, she often relied on her dog's movements and barking to warn her of heavy rainfall. Her children moved furniture away from windows and put plastic tarps over holes of the tin roof when it rained. Renee's vulnerability emerged in continuity with things that crosscut (non)human boundaries of the ordinary (Khan 2014). Her testimonial convinced VCA trainees that Sophia's emergency contact list should include not only phone numbers and home addresses but also the number of pets in households.

In contrast, not all of North Field's residents were committed to an ethos that equated the VCA with testimonials about vulnerability. In one interview, a North Field resident interjected in the middle of questioning to suggest that the VCA only matters if drainage improves. The VCA made him feel proud of Sophia but irritated by how he lives. He dramatized his point by making VCA trainees stand on top of an eroding canal embankment near his yard. Moved by their willingness to indulge him, he insisted that the VCA would only make North Field residents more accepting of floods.

At issue in his reprimand are concerns about the way private lives and flood hazards may often intersect but also are processes that can conjure competing imaginaries about daily life. The survey in North Field thus animates crisis ordinariness in two ways. First, any evidence of a potential flood is made a case for collecting more testimonials to get a richer sample of probable scenarios of vulnerability. Second, Sophia residents use these testimonials to question the VCA trainees' authority and their conventional social identities as "community advocates." Some like Renee claim to rise above water; others wear their vulnerability like a badge of honor, optimistic that with a bit more effort they can force other people and things to become (more) accountable. But is the VCA a tool to warn North Field residents of the vulnerabilities that might have not caught their attention, or is it intended to mobilize another kind of world?

VCA trainees attempted to address this ambiguity, particularly those who desired to put the survey to use beyond Red Cross activities. Some planned to create a flood library and research station at the community center to have information on hand to improve future VCAs. Others intended to use the survey to lobby the Ministry of Agriculture to dredge canals and improve embankments. They debated how to present the survey to state officials. A PowerPoint, they surmised, was a distraction that would make them appear too "well adapted" to climate change. They agreed that an informal presentation was the best way to communicate. The conversation would be directed by no more than ten residents, as to not overwhelm, and remind state officials that Sophia is a "cumbersome place." They desired to take on the persona of accommodating experts, who out of urgency and need could work with state agencies' limited resources. Surviving the everyday requires a light touch, and the ability to assimilate the possibilities and foreclosures flood hazards incite.

Despite these plans, they never made it to the ministry and instead drafted a letter that outlined their grievances. Vulnerability, so it is said, is socially constructed within narratives of identity and place, with varying structures and powers of authorization. The interplay of knowledge, self-presentation, eco-biological processes, and testimonials established through VCAs create a discernible communicative context for ethical commitments to participation. Yet, the VCA does not guarantee redress or even a better life. To say all this, of course, is not to dismiss outright VCAs and the moral economies in which they traffic as antipolitics (Ferguson 2006). It may be this, but it may not only be this.

The VCA demonstrates that participatory climate adaptation does not mark clear distinctions between expert and nonexpert methods for monitoring flood hazards. These distinctions have long been emphasized in biopolitical studies of vulnerability and biosecurity more broadly (Lakoff 2008). Instead, I have suggested that the increased frequency of abnormal rainfall due to climate change has blurred distinctions between expert and nonexpert in Guyana. This blurring creates the conditions for new thoughts, and as I suggest, inform contestations that emerge around relations of accountability.

These relations are quite different from what Bruno Latour calls "matters of concern," or the defense of facts for the sake of ideological or political gain (Latour 2004). This is because as long as they took initiative, VCA trainees believed that they were adapting and that their injuries due to flooding could be addressed on a case by case basis. VCA training began as a routinized effort to convey flood knowledge and a skill set in water filtration but shifted in the real time of data collection, and unfolded into a scene of adaptation itself. The VCAs are not the result of the technical or political compulsions of a few individuals, nor are they mere expressions of vulnerability that follow historically formalized understandings

———

of neoliberal development or, for that matter, state abandonment. Yet, they are not, for that reason, solely dependent on the local particularities of a hazardous place. VCA trainees understand that climate adaptation entails the constant adjustment of expectations about accountability and survival.

6. CONCLUSIONS

In this article, I described some of the attitudes and dispositions that VCA trainees hold toward participatory climate adaptation in Guyana. They hold a mix of indifference, fear, hope, and cynicism. VCAs are not a departure from the reduction and despair that so often absorbs genuine energy for humanitarian interventions. Rather, VCAs provide trainees guidelines to first build up the capacity to identify flood hazards, and second to learn to live with them. This sort of ecological realism can be stifling, just as much as it can be a foundation for change beyond pragmatism and insist on a new materialism. Between VCA trainees' testimonials and Steven's photography lies a difference not in textual interpretation or citation but in ethical sensibilities toward participation. An ethnographic focus on scenes of the ordinary helps scholars better explain why and how the circulation of climate change related data, models, and information matters to nontechnological and nonscientific publics. Berlant's analytic "crisis ordinariness" thus offers a means to track the epistemological and ontological demands of climatological expertise, as it transverses various worlds of nature and culture.

The past decade has yielded a wealth of debates about knowledge and vulnerability in the qualitative-oriented literature on participatory climate adaptation (Adger 2003, Pelling 2010). One common theme is that the "politics" of social elites and state actors effects where and how such projects can be implanted, and by extension the forms of expertise they rely on. But the VCA reminds us that politics are not predetermined by social capital alone but rather come into being through complex processes of expertise that are located in material, historical, geopolitical, economic, and nature/culture contexts (Stengers 2015). For instance, VCAs in Guyana demonstrate that participatory climate adaptation is constitutive of other crises related to Georgetown's housing stock, growing population diaspora, and waste disposal. Hence, the notion that VCAs can inherently

---

represent an effective alternative to the work of ill-resourced states is not a self-evident claim, nor is it necessarily emancipatory. Instead, I have demonstrated that these claims are regimented by how people's experiences of vulnerability contour landscapes, things, places, bodies, and desires in the everyday.

A range of activities (e.g., testimonials and surveys) dramatize the role that participatory decision-making plays in the VCA. These decisions may at first appear to be inconsequential. This is the case if we compare VCAs to geoengineering or conservation easements, practices often deemed by governmental institutions as necessary steps toward recalibrating a planet fractured by climate change. But in its mundane unfolding, participatory decision-making resonates with histories of development and North/South divides in technology and science that unfold against the backdrop of a changing climate. My focus on crisis ordinariness thus enables an analysis of participatory climate adaptation that does not assume its efficaciousness and who or what gets charged up enough to pursue survival.

Ethnography of participatory climate adaptation is not an exercise in representation or a critique of the possible publics that delimit its fields of accountability. Far from a definitive appraisal of vulnerability, politics, or ethics, it illuminates ways of knowing that inform ordinary life. It recognizes the hubris involved in such a task. At the same time, it gestures to the limits of human knowledge, while leaving open the possibility of finding other models of knowing (and living with) climate change.

NOTES

1. I refer to many of my informants by pseudonyms to protect their privacy.
2. Berlant uses the term *precarity* to describe political and economic fragility related to capitalism. In this reading, crisis ordinariness is engendered by globalized zones of capital accumulation and the migration of capital, features of the historical present which I recognize throughout this article. In doing so, Berlant associates precarity with an existential human condition shaped by the "loss of an object/scene of desire" (Berlant 2011, 10). However, my use of the term "vulnerability" instead of precarity is an attempt to highlight two related concerns. It is a term that makes clear the fragility of things in the world and the competing histories people use to narrate this fragility. In this respect, I find Berlant's crisis ordinariness a helpful analytic for making visible narratives other than those about capitalism.
3. Pelling, like others, has extended this critique of development and flooding to the

—

racial/political divisions between the majority Afro- and Indo-Guyanese populations. An in-depth analysis of race relations in Georgetown (as opposed to a national
framework) would be needed to contribute to this debate. However, I would add that
an ideal for interracial participation is dependent on various acts of recognition
across public/private spaces, and not simply electoral representation.

4. While Sophia is not represented in the national and municipal government as an
NDC, for practical purposes it is treated as a "neighborhood" of Georgetown even
though residents pay taxes and abide by city ordinances for land development. A
number of municipal maps, for instance, include Sophia. Since the early 2000s, a
number of Sophia residents have lobbied the national government to grant it NDC
status. Sophia offers a dramatic case of the lived contradictions of political representation, self-determination, and climate adaptation.

REFERENCES

Adger, N., 2003: Social capital, collective action, and adaptation to climate change. *Econ. Geogr.*, 79, 387–404, doi:10.1111/j.1944-8287.2003.tb00220.x.

Bankoff, G., G. Frerks, and D. Hilhorst, Eds., 2013: *Mapping Vulnerability: Disasters, Development and People.* Routledge Press, 256 pp.

Barad, K., 2011: Nature's queer performativity. *Qui Parle*, 19, 121–158. [Available online at https://muse.jhu.edu/journal/477.]

Berlant, L., 2011: *Cruel Optimism.* Duke University Press, 352 pp.

Blommestein, E., and Coauthors, 2005: Guyana: Socio-economic assessment of the damages and losses caused by the January– February 2005 flooding. UN Development Program/Economic Commission for Latin America and the Caribbean Rep., 14 pp. [Available online at http://www.cepal.org/publicaciones/xml/0/26950/l.031rev1part1.pdf.]

Braun, B., 2014: A new urban dispositif? Governing life in an age of climate change. *Environ. Plann.*, 32D, 49–64, doi:10.1068/ d4313.

Broad, K., and B. Orlove, 2007: Channeling globality: The 1997–98 El Niño climate event in Peru. *Amer. Ethnologist*, 34, 285–302, doi:10.1525/ae.2007.34.2.285.

Carey, M., M. Jackson, A. Antonello, and J. Rushing, 2016: Glaciers, gender, and science: A feminist glaciology framework for global environmental change research. *Prog. Hum. Geogr.*, 40, 770–793, doi:10.1177/0309132515623368.

Cavell, S., 1994: *Quest of the Ordinary: Lines of Skepticism and Romanticism.* University of Chicago Press, 208 pp.

Chakrabarty, D., 2012: Postcolonial studies and the challenge of climate change. *New Lit. Hist.*, 43, 1–18, doi:10.1353/nlh.2012.0007.

Corbin, H. P., and L. E. Aragon, 2014: Fluxos e usos das remessas da diáspora pelos domicílios receptores na Guiana. *Novos Cadernos NAEA*, 17, 325–347.

Crate, S. A., 2011: Climate and culture: Anthropology in the era of contemporary climate change. *Annu. Rev. Anthropol.*, 40, 175–194, doi:10.1146/annurev.anthro.012809.104925.

Dumm, T. L., 1999: *A Politics of the Ordinary*. NYU Press, 215 pp.

Edwards, R., S. C. Wu, and J. Mensah, 2005: Georgetown, Guyana. *Cities*, 22, 446–454, doi:10.1016/j.cities.2005.07.010.

Ferguson, J., 2006: *Global Shadows: Africa in the Neoliberal Order*. Duke University Press, 262 pp.

Hoffman, S. M., and A. Oliver-Smith, 2002: *Catastrophe and Culture: The Anthropology of Disaster*. School for Advanced Social Research Press, 328 pp.

Ifill, M., 2000: Policy response to the debt crisis: The IMF/World Bank Group 1977–1981. *Stabroek News*, February 10, 2000, p. 8.

IFRC, 2009: Independent evaluation of the second phase of the Preparedness for Climate Change programme ('PfCC2'). International Federation of Red Cross and Red Cross Societies, 20 pp. [Available online at http://www.climatecentre.org/downloads/files/programs/PFCC/AW_PfCC2_Evaluation_final.pdf.]

Khan, N., 2014: Dogs and humans and what Earth can be: Filaments of Muslim ecological thought. *HAU J. Ethnogr. Theory*, 4, 245–264, doi:10.14318/hau4.3.015.

Kirby, A., P. Meesen, and H. Ognik, 2006: Engineering Assessment of 2006 Floods. Report for the Government of Guyana, 47 pp. [Available upon request from the corresponding author.]

Lakoff, A., 2008: The generic biothreat, or, how we became unprepared. *Cult. Anthropol.*, 23, 399–428, doi:10.1111/j.1548-1360.2008.00013.x.

Latour, B., 2004: *The Politics of Nature: How to Bring the Sciences into Democracy*. Harvard University Press, 320 pp.

Lazrus, H., 2012: Climate change, water, and development in daily life in Tuvalu. *Water, Cultural Diversity, and Global Environmental Change*, B. R. Johnston et al., Eds., Springer, 88–92.

Marks, C., 2014: Sophia catchment area, fact sheet and information: The background and history. 6 pp. [Available upon request from the corresponding author.]

Mathur, N., 2015: "It's a conspiracy theory *and* climate change": Of beastly encounters and cervine disappearances in Himalayan India. *HAU J. Ethnogr. Theory*, 5, 87–111, doi:10.14318/hau5.1.005.

Peake, L., 2005: From cooperative socialism to a social housing policy? Declines and revivals in housing policy in Guyana. *Negotiating Caribbean Freedom: Peasants and the State in Development*, M. A. Crichlow, Ed., Lexington Books, 121–140.

Pelling, M., 1998: Participation, social capital and vulnerability to urban flooding in Guyana. *J. Int. Dev.*, 10, 469–486, doi:10.1002/(SICI)1099-1328(199806)10:4,469::AID-JID539.3.0.CO;2-4.

——, 1999: The political ecology of flood hazard in urban Guyana. *Geoforum*, 30, 249–261, doi:10.1016/S0016-7185(99)00015-9.

——, 2010: *Adaptation to Climate Change: From Resilience to Transformation*. Routledge Press, 224 pp.

Puri, R. K., 2015: The uniqueness of the everyday: Herders and invasive species in India. *Climate Cultures: Anthropological Perspectives on Climate Change*, J. Barnes and M. Dove, Eds., Yale University Press, 249–272.

———

Ranganathan, M., 2015: Storm drains as assemblages: The political ecology of flood risk in post-colonial Bangalore. *Antipode*, 47, 1300–1320, doi:10.1111/anti.12149.

Redfield, P., 2013: *Life in Crisis: The Ethical Journey of Doctors without Borders.* University of California Press, 338 pp.

Rodney, W., 1981: *A History of the Guyanese Working People, 1881–1905.* Johns Hopkins Press, 312 pp.

Somers, M., 2008: *Genealogies of Citizenship: Markets, Statelessness, and the Right to Have Rights.* Cambridge University Press, 338 pp.

Stengers, I., 2015: *In Catastrophic Times: Resisting the Coming Barbarism.* A. Goffey, translator, Open Humanities Press, 158 pp.

Stewart, K., 2005: Cultural poesis: The generativity of emergent things. *Handbook of Qualitative Research*, 3rd ed., N. Denzin and Y. Lincoln, Eds., Sage Publications, 1015–1030.

Thomas, C., 1984: *The Rise of Authoritarian States in Peripheral Societies.* Monthly Review Press, 288 pp.

Trotz, A., 2010: Shifting the ground beneath us: Social reproduction, grassroots women's organizing and the 2005 floods in Guyana. *Interventions*, 12, 112–124, doi:10.1080/13698010903553385.

Watts, M. J., 2014: Resilience as a way of life: Biopolitical security, catastrophism, and the food-climate change question. *Biosecurity and Vulnerability*, N. Chen and L. Sharp, Eds., School of Advanced Research Press, 145–172.

$$\textcircled{10}$$

WHAT THE SANDS
REMEMBER

VANESSA AGARD-JONES

environment:

all that surrounds our bodies:

what exists along/be/side us and what we have created:

what surrounds us because of what we surround

. . . . . requires an examination of the distinctions between the human and
    nonhuman . . . . . world

implies location, shelter, belonging, not belonging

. . . . . asks how we are both inside and outside, there because here, inter-
    connected

. . . . and therefore a center

becomes place and placeholder, repository of guilt and outrage, a satu-
    rated, empty syllable

    —TAMIKO BEYER, "NOTES TOWARDS A QUEER::ECO::POETICS"

D rawing this poem's evocation of "environment" into the Caribbean's
landscape, might we imagine Tamiko Beyer's "saturated, empty

Originally published as, Agard-Jones, V., 2012. What the Sands Remember. *GLQ: A Journal of Lesbian and Gay Studies*, 18(2–3), pp. 325–46. Copyright, 2012, Duke University Press. All rights reserved. Republished by permission of the copyright holder, Duke University Press. www.dukeupress.edu.

———

syllable" as something akin to a grain of sand? In the region, sand is ubiquitous; it is, as Beyer puts it, both place (beach) and placeholder (landscape marker). Here, on these islands, it "exists along" and "be/side us"; it "surrounds us." For Beyer, the syllable is a repository of feeling (of "guilt and outrage"), and in this essay I ask that we consider sand as a repository both of feeling and of experience, of affect and of history, in the Caribbean region. Here sand links us unswervingly to place, to a particular landscape that bears traces of both connection and loss. I imagine it to be "saturated" with the presence of people who have walked on and carried it, but simultaneously "empty" of the archaeological and forensic traces that would testify to that presence. If water is the romantic metaphor that has irredeemably made its place in Caribbean and African diasporic studies, sand is the less embraced referent that returns us to the body's messy realities. Water washes, makes clean.[1] Sand gets inside our bodies, our things, in ways at once inconvenient and intrusive. It smooths rough edges but also irritates, sticking to our bodies' folds and fissures. In this essay I ask what it might mean to pay close attention to sand, this object that exists at the point of nature's hesitation between land and sea. Heeding a call by Omise'eke Natasha Tinsley that in black queer studies our "metaphors be materially informed; [that] they be internally discontinuous, allowing for differences and inequalities between situated subjects," I propose that we experiment with sand in addition to water as a tool for that metaphorical thinking, to track fleeting references to same-sex desire and gender transgression in Martinique.[2]

This essay's aim is to bring together two strands of inquiry, first, into the meaning of what Makeda Silvera once (in)famously called the "invisibility of (Afro-) Caribbean lesbians [and gays]" and the endurance of narratives about their relationship to a presumably "silent" archive, and second, into the rapport between tropes of invisibility and the physical landscapes that people who might be called "queer" inhabit in the Caribbean region.[3] One of my concerns is the persistent bias toward what is imagined to be diaspora's radical potential both in academic figurations of "queer" lives in the Caribbean and in activist narratives about what it might take to make those lives qualitatively "better." While queer of color theorists have been doing quite a lot of powerful thinking about Caribbean queerness in relation to diaspora, in this essay I want to insist on a deeply local framing of these questions and to argue for a fine-pointed scholarly interest not particularly in movement, but in place and emplacement.[4]

Sand emerges as a compelling metaphor here, as a repository from which we might read traces of gender and sexual alterity on the landscape.[5] Ever in motion, yet connected to particular places, sand both holds geological memories in its elemental structure and calls forth referential memories through its color, feel between the fingers, and quality of grain. Today's sands are yesterday's mountains, coral reefs, and outcroppings of stone. Each grain possesses a geological lineage that links sand to a place and to its history, and each grain also carries a symbolic association that indexes that history as well. In her groundbreaking essay on the politics of erotic autonomy and decolonization in the Bahamas, M. Jacqui Alexander asks "how . . . sexuality and geography collide," and as diaspora continues to be idealized as the Caribbean's cutting edge, the fate of those who do not or cannot move in this vaunted age of mobility—people attached to local geographies—often drops out of analytic purview.[6] I think with sand here to understand that collision, to both question and document how people with access to only limited forms of mobility, like those of the shifting sands, live their genders and sexualities within the region.

This essay asks what it might mean to refute the idea that queerness does not and cannot exist, or must somehow remain invisible, in the Caribbean, and that it is only through diasporic movement that people gain their capacity to be legible, visible, and politically viable subjects. Rather than reject studies of movement and migration as both analytic frames and material experiences for Caribbean subjects, I ask what it can mean to pay equal attention to the rooted, to those Caribbean people who build lives for themselves right where they are, under conditions of both intense contradiction and sometimes, too, intense joy.[7] Spatial stabilities often profoundly mark the lives of same-sex-desiring and gender-transgressing subjects in the region, and this essay demonstrates that considering genders and sexualities in quotidian, place-specific terms can function as a critical dimension of how we join Caribbean to queer analyses.

The events that inform this work take place in Martinique, a territory where centuries-long debates about the ideal nature and extent of its autonomy from the French state continue to be struggled over and illuminated by sexual politics. Because the island is not independent, it operates

---

under a legal regime unique to the Caribbean vis-à-vis sexual rights. As just one example, in many countries in the region homosexuality is criminalized and "homosexual acts" are punishable by law, but these practices clash with France's legal code, which both affords protections and extends certain rights, like access to civil unions, to same-sex couples.[8] In the face of policies like these, local figures have argued that homosexual practices are unacceptable to 95 percent of the Martinican population because this population is said to hold "Christian" values different from those of French metropolitans.[9] This argument runs in tandem with a familiar narrative that displaces all same-sex desire onto the colonizer and onto depraved, decadent white bodies. Sited within the racialized politics of citizenship in France, these questions about community ethics and cultural sovereignty retain tremendous everyday importance for Martinican residents.

Like their heterosexual and cisgendered counterparts, same-sex-desiring and gender-transgressing Martinicans are forced to grapple with an intersection of epistemological violences as they navigate various social worlds. Throughout the region Martinicans continue to be understood as products of a kind of modernist failure, having not followed the standard postcolonial teleology to independence as did the majority of the other territories of the global South. Locally, same-sex-desiring and gender-transgressing people become subject to a culturalist agenda that rationalizes homophobia as an expression of cultural sovereignty and as a way to defend Martinican "local values" against those of the French state. These same people are also interpellated by a French universalist agenda proffered by metropolitan LGBT activists that requires the revindication of a particular type of (out, loud, and "proud") queer subject—an agenda that also, undoubtedly, violates.[10] This essay revisits tropes of queer invisibility and frames its analysis around a conscious attention to place in this particular (and somewhat peculiar) context, bearing in mind the complicated ways that this putatively (post)colonial situation affects the lives of my interlocutors on the island, both contemporary and long past.

So what, then, does or can it mean to think about queerness on France's Caribbean periphery? This essay seeks to unite a scattered archive of same-sex desire in Martinique, and, following José Muñoz's work in performance theory, it focuses on ephemera, on the traces left behind from moments of queer relation.[11] I use both popular literature and ethnography to track fleeting references to same-sex desire and gender transgression on the island, drawing a through-line between nonnormative practices across both space and time. Queer studies has largely had to define its archive through this kind of trace and absent-presence, searching for ways to both document and describe nonnormative modes of living and loving. Such theorists as Judith Jack Halberstam have compellingly described the assembly of archives, particularly those that unsettle normative interpretive regimes, as a process of scavenge; Mathias Danbolt has named the project of "touching [queer] history" as one shot through with ambiguities; Kara Keeling has written about the dual process of seeing a queer black past and producing it within the interstices; and Heather Love has urged that we understand why genealogies of this sort are at once ambivalent (as reminders of secrecy, violence, and shame) and urgent (as the groundings for future political projects).[12] Bearing in mind these structuring concerns, this essay thinks through the sexual politics of simultaneously memory and place, linking queer presence to the sands of two particular beaches on Martinique's coasts.

SAINT-PIERRE

In September 1635 Saint-Pierre became the colony of Martinique's first permanent settlement, established at the foot of Mount Pelée by French representatives of the Compagnie des Îles de l'Amérique. Seated on the island's western coast and opening out onto the Caribbean Sea, Saint-Pierre's port was Martinique's administrative and financial center for nearly 260 years. During the nineteenth century the city became known in colonial circuits as the Paris of the Antilles, as a cosmopolitan place where liberal sexual mores and a laxity about church membership were at the heart of the city's culture.[13] It housed the largest population of European migrants in the Caribbean region, and for that reason too it was a place of major social division. In a census taken in July 1901, Martinique's entire population was counted at 203,781 people, 36,011 of whom lived in Saint-Pierre. In the half century between emancipation (which came to French colonies in 1848) and Saint-Pierre's demise at the beginning of the twentieth century, fierce battles were fought in the public sphere among members of *béké* (white colonist) families, white functionaries from the

—

metropole, members of the growing *métisse* and *mulâtre* (mixed-race and fair-skinned) middle class, and the overwhelmingly black servant/worker majority. Saint-Pierre was also a city of contradiction, for while violent struggles for power were endemic to the city's workings, so too was a type of social mixture that was most evident in the private and, above all, sexual sphere. The city's theater, brothels, and carnival celebrations were legendary, attracting wealthy joy-seekers from all over the island and from other islands, too, all throughout the year. While a spirit of *libertinage* had come to characterize French landholdings in the Americas from New Orleans to Saint-Domingue, Saint-Pierre emerged as a central site in France's eighteenth- and nineteenth-century economic, political, and sexual conquest of the region.[14] As the Martinican author and cultural critic Raphaël Confiant has argued, "Saint-Pierre was the city of all excesses."[15]

But on the morning of May 8, 1902, Mount Pelée, the volcano that sits just above the city, erupted—killing nearly everyone in Saint-Pierre within five seconds. It was the kind of volcanic eruption that inspired divine interpretation: a boiling, three-hundred-degree cloud of gas, steam, dust, ash, and pumice formed within the mountain and then burst forth. Hugging the earth and moving laterally at five hundred kilometers per hour, the cloud engulfed the city before anyone had time to react. This feat of nature was later named a *nuée ardente*, or a pyroclastic cloud. It was a phenomenon that had never been seen or analyzed before by the era's geologists and volcanologists. While Plinian eruptions (eruptions that shoot straight up into the air and end in lava flows) were familiar to the scientists of the day, this "new" type, which came to be known as a Peléan eruption, seemed to have come out of nowhere.[16] The Caribs, the indigenous inhabitants of Martinique, surely knew of the dangers of this volcano—they called it "Fire Mountain"—but that knowledge was lost in the genocidal campaign that the French waged in the name of imperial expansion. By 1902 Pierrotins (as the residents were called) had grown accustomed to living at the foot of a volcano and had taken to enjoying the warm sulphurous waters at its base for their curative practices. While there had been minor eruptions at the mountaintop in 1792 and again in 1851, these had been judged insignificant final gasps of a volcano on the decline. No one suspected that by the end of 1902 a local priest would have published a memoir called *Funeral Pilgrimage in the Ruins of Saint-Pierre*, or that a children's book comparing

Saint-Pierre to Sodom and Gomorrah would claim to illustrate the wages of sin(s) gone too long unpunished.[17] Nor could residents anticipate that a year later, marking the first anniversary of the eruption, the island's newspaper would bear the headline: "Only Sodom is the analogy that we can make to the disaster at Saint-Pierre."[18]

The equation of Saint-Pierre with Sodom is of most interest for the present essay, particularly because the image of that doomed city is a recurrent one in Caribbean cultural imaginaries.[19] Alexander, commenting on the problems of invoking Sodom in the Caribbean, asserts that "Sodom requires no point of reference other than itself; it can assert authority without comparison, evidence, or parallel. Its power lies in the ability to distort, usurp, or foreclose other interpretative frameworks, other plausible explanations for its destruction, or other experiential dimensions of homosexuality [nonnormative practices] that oppose and refuse [dominant] constructions."[20] Here Alexander makes a compelling case for the metaphor's uselessness, for its power to obscure. But looked at differently, what might this repeated evocation of Sodom help us understand about the lives of Saint-Pierre's residents at the turn of the century? How might the image of Sodom have stood in for a range of things that could not be said or that could not have been spoken directly into the archive? Looked at differently, what traces might this image help us reveal?

When after the eruption Clémence Cassius de Linval, a longtime *béké* resident of Saint-Pierre and author of *Coeurs martiniquais*, wrote that "Sodom will sink because the volcano has vomited on the imprudent," or when a local priest criticized the city by calling it "the sad testimony to the impiety and immorality of this country: it is a real Sodom that God has punished," what did these writers communicate to their broader reading publics?[21] Rather than dismiss these writing strategies as reductive sleights of hand employed by chroniclers seeking the moral authority conveyed by biblical allusion, we might see these invocations of Sodom as a mode of indexing knowledge not only about same-sex desire but also about other modes of nonnormative relation and gender transgression, in pre-eruption Saint-Pierre. In an era when writing directly about these "queer" practices was taboo, calling Saint-Pierre the Sodom of the Antilles might have functioned as a privileged gesture—as a nod toward a mountain of things that could not be referenced directly.

Beyond these allusions, though, there remains at least one textual trace of Saint-Pierre's queerness: an erotic novel from the nineteenth century. While the relationship of fictional narrative to social analysis is not uncomplicated, it is clear that fiction captures something that social science often cannot. It moves beyond what can be readily observed, measured, and tabulated to more ephemeral phenomena that empirical methods often fail to capture. The novelist Samuel Delany warns about "generaliz[ing] from our fictions," but in this essay I ask that we consider them spaces for sustained inquiry and that we approach this work of pulp fiction as the location for an unstable, atomized archive of queer relation.[22]

Originally published in 1892 and rereleased in 1901, then recuperated and reprinted in 1992 and 1996, *Une nuit d'orgies à Saint-Pierre, Martinique* (*A Night of Orgies in Saint-Pierre, Martinique*) captures the social and linguistic registers of life in the city at the end of the nineteenth century.[23] Written in both French and Créole under the playful pseudonym Effe Géache (the initials F. G. H. in French), it is the story of three men who have long been running buddies, and in a classically French formula for narrative diversity, one is white (Philippe), one *mulâtre* (Jules), and one black (Hubert).[24] The erotic novel is the story of just one night, when after the friends have reunited they reminisce around a dinner table about old sexual liaisons and then head to a party in town. Confiant, in his preface to the 1992 edition, reminds readers that Géache's work is critical because it centers on experiences of misery, violence, and, of course, sex—experiences that, he maintains, were some of the most important dimensions of everyday life for residents of Saint-Pierre. Unlike the work of de Linval, who narrates life in Saint-Pierre as if it were a town populated only by *békés* and French metropolitans, Géache's story attempts a more realistic vision of the era's social context.[25] According to the historian Liliane Chauleau, after France's Third Republic was established in 1870, life in the capital took on a significantly more racially mixed character.[26] While misery and violence were undoubtedly an important part of that "mixed" life in the city, the representation of sex in *A Night of Orgies* is the narrative's most striking aspect. There Géache describes a range of sex acts for his readers, both consensual and not, sexual encounters enacted often in public: group sex, play with sex roles, female ejaculation, more cunnilingus and fellatio than can be counted on two hands, loads of anal play and penetration,

———

and doggie-style sex (that, it seems, was fairly transgressive for the time). But Géache also offers two moments in the novel that give readers indirect access to same-sex desire and gender transgression in pre-eruption Saint-Pierre.

Early on in the narrative, Hubert (the dandy of the bunch) is on his way to the port to meet Jules, who is arriving on a boat from Fort-de-France, when he happens on a group of five women on a street corner. With little fanfare, these women are said to be "comparing and poking at each others' pussies."[27] It is a striking, but still oblique image, and is quickly passed over when Hubert throws up one of the women's skirts and forces her into a brief and violent sex act in front of her friends. This becomes a scene of base sexual violence, but what kind of trace of queer relationality might that one moment, just as Hubert arrived, have given us access to? Who were these women and what were they doing when Hubert approached? These women are later referred to as a group of whores (*catins*), but it is never clear whether that is their profession or a moniker ascribed to them as a result of their practices. Almost all of the women in the novel are called whores at one time or another, no matter what their social position. Hubert has clearly had a relationship with one of the women in the group, Jeanne, who jealously pulls his penis out of the woman he is raping just as he is about to ejaculate. But long before Hubert's arrival, when the women were alone and connecting with each other, what allowed this group's intimate touching, particularly in public, to be narrated in such a fashion? The language makes it seem commonplace, as if they were admiring each other's hair. So what does it mean that they were "comparing" pussies? And "poking" them?

Theorists of women's same-sex desire have made important use of these kinds of fleeting presences. They have challenged conventional disciplines' privileging of visible, empirical evidence, interpreting those stances as indictments of women-desiring-women's practices and forms of identification as either "impossible" or unmentionable.[28] The anthropologist Serena Owusua Dankwa, for example, writes compellingly about everyday intimacies between women in Ghana and about "modes of sexual sociality . . . [that exist] beyond the subcultural language of sexual identity politics."[29] In her analysis, norms of discretion and indirection structure relationships between women, with codes legible only to and between them. This, she

—

argues, is not silence nor absence but a kind of tacit engagement that well reflects the kind of "queer" presence that has long been a legible part of life in Martinique: present yet not particularly remarked on, and represented only fleetingly.[30] These are the kinds of engagements that, as Jafari S. Allen has so elegantly described them, "require no parade and no declarations outside of [their] own cocoons of recognition."[31]

The second moment in the narrative that draws our queer attention comes midway through the novel, when the friends decide to leave the conviviality of their dinner table to attend a party at a place called Chez Babette, a bar and dancehall that actually existed before the volcano struck. Géache writes that Philippe helps his companions to "se travestir" before heading out into the night.[32] *Se travestir* is an ambiguous, polysemic term, meaning simultaneously to disguise oneself and to cross-dress, and would also have been so in nineteenth-century Martinique. In this instance, the fact of the companions' work to change their physical appearances may be an important one. Martinique is known throughout the Caribbean for its "unusual" Carnival practices. Whereas Carnival is a time of sexual excess nearly everywhere in the region, in Martinique it is also a moment when men—from all walks of life and with varying attachments to masculine identities—*se travestissent en femme*, dress as women.[33] This practice was said to have begun in Saint-Pierre, the center of the first Carnival celebrations on the island.[34]

By 1892, the date of the novel's publication, cross-dressing had been firmly anchored in the social life of Pierrotins. When just under ten years later Pélée erupted and many of the city's former residents were dispersed throughout the French Caribbean, they brought the practice elsewhere, most notably to French Guyana, where the familiar figure of *touloulous solidaires* are often men dressed as women in the prototypical head-to-toe Carnival disguise.[35] The anthropologist Thierry L'Étang, in his oral histories with descendants of Pierrotins, has explored popular reinterpretations of the disaster that focus on *malédiction*, or divine retribution, as the genesis of the eruption. While the logics that he elicits are largely confined to stories of residents' disrespect of religious figures, he also documents stories that suggest that magically related gender transgression may have been a part of the city's maligned reputation. His interlocutor Antoinette, for example, talks of hearing about "young boys who turned themselves into

---

dogs. They transformed into *diablesses* at noon, and *zombis* in the evening."[36] And his interlocutor George talks about a couple who always made their appearances in town "dressed as women . . . [who] frightened the young."[37]

Given this context of gender play and *travestissement*, Géache's mention of the men's redressing on their way to the dance could be read not simply as their dressing *up* but also as their assumption of nonnormative gender presentations. When Jules first arrives at the dock and Philippe proposes that they go out to this party, Jules laments that he has brought nothing to wear. That problem is easily solved later on, when Philippe presumably loans both men the necessary "disguises." Just as he had described the women on the corner, Géache writes this moment with little fanfare, yet both of these scenes highlight the indirect ways that moments of queer relation show up in Martinique's textual archive.

Like these moments unremarked upon yet inescapably present, when one drives the island's western coast today from the town of Carbet, up through Saint-Pierre, and on to the northernmost cove at Anse Couleuvre, it is impossible to miss the fact that the beaches' sands range from a light charcoal gray to deep, deep black.[38] Like the fleeting references to same-sex desire and gender transgression in *A Night of Orgies*, the sands in the area that surround Saint-Pierre are today a visual reminder of Mount Pelée's eruption. Like people, like places, like objects or ideas, sand has a history, a genealogy. The composition of sand varies, yet that variation is deeply dependent on its environment. Sand always carries a local imprint. In this area the beaches are black because particles in the sand are made up of basalt, which comes from volcanic ash. There the sands remember—or at least they reference—the eruption, and in doing so they call up all of the associations we might have with the city that once was. Those sands carry the imprint of the world that Mount Pelée both dispersed and destroyed on that day in 1902.

SAINTE-ANNE

Far to the south and east of Saint-Pierre, in an area that sits at the tip of a small outcropping on Martinique's other shore, lies a commune called Sainte-Anne. While pre-eruption Saint-Pierre was often imagined as a space of hedonistic racial mixture, Sainte-Anne has long held a far different reputation. During the 1950s the out-of-the-way commune was known as a refuge for rebels, for people who contested the continued dominance of *béké* and *mulâtre* elites in the lives of ordinary (mostly black) Martinicans, and was the center of the island's small cultural nationalist movement.[39] In the 1970s community members protested the building of the island's only Club Méditeranée and have since worked concertedly to thwart the development of a tourist industry in the commune.[40] After the local activist Garcin Malsa was elected mayor in 1989, he launched a campaign to remove all of the *tricolores* (the blue, white, and red French flags) from their official perches and to replace them with a red, black, and green flag, meant to declare Martinican independence from France. Today, when you drive into Sainte-Anne from the island's major highway, the first thing you see as you cross the boundary is a roundabout where the red, black, and green waves. But Sainte-Anne is known for another reason, too: it is home to one of the island's few meeting spaces for same-sex-desiring men, a secluded cove called Anse Moustique on the least visited part of its largest beach, Les Salines.

On my first visit to the island, I hiked out to Anse Moustique at midmorning. Not only was it long before noon, but it was also the middle of the week, and I found myself alone on the beach, wondering how this empty place squared with the stories that I had heard men tell about their liaisons there. It was just a cove flanked by trees and low-hanging brush, opening onto a shallow stretch of the sea. The waves there were gentle, and the sand freshly flattened by the high tide. I was beset by two questions that have remained with me since. The first: why make this cruising spot all the way out here, in Sainte-Anne? On a good traffic-free day, Anse Moustique is over an hour's drive from the island's urban center. While the capital seems to always have one operational cruising strip, alternating between the central waterfront, La Savane (a city park), and the port, this beach is the only drag that has remained constant for more than two decades. Distance is one good reason, but there are other beaches on the island, themselves equally difficult to access. That Anse Moustique sits in one of Martinique's two nationalist communes reminds us of the omnipresence of queer relation. Rather than restrict the archive of these presences to the decadent city that Saint-Pierre once was, often read as European, Anse Moustique takes us into the hinterlands, often read as the site for black

———

authenticity, to a context far different from the one described in Géache's novel. While Saint-Pierre was the embodiment of the island's cosmopolitanism, Sainte-Anne is a sleepy backwater. There unemployment rates sit at nearly 35 percent, and people remember vividly a not-so-distant time when many made their living by doing the tedious work of salt-collecting out on the flats.[41] People who live in the island's contemporary urban spaces often speak of places like Sainte-Anne, pejoratively, as being *en commune*. Said with a frown of the face and a roll of the eyes, they imagine the people in these places incapable of acquiring the sophistication assigned to the residents of more urban grounds.

As we sipped espresso in a café in Fort-de-France, I asked thirty-two-year-old Guillaume to describe Anse Moustique for someone who had never been there.[42] He and I had been talking about our experiences of the place, and most particularly about his first journey there, when a friend whom he had met online (through the website Adam 4 Adam) gave him a ride to the beach.[43] It was there that he first had oral sex with another man. This is what he said:

> GUILLAUME: Listen, it's not like it's on anyone's way anywhere else. Anse Moustique? Whew [he sucks his teeth]. You have to drive all the way out to Sainte-Anne first (And with the traffic here? That can take over an hour!) and then you have to continue, continue, continue . . . all along that smaller road to Les Salines. And then you still have to get to Anse Moustique—now that there's that new access road—you know the one I mean. That you took for the party?—no, I don't remember when they opened it . . . my memory's bad . . . but you know the road, with all of the rocks and potholes, and it gets flooded, too, every time it rains (and you know it rains all the time here!). And then even after you park, you have to put on your boots and hike! [he laughs] But when you get there, you know. You know that the guys who are there are in the same spirit as you.
>
> VANESSA AGARD-JONES: How does that feel?
>
> GUILLAUME: C'est magique, chérie. Tout à fait. C'est magique. [It's magic, my dear. Completely. It's magic.]

What makes Anse Moustique magic for Guillaume is the kind of shared space that it offers to the people who go there. This kind of experience is

———

a critical dimension of what might be called "queer" culture on the island. The beach is so far out of the way that those who find themselves on its sands are a self-selecting bunch. The men there do not usually call themselves gay—instead of embracing an identity, they identify with an affective state—they often say they are *chaud* (hot)—in a hot period, needing release. In addition to the space, this is the "spirit" (*esprit*) that they share, a shifting terrain of desire much like the sands that heat and cool throughout the day. Many, like Guillaume, have girlfriends and wives on other parts of the island and are able to make the long journey out to the beach only a few times a month. As Lionel, another of my interlocutors, said to me, *On vient pour koker—c'est ça le but*. (We come to fuck—that's the goal.) But other things happen, too, at Anse Moustique. Men come to know and recognize each other, an important, but also potentially risky process on an island as small as Martinique, where propinquity feeds the gossip mill. Men who have come by bus and on foot often leave with others who have cars. Drinks and joints are brought and shared. Men play and bathe and rest in the sea. The magic is sexual but also social, equally about what Guillaume described as the "best blow job of [his] life" as about the kinds of connections, however tenuous, that the space offers for its users.

I think of Anse Moustique as another example of what Delany describes in his powerful set of essays *Times Square Red, Times Square Blue*, where he recounts the kinds of relationships that men built in Manhattan's porn theaters in the 1970s and 1980s. Refusing an easy nostalgia, Delany writes, "Were the porn theaters romantic? Not at all. But because of the people who used them, they were humane and functional, fulfilling needs that most of our society does not yet know how to acknowledge."[44] For Delany, these were places that fulfilled sexual needs, but also social ones—allowing for a kind of cross-class contact that was otherwise rare in his daily life. In Martinique, this kind of contact is even more rarified, as the island's class stratification is exacerbated by disparities in access to transportation and by the fact that living without a car limits access to a wide range of places on the island. This is not Delany's New York City, where, however cynically we might think about it, even the mayor rides public transportation. In Martinique, public buses run only in the capital, and they operate only Monday through Friday from 5 a.m. to 6 p.m. and on Saturdays until noon. Collective taxis get people without cars from town to town, but they are unscheduled and unreliable, and only go to the town centers rather than to more out-of-the-way places, like Anse Moustique.

Through Guillaume I met Bruno, an HIV-positive man in his forties who lives on social assistance in a small apartment in Fort-de-France. He scrapes to get by most months, supplementing his state income with a variety of hustles.[45] While he does not have access to a car, he travels to Anse Moustique fairly regularly, either by bus or hitchhiking to make his way to that other shore. When I asked him to describe a particularly memorable moment at Anse Moustique, he said this:

> BRUNO: It was a Sunday a couple of years back, and I met a young man, a *béké*, who was seventeen years old . . . I saw him walking with a piece of wood, swinging it like this, and he had on hiker shorts—and I asked him, "Are you lost?" He said "No, no, no. I'm just taking a walk." I asked, "Do you know where you are?" And he said, "I know this route." So I did a U-turn and came back to him and said, "Do you know there are a lot of homos here?" And he said, "Oh yes? I didn't know." And I said, "You didn't know?" "(You know when they say they don't know, they really know.)" And he said, "And you, are you homo?" And I said, "Yes, I'm homo—but don't be afraid." And he said, "I'm not afraid!" But he was scared to be penetrated, you know, because I had on a cap and baggy jeans, I was looking very BadBoy, and he had this idea about what was going to happen to him—but when I offered to suck him off he said—*tout de suite!*—*On va où?* (Where can we go?) *Tout de suite!* (Right away!) So we walked across the mangrove, and laid down a towel, and we made love there but that young man he was seventeen—and he was a *béké*! And we talked for a long time afterward—he told me that he was a *béké*, and that he was in high school at the rich people's school, the private one in Fort-de-France. That's a story that I would love to see happen again—no, I haven't seen him again yet, but when we see each other . . . that would be something nice.

Bruno's story about his encounter with the young *béké* highlights the function of the beach as a space of both cross-class and interracial connection. In Martinique, *békés* are the descendants of the white colonial elite, the planter class that continues to dominate the island economically, though no longer politically. *Békés* are notorious for their remove from the rest of the

—

island, for their enclosed communities on the east coast in and around Le François, and for their continued staunch refusal to "mix" with the rest of the island's population.[46] For Bruno, having this liaison—and, particularly, this postcoital conversation with a *béké*—remained in his memory as a singularly significant moment in his nearly twenty years of frequenting Anse Moustique. The conventional racial scripts that would have made their connection unlikely are disrupted here by the prospect of a blow job, by the potential for a moment of shared pleasure. Like Guillaume, who thinks of the beach in magical terms, Bruno appreciates it not just for the sex but also for the other kinds of social connection that the place makes possible.

While most evenings Anse Moustique is a cruising space for men alone, a few times a year a promoter named Jean-Marc throws large parties on the beach, trucking in a generator, DJ equipment, tiki torches, and party lights to welcome nearly two hundred people to dance and connect. Everyone brings a bottle to contribute to the bar (a requirement for admission), and after drinking and dancing most of the night away there is time for sea baths at dawn.

I arrive at 2 a.m., just as the party is getting under way. The sandy dance floor is already marked by the footprints of ecstatic dancers, moved by the DJ's facility with diasporic music—he moves seamlessly from soca to zouk, through calypso and dancehall, back to hip hop and R&B, and then again to something close to, though not quite, Chicago house. Women come to these parties in striking numbers, setting up their towels in a cove slightly separate from the men's side of the beach. Like their male counterparts, they drink and dance, often leading the more raucous line-dancing interludes orchestrated by the DJ. They too are the first to the sandy dance floor when the selector plays a slow zouk, and their grinding and twirling entices the male couples to join, swaying to the syncopated beats, forehead to forehead, crotches intertwined. There is a good deal of semipublic sex on these evenings among both men and women, who use the cover of night's darkness and the privacy of the surrounding brush to consummate their unions, however tenuous.

The day after one such party I called a woman in her forties named Karine to talk about the night's events. Karine works as a security guard and identifies herself by the French term *garçon manqué*, or "missed boy" (tomboy). In the years that I have known her, she has never had a serious relationship, but at these beach parties she is quite popular and is usually surrounded by a group of women of varying gender identifications. I had seen Karine head off down a path with a younger woman just as I was getting ready to leave the party. On the phone, I asked her what it was that she remembered most about the evening. In response, she said this: "*Seigneur* (God), I woke up this afternoon with sand in my ass and all I could think about was that hot little *chabine* that I had on the beach."[47] Powerfully mediated through her experience of sand lodged in an uncomfortable place, Karine's corporeal association of the beach with her lovemaking made me wonder anew what the sand might offer us as a repository for queer memory.

Beyond the stories that Guillaume, Bruno, and Karine are able to recount, what remains of the vibrant sexual encounters that they have had at Anse Moustique? After the parties are over, and the blankets, empty bottles, and sound system cleared away, what reminds us of the importance of this site, for so many people? On that beach, the sand that people dance and lie down on holds something of those experiences—perhaps not materially, but metaphysically. Thinking about how we might understand this phenomenon, the second question that has beset me since my first solitary visit to that cove is this: what could an empty place tell me, an ethnographer, about same-sex desire on the island? Perhaps it is in the sands that I have my answer. The sand tracks this presence in a place where the archive is shallow, and where the ravages of the plantation, then later of the colony, and even worse still, of the salinated air, has meant the slow erosion of all things putatively concrete. Sand is born of, and speaks of, that erosion. On a beach where people live and love and dance together, there can be no definitive record. But far from V. S. Naipaul's condemnation of the Caribbean as a site of "ruination," the sand, even in its erosion, has its own integrity and retains its own history. The sand's memory is "a resolute commitment to those with whom . . . we are still dancing," a diffuse and oblique archive of movement in place, of loving on a local scale.[48]

SAND IS HISTORY

In his magisterial and now-iconic poem, St. Lucian writer and Nobel laureate Derek Walcott contends that, for the Caribbean region, "sea is history."[49] Invoked time and again as the ideal metaphor to index the complicated calculus of presence, loss, and absence that attends the history of the African diaspora in the Americas, Walcott's articulation of the sea is much like those of a cadre of literary workers and cultural critics who employ watery metaphors to help us better grasp and understand this history.

Working from a different angle, in my attempt to pay close attention to place, this essay invokes the most fine-grained element—quite literally—of the place where I work: the sand. From the sand on the beaches of Saint-Pierre, to the morning-after sand in Karine's ass, sand is everywhere in Martinique (as it is throughout the region). It is, of course, on the beaches, but it is also carried on the wind and on our bodies. It ends up on the kitchen floor, in the backseat of the car, in the bottom of my handbag, and in all manner of bodily orifices. While we have work that inspires and elucidates using metaphors of the mangrove and of the sea in Caribbean cultural studies, the sand has received no such attention. But what can the sand tell us?

Nearly everywhere on earth, sand is principally made up of one element—in some places silica, in others limestone. Ninety percent of a grain is almost always just one of those two elements. But the other 10 percent is the percentage with a difference—the percentage that, in its difference, matters—the percentage that can tell us something about the history of a place. In Saint-Pierre and its surroundings, that variable 10 percent is made up of the basalt that makes the sands black.[50] In Sainte-Anne, there is no geological marker in those grains, but they hold something all the same. While the sand's referents are far from concrete, they provide a model for one way to understand the memory of same-sex desire and gender transgression on the island—as diffuse yet somehow omnipresent. "Queerness," then, retains a kind of oblique permanence in Martinique that has resonance both in the structure of the sand and in the connections made on the island's shores. Rather than invoke ideas about absence and invisibility as the condition of same-sex-desiring and gender-transgressing people, turning to sand as a metaphor for the repository of memory may help our analyses engage with more fine-grained and ephemeral presences than our usual archives would allow.

NOTES

I would like to thank Jafari S. Allen, Alex Bell, Mathias Danbolt, Dána-Ain Davis, A. Naomi Jackson, and Ram Natarajan for their ongoing engagement with this work and for their astute feedback as it moved from talk to essay. My arguments were also productively honed through presentations at the 2010 "Queer Again? Power, Politics, Ethics" conference in Berlin, hosted by the generous and engaging members of the Gender as a Category of Knowledge Research Group, in a 2011 iteration of Simone Leigh's "Be Black Baby" art and performance event at Recess Art Gallery, and at the 2011 Caribbean Studies Association's annual conference in Curaçao, where discussions with my copanelists Lyndon K. Gill and Omise'eke N. Tinsley were beyond my imaginings and proved truly priceless. I am particularly grateful for Deborah A. Thomas, who has supported this work in all ways—(very!) big and small. My colleagues at Linköping University's Tema Genus and in Stockholm's broader gender/queer/feminist studies networks were extraordinarily helpful as I made my way through the revision process, even at the height of Swedish summer. Finally, I thank *GLQ*'s three anonymous reviewers for their insightful and incisive readings, and hope to continue to engage their feedback as the broader project that includes this work develops. During the time that I developed this essay, my research was generously supported by a National Science Foundation Graduate Research Fellowship (and its Nordic Research Opportunity) under grant number DGE-0813964, as well as by the Bourse Chateaubriand of the Embassy of France in the United States.

1. This is not to discount the deep associations of water with both physical and emotional pain, with death and drowning, or of specific bodies of water (and their boundaries) with militarism. My point is also not to set sand in brutal opposition to water but to highlight the different kind of work that it might do given its material constraints, in its moderation of ideas about fluidity and motion. For important discussions of water, pain, and black historical memory, see Omise'eke Natasha Tinsley, *Thiefing Sugar: Eroticism between Women in Caribbean Literature* (Durham, NC: Duke University Press, 2010); and Marcus Wood, *Blind Memory: Visual Representations of Slavery in England and America, 1780–1865* (Manchester: Manchester University Press, 2000).

2. Omise'eke Natasha Tinsley, "Black Atlantic, Queer Atlantic: Queer Imaginings of the Middle Passage," *GLQ* 14 (2008): 204.

3. Makeda Silvera, "Man Royals and Sodomites: Some Thoughts on the Invisibility of Afro-Caribbean Lesbians," *Feminist Studies* 18, no. 3 (1992): 521–32. While Silvera's argument is pegged specifically to *lesbian* invisibility, and the particular silences/erasure that she argues condition our lives, I believe her broader critique would extend to same-sex-desiring Afro-Caribbean people more generally. I use the words *queer* and *queerness* here as a shorthand, fully cognizant of the fact that they are not words that appear in the lexicon of same-sex-desiring and gender-transgressing subjects in Martinique. For a masterful analysis of the challenges of fitting language to our interlocutors' form/s and practice/s in black queer studies, see Tinsley, *Thiefing Sugar*, 5–15.

---

4. For work on queer Caribbean diasporas, see, for example, Ronald Cummings, "(Trans)nationalisms, Marronage, and Queer Caribbean Subjectivities," *Transforming Anthropology* 18, no. 2 (2010): 169–80; Lawrence La Fountain-Stokes, *Queer Ricans: Cultures and Sexualities in the Diaspora* (Minneapolis: University of Minnesota Press, 2009); Rinaldo Walcott, "Queer Returns: Human Rights, the Anglo-Caribbean, and Diaspora Politics," *Caribbean Review of Gender Studies*, no. 3 (2009); Timothy Chin, "The Novels of Patricia Powell: Negotiating Gender and Sexuality across the Disjunctures of the Caribbean Diaspora," *Callaloo* 30, no. 2 (2007): 533–45.

5. I am inspired here by feminist technoscience studies and by efforts to theorize a "posthumanities" that breaks down boundaries both between academic disciplines and between bodies and their surroundings. For example, Anneke Smelik and Nina Lykke argue that "the human body can no longer be figured either as a bounded entity or as a naturally given and distinct part of an unquestioned whole that is itself conceived as the 'environment.' The boundaries between bodies and their components are being blurred, together with those between bodies and larger ecosystems" (x). This essay's use of sand as both material and metaphor resonates with Smelik and Lykke's concept "bits of life" (xxi) and their theorization of people simultaneously with the biological/geological/chemical environments in which they live. Similarly, in her bid for complex systems thinking across disciplinary divides, Elizabeth Wilson calls for "some middle ground of conceptual advocacy in which the metaphoricity of depression and the neurobiology of depression cohabit, entwine and are inherently shaped by one another" (292). Like Smelik and Lykke, she works productively between metaphor and science, across the literary and the empirical, in ways that this essay also seeks to situate its work. See Anneke Smelik and Nina Lykke, "Bits of Life: An Introduction," in *Bits of Life: Feminism at the Intersections of Media, Bioscience, and Technology*, ed. Anneke Smelik and Nina Lykke (Seattle: University of Washington Press, 2008), x, xxi; and Elizabeth Wilson, "Neurological Entanglements: The Case of Paediatric Depressions, SSRIs, and Suicidal Ideation," *Subjectivity* 4, no. 3 (2011): 277–97; quotation on 292.

6. M. Jacqui Alexander, *Pedagogies of Crossing: Meditations on Feminism, Sexual Politics, Memory, and the Sacred* (Durham, NC: Duke University Press, 2006).

7. The anthropologist Gloria Wekker has long done this work in Suriname, and her *Politics of Passion: Women's Sexual Culture in the Afro-Surinamese Diaspora* (New York: Columbia University Press, 2006) is a compelling examination of many of the concerns with which I am preoccupied here.

8. N.B.: "homosexual acts" often serves as a gloss for anal penetration, a practice engaged in by people across sexual spectra, yet used to single out and penalize male same-sex couples for their lovemaking.

9. See, for example, an interview with Vauclin's mayor Raymond Occolier from 2007, just before the French national election campaign: www.dailymotion.com/video /x1i170_occo-bondamanjak_news. Beginning at 3:20 he describes his stance as an "élu chrétien" (itself an oxymoron to the French state) as one that requires that he take a position against marriage, adoption, and other legal reforms for LGBT people.

———

In the interview he purports to speak for the great majority of Martiniquai(se)s when he declares himself to be against sexual acts he calls "against nature," yet emphasizes that his positions on these issues do not, in his view, make him homophobic.

10. Vanessa Agard-Jones, "Le Jeu de Qui? Sexual Politics at Play in the French Caribbean," in *Sex and the Citizen: Interrogating the Caribbean*, ed. Faith Smith (Charlottesville: University of Virginia Press, 2011).

11. José Esteban Muñoz, "Gesture, Ephemera, Queer Feeling," in *Dancing Desires: Choreographing Sexualities on and off the Stage*, ed. Jane Desmond (Madison: University of Wisconsin Press, 2001).

12. Judith Halberstam, *In a Queer Time and Place: Transgender Bodies, Subcultural Lives* (New York: New York University Press, 2005); Mathias Danbolt, "Touching History: Archival Relations in Queer Art and Theory," in *Lost and Found: Queerying the Archive*, ed. Jane Rowley, Louise Wolthers, and Mathias Danbolt (Copenhagen: Nikolaj, Copenhagen Center of Contemporary Art and Bildmuseet Umeå University, 2010); Kara Keeling, "Looking for M—: Queer Temporality, Black Political Possibility, and Poetry from the Future," *GLQ* 15 (2009): 565–82; Heather Love, *Feeling Backward: Loss and the Politics of Queer History* (Cambridge, MA: Harvard University Press, 2007).

13. Claude Rives and Frédéric Denhez, *Les épaves du volcan* (Grenoble: Editions Glénat, 1997).

14. Doris Garraway, *The Libertine Colony: Creolization in the Early French Caribbean* (Durham, NC: Duke University Press, 2005).

15. Raphaël Confiant, "Libertinage à la Créole," in *Une nuit d'orgies à Saint-Pierre, Martinique*, by Effe Géache (Paris: Arléa, 1992). Unless stated otherwise, all translations from French and Martinican Créole are my own.

16. Alwyn Scarth, *La Catastrophe: The Eruption of Mount Pelée, the Worst Volcanic Eruption of the Twentieth Century* (Oxford: Oxford University Press, 2002).

17. U. Moerens, *Pèlerinage funèbre aux ruines de Saint-Pierre, Martinique* (Lille: Société Saint-Augustin, 1903).

18. Patrice Louis, *L'enfer à Saint-Pierre: Dictionnaire de la catastrophe de 1902* (Martinique: Ibis Rouge, 2002), 151.

19. This also holds true for sexual politics in other regions, wherever the influence of the biblical tale retains cultural meaning. For an analysis of the threat of Sodom-like destruction in early New England, see Jonathan Ned Katz, "The Age of Sodomitical Sin, 1607–1740," in *Reclaiming Sodom*, ed. Jonathan Goldberg (New York: Routledge, 1994).

20. M. Jacqui Alexander, "Erotic Autonomy as a Politics of Decolonization," in *Pedagogies of Crossing*, 51.

21. Louis, *L'enfer à Saint-Pierre*; Scarth, *La Catastrophe*.

22. Samuel R. Delany, *Times Square Red, Times Square Blue* (New York: New York University Press, 2001), 147.

23. Effe Géache, *Une nuit d'orgies à Saint-Pierre, Martinique* (Paris: Calivran, 1978).

24. This formula, echoed in more contemporary film and fiction as a black/blanc/beur triad, activates tropes of cross-racial friendship and common French citizenship

———

while eliding both historical and contemporary structures of racial violence. For masterful analyses of antiblack racism within French multiculturalist imaginaries, see Pap Ndiaye, "Pour une histoire des populations noires en France: Préalables théoriques," *Le mouvement social* 213, no. 4 (2005); Ndiaye, *La condition noire: Essai sur une minorité française* (Paris: Calmann-Lévy, 2008); and Tricia D. Keaton, "The Politics of Race-Blindness: (Anti)blackness and Category-Blindness in Contemporary France," *Du Bois Review: Social Science Research on Race* 7, no. 1 (2010): 103–31.

25. For a searing critique of de Linval's whitewashed representations of the city, see Alain Yacou, *Les catastrophes naturelles aux Antilles: D'une soufrière à une autre* (Paris: Karthala Editions, 1999).

26. The archivist and historian Liliane Chauleau has chronicled these everyday conditions in two separate publications: *Le Saint-Pierre d'antan: Quelques aspects de la vie des Pierrotins d'autrefois: Conférence faite au Rotary à l'occasion de son 5e anniversaire, le 9 mai 1975* (Fort-de-France: Les Archives départementales de la Martinique, 1975), and *Pierrotins et Saint-Pierrais: La vie quotidienne dans la ville de Saint-Pierre avant l'éruption de la montagne Pelée de 1902* (Paris: Editions L'Harmattan, 2002).

27. Géache, *Une nuit*, 8.

28. Gayatri Gopinath, *Impossible Desires: Queer Diasporas and South Asian Public Cultures* (Durham, NC: Duke University Press, 2005).

29. Serena Owusua Dankwa, "'It's a Silent Trade': Female Same-Sex Intimacies in Post-Colonial Ghana," *Nora-Nordic Journal of Feminist and Gender Research* 17, no. 3 (2009): 193.

30. I take my naming of "tacit" forms and unremarked upon presences from Carlos U. Decena, "Tacit Subjects," *GLQ* 14 (2008): 339.

31. Jafari Sinclaire Allen, "For 'the Children': Dancing the Beloved Community," *Souls: A Critical Journal of Black Politics, Culture, and Society* 11, no. 3 (2009): 315.

32. Géache, *Une nuit*, 108.

33. On Carnival and sexuality more generally in the Caribbean, see Kamala Kempadoo, "Theorizing Sexual Relations in the Caribbean," in *Confronting Power, Theorizing Gender: Interdisciplinary Perspectives in the Caribbean*, ed. Eudine Barriteau (Mona: University of the West Indies Press, 2003); and Linden Lewis, *The Culture of Gender and Sexuality in the Caribbean* (Gainesville: University Press of Florida, 2003). On the francophone Caribbean, see Thomas Spear, "Carnivalesque Jouissance: Representation of Sexuality in the Francophone West Indian Novel," *Jouvert: A Journal of Postcolonial Studies* 2, no. 1 (1998); on Martinique in particular, David A. B. Murray, "Defiance or Defilement? Undressing Cross-Dressing in Martinique's Carnival," *Sexualities* 1, no. 3 (1998): 343–54; also see Patrick Bruneteaux and Véronique Rochais, *Le Carnaval des travestis: Les travestis makoumè* (Case Pilote: Éditions Lafontaine, 2006), which in calling attention to wide-ranging participation in the practice, insists that the phenomenon of *travestissement* was (and remains) "transclassiste."

34. While cross-dressing is also part of celebrations in Brazil, it is rarer in the insular Caribbean and does not hold the kind of traditional permanence that the spectacle of *travestis makoumè* holds in Martinique.

——

35. Isabelle Hidair, *Anthropologie du Carnaval cayennais: Une représentation en réduction de la société créole cayennaise* (Paris: Editions Publibook, 2005), 43.

36. The *diablesse* (*guiablesse*, *djablès*) is a popular folk figure, a female consort of the devil whose beauty is reputed to seduce men to their deaths. See also Lafcadio Hearn, "Martinique Sketches: La Guiablesse," for a nineteenth-century rendering in *Two Years in the French West Indies* (New York: Harper and Brothers, 1903).

37. Thierry L'Étang, "Saint-Pierre, Martinique: Mémoire orale d'une ville martyre et eschatologie de la catastrophe," in *Saint-Pierre: Mythes et réalités de la cité créole disparue*, ed. Léo Ursulet (Guyane: Ibis Rouge Editions, 2004), 25–26.

38. Édouard Glissant has written extensively about Martinique's black sands, most notably in "La Plage Noir" ("The Black Beach"), where he uses the beach's mutations (in this case, the one at Diamant) to think through both relationality and disorder in Martinican politics. See Édouard Glissant, *Poétique de la Relation* (Paris: Messageries du Livre, 1990).

39. See Sainte-Anne's longtime mayor Garcin Malsa's memoir for one perspective on this history: *L'écologie ou la passion du vivant: Quarante ans d'écrits écologiques* (Paris: L'Harmattan, 2008).

40. Éric Coppet, "L'avenir, Sainte-Anne et le marin," *Politiques publiques*, October 5, 2010.

41. For employment rates, see Institut National de la Statistique et des Études Économiques statistics, 2010 (www.insee.fr).

42. All names are pseudonyms.

43. Adam 4 Adam (www.adam4adam.com/) is an online dating and chat site for men who have sex with men, used often in Martinique by men seeking casual sexual partners, as well as friends.

44. Delany, *Times Square Red, Times Square Blue*, 90.

45. The anthropologist Katherine Browne, in *Creole Economics: Caribbean Cunning under the French Flag* (Houston: University of Texas Press, 2004), provides an important analysis of the ways that people make ends meet on the island, through a combination of legal and extralegal economic pursuits.

46. Emily Vogt's unpublished doctoral dissertation is one important source for this history, "Ghosts of the Plantation: Historical Representations and Cultural Difference among Martinique's White Elite" (University of Chicago, 2005), as is Édith Kováts Beaudoux, *Les blancs créoles de la Martinique: Une minorité dominante* (Paris: L'Harmattan, 2002), the belated publication from her field research on the island in the 1960s.

47. In Martinique, as in other parts of the French Caribbean, a *chabin/e* designates a person of African descent with light (often very light) skin, but "African" features. These distinctions are well documented in Jean Luc Bonniol, *La couleur comme maléfice: Une illustration créole de la généalogie des "blancs" et des "noirs"* (Paris: Albin Michel, 1992) as well as in the anthropologist Stéphanie Mulot's doctoral dissertation, "'Je suis la mère, je suis le père!' L'énigme matrifocale. Relations familiales et rapports de sexe en Guadeloupe" (École des Haute Études en Sciences Sociales, 2000).

48. Allen, "For 'the Children,'" 320.

———

49. Derek Walcott, "The Sea Is History," in *Collected Poems, 1948–1984* (New York: Farrar, Straus and Giroux, 1986).

50. My understandings of sand's composition are drawn from Michael Helland, *Sand: The Neverending Story* (Berkeley: University of California Press, 2009); Bernard W. Pipkin, D. D. Trent, Richard Hazlett, and Paul Bierman, *Geology and the Environment* (New York: Cengage, 2007); and F. Michel and H. Conge's film *Histoire d'un grain de sable* (2004).

CONTRIBUTORS

VANESSA AGARD-JONES is an assistant professor of anthropology at Columbia University. She is coeditor of *Transnational Blackness: Navigating the Global Color Line*.

SHAILA SESHIA GALVIN is an associate professor in the Department of Anthropology and Sociology at the Geneva Graduate Institute in Switzerland. She studies processes of environmental and agrarian change and is author of *Becoming Organic: Nature and Agriculture in the Indian Himalaya*.

RADHIKA GOVINDRAJAN is an associate professor of anthropology and international studies at the University of Washington, Seattle. She is author of *Animal Intimacies: Interspecies Relatedness in India's Central Himalayas*.

HIʻILEI JULIA KAWEHIPUAAKAHAOPULANI HOBART (Kanaka Maoli) is an assistant professor of Native and Indigenous studies at Yale University. She is coeditor of the special issue "Radical Care" for *Social Text* (2020) and author of *Cooling the Tropics: Ice, Indigeneity, and Hawaiian Refreshment*.

—

CINDY ISENHOUR is an associate professor with a joint appointment in the Department of Anthropology and the Climate Change Institute at the University of Maine. Isenhour specializes in environmental governance and policy with a focus on sustainable systems of consumption and production and waste. She is coeditor of three books—*Sustainability in the Global City: Myth and Practice, Power and Politics in Sustainable Consumption Research*, and *Status, Consumption and Sustainability: Ecological and Anthropological Perspectives*—as well as more than fifty peer reviewed journal articles.

MYLES LENNON is an environmental anthropologist, Dean's Assistant Professor of Environment and Society and Anthropology at Brown University, and a former sustainable energy policy practitioner. His research has been supported by the US National Science Foundation, the Ford Foundation, and the Wenner-Gren Foundation.

DÁILAN J. LONG is a Medicaid consultant and a broker for managed care services in New Mexico. Long advocates for individuals with disabilities, and he represents uranium workers who seek compensation from the Department of Justice. Long is also a statewide trainer for various pilot programs to increase health services using mobile technology.

SARAH R. OSTERHOUDT is an associate professor of anthropology at Indiana University. She is author of *Vanilla Landscapes: Meaning, Memory, and the Cultivation of Place in Madagascar*.

DANA E. POWELL is an associate professor of anthropology at Appalachian State University and affiliate faculty in the College of Indigenous Studies at National Dong Hwa University. She is engaged in environmental justice and health humanities collaborative research at the intersection of extractivism, climate change, and self-determination in comparative settler-colonial contexts.

JOHN CHARLES RYAN is an adjunct associate professor at Southern Cross University, Australia, and an adjunct senior research fellow at the Nulungu Institute, University of Notre Dame, Australia. His research

———

focuses on ecopoetics, the environmental humanities, and transdisciplinary plant studies. His recent publications include the coedited book *Postcolonial Literatures of Climate Change*.

K. SIVARAMAKRISHNAN is Dinakar Singh Professor of Anthropology, professor in the School of the Environment, and codirector of the Program in Agrarian Studies at Yale University. His recent books include *Death and Life of Nature in Asian Cities*, edited with Anne Rademacher, and *Nature Conservation in the New Economy: People, Wildlife and the Law in India*, edited with Ghazala Shahabuddin.

SARAH E. VAUGHN is an assistant professor in the Department of Anthropology at the University of California, Berkeley. Her research focuses on the intersections of climate change and technopolitics in the circum-Caribbean. She is author of *Engineering Vulnerability: In Pursuit of Climate Adaptation*.

AMY ZHANG is an environmental anthropologist whose research investigates the intersection of ecology, technology, labor, and urban life. Her forthcoming book project explores how waste infrastructures, materials, and technical interventions ground and condition the forms, possibilities, and limits of China's emerging urban environmental politics. She is an assistant professor of anthropology at New York University.

—

INDEX

Note: Pages in *italics* indicate illustrations or their captions.

Denístsah bit'óh (Ram Springs), 168–69.
See also Burnham, NM
Department of Energy (DOE, US), 174, 184,
187, 189, 190
Department of Health (DOH, Hawai'i),
85–86
Derrida, Jacques, 268
Desert Rock, 168–69. See also Burnham, NM
Desert Rock Energy Project (DREP): activists' meeting with journalists about,
169–70; benefits of, 176; as convergence point for concerns, 193; cost
of delivered energy from, 186; Draft
Environmental Impact Statement,
174, 176–77, 184, 186; global story of,
187; history of Burnham activism
and, 175; Navajo government, Diné
Fundamental Laws, and, 183; plans
for, 173; productive public dialogue
on, 171; tribal ownership of, 176,
197n19. See also renewable energy
activism: opposition to DREP
devbhumi (land of gods), 254–55, 260
Devi, Savita, 59
Devi, Usha, 51
devi-devta (local goddesses and gods), 248;
animals' connection with, 245, 254,
257–58, 260; animal souls and, 250;
destructive weather and, 244–45,
256; high gods and, 255; leopards'
devotion to, 253
Devidutt (elderly man, Uttarakhand),
244–45, 246, 256–57
DFL. See Diné Fundamental Laws
Dharampur Block (Uttarakhand), 53, 55
diaries, 42. See also organic certification:
farmers' diaries
diaspora, 336–37, 352
diet, 77, 90n24
difference: gendered, 181; geographical,
108, 118; ontology of, 192; persistence of, 80; racial, 226
Dilkon, AZ, 178, 187–88

Diné Bikéyah. See renewable energy
activism
Diné Citizens Against Ruining Our
Environment (Diné CARE), 178–79,
183–84, 187, 192–93, 197n27
Diné Fundamental Laws (DFL), 172, 183,
185, 191–92, 198n38, 198n42
Diné Natural Resources Protection Act
(DNRPA), 172–73, 183
Diné peoples. See Navajo community and
people
Diné Policy Institute, 183
Diné Power Authority (DPA), 170, 173
Dinesh (migrant from the mountains to
Delhi), 260
displacement, 9, 15, 25, 85, 182, 233, 317, 326
dispossession. See land dispossession
divine retribution, 245, 256, 341, 344
documentation. See organic certification:
farmers' diaries; organic certifica-
tion: other documentation for
DOE. See Department of Energy
DOH (Department of Health, Hawai'i),
85–86
Doniger, Wendy, 252
Doodá Desert Rock (No Desert Rock), 179
Doon Valley (Uttarakhand). See organic
certification
double fetishism in biotech boosterism, 141
Draft Environmental Impact Statement
(DEIS), 174, 176–77, 184, 186
drainage, 315–16, 318, 322, 324, 328
Dreaming, Aboriginal, 295, 298
DREP. See Desert Rock Energy Project
Durkheim, Emile, 248–49
dynamism, 290–91

East Demerara Water Conservancy
(EDWC), 312, 315, 320, 321
eating, 81–82, 87
ecocentrism, 10–11, 15, 211
eco-efficiencies, 104, 105–8, 109–10, 111,
112–13, 115–16, 120

CULTURE, PLACE, AND NATURE

STUDIES IN ANTHROPOLOGY AND ENVIRONMENT